Symbols and Notations

⬩	Any source of drinking water	⌂	Post Office
◌	Seasonal water source	✉	Will hold mail
⊏(x)	AT Shelter and (capacity)	☽	Privy
⛺	Camping, tentsite	🚻	Public restroom
🛏	Hostel	🗑	Trailhead trash can
🛌	Hotel, Cabin or B&B	⎓	Laundry
🚿	Shower available w/o stay	💻	Computer available
🚶	Outfitter	📶	Wireless (WiFi)
🚌	Shuttle, Bus or Taxi	🚉	Train Station
🍴	Any place that serves food	✈	Airport
🛒	Long term resupply	℞	Pharmacy
🏪	Short term resupply	✚	First Aid
🔨	Hardware store	🐕	Vet or kennel
💲	Bank or ATM	✂	Barber
📷	View	ℹ	Info center
🗼	Lookout tower	🍸	Lounge
🛶	Boating or aquablaze	🎥	Movie Theater
✳	Flora	+	Intersection
🛆	Picnic table	🏊	Swimming area

⊛ New in 2014. Hikers can acquire an "AT Passport" and have it stamped at more than 60 hiker friendly lodgings and at other landmarks along the trail. Patterned after the Camino de Santiago passport, it makes for a truly memorable keepsake for both thru and section hikers. Details and ordering info at ⟨www.ATPassport.com⟩

⚠ Warning: watch for trail ⟨...⟩

🅿 Parking. Many have GPS ⟨...⟩ entered into a vehicle's G⟨...⟩ parking lots. GPS system ⟨...⟩ a course to remote locati⟨...⟩.

◂▸ Southbound / Northbound. Used to show distances to next shelter, and to show a transition of trails in the White Mountain National Forest.

☎ Public phone - nearly obsolete, no longer maintained

■ Not categorized by other symbols; only on maps.

(pg.xx) More information on page xx

B/L/D Breakfast/Lunch/Dinner

$nnS, $nnD, $nnPP, $nnEAP: Room prices: single, double, per-person, each additional person.

Contents

The A.T. Guide

Jerelyn Press
Titusville, FL
www.Jerelyn.com

Contributors: Bill Bancroft, Tripp Clark, Chase Davidson, John Gordon (Teej), Rick Hatcher (Bearfoot), Dave Hennel (Gourmet Dave), Jim Houck, Raymond Johnson (Flatfoot), Dave Levy (Survivor Dave), Ryan Linn (Guthook), Juli Miller, Raymond Myers (Rain Man), Nicolas Sirot (Bear Bell), Bill Spach, John Stempa (Mechanical Man), Brian & Amy Sweet (Movinon & Swell), Jeff Taussig, Pete Zuroff

Maildrop Guidelines

▶ Use your real name (not a trail name), and include an ETA.
▶ Only send "General Delivery" mail to a Post office.
▶ FedEx and UPS packages cannot be addressed to PO boxes.
▶ USPS will forward unopened general delivery mail for free if it was shipped by Priority Mail.
▶ Be prepared to show an ID when you retrieve your mail.
▶ The "C/O" name is essential when mailing to a business's PO Box; without it, they may not be able to retrieve your mail.
▶ Send maildrops to a lodging facility only if you plan to stay there. If your plans change, offer to pay for the service of holding your mail.

Packages sent to post offices:

```
John Doe
C/O General Delivery
Trail Town, VA 12345

Please hold for AT hiker
ETA May 16, 2014
```

Packages sent to businesses:

```
John Doe
C/O Hiker Hostel
2176 Appalachian Way
Trail Town, VA 12345
Please hold for AT hiker
ETA May 16, 2014
```

Visit the Website: www.theATguide.com

The website contains the most recent updates, additions and corrections to the information contained in this book. Please let us know if there is anything we can do to improve the material or its presentation.
email: david@AWOLonTheTrail.com

Directions

North/ South

At many points along the trail, a northbound hiker will be heading some direction other than compass north, but this book will always refer to "north" as the direction on the AT that ultimately leads to Katahdin, and "south" leads to Springer Mountain. When reference is made to the true bearing, the word "compass" will precede the direction (e.g.: "compass south"). If the trail joins a section of road, enters a park, or enters a town, the "south" end is where a northbound hiker first arrives, and the "north" end is where he leaves.

East/West

"East" is to the right of the trail for a northbound hiker and "west" is to his left, regardless of the compass reading. Most east-west directions are abbreviated along with a distance in miles. For example, three-tenths of a mile east is written "0.3E."

Left/Right

If a road leads to a town that is to the west, then a northbound hiker would go to his left, and the southbound hiker to his right. Once on the road both hikers are headed in the same direction, so any additional directions are given using the words "left" and "right." "Left" and "right" are also used to describe features near a shelter, from the perspective of a person outside of the shelter looking in.

Book Organization - A spread is the pair of pages seen when the book is laid open. *The A.T. Guide* contains trail data and services in alternating spreads; a spread containing trail data is followed by a spread detailing services available to hikers within that section. Occasionally the information is not distributed evenly and there are back-to-back spreads of data or services.

Data Spread - Data Spreads contain a table of landmarks, mileages and elevations. Every spread covers approximately 40.4 miles of trail (20.2 miles per page). An elevation profile is "watermarked" on the data. The lines of text that describe the landmarks are spaced so that they intersect the profile map at the approximate location of each landmark. Small triangular pointers below the profile line identify shelter locations. The vertical exaggeration of the profile maps is 8:1.

Services Spread - The Services Spreads provide resupply information in towns that the trail passes through or near. Businesses are selectively included, and maps may only show a portion of town closest to the trail.

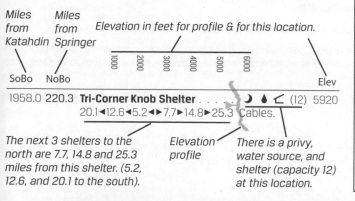

Miles from Katahdin

Miles from Springer

Elevation in feet for profile & for this location.

SoBo   NoBo

1000 2000 3000 4000 5000 6000

Elev

1958.0 220.3 **Tri-Corner Knob Shelter** . . . . ☽ ♦ ⊏ (12) 5920
20.1◄12.6◄5.2◄►7.7►14.8►25.3 Cables.

The next 3 shelters to the north are 7.7, 14.8 and 25.3 miles from this shelter. (5.2, 12.6, and 20.1 to the south).

Elevation profile

There is a privy, water source, and shelter (capacity 12) at this location.

When a map is provided, information presented in the map is not repeated in the text unless more elaboration is needed. Post office information will be on the map and is not repeated in the text. The width of the mapped area is at the bottom of the map and maps are proportionally scaled. Places of business that appear to be adjacent may be separated by one or more unspecified buildings or roads.

Prices are listed as given in fall of 2013. **No establishment is obliged to maintain these prices.** Lodging prices are particularly volatile, but most facilities listed will do their best for hikers. Let them know if you are thru-hiking; there may be a "thru-hiker rate."

DISPOSE OF WASTE PROPERLY

Improper waste disposal can spread disease, change the habits of wildlife and spoil the scenery.

• Pack it in; pack it out. Leave any donated items at hiker boxes in town rather than at campsites or shelters.

• Walk at least 100 feet (40 steps) away from shelters, water sources and campsites to dispose of urine, toothpaste, cooking water and strained dishwater, and to wash bodies, dishes or clothing. Minimize any use of soap.

• Use the privy only for human waste and toilet paper. Pack out disposable wipes and hygiene products.

• If there is no privy, walk at least 200 feet (80 steps) away from campsites, shelters, trails and water sources to bury feces in a hole 6 to 8 inches deep. Bury or carry out toilet paper.

Read more of the Leave No Trace techniques developed for the A.T.: www.appalachiantrail.org/LNT

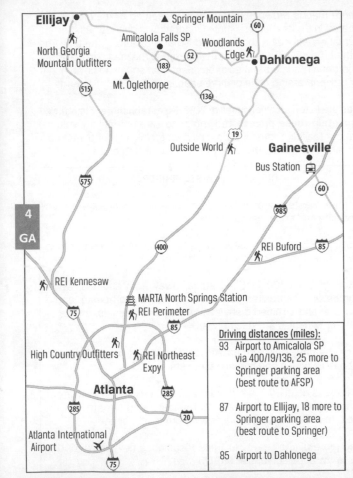

Driving distances (miles):
93 Airport to Amicalola SP
    via 400/19/136, 25 more to
    Springer parking area
    (best route to AFSP)

87 Airport to Ellijay, 18 more to
    Springer parking area
    (best route to Springer)

85 Airport to Dahlonega

Trail Etiquette

Avoid using a cell phone anywhere within the trail corridor, especially in shelters or within earshot of other hikers. Turn ringer off.

When hikers approach one another on the trail, the uphill hiker has the right-of-way, but the rule is irrelevant. If a hiker is approaching, look for an opportunity to step aside, regardless of your position. Be aware of hikers approaching from behind, and step aside so that they may pass.

Take only as much shelter space as you need to sleep. Shelter spaces cannot be reserved for friends who have yet to arrive. If you bring alcohol to a shelter or campsite, do so discreetly. Soon after dark is bedtime for most hikers.

The AT is liberating, and outlandish behavior is part of AT lore. Be considerate; boisterous and erratic behavior may be unsettling to strangers stuck in the woods with you. Conversely, hikers seeking a serene experience should be aware that AT hiking is, for many, a social experience. Be tolerant. Stay flexible and be prepared to move on rather than trying to convince others to conform to your expectations.

Town Etiquette

Ask permission before bringing a pack into a place of business.

Don't expect generosity, and show appreciation when it is offered. If you are granted work-for-stay, strive to provide service equal to the value of your stay.

Assume that alcohol is not permitted in hostels & campsites until told otherwise.

Respect hotel room capacities; hotel owners should know how many people intend to stay in a room. Try to leave hotel rooms as clean as a car traveler would. If a shower is available, use it.

Getting to Springer Mountain

The southern terminus of the trail is atop Springer Mountain, and is accessible only by foot. The 8.8-mile Approach Trail, originating at the Visitor Center in Amicalola Falls State Park, is one means of getting there. An alternative is to drive to Big Stamp Gap via USFS 42, a dirt road passable by most vehicles unless there is snow or bad-weather washout. From the gap, hike one mile south to Springer Mountain. Your hike would begin by retracing your steps. (See Start of Trail map on pg. 10)

The closest major city is Atlanta, GA, 82 miles south. If you fly or take AMTRAK into Atlanta, take the MARTA rail system to the North Springs Station, and a shuttle service can pick up from there. There is also Greyhound bus service to Gainesville, GA, 38 miles from the park.

🚌 **Hiker Hostel** Package deal including shuttle, see pg. 11.

🚌 🥾 **Survivor Dave's Trail Shuttle** 678-469-0978 (No texts please) ⟨www.atsurvivordave.com⟩ Shuttle service to/from Atlanta Airport and North Springs MARTA Station to Amicalola Falls State Park, Springer Mountain, and all trailheads as far north as Fontana Dam. Long haul shuttles to/from North Georgia directly to Clingmans Dome, Newfound Gap, Davenport Gap, and Hot Springs, NC are also available. Will stop at outfitter and/or supermarket for supplies (time permitting). Stove fuels available at cost. Well behaved dogs welcome. 24 hours' notice please. Will respond promptly to phone messages.

🚌 **Wes Wisson** 706-747-2671, dwisson@alltel.net Based in Suches, GA. Will shuttle year-round, up to four hikers. MARTA to Amicalola or to Big Stamp Gap.

🚌 🔼 **Ron Brown** Home: 706-636-2825, Cell: 706-669-0919 hikershuttles@outlook.com. Shuttle range Atlanta to Fontana.

🚌 **Ron Hulbert and Sam Duke** 706-781-7641 or 706-745-1596 Centered in Blairsville, shuttle range Atlanta to Fontana.

Outfitters Near the Southern Terminus

🥾 **Mountain Crossings** 706-745-6095 (see pg. 11)

🚶 **North Georgia Mountain Outfitters** 706-698-4453 ⟨hikeNorthGeorgia.com⟩ 583 Highland Crossing, Suite 230, East Ellijay, GA 30540 Full service outfitter.

🥾 **Woodlands Edge** 706-864-5358 Open 10-5, 363 days a year (closed Easter and Christmas Day). Full service outfitter, fuel/oz, ask about shuttles. 36 North Park Street Dahlonega, GA 30533

🥾 **Outside World** 706-265-4500 471 Quill Drive, Dawsonville, GA 30534

🥾 **Half Moon Outfitters** 404-249-7921 1034 N. Highland Ave. NE, Atlanta, GA 30306

🥾 **High Country Outfitters** 404-814-0999 3906 Roswell Rd. #B, Atlanta, GA 30342

🥾 **REI** Four Atlanta area stores:
1800 Northeast Expy NE, Atlanta, GA 30329, 404-633-6508
1165 Perimeter Ctr W Suite 200, Atlanta, GA 30338, 770-901-9200
740 Barrett Parkway Suite 450, Kennesaw, GA 30144, 770-425-4480
1600 Mall of Georgia Blvd, Buford, GA 30519, 770-831-0676

1. Plan Ahead and Prepare
2. Travel and Camp on Durable Surfaces
3. Dispose of Waste Properly
4. Leave What You Find
5. Minimize Campfire Impacts
6. Respect Wildlife
7. Be Considerate of Other Visitors

leave no trace

This copyrighted information has been reprinted with permission from the Leave No Trace Center for Outdoor Ethics: ⟨www.LNT.org⟩

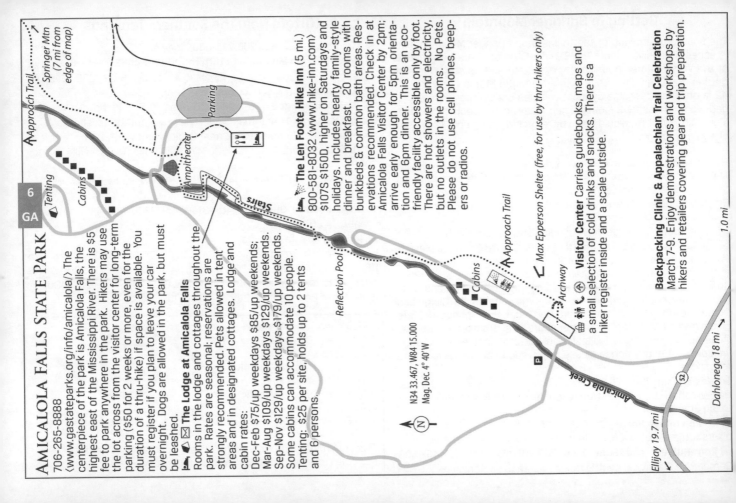

AMICALOLA FALLS STATE PARK

706-265-8888

⟨www.gastateparks.org/info/amicalola/⟩ The centerpiece of the park is Amicalola Falls, the highest east of the Mississippi River. There is $5 fee to park anywhere in the park. Hikers may use the lot across from the visitor center for long-term parking ($50 for 2 weeks or more, even for the duration of a thru-hike) if space is available. You must register if you plan to leave your car overnight. Dogs are allowed in the park, but must be leashed.

The Lodge at Amicalola Falls

Rooms in the lodge and cottages throughout the park. Rates are seasonal; reservations are strongly recommended. Pets allowed in tent areas and in designated cottages. Lodge and cabin rates:

Dec-Feb $75/up weekdays $85/up weekends;
Mar-Aug $109/up weekdays $129/up weekends.
Sep-Nov $129/up weekdays $179/up weekends.
Some cabins can accommodate 10 people.
Tenting: $25 per site, holds up to 2 tents and 6 persons.

The Len Foote Hike Inn (5 mi.) 800-581-8032 ⟨www.hike-inn.com⟩ $107S $150D, higher on Saturdays and holidays. Includes hearty family-style dinner and breakfast. 20 rooms with bunkbeds & common bath areas. Reservations recommended. Check in at Amicalola Falls Visitor Center by 2pm; arrive early enough for 5pm orientation and 6pm dinner. This is an eco-friendly facility accessible only by foot. There are hot showers and electricity, but no outlets in the rooms. No Pets. Please do not use cell phones, beepers or radios.

Visitor Center Carries guidebooks, maps and a small selection of cold drinks and snacks. There is a hiker register inside and a scale outside.

Backpacking Clinic & Appalachian Trail Celebration March 7-9. Enjoy demonstrations and workshops by hikers and retailers covering gear and trip preparation.

Springer Mtn (7 mi from edge of map)

Approach Trail

Parking

Tenting

Cabins

Amphitheater

Stairs

Reflection Pool

N34 33.467, W84 15.000
Mag. Dec. 4° 40'W

Cabins

Approach Trail

Max Epperson Shelter (free, for use by thru-hikers only)

Archway

Amicalola Creek

Ellijay 19.7 mi

Dahlonega 18 mi

1.0 mi

N

The Approach Trail

Elev	NoBo	SoBo	Description
1800	0.0	8.8	**Amicalola Falls State Park,** archway behind Visitor Center
1858	0.1	8.7	**Max Epperson Shelter,** for thru-hiker use only
2003	0.4	8.4	Reflection Pond at base of falls
2216	0.7	8.1	Staircase - 604 steps to the top of the Falls
2639	1.1	7.7	Parking, side trail to Lodge
2642	1.2	7.6	Lodge Road (lodge to east)
2656	1.3	7.5	Trail to **Len Foote Hike Inn** (5.0E) blazed lime-green
2584	1.5	7.3	USFS Road 46, steps on north side
2841	3.2	5.6	High Shoals Road
3384	4.8	4.0	Frosty Mountain. Spring (0.2E) is unreliable.
3178	5.1	3.7	Frosty Mountain Road, USFS Road 46
3353	5.4	3.4	Trail to **Len Foote Hike Inn** (1.0E) blazed lime-green
3406	5.7	3.1	Woody Knob.
3100	6.0	2.8	Nimblewill Gap, USFS Road 28
3419	6.2	2.6	Spring (left of trail), unreliable
3300	7.3	1.5	**Black Gap Shelter** (0.1W) Spring is on opposite side of the Approach Trail (0.1E).
3782	8.8	0.0	Springer Mountain

(pg. 6)

7
GA

SoBo	NoBo		Elev
2185.3	0.0	Springer Mountain southern terminus, register on back of rock with plaque. ⟡	3782
2185.1	0.2	**Springer Mountain Shelter** (0.2E) Use designated tent pads. (12)	3733
2184.3	1.0	0.0◀0.0◀0.0◀▶2.6▶7.9▶15.6 150 yards north, Benton MacKaye Trail to east. Big Stamp Gap, USFS 42. N34 38.257 W84 11.725 [P]	3350
2183.3	2.0	Benton MacKaye Trail.	3279
2182.6	2.7	Footbridge, stream. (16)	2947
2182.5	2.8	**Stover Creek Shelter** (0.1E) (2006).	2932
2182.4	2.9	0.0◀0.0◀2.6◀▶5.3▶13.0▶25.3 Footbridge, stream.	2890
2181.9	3.4	Stream.	2707
2181.1	4.2	Benton MacKaye / Duncan Ridge Trail to east.	2586
2181.0	4.3	Three Forks, USFS 58, footbridge.	2530
2180.6	4.7	Campsites to west, between trail and creek.	2550
2180.1	5.2	Benton MacKaye / Duncan Ridge Trail to west. Trail to Long Creek Falls.	2800
2179.1	6.2	Dirt road, 0.2W to Hickory Flats Cemetery, pavillion.	3000
2177.2	8.1	**Hawk Mountain Shelter** (0.2W) (1993). 0.0◀7.9◀5.3◀▶7.7▶20.0▶21.2 Water south on AT and 0.1 mile behind shelter. (12)	3209
2176.7	8.6	Hightower Gap, junction USFS 42 & 69. N34 39.809 W84 7.779 [P]	2854

✳ **Mayapple** – White flower ball dangling under an umbrella of broad leaves. Plant is about a foot tall.

SoBo	NoBo		Elev
2174.8	10.5	Horse Gap.	2681
2173.8	11.5	Sassafras Mountain.	3342
2173.0	12.3	Cooper Gap, USFS 15, 42 & 80. N34 39.180 W84 5.078 [P]	2940
2172.5	12.8	Justus Mountain.	3226
2171.8	13.5	Dirt road.	2743
2170.9	14.4	Justus Creek, rock-hop. Use designated campsites north of creek, to west.	2619
2170.4	14.9	Stream.	2646
2169.8	15.5	Blackwell Creek.	2674
2169.5	15.8	**Gooch Mountain Shelter** (0.1W) (2001) Water behind shelter. 15.6◀13.0◀7.7◀▶12.3▶13.5▶22.6 Designated tentsites, cables. (14)	2821
2168.4	16.9	Spring to the east.	2879
2168.1	17.2	Gooch Gap, USFS 42 (gravel) N34 39.1256 W84 1.9402 [P] ◆ (pg.10-11) **Suches, GA** (2.7W) water north of road 0.1E on marked trail	2837
2167.1	18.2	Roadbed.	2969
2166.9	18.4	Liss Gap.	3064
2166.3	19.0	Ramrock Mountain.	3266

Elev	Features	NoBo	SoBo
3263 △	Seasonal springs	20.4	2164.9
3283	Woody Gap, GA 60 . . . N34 40.659 W84 0.000 P 🚻🏕♦ (pg.10–11); Suches, GA (2.0W); Hostel (6.0E); spring north of road 0.2W.	21.0	2164.3
3589 📷	Preaching Rock, view to east. Woody Lake in Suches in view to west.	21.8	2163.5
3737	Big Cedar Mountain, rock ledges and views.	22.1	2163.2
3662	Spring to west.	22.3	2163.0
3305	Spring to west	23.1	2162.2
3036	Dockery Lake Trail	23.9	2161.4
2880	Lance Creek, camp in designated sites north of footbridge	24.3	2161.0
3080 P	Henry Gap (unmarked) is 70 yards west on side trail, woods road to GA 180.	25.1	2160.2
	⚠ A hard-shell bear-resistant canister is required for hikers overnighting between Jarrard Gap and Neel Gap from Mar 1 – Jun 1. No fires (year-round) from Slaughter Creek Trail to Neel Gap.		
3250	Jarrard Gap, dirt road. . . . . . . ♦(0.3W) (pg.10–11)	26.7	2158.6
3394	Gaddis Mountain	26.9	2158.4
3751	Turkey Stamp	28.1	2157.2
3720	**Woods Hole Shelter** (0.2W) 25.3◄20.0◄12.3▶1.2▶10.3▶15.1 . . . ☾△⊏(7)	28.2	2157.1
3797	Bird Gap, Freeman Trail east bypasses Blood Mtn & rejoins AT at Flatrock Gap	28.5	2156.8
4178	Slaughter Creek Trail, spring on AT, campsite 0.1 south on AT Duncan Ridge Trail, Coosa Trail to west	28.9	2156.4
4461	**Blood Mountain Shelter** (1934) 21.2◄13.5◄1.2▶9.1▶13.9▶21.2 . . . 📷☾⊏(8) Privy 50 yards south. No fires. Stream (0.8S). Many views from AT south of shelter	29.3	2156.0
3486	Flatrock Gap, Freeman Trail east bypasses Blood Mtn; west. P ♦(0.2W) to Byron Reece parking area. Balance Rock 150 yards north.	30.6	2154.7
3125 P	Neel Gap, US 19 . . . N34 44.464 W83 55.237 P (pg.11)	31.7	2153.6
3683	Bull Gap, spring 0.1W	32.8	2152.5
3836 📷	Leveland Mountain, view	33.4	2151.9
3527	Swaim Gap, spring to west, campsites within 0.1 to north and south.	34.6	2150.7
3766 📷	Wolf Laurel Top, campsite with views to east.	35.3	2150.0
3842 📷	Cowrock Mountain	36.7	2148.6
3138 P	Tesnatee Gap, GA 348, Russell Hwy . . . N34 43.570 W83 50.853 P	37.7	2147.6
3554 📷	Wildcat Mountain.	38.2	2147.1
3650	**Whitley Gap Shelter** (1.2E) 22.6◄10.3◄9.1▶4.8▶12.1▶20.2 Spring 0.3 mile behind shelter. Campsite 0.1E with view just beyond. 📷☾♦⊏(6)	38.4	2146.9
3468 P	Hogpen Gap, GA 348, Water south of rd. east of AT N34 43.551 W83 50.395 ♦	38.6	2146.7
3470	White Oak Stamp	39.5	2145.8

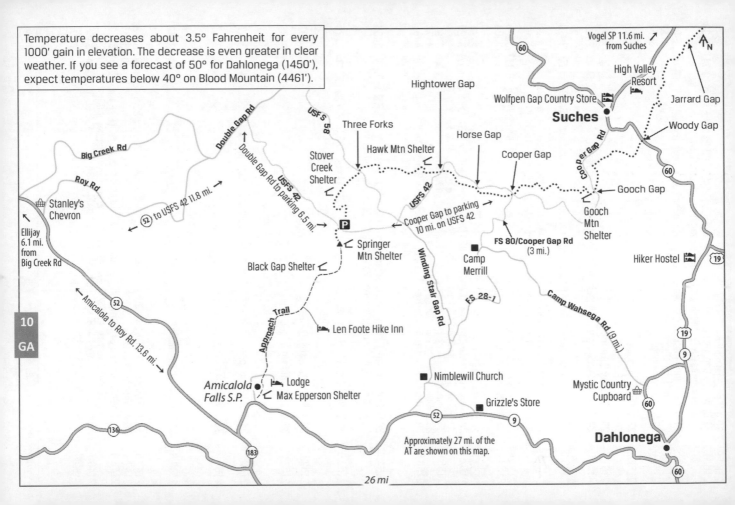

Temperature decreases about 3.5° Fahrenheit for every 1000' gain in elevation. The decrease is even greater in clear weather. If you see a forecast of 50° for Dahlonega (1450'), expect temperatures below 40° on Blood Mountain (4461').

60

Vogel SP 11.6 mi. ↗
from Suches

High Valley Resort

Wolfpen Gap Country Store

Jarrard Gap

Suches

Woody Gap

60

USFS 58

Hightower Gap

Three Forks

Hawk Mtn Shelter

Horse Gap

Cooper Gap

Cooper Gap Rd

Big Creek Rd

Stover Creek Shelter

Gooch Gap

Roy Rd

USFS 42

Double Gap Rd

Double Gap Rd to parking 6.5 mi.

Stanley's Chevron

52 to USFS 42 11.8 mi.

USFS 42

Cooper Gap to parking 10 mi. on USFS 42

Gooch Mtn Shelter

Ellijay 6.1 mi. from Big Creek Rd

P

FS 80/Cooper Gap Rd (3 mi.)

Hiker Hostel

19

Springer Mtn Shelter

Camp Merrill

Black Gap Shelter

Winding Stair Gap Rd

FS 28-1

Camp Wahsega Rd (9 mi.)

10
GA

52 Amicalola to Roy Rd. 13.6 mi.

Approach Trail

Len Foote Hike Inn

19

9

Amicalola Falls S.P.

Lodge

Max Epperson Shelter

Nimblewill Church

Mystic Country Cupboard

60

136

183

Grizzle's Store

52

9

Dahlonega

60

Approximately 27 mi. of the AT are shown on this map.

26 mi

17.2   Gooch Gap, USFS 42

21.0   Woody Gap, GA 60

🏠🔆⛺🚐📶🖥📧 (6.0E) **Hiker Hostel** 770-312-7342 ⟨www.hikerhostel.com⟩ hikerhostel@yahoo.com Open year-round. $18PP Bunks $42 Private room for 2. Overnight stay includes breakfast, bed linens, towel & shower. Computer w/ internet & wireless available. Laundry $3. SPECIAL(Feb 24-Apr 20): $80 pickup from Atlanta North Springs MARTA Station or Gainesville, overnight stay in bunk, breakfast, shuttle to Amicalola or Springer, 8oz of white gas/alcohol. Canister fuel available for purchase. Feb 24-Apr 27 5pm daily pickup at Woody Gap. Shuttles from Atlanta to Dick's Creek Gap by reservation for hostel guests. Maildrops: (USPS) PO Box 802 or (FedEx/UPS) 7693 Hwy 19N, Dahlonega, GA 30533.

Suches, GA 30572 (2W)

📮 M-F 12:15-4:15, 706-747-2611

🏠🍴🏛💲⛺📧 **Wolfpen Gap Country Store** 706-747-2271 M-Sat 7:30-8, Su 9-6, open later in summer. Bunks $15. Laundry $5/load. Beer, soda, hiker foods, pizza and BBQ. Coleman/oz and canisters. Will pickup at Woody Gap. Accepts MC/Disc. Maildrops: 41 Wolf Pen Gap Rd, Suches, GA 30572.

🛏🏠🔆⛺📶 **High Valley Resort** (0.7W) of PO, 404-720-0087 ⟨www.highvalleyresort.com⟩ Camping $15PP, bunkhouse $45PP. Tenters and bunkhouse have access to bathhouse, showers and lodge with satellite TV. Cabins $100/night Su-Wed; $165 Th-Sat, some sleep 4, some sleep up to 8 persons.

🛏🏠🔆🍴🏛 **Wildcat Lodge and Campground** 706-747-1011. (7W) $15 bunkroom, $12 camping. Also lodge rooms. Sometimes can pickup & return. Well-stocked camp store has Coleman & canisters. Diner serves B/L.

🚐 **Wes Wisson** 706-747-2671 Shuttles cover Atlanta thru GA.

➕ **Don Pruitt** 706-747-1421, M, Tu, Th, F 8-3, walk-ins 9-10.

26.7   Jarrard Gap

🔥🚿 (1.0W) **Lake Winfield Scott Recreation Area** tent sites $12 for up to 5 persons, showers & bathrooms, leash dogs.

31.7   Neel Gap, US 19

🚶🛏🏠🍴🚿⛺🚐📧🖥 **Mountain Crossings** 706-745-6095 ⟨www.mountaincrossings.com⟩ Full-service outfitter, full resupply, gear shakedown, alcohol/oz., bunkroom (remodeled fall 2013) $17PP includes shower w/towel. Shower without stay $4. No pets. Ask about shuttles. Maildrops: (USPS/UPS/FedEx) held for 2 weeks, $1 fee at pickup, 12471 Gainesville Hwy, Blairsville, GA 30512.

🛏⛺ (0.3E) **Blood Mountain Cabins** ⟨www.bloodmountain.com⟩ 800-284-6866 Thru-hiker rate $60. Cabin w/ kitchen and satellite, holds 4 adults & 2 children under the age of 13. Laundry free w/stay. WiFi at lodge. No pets.

🔥🏛🚿⛺🅿 (3W) **Vogel State Park** 706-745-2628 ⟨www.gastateparks.org⟩ Tent sites with shower $19, cabins for 2 to 10 persons $90-$160, $2 shower w/o stay. Long term parking $5.

🛏⛺🚐🅿 (3.5W) **Goose Creek Cabins** 706-745-5111, 706-781-8593 Cabins with washer/dryer for 3-6 persons $30PP/up. Shuttle to Blairsville for dinner or to Hogpen Gap $25 for up to 6 persons. Other shuttles can be arranged and parking is available for section hikers using shuttle service.

🚐 **Ron Hulbert and Sam Duke** 706-781-7641 or 706-745-1596 Centered in Blairsville, shuttle range Atlanta to Fontana.

Blairsville, GA 30514 (14W) All major services.

🚶 **Blairsville Hikes and Bikes** 706-745-8141 Packs, poles, fuel & hiker food.

Dahlonega, GA 30597 (17E) All major services.

12
GA

> ⚠ Get the most out of your guidebook: pay attention to lines that end with a page number. The page that is referenced will list the services available at or near the trailhead.

SoBo	NoBo	Feature	Elev
2144.7	40.6	Poor Mountain	3620
2143.0	42.3	Sheep Rock Top.	3576
2142.1	43.2	**Low Gap Shelter** 15.1◄13.9◄4.8◄►7.3►15.4►22.8. Water 30 yards in front of shelter. Cables. Privy on steep hill beyond shelter.	3054
2141.7	43.6	Stream.	3216
2140.7	44.6	Poplar Stamp Gap, spring 0.1E, gap and side trail unmarked.	3367
2140.0	45.3	Spring to west	3563
2138.7	46.6	Stream with cascade, several streams in area.	3491
2138.2	47.1	Cold Springs Gap	3490
2137.1	48.2	Chattahoochee Gap, Jacks Knob Trail to west, spring 0.5E	3480
2136.4	48.9	Red Clay Gap (pg.14)	3485
2135.7	49.6	Site of former Rocky Knob Shelter	3636
2135.5	49.8	Spring west of trail down slope	3620
2134.8	50.5	**Blue Mountain Shelter** 21.2◄12.1◄7.3◄►8.1►15.5►23.6 Spring on AT (0.1S), bear cables.	3906
2133.9	51.4	Blue Mountain	4025
2132.4	52.9	Unicoi Gap, GA 75, **Helen, GA** (9.0E) N34 48.101 W83 44.570 P (pg.14) **Hiawassee, GA** (12.0W)	2949
2131.7	53.6	Stream.	3514
2131.5	53.8	Rocky Mountain Trail to west	3709
2131.0	54.3	Rocky Mountain, views from AT 0.1 north of summit	4017
2129.7	55.6	Indian Grave Gap, USFS 283 N34 47.563 W83 42.855 P Andrews Cove Trail to east.	3113
2129.0	56.3	Tray Mountain Rd (gravel), USFS 79, piped stream east on road.	3580
2128.7	56.6	Cheese factory site, water (0.1W) on blue-blazed Trail	3638
2128.0	57.3	Tray Gap, Tray Mountain Rd, USFS 79 N34 47.959 W83 41.461 P	3847
2127.2	58.1	Tray Mountain.	4430
2126.7	58.6	**Tray Mountain Shelter** (0.2W) 20.2◄15.4◄8.1◄►7.4►15.5►22.8 Spring 0.1 mile behind shelter. Cables.	4199
2125.5	59.8	Wolfpen Gap	3568
2125.0	60.3	Steeltrap Gap, water 0.5E	3493

Appalachian Trail elevation profile — Georgia

NoBo	SoBo	Feature	Elev
		(top)	3764
60.9	2124.4	Young Lick Knob	
63.3	2122.0	Sassafras Gap, water 0.1E on steep blue-blazed trail	3500
64.2	2121.1	Addis Gap. Campsite 0.5E down old fire road, stream to right of campsite.	3304
65.2	2120.1	Kelly Knob, trail skirts summit, water 0.1E down steep trail	4171
66.0	2119.3	**Deep Gap Shelter** (0.3E) 22.8◄15.5◄7.4◄▶8.1▶15.4▶20.3 ☾ ⊏(12) Water 0.1 before shelter.	3583
67.1	2118.2	"Vista" blue-blaze leads 0.1E to campsite.	3891
67.4	2117.9	Powell Mountain	3850

No phone signal at Dicks Creek Gap. If you need ride, call from Shelter or Powell Mtn.

NoBo	SoBo	Feature	Elev
68.6	2116.7	Moreland Gap, water to east	2990
69.6	2115.7	Dicks Creek Gap, US 76 N34 54.728 W83 37.130 P ◆ (pg.14-15) Water, picnic tables at the gap, **Hiawassee, GA** (11.0W)	2675
70.6	2114.7	Campsite, water	3176
71.4	2113.9	Cowart Gap	2900
72.7	2112.6	Buzzard Knob	3750
72.9	2112.4	Bull Gap	3690
73.6	2111.7	Spring	3331
74.1	2111.2	**Plumorchard Gap Shelter** (0.2E) Privy 0.2 mile down steep trail ☾◆◆⊏(14) 23.6◄15.5◄8.1◄▶7.3▶12.2▶19.8 Creek on trail to shelter & spring (0.1W) of AT.	3165
74.8	2110.5	As Knob	3460
75.3	2110.0	Blue Ridge Gap, dirt road	3078
76.3	2109.0	Spring to west, campsite	3387
77.0	2108.3	Rich Cove Gap	3504
77.2	2108.1	Rocky Knob	3579
78.5	2106.8	**GA-NC** border	3833
78.6	2106.7	Bly Gap, spring west 30 yards Old and twisted tree often photographed.	3840
79.9	2105.4	Couthouse Bald, summit 0.1W	4666
80.5	2104.8	Sassafras Gap	4300
80.8	2104.5	Piped Spring	4517

NoBo   SoBo

13 GA

48.9   Red Clay Gap

🛏 🏕🔥⚕ ⛺🚿🏠✉ **Enota Mountain Retreat** 706-896-9966, 1.4W from Red Clay Gap. No sign & trail not blazed; be certain of location if you walk. Marked on some maps by its previous name "Camp Pioneer." Trail is downhill to Joel's Creek and follows creek into camp. Driving from Unicoi Gap: 2.4W on Hwy 17, then left 2.4 mi. on Hwy 180. Rides sometimes available. Tentsites, cabins, bunkrooms ($25), and laundry. Store with snacks and small gear items. Dining room open when there is enough guests. Beautiful waterfall, trout pond, work for stay possible on organic farm. Maildrops (guests only): 1000 Highway 180 Hiawassee, GA 30546

52.9   Unicoi Gap, GA 75
          Enota Mountain Retreat (4.8W, see listing above)
          Helen, GA 30545 (9E)

🏠 M–F 9–12:30 & 1:30-4, Sa 9-12, 706-878-2422
Tourist town with many hotels, restaurants, gift shops, ice cream shops, river rafting and tubing rentals. Visitor Center on Bruckenstrasse (near the PO) has information about places to stay and a free phone for making reservations.

🛏🚿🖥 **Best Western Motel** 706-878-2111 Hiker rate Mar 15-Apr 30; $50S + $5EAP up to 4. Includes breakfast buffet. Ride to/from trail weekdays only when staff is available.

🛏⛺🚿🖥 **Helendorf River Inn** 800-445-2271 Prices for 1 or 2 persons Su-Th; weekends are more: Dec-Mar $34, Apr-May $44, Jun-Sep $59, $10EAP, pets $20. Includes cont B. Visa/MC/Disc accepted.

🛏🚿 **Super 8 Motel** 706-878-2191, ask for hiker room $49+tax for 1 or 2 persons, no pets.

🛏🚿**Econo Lodge** 706-878-8000 Weekdays $60, weekends higher, includes cont. bfast. Pets under 20 pounds allowed with $20 fee.

🛏🚿🖥 **Country Inn and Suites** (706) 878-9000, indoor pool

🏪 **Betty's Country Store** 706-878-2943 open 7 days 7am-9pm.

⛺ **laundromat**

          Hiawassee, GA 30545 (12E) *(see Dicks Creek Gap)*

69.6   Dicks Creek Gap, US 76

🏕🔥⛺🏔⛺✉ (3.4W) **Blueberry Patch Hostel** 706-896-4893 Christian ministry operated since 1993 by Gary and Lennie Poteat. Gary is a 1991 thru-hiker. Open mid-February until the end of April. Bunks and tentsites; donations accepted. Please check in between 10am-6pm. Shower, laundry, breakfast and 9:30 shuttle back to Dick's Creek Gap, white gas/alcohol/oz. No pets; no alcohol or drugs. Maildrops: 5038 Hwy 76 East, Hiawassee, GA 30546.

🛏⛺🚿🖥✉ **Henson Cove B&B** (5W) 800-714-5542 relax@ henson-cove-place.com. Small cabin for 1-6 persons with full kitchen, 3 beds, 1.5 baths. $100 for 3 people, $120 for 6. Breakfast $7PP. Standard B&B rooms $100D, breakfast included. All stays include free ride to/from AT from Dick's Creek Gap or Unicoi Gap, or into town for provisions, free use of laundry and internet. Credit cards OK. Well behaved pets OK. Mail drops: 1137 Car Miles Rd, Hiawassee, GA 30546.

          Hiawassee, GA 30546 (11W)

🛏🏔⛺🚌🚿🖥✉ **Budget Inn** 706-896-4121 ⟨hiawasseebudgetinn.com⟩ $39.99S, $5EAP, pets $10, coin laundry. For guests, free ride to/from Dick's Creek Gap or Unicoi Gap (9 & 11am) Mar-Apr. Non-guest shuttles for a fee. Three Eagles Satellite on-site. Accepts Visa/MC. Complimentary guest maildrop transfer to Franklin Budget or Sapphire Inn. Maildrops: 193 South Main Street, Hiawassee, GA 30546.

🛏🚌🚿✉ **Mull's Motel** 706-896-4195 $45/up, no pets, shuttles by arrangement. Guest maildrops: 213 N Main St, Hiawassee, GA 30546.

🛏⛺🚿🖥✉ **Holiday Inn Express** 706-896-8884 $79/up, accepts all major credit cards. Full hot breakfast included, indoor pool and hot tub, no pets. Maildrops: 300 Big Sky Drive, Hiawassee, GA 30546.

🛏🍴⛺🚿🖥**Ramada Lake Chatuge Lodge** 706-896-5253

$89/up includes continental breakfast. **Chophouse Restaurant** on site.

🚶 **Three Eagles Satellite** 828-524-9061 Open Mar-Apr 8:30-1:30, 7 days. Footwear, hiking gear, rain gear, clothing, fuel/oz, food, shipping services, free "bumps" to Franklin store.

🚶🏠 **Buckhead House** 706-896-0028 Hiker friendly, carries boots, clothes and small gear, freeze-dried food, canister fuel, denatured/white gas/oz.

🛒🍴📷 **Ingles** 7-10, 7 days. Pharmacy, Starbucks, deli, bakery, salad bar.

🚌 **Bill's Wheels of Georgia** 865-202-1041 (Cell) BillsWheelsOfGeorgia@yahoo.com Shuttles to/from airports, bus & train stations and trailheads from Atlanta to NOC in Wesser, NC. Available 365 days a year at any hour, however extremely early or extremely late shuttles are price-adjusted accordingly. Advance notice appreciated.

■ **Goin' Postal** 706-896-1844 FedEx and UPS shipping 9-5 M-F.

⚠ Visit the website www.theATguide.com regularly to get updates, additions and corrections. Please let us know if you've found anything that should be added or corrected.

⚠ Prices are subject to change, particularly at hotels. Prices published in this guidebook were given in fall of 2013 and often represent a significant discount for hikers. Businesses *intend* to keep these prices throughout 2014, but they are not obliged to do so.

⚠ Many of the water sources listed in this book are springs and small streams that can go dry. Never carry just enough water to reach the next water source.

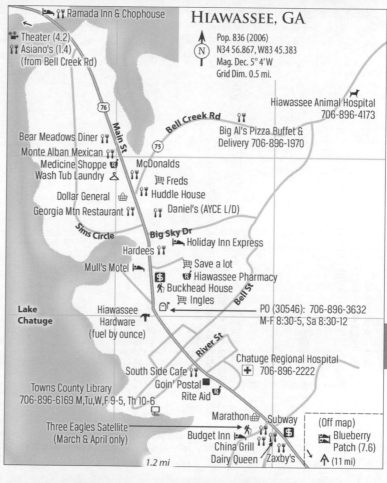

HIAWASSEE, GA

Pop. 836 (2006)
N34 56.867, W83 45.383
Mag. Dec. 5° 4'W
Grid Dim. 0.5 mi.

Ramada Inn & Chophouse
Theater (4.2)
Asiano's (1.4)
(from Bell Creek Rd)

Bell Creek Rd
Hiawassee Animal Hospital 706-896-4173
Big Al's Pizza Buffet & Delivery 706-896-1970

Bear Meadows Diner
Monte Alban Mexican
Medicine Shoppe
Wash Tub Laundry
Dollar General
Georgia Mtn Restaurant

Main St
McDonalds
Freds
Huddle House
Daniel's (AYCE L/D)

Sims Circle
Big Sky Dr
Holiday Inn Express
Hardees
Save a lot
Mull's Motel
Hiawassee Pharmacy
Buckhead House
Ingles

Lake Chatuge
Hiawassee Hardware (fuel by ounce)

Bell St
PO (30546): 706-896-3632
M-F 8:30-5, Sa 8:30-12

River St
Chatuge Regional Hospital
706-896-2222

South Side Cafe
Goin' Postal
Rite Aid

Towns County Library
706-896-6169 M,Tu,W,F 9-5, Th 10-6

Three Eagles Satellite
(March & April only)

Marathon
Subway
Budget Inn
China Grill
Dairy Queen
Zaxby's

(Off map)
Blueberry Patch (7.6)
(11 mi)

1.2 mi

15
GA

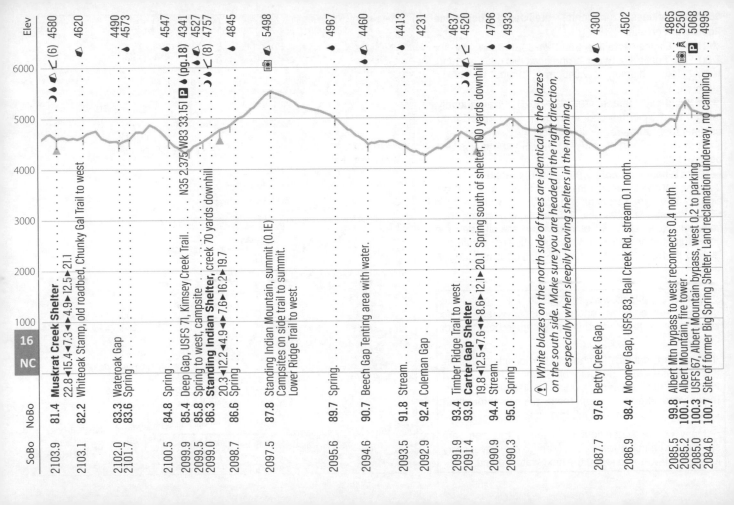

SoBo	NoBo	Feature	Elev
2103.9	81.4	**Muskrat Creek Shelter** 22.8◀15.4◀7.3◀▶4.9▶12.5▶21.1	4580
2103.1	82.2	Whiteoak Stamp, old roadbed, Chunky Gal Trail to west	4620
2102.0	83.3	Wateroak Gap	4490
2101.7	83.6	Spring	4573
2100.5	84.8	Spring	4547
2099.9	85.4	Deep Gap, USFS 71, Kimsey Creek Trail. N35 2.375 W83 33.151	4341
2099.5	85.8	Spring to west, campsite	4527
2099.0	86.3	**Standing Indian Shelter,** creek 70 yards downhill 20.3◀12.2◀4.9▶7.6▶16.2▶19.7	4757
2098.7	86.6	Spring	4845
2097.5	87.8	Standing Indian Mountain, summit (0.1E) Campsites on side trail to summit. Lower Ridge Trail to west.	5498
2095.6	89.7	Spring.	4967
2094.6	90.7	Beech Gap Tenting area with water.	4460
2093.5	91.8	Stream.	4413
2092.9	92.4	Coleman Gap	4231
2091.9	93.4	Timber Ridge Trail to west	4637
2091.4	93.9	**Carter Gap Shelter** 19.8◀12.5◀7.6▶8.6▶12.1▶20.1 Spring south of shelter, 100 yards downhill.	4520
2090.9	94.4	Stream.	4766
2090.3	95.0	Spring	4933
2087.7	97.6	Betty Creek Gap.	4300
2086.9	98.4	Mooney Gap, USFS 83, Ball Creek Rd, stream 0.1 north.	4502
2085.5	99.8	Albert Mtn bypass to west reconnects 0.4 north.	4865
2085.2	100.1	Albert Mountain, fire tower.	5250
2085.0	100.3	USFS 67, Albert Mountain bypass, west 0.2 to parking.	5068
2084.6	100.7	Site of former Big Spring Shelter. Land reclamation underway, no camping	4995

White blazes on the north side of trees are identical to the blazes on the south side. Make sure you are headed in the right direction, especially when sleepily leaving shelters in the morning.

16 NC

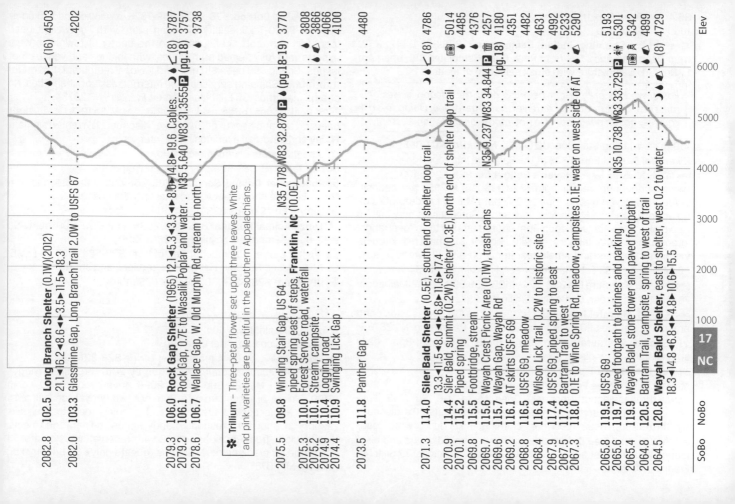

Page 17 — NC

NoBo	SoBo	Description	Elev
102.5	2082.8	**Long Branch Shelter** (0.1W)(2012) 🌙 ⌒(16)	4503
		21.1◄16.2◄8.6◄▶3.5▶11.5▶8.3	
103.3	2082.0	Glassmine Gap, Long Branch Trail 2.0W to USFS 67	4202
106.0	2079.3	**Rock Gap Shelter** (1965) 12.1◄5.3◄3.5◄▶8.0▶14.8▶19.6 Cables. 🌙 ⌒(8)	3787
106.1	2079.2	Rock Gap, 0.7E to Wasalik Poplar and water. N35 5.640 W83 31.3555 **P** (pg.18)	3757
106.7	2078.6	Wallace Gap, W. Old Murphy Rd, stream to north. ◆	3738
109.8	2075.5	Winding Stair Gap, US 64. N35 7.178 W83 32.878 **P** ◆ (pg.18-19)	3770
		piped spring east of steps, **Franklin, NC** (10.0E)	
110.0	2075.3	Forest Service road, waterfall ◆	3808
110.1	2075.2	Stream, campsite ◆	3866
110.4	2074.9	Logging road	4066
110.9	2074.4	Swinging Lick Gap	4100
111.8	2073.5	Panther Gap	4480
114.0	2071.3	**Siler Bald Shelter** (0.5E), south end of shelter loop trail 🌙 ⌒(8)	4786
		13.3◄11.5◄8.0◄▶6.8▶11.6▶17.4	
114.4	2070.9	Siler Bald, summit (0.2W), shelter (0.3E), north end of shelter loop trail	5014
115.2	2070.1	Piped spring ◆	4485
115.5	2069.8	Footbridge, stream	4376
115.6	2069.7	Wayah Crest Picnic Area (0.1W), trash cans	4257
115.7	2069.6	Wayah Gap, Wayah Rd N35 9.237 W83 34.844 **P** 🏛 (pg.18)	4180
116.1	2069.2	AT skirts USFS 69	4351
116.5	2068.8	USFS 69, meadow	4482
116.9	2068.4	Wilson Lick Trail, 0.2W to historic site	4631
117.4	2067.9	USFS 69, piped spring to east ◆	4992
117.8	2067.5	Bartram Trail to west	5233
118.0	2067.3	0.1E to Wine Spring Rd, meadow, campsites 0.1E, water on west side of AT ◆	5290
119.5	2065.8	USFS 69	5193
119.7	2065.6	Paved footpath to latrines and parking N35 10.738 W83 33.729 **P** 🚻	5301
119.9	2065.4	Wayah Bald, stone tower and paved footpath	5342
120.5	2064.8	Bartram Trail, campsite, spring to west of trail	4899
120.8	2064.5	**Wayah Bald Shelter**, east to shelter, west 0.2 to water 🌙 ⌒(8)	4729
		18.3◄14.8◄6.8◄▶4.8▶10.6▶15.5	

❋ Trillium – Three-petal flower set upon three leaves. White and pink varieties are plentiful in the southern Appalachians.

SoBo   NoBo   Elev

| 85.4 | Deep Gap, USFS 71 |
| 106.1 | Rock Gap |

🔥⛺🚿 **Standing Indian Campground** 828-369-0442 3.7W from Deep Gap and 1.5W from Rock Gap. Campsites $16, open Apr 1 - Nov 30. Camp store with small selection of foods.

> *Postal workers are present before & after the window closes at most post offices, and may retreive a package for you. Doing so is a courtesy not an obligation. Do not impose on them unnecessarily.*

| 109.8 | Winding Stair Gap, US 64 | ***Franklin, NC*** (10E) |

Hiker Fool Bash March 28-29 at the Sapphire Inn. Food, fun & games.
🛏🏨⚛✂⛺🚌🖥🖂 **Haven's Budget Inn** 828-524-4403 ⟨www.budgetinnoffranklin.com⟩ $39.99S, $5EAP, $50 pet deposit. Owner Ron Haven makes trips at 9 & 11am Mar-Apr to drop off/pick up at Rock, Wallace & Winding Stair Gaps. Motel guests may call for free pickup Mar-Apr, and get a 4pm shuttle around town for errands. Internet and coin laundry on-site. Hostel $15 has full kitchen, vending machines and used gear items on-site. Shower w/o stay $5. Maildrops: 433 East Palmer Street, Franklin, NC 28734.

🛏⚛🖥🖂 **Sapphire Inn** 828-524-4406, $39.99S, $5EAP Maildrops: 761 East Main Street, Bus 441, Franklin, NC 28734.

🛏📶🖥🖂 **Microtel Inn & Suites** 888-403-1700 Prices vary, cont. breakfast, pet fee $20. Maildrops: 81 Allman Dr, Franklin, NC 28734
🍴 **Sunset Restaurant** Homestyle B/L/D M-Sa 6am-8pm, daily specials, 10% hiker discount.
🍴 **Fun Factory** AYCE pizza lunch M-Sa.

🧗🍴📶🖥🖂 **Three Eagles Outfitters** 828-524-9061 ⟨www.threeeaglesoutfitters.net⟩ Open M-Sa 9-6, Su 12-5. Full-service outfitter serving AT hikers for over 20 years. 10% discount for thru-hikers. Gear, footwear, clothing, hiker food, white gas/alcohol/oz. **Trail Tree Cafe** inside; coffee bar, baked goods and hiker lounge with internet access. In-town shuttle. Maildrops: 78 Siler Rd, Franklin, NC 28734.

🧗🚌📶🖥🖂 **Outdoor 76** 828-349-7676 ⟨www.outdoor76.com⟩ Open M-Sa 10-7. Specialty AT hiking store with lightweight gear, food, fuel and draft beer, located in the center of town. Footwear experts with fully trained staff to deal with injuries and various foot issues. Spend $50 get a $10 gift card for local restaurant. 10% off for thru-hikers. Shipping services, free internet, ask about shuttles. No charge maildrops: 35 East Main Street, Franklin, NC 28734.

🍺📶 **Rock House Lodge** Inside of Outdoor 76, M-Sa 10-7. Quality draft beers on tap and beer to go. 10% hiker discount. Live entertainment Friday and Saturday evenings. Free internet.

🔧 **Ace Hardware** Coleman/alcohol/oz
🚌 **City Taxi** 828-369-5042, by appt. until 6 pm.
🚌 **Roadrunner Driving Services** 706-201-7719 where2@mac.com Long distance shuttles covering Atlanta to Damascus.
🚌 **Larry's Taxi Service** 828-421-4987, shuttles anywhere.
✈ **Lenzo Animal Hospital** 828-369-2635 M-F 8:30-5:00, some Sa 8:30-noon. Emergency clinic 828-665-4399.
ℹ **Visitor Center** (Chamber of Commerce) 828-524-3161 M-F 9-5, Sa 10-4, closed Sunday. List of hiker services and shuttles.
🖂 **UPS Store** 828-524-9800, M-F 8-6, Sa 10-3.

115.7	Wayah Gap, Wayah Rd.
124.4	Burningtown Gap, NC 1397
129.2	Tellico Gap, Otter Creek Rd.

🛏🏨⚛🍴⛺🚌🖂 **Aquone Hiker Lodge** 828-321-2340 ⟨www.aquonecabins.com/at.html⟩ Run by 2010 thru-hiker "Wiggy". Open Feb 25 - May 25. Bunkroom $20PP, private room $50D, cabin $110D. Pickup or return from/to Burningtown, Wayah or Tellico $4 per trip. Home cooked breakfast and evening meal is available. Laundry $4. Short term resupply, candy, sodas and packaged meals. Slackpacking from Rock Gap to NOC with reservations. No pets. $3 surcharge for credit cards. Maildrops (guests only): 63 Britannia Dr, Aquone, NC 28781.

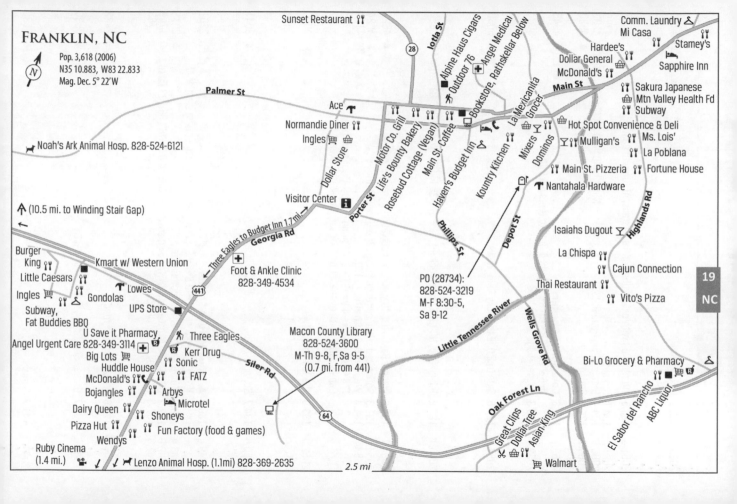

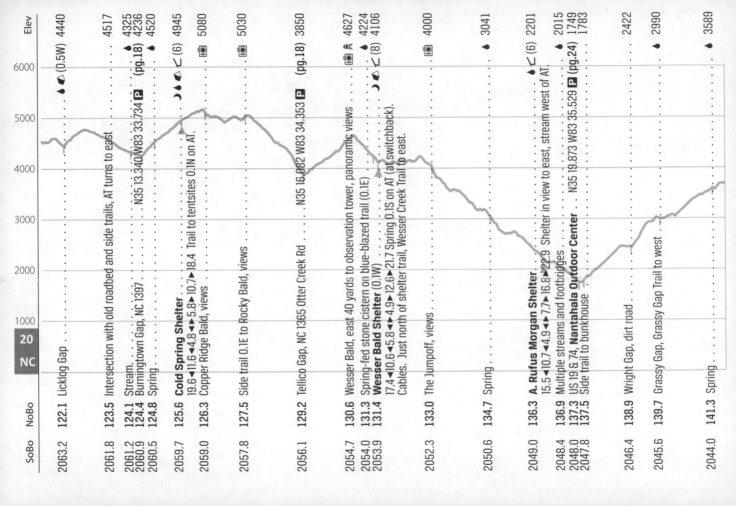

SoBo	NoBo		Elev
2063.2	122.1	Licklog Gap	4440
2061.8	123.5	Intersection with old roadbed and side trails, AT turns to east	4517
2061.2	124.1	Stream.	4325
2060.9	124.4	Burningtown Gap, NC 1397 N35 13.340 W83 33.734 P (pg.18)	4236
2060.5	124.8	Spring	4520
2059.7	125.6	**Cold Spring Shelter** 19.6◄11.6◄4.8▶5.8▶10.7▶18.4 Trail to tentsites 0.1N on AT	4945
2059.0	126.3	Copper Ridge Bald, views	5080
2057.8	127.5	Side trail 0.1E to Rocky Bald, views	5030
2056.1	129.2	Tellico Gap, NC 1365 Otter Creek Rd N35 16.082 W83 34.353 P (pg.18)	3850
2054.7	130.6	Wesser Bald, east 40 yards to observation tower, panoramic views	4627
2054.0	131.3	Spring-fed stone cistern on blue-blazed trail (0.1E)	4224
2053.9	131.4	**Wesser Bald Shelter** (0.1W) 17.4◄10.6◄5.8▶4.9▶12.6▶21.7 Spring 0.1S on AT (at switchback). Cables. Just north of shelter trail, Wesser Creek Trail to east.	4106
2052.3	133.0	The Jumpoff, views	4000
2050.6	134.7	Spring	3041
2049.0	136.3	**A. Rufus Morgan Shelter** 15.5◄10.7◄4.9▶7.7▶16.8▶22.9 Shelter in view to east, stream west of AT.	2201
2048.4	136.9	Multiple streams and footbridges	2015
2048.0	137.3	US 19 & 74, **Nantahala Outdoor Center** N35 19.873 W83 35.529 P (pg.24)	1749
2047.8	137.5	Side trail to bunkhouse	1783
2046.4	138.9	Wright Gap, dirt road	2422
2045.6	139.7	Grassy Gap, Grassy Gap Trail to west	2990
2044.0	141.3	Spring	3589

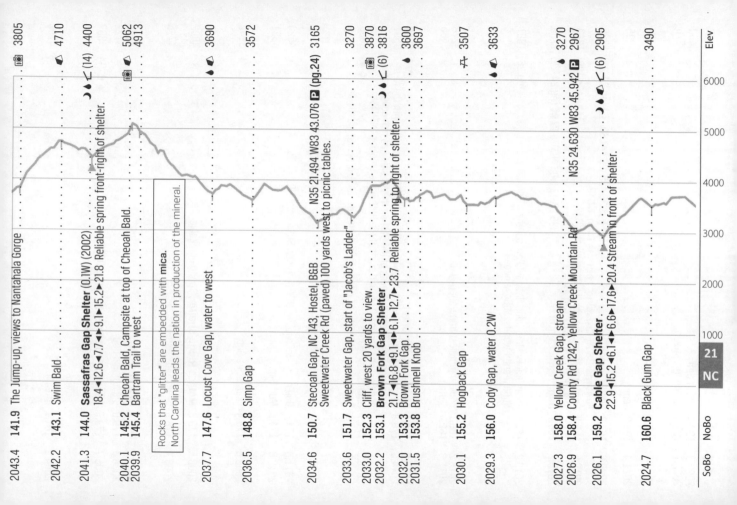

SoBo	NoBo	Description	Elev
2043.4	141.9	The Jump-up, views to Nantahala Gorge	3805
2042.2	143.1	Swim Bald	4710
2041.3	144.0	**Sassafras Gap Shelter** (0.1W) (2002) 18.4◀12.6◀7.7◀▶9.1▶15.2▶21.8 Reliable spring front-right of shelter.	(14) 4400
2040.1	145.2	Cheoah Bald, Campsite at top of Cheoah Bald.	5062
2039.9	145.4	Bartram Trail to west	4913
2037.7	147.6	Locust Cove Gap, water to west	3690
2036.5	148.8	Simp Gap	3572
2034.6	150.7	Stecoah Gap, NC 143, Hostel, B&B N35 21.494 W83 43.076 P (pg.24) Sweetwater Creek Rd (paved) 100 yards west to picnic tables.	3165
2033.6	151.7	Sweetwater Gap, start of "Jacob's Ladder"	3270
2033.0	152.3	Cliff, west 20 yards to view.	3870
2032.2	153.1	**Brown Fork Gap Shelter** 21.7◀16.8◀9.1◀▶6.1▶12.7▶23.7 Reliable spring to right of shelter.	(6) 3816
2032.0	153.3	Brown Fork Gap	3600
2031.5	153.8	Brushnell Knob	3697
2030.1	155.2	Hogback Gap	3507
2029.3	156.0	Cody Gap, water 0.2W	3633
2027.3	158.0	Yellow Creek Gap, stream	3270
2026.9	158.4	County Rd 1242, Yellow Creek Mountain Rd N35 24.630 W83 45.942 P	2967
2026.1	159.2	**Cable Gap Shelter** 22.9◀15.2◀6.1◀▶6.6▶17.6▶20.4 Stream in front of shelter.	(6) 2905
2024.7	160.6	Black Gum Gap	3490

Rocks that "glitter" are embedded with **mica**.
North Carolina leads the nation in production of the mineral.

21
NC

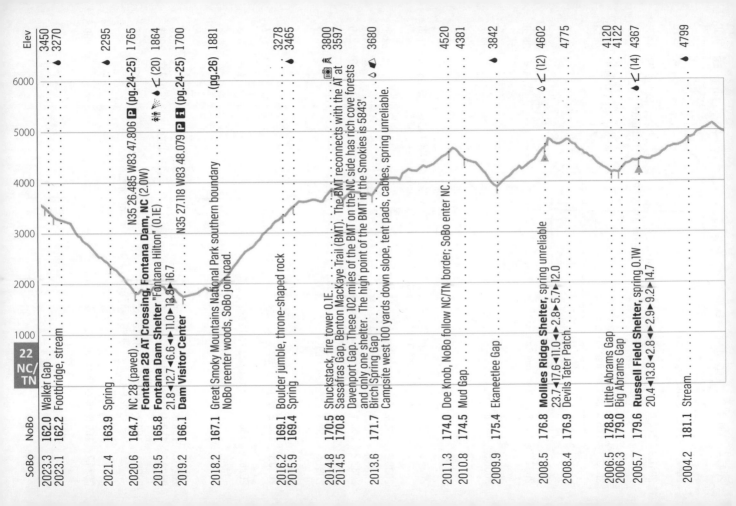

Elev	SoBo	NoBo	Feature
3450	2023.3	162.0	Walker Gap
3270	2023.1	162.2	Footbridge, stream
2295	2021.4	163.9	Spring
1765	2020.6	164.7	NC 28 (paved). N35 26.485 W83 47.806 **P** (pg.24-25) (2.0W)
1864	2019.5	165.8	**Fontana 28 AT Crossing, Fontana Dam, NC** ... **Fontana Dam Shelter** "Fontana Hilton" (0.1E) ⌂ (20)
1700	2019.2	166.1	21.8◄12.7◄6.6◄▶11.0▶13.8▶16.7 **Dam Visitor Center** N35 27.118 W83 48.079 **P**
1881	2018.2	167.1	Great Smoky Mountains National Park southern boundary. NoBo reenter woods, SoBo join road. (pg.26)
3278	2016.2	169.1	Boulder jumble, throne-shaped rock
3465	2015.9	169.4	Spring
3800	2014.8	170.5	Shuckstack, fire tower 0.1E.
3597	2014.5	170.8	Sassafras Gap, Benton MacKaye Trail (BMT).
3680	2013.6	171.7	Birch Spring Gap. Campsite west 100 yards down slope, tent pads, cables, spring unreliable. △
4520	2011.3	174.0	Doe Knob, NoBo follow NC/TN border; SoBo enter NC.
4381	2010.8	174.5	Mud Gap.
3842	2009.9	175.4	Ekaneetlee Gap.
4602	2008.5	176.8	**Mollies Ridge Shelter**, spring unreliable 23.7◄17.6◄11.0◄▶2.8▶5.7▶12.0 △ ⌂ (12)
4775	2008.4	176.9	Devils Tater Patch.
4120	2006.5	178.8	Little Abrams Gap
4122	2006.3	179.0	Big Abrams Gap
4367	2005.7	179.6	**Russell Field Shelter**, spring 0.1W 20.4◄13.8◄2.8◄▶2.9▶9.2▶14.7 ⌂ (14)
4799	2004.2	181.1	Stream.

The BMT reconnects with the AT at Davenport Gap. These 102 miles of the BMT on the NC side has rich cove forests and only one shelter. The high point of the BMT in the Smokies is 5843'.

NoBo		Elev
2002.8	**Spence Field Shelter** (0.2E) on Eagle Creek Trail ♪ ◊ ⊂ (12)	4921
	16.7◄5.7◄2.9◄►6.3►11.8►13.5 100 yards north, Bote Mountain Trail to west.	
2002.4	Jenkins Ridge trail to east.	4935
2001.6	Rocky Top, views	5440
2001.0	Thunderhead Mountain	5527
2000.3	Water to west. ●	4922
❋	Sarvis Tree – Also called "serviceberry." Blooms with plentiful petite white petaled flowers.	
1998.4	Starkey Gap.	4555
1997.6	Sugar Tree Gap.	4435
1996.5	**Derrick Knob Shelter** ● ◊ ⊂ (12)	4901
	12.0◄9.2◄6.3◄►5.5►7.2►13.5 Reliable spring near shelter. Cables.	
1996.2	Sams Gap, Greenbrier Ridge Trail to west ●	4775
1994.2	Cold Spring Knob	5187
1993.9	Miry Ridge Trail to west.	4929
1993.7	Buckeye Gap ●	4817
1991.0	**Silers Bald Shelter**, spring 75 yard to right of shelter. ⊂ (12)	5454
	14.7◄11.8◄5.5◄►1.7►8.0►15.5	
1990.8	Silers Bald, survey mark on boulder, AT turns to east.	5607
1990.6	Welch Ridge Trail to east.	5444
1989.3	**Double Spring Gap Shelter** 13.5◄7.2◄1.7◄►6.3►13.8►21.2 ● ⊂ (12)	5511
	Best water 15 yards from crest on NC side. Water is also 35 yards down TN side.	
1988.7	Goshen Prong Trail to west.	5768
1986.8	Mt Buckley	6585
1986.7	Trail 0.5E to Clingman's parking area (NoBo be careful at this fork).	6553
1986.4	Clingmans Tower Path, paved path between tower and parking area	6643
1986.2	Clingmans Dome, tower to east Ⓐ (pg.26)	6655
1985.2	Mt Love	6446
1984.1	Collins Gap	5764
1983.4	Mt Collins	6182
1983.0	Sugarland Mtn Trail, **Mt Collins Shelter** (0.5W) ♪ ● ⊂ (12)	5970
	13.5◄8.3◄6.3◄►7.5►14.9►20.1 Cables. Small spring 0.1 beyond shelter.	

SoBo

137.3   US 19 & 74

⊛⊕ ⛺🚐📞 **Nantahala Outdoor Center** 888-905-7238 ⟨www.noc.com⟩ Complex with lodging, food, gear & whitewater rafting. Coin-op showers available to non-guests Apr-Oct. In-season office hours 8-5. Reservations recommended, even for the hostel. If you walk in without reservation, go to General Store to check in, or to the River's End Restaurant if the store is closed.

🛏 Motel rooms $59/up. Prices higher mid-summer, weekends and holidays. Baisc rooms do not have TV or phone. Rooms with more amenities are available at **Nantahala Inn** 1.5 miles away. For large groups, it can be economical to rent a cabin; ask about prices.

🛏 **Base Camp (hostel)** $19.387 includes tax, shower and use of common area and kitchen. Check in at general store.

🍴📶 **River's End Restaurant** (B/L/D); **Big Wesser BBQ/ Pourover Pub** Live music, opens mid-April.

🥾🚮🚐📧 **NOC Outfitters** Full service outfitter, fuel/oz. Experienced staff, gear shakedowns, Full line of gear and trail food. Open 7 days, extended hours in summer. Ask about shuttles. Maildrops: dated & marked "Hold for AT Hiker", 13077 Hwy 19W, Bryson City, NC 28713.

🏪 **Wesser General Store**

🚐 **Jude Julius** 828-736-0086 In Bryson City, NC. Shuttle range Standing Indian to Fontana.

150.7   Stecoah Gap, NC 143

🛏🛏🍴⛺🚐📶📧 **The Cabin in the Woods** Phil Capper 828-735-3368 or 828-735-1930 ⟨www.thecabininthewoods.com⟩ Lodging includes ride to/from the trail up to 15 miles each way. 2 cabins $65 or $70, are often booked so reserve early. The loft accommodates 2 hikers; $30 includes ride, shower, bathroom. $15 resupply trip up to 4 persons. Shuttles anywhere 50 cents per mile. Family style breakfast $6, dinner $10, laundry $3/load. Pets ⟨40 pounds. Maildrops: 301 Stechoa Heights Rd. Robbinsville, NC 28771

🛏⛺📶📧 **Buffalo Creek B&B** 828-479-3892 RobMason@rocketmail.com. Hiker rate (no drive-ins) $70 for single or double includes pickup/return from Stecoah Gap or Fontana Dam, a resupply stop in Robbinsville, laundry and breakfast. Open April-October, call for availability in other months. The B&B offers WiFi and you may print your Smokies permit here. Maildrops (guests only): 4989 W. Buffalo Creek Rd, Robbinsville, NC 28771.

🛏⛺📶 **Appalachian Inn** 828-479-8450 Luxurious log cabin with great views $130-150 double, 1.2E from Stechoa Gap. Includes pickup/return from Stecoah Gap, laundry and full country breakfast. Additional charge for lunch/dinner. Some rooms have jacuzzi tubs.

Robbinsville, NC 28771 (8W) Compact town center with motel, restaurants, PO, grocery, pharmacy and laundromat within walking distance of each other.

🏤 M–F 9–4:30, 828-479-3397

🛏📶 **San Ran Motel** 828-479-3256 Non-smoking rooms with fridge and microwave. No pets.

164.6   NC 28

🚻🚐 **Fontana 28 AT Crossing** Bathrooms, vending machines, GSMNP maps ($1), and house phone to call for shuttle. More snacks and canned meats available from bait store on dock 0.1E. $3 for shuttle   between here or shelter to/from Fontana Village 8:30-6 daily 2/15-5/15.

Peter Barr ("Whippersnap" GA-ME 2010), author of **Hiking North Carolina's Lookout Towers,** *recorded the track and landmarks that are the core of this book.*

24
NC

Fontana Village, NC (2W from NC 28) For all facilities contact: 800-849-2258 or 828-498-2211

🛏️✉️🖥️💲 **Fontana Lodge** Ask for thru-hiker rate $59 Su-Th, $89 F-Sa, room holds up to 4, no pets. Price may be higher on high-demand nights. Cabins $99/up. Maildrops: Fontana Village Resort, ATTN: Front Desk, 300 Woods Dr., Fontana Dam, NC 28733.

🛒🖥️ **General Store** Grocery store, freeze-dried food, Coleman/alcohol/oz, isobutane canisters during thru-hiker season, small selection of gear items. 10% discount for thru-hikers on non-food items. Open Mar 7-Nov 28.

🍴 **Mountainview Bistro** is pricey; the **Wildwood Grill** does not open until May 1; the **Fontana Pit Stop** offers hot dogs, nachos and microwave fare.

⛺ **Laundromat** 7 days, open year-round.

166.1 Fontana Dam Visitor Center

ℹ️🏛️🚻🚿 Sodas, snacks, camera supplies, free showers, GSMP self-registration permits. Open 9am-6pm daily May-Oct. Verizon and AT&T cell phones may get signal at the overlook near the shelter parking area.

🛏️⛺🚌 (6.3E) **The Hike Inn** 828-479-3677 ⟨www.thehikeinn.com⟩ hikeinn@graham.main.nc.us. A hiker only service owned and operated by Jeff and Nancy Hoch since 1993. They offer Thru-hiker/long distance hiker packages, section/day hiker rates, shuttles by arrangement as well as a variety of other hiker services. Please call, e-mail or visit their website for more information, reservations and directions.

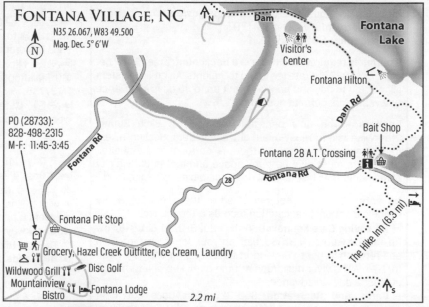

FONTANA VILLAGE, NC

N35 26.067, W83 49.500
Mag. Dec. 5°6'W

PO (28733):
828-498-2315
M-F: 11:45-3:45

Fontana Rd

Fontana Pit Stop

Grocery, Hazel Creek Outfitter, Ice Cream, Laundry

Wildwood Grill
Mountainview Bistro   Disc Golf
Fontana Lodge

2.2 mi

Dam

Fontana Lake

Visitor's Center

Fontana Hilton

Dam Rd

Bait Shop

Fontana 28 A.T. Crossing

Fontana Rd

The Hike Inn (6.3 mi)

APPALACHIAN TRAIL
CONSERVANCY®

Great Smoky Mountains NP ⟨www.nps.gov/grsm⟩
Backcountry Info: 865-436-1297
Reservations: 865-436-1231

A permit is required and there is a backcountry fee - $4PP per night or $20PP flat rate fee for up to 7 nights. An on-line system allows you to pay and print a permit up to 30 days in advance ⟨www.smokiespermits.nps.gov⟩

Shelters - The only near-trail campsite is Birch Spring. Otherwise hikers must overnight at shelters. Section hikers must make reservations. If there is no room in the shelter, thru-hikers must give up bunk space and tent in the vicinity of the shelter. All hikers must use bear cables to secure food.

No pets - Dogs are not permitted in the park. Below are kenneling options, vaccination records often required:

🐾 ✉ **Loving Care Kennels** 865-453-2028, 3779 Tinker Hollow Rd, Pigeon Forge, TN 37863. Pick up your dog at Fontana Dam and return him/her to Davenport Gap. $325 for one dog, $450 for two. Will deliver maildrops at time of pickup or return. Call at least 2 days in advance.

🐾 **Barks and Recreation** 865-325-8245 Does not offer rides, but you can drop off/pickup from 2159 East Parkway Gatlinburg, TN. M-F 7am-8pm, Su 10-6.

🐾 **Standing Bear Farm** (see pg. 32)

199.1   **Clingmans Dome** N35 33.433 W83 29.634 🅿 🚻
This is the highest point on the Appalachian Trail. Parking lot and restrooms are 0.5E on a paved walkway. It's 7 mi. from the parking area to Newfound Gap on Clingmans Dome Rd, and the road is closed to cars Dec 1 - Apr 1. There are no sinks in the restrooms. Gift shop near parking area sometimes sells drinks and snacks.

206.8   Newfound Gap, US 441   *Gatlinburg, TN* (15W)
🛏🏕🚗🛜🖥 **Grand Prix Motel** 865-436-4561, $29.95/up, coin laundry. Shuttle up to 4 persons to Newfound Gap $30 or Clingmans Dome for $35. Maildrops: 235 Ski Mtn Rd, Gatlinburg, TN 37738.

🛏🛜✉ **Microtel Gatlinburg** 865-436-0107 $44.95/up, cont B, pets $10. Maildrop with reservation only: 211 Historic Nature Trail, Gatlinburg, TN 37738.

🛏🛜✉ **Motel 6** 865-436-7813 Room for 2: $40 weekdays, $50 weekends, room for 4: $46 weekdays, $56 weekends. Pool, pets $10. Trolley stops at the front door. All major CC. Maildrops: 309 Ownby St, Gatlinburg, TN 37738.

🛏🛜 **Days Inn** 865-436-5811
🛏🛜 **Best Western** 865-436-5121

🚶🍴🚗✉ **NOC Great Outpost** 865-277-8209 Open 7 days 10-9, 10-6 in winter (Jan-May). Full line of gear and white gas/denatured/oz. Free showers & pack storage, call for trailhead shuttle schedule. Maildrops: 1138 Parkway, Gatlinburg, TN 37738.

🚶 **The Day Hiker** 865-430-0970 Small shop with shoes and fuel.
🚗 **Highlands Shuttle Service** (Ron McGaha) 423-625-0739 or 865-322-2752 mdron@bellsouth.net, shuttles from Standing Indian (NC) to Damascus, VA. Also pick up/drop off at Knoxville and Asheville airports and bus stations.

🚗 **A Walk in the Woods** 865-436-8283 ⟨www.aWalkintheWoods.com⟩ GSMNP guides Vesna and Erik Plakanis shuttle anywhere from Springer to Damascus. Can help with resupply & dog shuttling while you are in the Smokies.

🚗 **Cherokee Transit** 866-388-6071 ⟨www.cherokeetransit.com⟩
■ **Roger Bailey, LMT** 865-250-0676 Special thru-hiker rate $50 for one-hour massage.

Cherokee, NC (21E) Large town, many services.
🛏🏕🚗🛜🖥☎ **Microtel Inn & Suites** 828-497-7800 $65, higher on wkends, includes breakfast, free local/long distance phone. Coin laundry, pool. Adjacent supermarket, fast-food, shoe store.

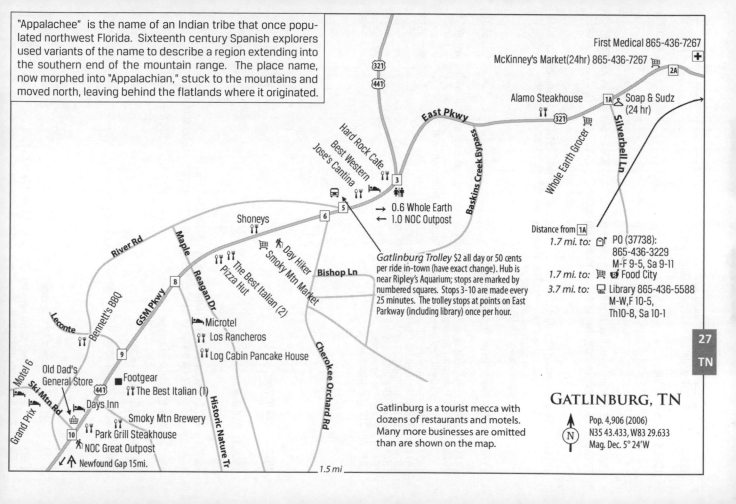

"Appalachee" is the name of an Indian tribe that once populated northwest Florida. Sixteenth century Spanish explorers used variants of the name to describe a region extending into the southern end of the mountain range. The place name, now morphed into "Appalachian," stuck to the mountains and moved north, leaving behind the flatlands where it originated.

First Medical 865-436-7267

McKinney's Market(24hr) 865-436-7267

Alamo Steakhouse

Soap & Sudz (24 hr)

Whole Earth Grocer

Hard Rock Cafe
Best Western
Jose's Cantina

East Pkwy

Baskins Creek Bypass

Silverbell Ln

→ 0.6 Whole Earth
← 1.0 NOC Outpost

Shoneys

Day Hiker
Smoky Mtn Market

Bishop Ln

Gatlinburg Trolley $2 all day or 50 cents per ride in-town (have exact change). Hub is near Ripley's Aquarium; stops are marked by numbered squares. Stops 3-10 are made every 25 minutes. The trolley stops at points on East Parkway (including library) once per hour.

Distance from 1A
1.7 mi. to: PO (37738): 865-436-3229 M-F 9-5, Sa 9-11
1.7 mi. to: Food City
3.7 mi. to: Library 865-436-5588 M-W,F 10-5, Th10-8, Sa 10-1

River Rd

Maple

The Best Italian (2)
Pizza Hut

Reagan Dr

GSM Pkwy

Bennett's BBQ

Leconte

Microtel
Los Rancheros
Log Cabin Pancake House

Cherokee Orchard Rd

27
TN

Motel 6
Old Dad's General Store
Footgear
The Best Italian (1)
Days Inn
Smoky Mtn Brewery
Park Grill Steakhouse
NOC Great Outpost
Newfound Gap 15mi.

Ski Mtn Rd
Grand Prix

Historic Nature Tr

Gatlinburg is a tourist mecca with dozens of restaurants and motels. Many more businesses are omitted than are shown on the map.

GATLINBURG, TN

Pop. 4,906 (2006)
N35 43.433, W83 29.633
Mag. Dec. 5° 24'W

1.5 mi

28
NC/TN

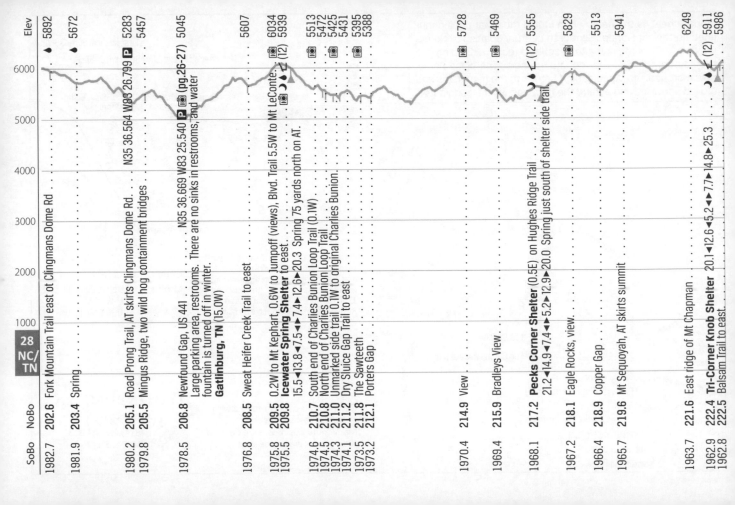

SoBo	NoBo	Description	Elev
1982.7	202.6	Fork Mountain Trail east ot Clingmans Dome Rd	5892
1981.9	203.4	Spring	5672
1980.2	205.1	Road Prong Trail, AT skirts Clingmans Dome Rd. N35 36.564 W83 26.799 P	5283
1979.8	205.5	Mingus Ridge, two wild hog containment bridges	5457
1978.5	206.8	Newfound Gap, US 441. N35 36.669 W83 25.540 P (pg.26-27) Large parking area, restrooms. There are no sinks in restrooms, and water fountain is turned off in winter. **Gatlinburg, TN** (15.0W)	5045
1976.8	208.5	Sweat Heifer Creek Trail to east	5607
1975.8	209.5	0.2W to Mt Kephart, 0.6W to Jumpoff (views), Blvd. Trail 5.5W to Mt LeConte	6034
1975.5	209.8	**Icewater Spring Shelter** to east. 15.5◀13.8◀7.5◀▶12.6▶20.3 Spring 75 yards north on AT.	5939
1974.6	210.7	South end of Charlies Bunion Loop Trail (0.1W)	5513
1974.5	210.8	North end of Charlies Bunion Loop Trail.	5472
1974.3	211.0	Unmarked side trail 0.1W to original Charlies Bunion.	5425
1974.1	211.2	Dry Sluice Gap Trail to east	5431
1973.5	211.8	The Sawteeth	5395
1973.2	212.1	Porters Gap	5388
1970.4	214.9	View	5728
1969.4	215.9	Bradleys View	5469
1968.1	217.2	**Pecks Corner Shelter** (0.5E) on Hughes Ridge Trail 21.2◀14.9◀7.4◀▶5.2▶12.9▶20.0 Spring just south of shelter side trail	5555
1967.2	218.1	Eagle Rocks, view.	5829
1966.4	218.9	Copper Gap	5513
1965.7	219.6	Mt Sequoyah, AT skirts summit	5941
1963.7	221.6	East ridge of Mt Chapman	6249
1962.9	222.4	**Tri-Corner Knob Shelter** 20.1◀12.6◀5.2◀▶7.7▶14.8▶25.3	5911
1962.8	222.5	Balsam Trail to east.	5986

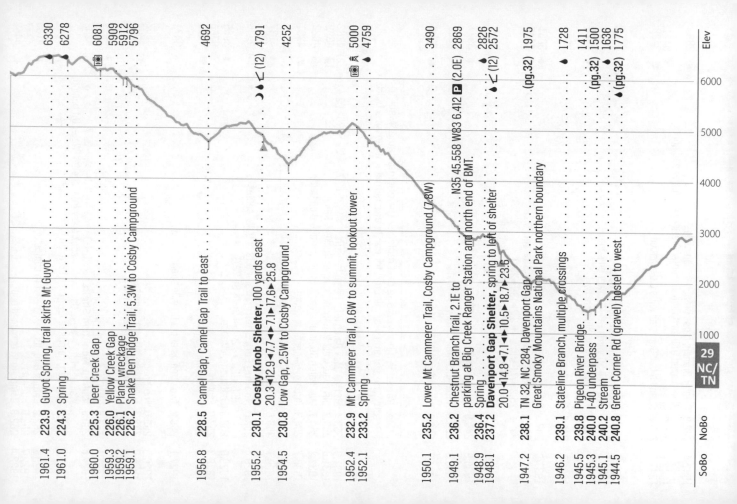

SoBo	NoBo	Description	Elev
1961.4	223.9	Guyot Spring, trail skirts Mt Guyot	6330
1961.0	224.3	Spring	6278
1960.0	225.3	Deer Creek Gap	6081
1959.3	226.0	Yellow Creek Gap	5909
1959.2	226.1	Plane wreckage	5912
1959.1	226.2	Snake Den Ridge Trail, 5.3W to Cosby Campground	5796
1956.8	228.5	Camel Gap, Camel Gap Trail to east	4692
1955.2	230.1	**Cosby Knob Shelter,** 100 yards east 20.3◄12.9◄7.7◄►7.1►17.6►25.8	4791
1954.5	230.8	Low Gap, 2.5W to Cosby Campground.	4252
1952.4	232.9	Mt Cammerer Trail, 0.6W to summit, lookout tower.	5000
1952.1	233.2	Spring	4759
1950.1	235.2	Lower Mt Cammerer Trail, Cosby Campground (7.8W)	3490
1949.1	236.2	Chestnut Branch Trail, 2.1E to parking at Big Creek Ranger Station and north end of BMT. N35 45.558 W83 6.412 **P** (2.0E)	2869
1948.9	236.4	Spring	2826
1948.1	237.2	**Davenport Gap Shelter,** spring to left of shelter 20.0◄14.8◄7.1◄►10.5►18.7►23.6	2572
1947.2	238.1	TN 32, NC 284, Davenport Gap Great Smoky Mountains National Park northern boundary (pg.32)	1975
1946.2	239.1	Stateline Branch, multiple crossings	1728
1945.5	239.8	Pigeon River Bridge.	1411
1945.3	240.0	I-40 underpass (pg.32)	1500
1945.1	240.2	Stream	1636
1944.5	240.8	Green Corner Rd (gravel) hostel to west. (pg.32)	1775

Appalachian Trail elevation profile — NC/TN, page 30

SoBo	NoBo	Feature	Elev
1942.4	242.9	Painter Branch, cross branch to campsites. Blue-blazed trail east across Painter Creek to campsite and spring.	2893
1942.1	243.2	Stream.	3121
1941.5	243.8	Spanish Oak Gap, trail joins old roadbed	3489
1940.1	245.2	Snowbird Mountain, grassy bald, side trail 50 yards to FAA tower on summit.	4263
1939.3	246.0	Wildcat Spring uphill from trail	4075
1938.7	246.6	Turkey Gap	3648
1937.8	247.5	Spring	3061
1937.6	247.7	Deep Gap, **Groundhog Creek Shelter** (0.2E) 25.3◀17.6◀10.5▶8.2▶13.1▶23.0 Stone shelter with reliable spring to left. Cables.	2929
1935.8	249.5	Spring downhill, east 30 yards	3577
1935.3	250.0	Rube Rock Trail to Hawks Roost.	3855
1934.7	250.6	Brown Gap, USFS 148A	3500
1932.2	253.1	Cherry Creek Trail	4344
1931.9	253.4	SR 1182, Max Patch Rd., stream to north. N35 47.776 W82 57.762 (pg.32)	4262
1931.6	253.7	Dirt road, west to parking, east to Buckeye Ridge	4392
1931.2	254.1	Max Patch Summit (campfires not permitted on bald)	4629
1930.7	254.6	Stream, campsite to south.	4391
1930.3	255.0	Roadbed, Buckeye Ridge Trail to east	4226
1929.7	255.6	Stream.	4137
1929.5	255.8	Water to east (signed)	4057
1929.4	255.9	**Roaring Fork Shelter**, water 0.1S or 0.4N, cables 25.8◀18.7◀8.2▶4.9▶14.8▶29.0	4036
1929.0	256.3	Footbridge, stream	3955
1928.3	257.0	Footbridge	3765
1927.9	257.4	Stream (many in area)	3654
1927.1	258.2	Two streams about 0.1 mile apart	3471
1926.3	259.0	Footbridge	3562
1926.0	259.3	Footbridge, stream, campsite	3504
1925.8	259.5	Lemon Gap, NC 1182, TN 107	3550
1925.1	260.2	Stream.	3963
1924.6	260.7	Walnut Mountain, grassy clearing	4305
1924.5	260.8	**Walnut Mountain Shelter** 23.6◀13.1◀4.9▶9.9▶24.1▶32.7 Walnut Mt tr. to west. Use cables, cook away from shelter. Water 0.1 behind.	4262
1923.8	261.5	Kale Gap, campsite 125 yards north on AT.	3714
1923.1	262.2	Catpen Gap, 100 yards east to campsite	4135
1922.7	262.6	Streams	4277
1922.4	262.9	Campsite in unnamed gap	4452

"Max Patch" is a homophone that replaced the original name "Mack's Patch". The summit was cleared for cattle and is maintained as a bald.

30
NC/TN

SoBo	NoBo	Description	Elev
1922.1	263.2	Bluff Mountain	4686
1921.4	263.9	Spring 50 yards west.	4210
1920.8	264.5	Old roadbed, spring.	3939
1920.5	264.8	Big Rock Spring located in ravine	3730
1919.9	265.4	Dirt road	3427
1919.3	266.0	Brook with cascades	2995
1918.9	266.4	Old Rd	2715
1918.0	267.3	Garenflo Gap, Shut-In Trail to west . . . N35 51.206 W82 52.556 P	2500
1917.3	268.0	Taylor Hollow Gap, two footbridges, one over a stream	2663
1914.6	270.7	**Deer Park Mountain Shelter** (0.2E) water at gap west of AT. 23.0◄14.8◄9.9◄ ►14.2►22.8►29.6 Cables. Gragg Gap 0.1 north on AT,	2339
1913.8	271.5	Deer Park Mountain.	2583
1911.4	273.9	NC 209 + US 25/70 . . . N35 53.371 W82 49.937 P (pg.32-33)	1326
1911.0	274.3	**Hot Springs, NC** French Broad River, US 25/70 bridge	1326
1910.5	274.8	NoBo turn east (hop guardrail) immediately after crossing river. 50 yards east to campsite by river	1330
1910.1	275.2	Lovers Leap Rock, several rock outcroppings, Silver Mine Trail to west	1682
1909.4	275.9	Campsite to east	2210
1908.1	277.2	Pump Gap, trail crossing	2130
1907.4	277.9	Springs	2336
1906.5	278.8	Campsite, north intersection with Pump Gap Loop Trail	2490
1906.2	279.1	Pond with boxed spring, campsite.	2529
1906.0	279.3	NoBo: AT 0.3W on dirt road. Cross Mill Ridge to gravel road.	2646
1905.7	279.6	(double-blazed oak tree). Go 0.1W on gravel road and reenter woods to east. Stream.	
1905.5	279.8	Tanyard Gap, US 25/70 overpass . . . N35 54.597 W82 47.46i P	2454 / 2270
1904.1	281.2	Piped spring	3044
1903.6	281.7	Roundtop Ridge Trail west 3.5 miles to Hot Springs (former path of AT)	3246
1903.1	282.2	Side trail 0.1W to Rich Mountain Lookout Tower,	3543
1902.6	282.7	Spring . . . piped spring and campsite north on AT.	3218
1902.2	283.1	Hurricane Gap, northmost of two gravel road crossings	2982

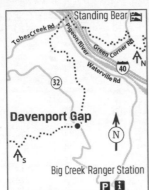

Standing Bear
TobesCreek Rd
Pigeon River
Green Corner Rd
Waterville Rd
40
32
Davenport Gap
Big Creek Ranger Station

238.1 TN 32, NC 284, Davenport Gap **Great Smoky Mountain NP**
(1.3E) **Big Creek Ranger Station** 828-486-5910
(2.3E) **Big Creek Campground** 865-436-1261 $14/site, no showers or electricity. Open Apr 1 - Oct 31. Chestnut Branch Tr (2.0mi) connects campground to AT 0.1S of Davenport Gap Shelter.

240.0 I-40 **Melissa Browning** 423-623-7074 shuttles from I-40 or Davenport Gap to Newport (town has hotels, restaurants, Walmart) or Hot Springs.

240.8 Green Corner Rd
Standing Bear Farm (0.1W) 423-487-0014 curtisvowen@gmail.com; Hosted by Maria & Curtis. $20PP cabin, $15 bunkhouse or tenting. Food for sale that you can cook yourself. Reasonably-priced resupply. White gas/alcohol/oz, canister fuel. Daypack loaner for slackpackers. Shuttles anywhere. Dogs must be kept on a leash while on property. Kennel service available while you hike Smokies; ask about rates. Directions: Green Corner Rd is gravel road 1.0 north of I-40, go west 200 yards to white farmhouse (see map). Parking: short term $5/car/day, long term $3/car/day. Maildrops: 4255 Green Corner Rd, Hartford, TN 37753.

HOT SPRINGS, NC

Pop. 637 (2007)
N35 53.700, W82 49.717
Mag. Dec. 5°58'W

PO (28743):
828-622-3242
M-F 9-11:30 & 1-4,
Sa 9-10:30

Mountain Magnolia Inn
Still Mtn Restaurant
Creekside Court
Spring Creek Tavern
Hiker's Ridge Ministries
Bill Whitten Center
Wash Tub
Hot Springs Resort and Campground
Hot Springs Medical Center
828-622-3245
Harvest Moon
Hillbilly Market
Dollar General
Smoky Mtn Diner
Elmer's Sunnybank Inn
Hostel at Laughing Heart Lodge
Bridge St
Welcome Center
Library: 828-622-3584 M,Tu,Th 10-6, F 10-5, W,Sa 10-2
Alpine Court
Gentry Hardware
Bluff Mtn Outfitter & Trailside Natural Foods
Artisun Gallery
Iron Horse Station Inn and Restaurant
Spring Brook Cottages
L&K's
Walnut St
Spring St
Andrews Ave
Surpentine Ave
209
25
70
32
NC
French Broad River
Zack's Smokehouse BBQ
0.7 mi

253.4 Max Patch Rd (8.0E to hostel)
Hostel of the Mountain 217-597-0718 Hostelofthemountain@gmail.com. $25 includes bunkroom & dinner. $20 for pickup and return from Max Patch Rd or Hot Springs. Even with ride there is a 2 mile walk to cabin on picturesque Sandy Mush Bald devoted to sustainable living practices. Drink/smoke responsibly. Work-for-stay sometimes available. No pets. Maildrops with reservation: 19001 NC HWY 209 Hot Springs,NC 28743.

273.9 NC 209, US 25/70 *Hot Springs, NC* Home to **Trailfest** on April 11-13, Friday night spaghetti dinner $5 at the Comm. Center, activities all day Saturday and Sunday breakfast.
Elmers Sunnybank Inn 828-622-7206 ⟨www.sunnybankretreatassociation.org⟩ Long-distance hikers (100+ miles) stay for $20PP private room, includes linens, towel and shower. Guests only can purchase breakfast $6 and dinner $12; gourmet organic vegetarian meals.

No pets, no smoking, no credit cards. Historic Sunnybank Inn has offered hospitality to AT hikers since 1947. Staffed by former thru-hikers, the Inn offers an extensive library & well-equipped music room. Work exchange possible. Maildrops: PO Box 233, Hot Springs, NC 28743.

🛏️�🔥⛺🚿🚌📶✉ **Hostel at Laughing Heart Lodge** 813-763-7868 At south trailhead parking lot. $15pp bunkroom, $25 single private, $40 double private. All rooms include shower & towel, movies, reading room, full kitchen, wireless access. Pet friendly. Tenting with shower $10, shower only $5. Quiet time 10pm-7am. Lodge rooms $75-100 include continental breakfast. Hosted by hikers Chuck Norris & Tigger. Maildrops: 289 NW Hwy 25/70, Hot Springs, NC 28743.

🛏️🍴📶 **Iron Horse Station** 866-402-9377 Hiker rate $55D. Restaurant, tavern and coffee shop. Serves L/D, and offers some vegetarian options. Live music Tu, Wed, Fri & Saturday.

🛏️📶✉ **Alpine Court Motel** 828-206-3384 Hiker rate Mar-Jun $42S, $55D. No credit cards. Maildrops: 50 Bridge St, Hot Springs, NC 28743.

🛏️📶 **Creekside Court** 828-215-1261 $75D, lower on weekdays, ask for hiker discount, pets allowed.

🛏️🔥🚿🏠🍴📶 **Hot Springs Resort Cabins Campground & Spa** 828-622-7267 ⟨www.nchotsprings.com⟩ Tenting $10S, $24 up to 4. Cabins $50 sleeps 5 with common bath & hot showers, $66 cabin sleeps 8. Pet fee $10. Shower w/o stay $5. Famous Hot Springs mineral water spa $15S before 6pm; 3-person rate $30 before 6pm, $35 after 6pm. The Camp store carries snacks and some supplies. Also offers massage therapy. Accepts Visa/MC/Disc.

🛏️🍴📶 **Mountain Magnolia Inn** 800-914-9306 Discount hiker rates when rooms available $65-$130 includes AYCE breakfast. Dinner Th-M open to all. Maildrops: 204 Lawson St, Hot Springs, NC 28743.

🛏️ **Creekside Court Cabins and Restaurant** 828-215-1261

🍴 **Smoky Mountain Diner** Hiker special 12 oz burger.

🍴 **Spring Creek Tavern** 50 varieties of beer, outdoor deck overlooking creek, live music Thurs-Sunday nights.

🍴📶✉ **ArtiSun Gallery** 828-622-3573 Coffee, baked goods, ultimate local ice cream, 50% off ALDHA membership, may use phone. AT hiker artwork. UPS or FedEx maildrops: 16 S. Andrews Ave, Hot Springs, NC 28743.

🚶📶🖥️ **Hiker's Ridge Ministries Resource Center** Open M-Sa 9-3, Mar 15-May 15. Place to relax, coffee, drinks, doughnuts, kitchen internet, restroom.

🍴 **Harvest Moon** Coffee, fresh lemonade, tincture. Next to PO; feel free to spread out on lawn and sort through your maildrops.

🚶🛒💲🚌🖥️✉ **Bluff Mountain Outfitters** 828-622-7162, Su-Th 9-5, F-Sa 9-6 ⟨www.bluffmountain.com⟩ Full service outfitter, fuel/oz. Natural foods grocery and other foods make this a one-stop location for complete resupply. Computer for internet access, free 30 min for hikers. ATM and scale inside. Shuttles Springer to Roanoke & area airports. SoBo hikers can print Smoky Mtn NP permits here. Ships UPS packages. Maildrops: (USPS) PO Box 114 Hot Springs, NC 28743 or (FedEx/UPS) 152 Bridge St.

290.2   Log Cabin Drive (dirt/gravel road)

🛏️🚲🔥🏠🚌 🅿🚌📶✉ **(0.7W) Hemlock Hollow Inn & Paint Creek Cafe** 423-787-0917 ⟨www.hemlockhollowinn.com⟩ West on Log Cabin Dr. to paved Viking Mountain Rd. Cabin $50/75 (up to 3) w/linens. Single $25 w/linens, $20 without. All cabins heated. Tent site $12PP. Pets $5 extra. All stays include shower, free return ride to trail. Non-guests can get shower & towel for $4. Camp store stocked with long term resupply, some gear, cold drinks, foods, fruit, stove fuels. Cafe open 7 days in hiker season, open-season if 4 or more. Shuttles available, slack-packing welcomed. Parking free for guests, $2/day for non-guests. Accepts Visa, M/C, Discover. Maildrops (ETA mandatory): 645 Chandler Circle, Greeneville, TN 37743.

309.0   Devil Fork Gap, NC 212

⚠ AT northbound is headed due south; trading post is "trail east" (to the right for northbounders) but compass west.

🚌🔥🏠🚿⛺ **(2.5E) Laurel Trading Post** 828-656-2492 M-Sa 7-7 Bunkroom $25, tenting $10, laundry $10, shower & towel w/o stay $5.

317.4   Sams Gap, US 23

🍴 **Little Creek Cafe** (2.8E) 828-689-2307 M-Th & Sa 6am-2pm, F 7-7.

🏠💲 **Wolf Creek Market** (3.3E) Open 7 days

		Elev

Top-right elevation axis with values and feature descriptions, elevation grid from 1000 to 6000.

SoBo	NoBo	Description	Elev
1901.8	283.5	Grave stone	2997
1900.4	284.9	**Spring Mountain Shelter** 29.0◄24.1◄14.2◄► 8.6►15.4►21.3 Water 75 yards down blue-blazed trail on east side of AT. Cables.	3556
1898.6	286.7	Deep Gap, Little Paint Creek Trail, west 200 yards to spring	2933
1897.2	288.1	Spring in ravine 30 yards west	2777
1896.6	288.7	NC 208, TN 70, Allen Gap, water 0.2W	2246
1895.6	289.7	AT skirts gravel road	2370
1895.1	290.2	Log Cabin Drive, private home in view 200 yards east, hostel to west . . . . (pg.33)	2383
1891.8	293.5	**Little Laurel Shelter** 32.7◄22.8◄8.6◄►6.8►12.7►21.5 Boxed spring 100 yards down blue-blazed trail behind shelter. Campsites west side of AT, south of shelter. Cables.	3670
1890.5	294.8	Pounding Mill Trail to east. 0.2W to Camp Creek Bald Lookout Tower. Tower is beyond first cluster of buildings and catwalk is locked (no view)	4750
1889.7	295.6	Jones Meadow, campsites 0.2W, spring 100 yards south	4452
1888.7	296.6	Trail west to Jones Meadow, 30 yards east to Whiterock Cliff.	4467
1888.5	296.8	0.1W to Blackstack Cliffs	4503
1888.3	297.0	Bearwallow Gap, Jerry Miller Trail to east, Firescald bypass to west reconnects with AT 1.5 miles north. AT between bypass points is rocky and strenuous.	4438
1887.6	297.7	Big Firescald Knob	4549
1886.7	298.6	Firescald bypass to west, reconnects with AT 1.5 miles south.	4192
1886.0	299.3	Round Knob Trail to west.	4294
1885.2	300.1	Fork Ridge Trail to east.	4289
1885.0	300.3	Chestnut Log Gap, **Jerry Cabin Shelter** 29.6◄15.4◄6.8◄►5.9►14.7►24.8 Water opposite shelter. Cables.	4166
1884.2	301.1	Bald Ridge	4529
1883.8	301.5	Sarvis Cove Trail to west	4540
1883.4	301.9	Howard C. Bassett Memorial, old roadbed before and after	4635
1883.1	302.2	Big Butt Mountain, summit to west, short bypass trail. ⚠ Squibb Creek Trail is "straight ahead," NoBo: AT east on gravel road for 1.5 mi.	4750

34
NC/
TN

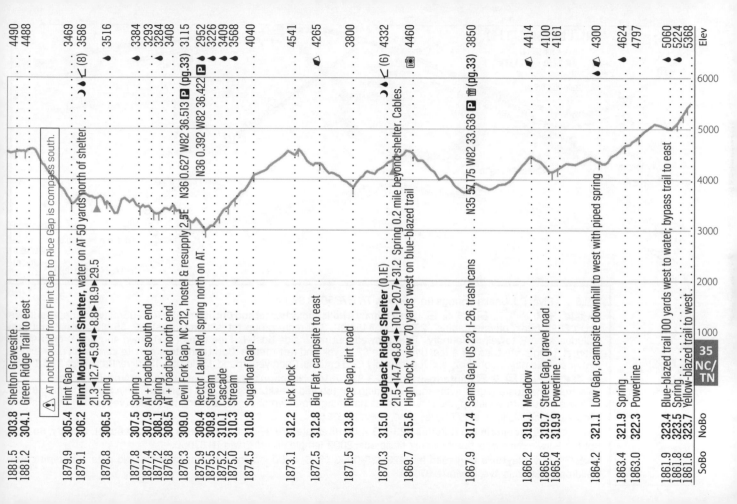

Elevation profile — page 35, NC/TN

SoBo	NoBo	Description	Elev	Symbols
1881.5	303.8	Shelton Gravesite	4490	
1881.2	304.1	Green Ridge Trail to east	4488	
		At nothbound from Flint Gap to Rice Gap is compass south.		
1879.9	305.4	Flint Gap	3469	
1879.1	306.2	**Flint Mountain Shelter,** water on AT at 50 yards north of shelter. 21.3◀12.7◀5.9◀▶8.8▶18.9▶29.5	3586	☾◑⊂(8)
1878.8	306.5	Spring	3516	◆
1877.8	307.5	Spring	3384	◆
1877.4	307.9	AT + roadbed south end	3293	◆
1877.2	308.1	Spring	3284	◆
1876.8	308.5	AT + roadbed north end	3408	◆
1876.3	309.0	Devil Fork Gap, NC 212, hostel & resupply 2.5E. N36 0.627 W82 36.513 P (pg.33)	3115	
1875.9	309.4	Rector Laurel Rd, spring north on AT. N36 0.392 W82 36.422 P	2952	◆
1875.5	309.8	Stream	3226	◆
1875.2	310.1	Cascade	3409	◆
1875.0	310.3	Stream	3568	◆
1874.5	310.8	Sugarloaf Gap	4040	
1873.1	312.2	Lick Rock	4541	
1872.5	312.8	Big Flat, campsite to east	4265	◭
1871.5	313.8	Rice Gap, dirt road	3800	
1870.3	315.0	**Hogback Ridge Shelter** (0.1E). Spring 0.2 mile beyond shelter. Cables. 21.5◀14.7◀8.8◀▶10.1▶20.7▶31.2	4332	☾◑⊂(6)
1869.7	315.6	High Rock, view 70 yards west on blue-blazed trail	4460	📷
1867.9	317.4	Sams Gap, US 23, I-26, trash cans. N35 57.175 W82 33.636 P 🏛 (pg.33)	3850	
1866.2	319.1	Meadow	4414	◭
1865.6	319.7	Street Gap, gravel road	4100	◭
1865.4	319.9	Powerline	4161	
1864.2	321.1	Low Gap, campsite downhill to west with piped spring	4300	◭
1863.4	321.9	Spring	4624	◆
1863.0	322.3	Powerline	4797	
1861.9	323.4	Blue-blazed trail 100 yards west to water; bypass trail to east	5060	◆
1861.8	323.5	Spring	5224	◆
1861.6	323.7	Yellow-blazed trail to west	5368	

SoBo · NoBo · Elev

35 NC/TN

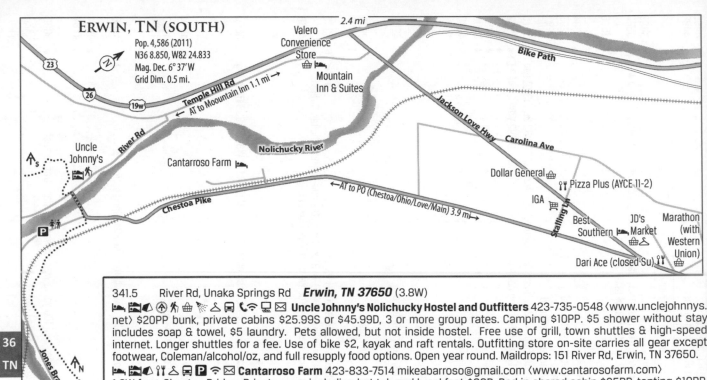

ERWIN, TN (SOUTH)

Pop. 4,586 (2011)
N36 8.850, W82 24.833
Mag. Dec. 6° 37'W
Grid Dim. 0.5 mi.

2.4 mi

Bike Path

Valero Convenience Store

Temple Hill Rd

Mountain Inn & Suites

← AT to Moountain Inn 1.1 mi →

Jackson Love Hwy

Carolina Ave

River Rd

Uncle Johnny's

Nolichucky River

Cantaroso Farm

Dollar General

Pizza Plus (AYCE 11-2)

IGA

Stalling Ln

←AT to PO (Chestoa/Ohio/Love/Main) 3.9 mi→

Chestoa Pike

P

Best Southern

JD's Market

Marathon (with Western Union)

Dari Ace (closed Su)

Jones Branch

Nolichucky Gorge Campground

36
TN

341.5   River Rd, Unaka Springs Rd   *Erwin, TN 37650* (3.8W)

Uncle Johnny's Nolichucky Hostel and Outfitters 423-735-0548 ⟨www.unclejohnnys. net⟩ $20PP bunk, private cabins $25.99S or $45.99D, 3 or more group rates. Camping $10PP. $5 shower without stay includes soap & towel, $5 laundry. Pets allowed, but not inside hostel. Free use of grill, town shuttles & high-speed internet. Longer shuttles for a fee. Use of bike $2, kayak and raft rentals. Outfitting store on-site carries all gear except footwear, Coleman/alcohol/oz, and full resupply food options. Open year round. Maildrops: 151 River Rd, Erwin, TN 37650.

Cantarroso Farm 423-833-7514 mikeabarroso@gmail.com ⟨www.cantarosofarm.com⟩ 1.0W from Chestoa Bridge. Private room including hot tub and breakfast $90D. Bed in shared cabin $25PP, tenting $10PP. All stays include free pickup and return. Additional charge for town shuttles, laundry, breakfast (vegetarian options) and secure parking. Maildrops: 777 Bailey Lane, Erwin TN 37650.

Mountain Inn & Suites 423-743-4100 Hiker rate $79.99 up to 4 includes breakfast buffet, laundry, no pets. Hot tub & swimming pool summer only. Maildrops: 2002 Temple Hill Rd, Erwin TN 37650.

Clayton's Dogwood Inn 423-735-0093 $50S, $65D includes full hot breakfast. No pets, no credit cards. Maildrops: 430 Ohio Ave, Erwin TN 37650.

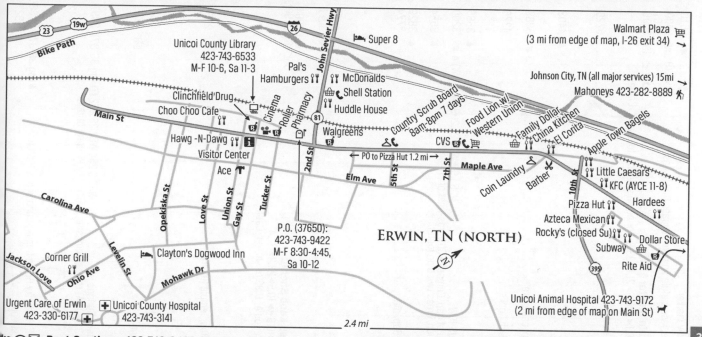

ERWIN, TN (NORTH)

Walmart Plaza (3 mi from edge of map, I-26 exit 34)

Johnson City, TN (all major services) 15mi
Mahoneys 423-282-8889

Super 8

Unicoi County Library
423-743-6533
M-F 10-6, Sa 11-3

Pal's Hamburgers
McDonalds
Shell Station
Huddle House

Clinchfield Drug
Choo Choo Cafe
Cinema
Roller
Pharmacy

Hawg -N-Dawg
Visitor Center
Ace

Country Scrub Board 8am-8pm 7 days
Walgreens

Food Lion w/ Western Union
Family Dollar
China Kitchen
El Corita
Apple Town Bagels
CVS

← PO to Pizza Hut 1.2 mi →

Elm Ave
Coin Laundry
Barber
Maple Ave

Little Caesars
KFC (AYCE 11-8)
Hardees
Pizza Hut
Azteca Mexican
Rocky's (closed Su)
Subway
Dollar Store
Rite Aid

Main St
Carolina Ave
Opekiska St
Love St
Union St
Gay St
Tucker St
2nd St
5th St
7th St
10th St

P.O. (37650):
423-743-9422
M-F 8:30-4:45,
Sa 10-12

Corner Grill
Jackson Love
Ohio Ave
Levelln St
Mohawk Dr
Clayton's Dogwood Inn

Urgent Care of Erwin
423-330-6177
Unicoi County Hospital
423-743-3141

Unicoi Animal Hospital 423-743-9172
(2 mi from edge of map on Main St)

399

2.4 mi

Best Southern 423-743-6438 $39.95S, $49.95D, no pets, Maildrops: 1315 Jackson Love Hwy, Erwin, TN 37650.

Super 8 423-743-0200, $49.99S, $59.99D includes breakfast, no pets. Maildrops: 1101 N Buffalo St, Erwin TN 37650.

Cherokee Adventures 800-445-7238 $10PP bunkhouse, $5PP camping. Open Mar-Oct. Call ahead; rides sometimes available.

Azteca (north end of town) Serves beer.

Shuttles by Tom 423-330-7416, 910-409-2509 Springer to Rockfish Gap including pickups at Asheville, Tri-Cities Knoxville

airports. Maildrops: Tom Bradford, ATTN: [hiker name], 620 Grove Ave. Erwin, TN 37650.

NetTrans 423-461-8288 ⟨www.NetTrans.org⟩ Erwin Connex on-demand service to Walmart $2. Regularly-scheduled shuttles from Walmart to Johnson City $3 approx. 6 times daily.

343.2   Side trail to:

Nolichucky Gorge Campground 423-743-8876, ⟨www.nolichucky.com⟩ Tent site $10, cabin $80/up, primarily caters to river recreation.

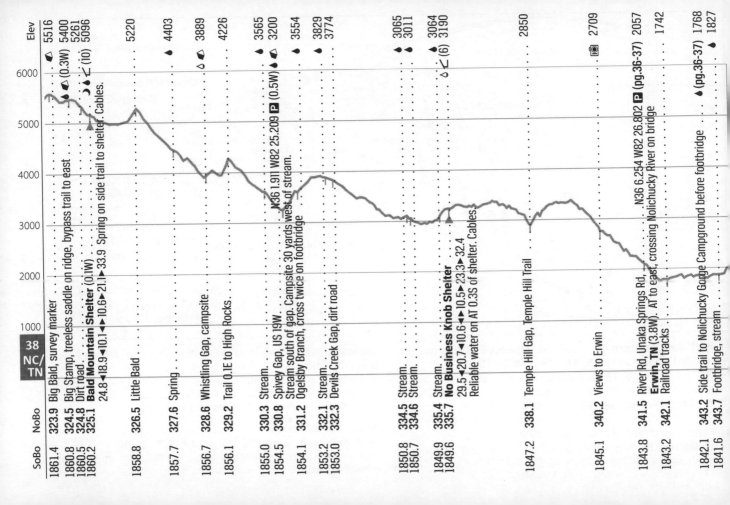

Elev	NoBo	SoBo	Description
5516	323.9	1861.4	Big Bald, survey marker
5400	324.5	1860.8	Big Stamp, treeless saddle on ridge, bypass trail to east (0.3W)
5261	324.8	1860.5	Dirt road.
5096	325.1	1860.2	**Bald Mountain Shelter** (0.1W) Spring on side trail to shelter. Cables. 24.8◀18.9◀10.1◀▶10.6▶21.1▶33.9
5220	326.5	1858.8	Little Bald
4403	327.6	1857.7	Spring
3889	328.6	1856.7	Whistling Gap, campsite
4226	329.2	1856.1	Trail 0.1E to High Rocks.
3565	330.3	1855.0	Stream.
3200	330.8	1854.5	Spivey Gap, US 19W. N36 1.911 W82 25.209 P (0.5W)
3554	331.2	1854.1	Stream south of gap. Campsite 30 yards west of stream. Ogelsby Branch, cross twice on footbridge
3829	332.1	1853.2	Stream.
3774	332.3	1853.0	Devils Creek Gap, dirt road
3065	334.5	1850.8	Stream.
3011	334.6	1850.7	Stream.
3064	335.4	1849.9	Stream.
3190	335.7	1849.6	**No Business Knob Shelter** 29.5◀20.7◀10.6◀▶10.5▶23.3▶32.4 Reliable water on AT 0.3S of shelter. Cables.
2850	338.1	1847.2	Temple Hill Gap, Temple Hill Trail
2709	340.2	1845.1	Views to Erwin
2057	341.5	1843.8	River Rd, Unaka Springs Rd, N36 6.254 W82 26.802 P (pg.36-37) **Erwin, TN** (3.8W). AT to east, crossing Nolichucky River on bridge
1742	342.1	1843.2	Railroad tracks
1768	343.2	1842.1	Side trail to Nolichucky Gorge Campground before footbridge (pg.36-37)
1827	343.7	1841.6	Footbridge, stream

SoBo	NoBo		Elev
1841.3	**344.0**	Footbridge, stream	1944
1840.9	**344.4**	Stream.	2039
1840.6	**344.7**	Footbridge	2143
1840.4	**344.9**	Footbridge, campsite to east ◁	2245
1839.1	**346.2**	**Curley Maple Gap Shelter,** water south of shelter ◁(14) ◆	3083
		31.2◀21.1◀10.5▶12.8▶21.9▶29.8	
1838.6	**346.7**	Spring ◆	3237
1838.0	**347.3**	Stream ◆	3338
1837.8	**347.5**	Stream	3319
1836.5	**348.8**	Campsite ◁	3159
1835.0	**350.3**	Indian Grave Gap, TN 395	3350
		Water 0.1E outside of curve in road, campsites south on AT. 3.3W to USFS **Rock Creek Recreation Area** $10 tent sites up to 6 persons, restrooms, showers. N36 6.578 W82 21.696 [P] ◆ ◁	
1834.5	**350.8**	Survey marker (USFS 381-28)	3703
1834.3	**351.0**	Powerline	3743
1833.9	**351.4**	USFS 230, Red Fork Rd (gravel)	3760
1831.6	**353.7**	Beauty Spot Gap, clearing N36 6.9796 W82 20.2321 [P]	4312
		Parking to west, trail parallel to USFS 230 from here north to Deep Gap.	
1831.1	**354.2**	Piped spring & campsites 100 yards west across USFS 230. ◆ ◁	4114
1830.7	**354.6**	AT skirts Red Fork Rd	4546
1829.6	**355.7**	Unaka Mountain, dense spruce forest.	5180
1827.4	**357.9**	Low Gap, campsite, weak stream 0.1W △	3900
1826.5	**358.8**	Footbridge, stream ◆	4130
1826.3	**359.0**	**Cherry Gap Shelter** 33.9◀23.3◀12.8▶9.1▶17.0▶22.2 ◁(6)	4012
		Spring 120 yards on blue-blazed trail behind shelter to the left.	
1825.9	**359.4**	Unmarked trail crossing	3924
1824.9	**360.4**	Little Bald Knob, trail skirts summit	4347
1824.7	**360.6**	Stream. ◆	4289
1823.2	**362.1**	Iron Mountain Gap, TN 107, NC 226 N36 8.600 W82 13.990 [P] (pg.42)	3723
		✳ **Golden ragwort** – Small flower with yellow center and small floppy petals. "Field flower" that can create a sea of yellow.	
1821.9	**363.4**	Campsite, water 0.1W from signpost near north end of clearing ◆ ◁	4021

39
NC/TN

40
NC/TN

Elev	NoBo	SoBo	Description
4430	364.5	1820.8	Rock pillar.
4034			(pg.42)
4140	366.2	1819.1	Greasy Creek Gap, campsite at gap, water 0.2W, **Greasy Creek Hostel** 0.6E
	367.0	1818.3	Campsite, weak spring 0.1W
4514	368.1	1817.2	**Clyde Smith Shelter** (1976) (0.1W) 32.4◄21.9◄9.1◄►7.9►13.1►15.0 Water 0.1 left of shelter, tent sites behind.
4918	369.0	1816.3	Little Rock Knob, views to west, south of summit
4749	369.3	1816.0	Stream. *Here north to Roan parking, NoBo trail bearing is compass south.*
4387	370.1	1815.2	Stream.
4040	371.2	1814.1	Hughes Gap, TN 1330, Hughes Gap Rd. N36 8.206 W82 8.457
4244	371.6	1813.7	Water 50 yards east
5350	374.2	1811.1	Ash Gap, campsite at gap, water 0.1E
6212	375.4	1809.9	Toll House Gap, saddle between Roan N36 6.238 W82 7.984
6144	375.5	1809.8	High Bluff & Knob, 0.1E to parking, picnic area, restrooms, trash cans.
6194			Chimney (remnant)
	376.0	1809.3	**Roan High Knob Shelter** (0.1E). 29.8◄17.0◄7.9◄►5.2►7.1►25.1 Piped spring, highest shelter on AT. NoBo: watch for AT turning west, leaving wide treadway
5794	376.8	1808.5	Several footbridges, streams
5527	377.4	1807.9	Carvers Gap, TN143, NC 261 N36 6.406 W82 6.633
5512	377.5	1807.8	Access road to summit (1.9mi) open approx. Memorial day - Oct 1
5818	378.2	1807.1	Round Bald, 30 yards east to summit, views
5794	378.9	1806.4	Jane Bald, big rock slab, views back to Roan Mtn
5900	379.5	1805.8	Side trail 0.5E to Grassy Ridge Bald and views, AT to west.
5875	379.7	1805.6	Springs
5386	380.6	1804.7	Campsite to west.
5063	381.2	1804.1	**Stan Murray Shelter** 22.2◄13.1◄5.2◄►1.9►19.9►29.5 Spring on blue-blazed trail opposite shelter.
4654	383.1	1802.2	**Overmountain Shelter** (0.3E) Yellow Mountain Gap. 15.0◄7.1◄1.9◄►18.0►27.6►35.8 Converted barn. Water on way to shelter.
5198	384.1	1801.2	Two intersections with old roadbed
5301	384.3	1801.0	Side trail 0.1E to Big Yellow Mountain

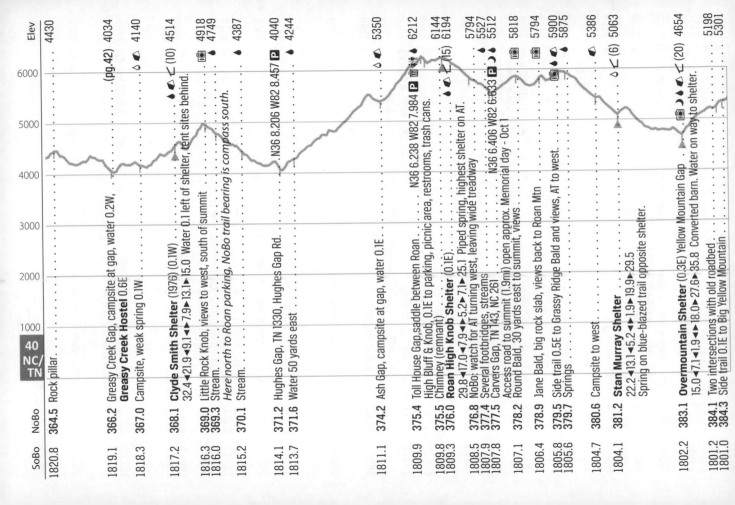

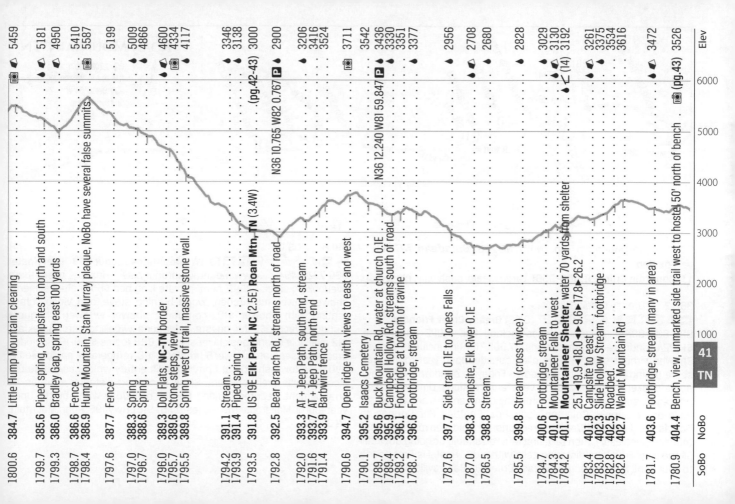

Appalachian Trail elevation profile — TN, page 41

SoBo	NoBo	Feature	Elev	Notes
1800.6	384.7	Little Hump Mountain, clearing	5459	
1799.7	385.6	Piped spring, campsites to north and south	5181	
1799.3	386.0	Bradley Gap, spring east 100 yards	4950	
1798.7	386.6	Fence	5410	
1798.4	386.9	Hump Mountain, Stan Murray plaque, NoBo have several false summits	5587	
1797.6	387.7	Fence	5199	
1797.0	388.3	Spring	5009	
1796.7	388.6	Spring	4866	
1796.0	389.3	Doll Flats, NC-TN border	4600	
1795.7	389.6	Stone steps, view	4334	
1795.5	389.8	Spring west of trail, massive stone wall.	4117	
1794.2	391.1	Stream.	3346	
1793.9	391.4	Piped spring	3138	
1793.5	391.8	US 19E Elk Park, NC (2.5E) Roan Mtn, TN (3.4W)	3000	(pg.42-43)
1792.8	392.5	Bear Branch Rd, streams north of road	2900	N36 10.765 W82 0.767 P
1792.0	393.3	AT + Jeep Path, south end, stream.	3206	
1791.6	393.7	AT + Jeep Path, north end	3416	
1791.4	393.9	Barbwire fence	3524	
1790.6	394.7	Open ridge with views to east and west	3711	
1790.1	395.2	Isaacs Cemetery	3542	
1789.7	395.6	Buck Mountain Rd, water at church 0.1E	3436	N36 12.240 W81 59.847 P
1789.4	395.9	Campbell Hollow Rd, streams south of road	3330	
1789.2	396.1	Footbridge at bottom of ravine	3351	
1788.7	396.6	Footbridge, stream	3377	
1787.6	397.7	Side trail 0.1E to Jones Falls	2956	
1787.0	398.3	Campsite, Elk River 0.1E	2708	
1786.5	398.8	Stream.	2680	
1785.5	399.8	Stream (cross twice)	2828	
1784.7	400.6	Footbridge, stream	3029	
1784.3	401.0	Mountaineer Falls to west	3130	
1784.2	401.1	Mountaineer Shelter, water 70 yards from shelter 25.1◄19.9◄18.0◄►9.6►17.8►26.2	3192	(14)
1783.4	401.9	Campsite to east	3261	
1783.0	402.3	Slide Hollow Stream, footbridge	3375	
1782.8	402.5	Roadbed.	3534	
1782.6	402.7	Walnut Mountain Rd	3616	
1781.7	403.6	Footbridge, stream (many in area)	3472	
1780.9	404.4	Bench, view, unmarked side trail west to hostel, 50' north of bench	3526	(pg.43)

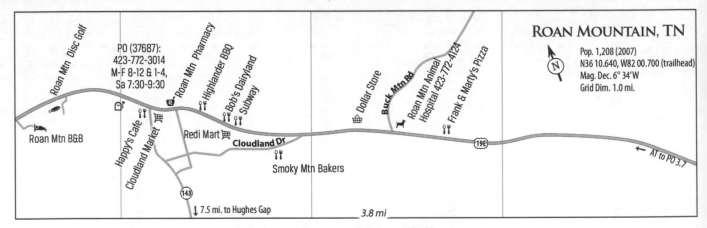

Pop. 1,208 (2007)
N36 10.640, W82 00.700 (trailhead)
Mag. Dec. 6° 34'W
Grid Dim. 1.0 mi.

Roan Mtn Disc Golf

PO (37687):
423-772-3014
M-F 8-12 & 1-4,
Sa 7:30-9:30

Roan Mtn Pharmacy

Highlander BBQ

Bob's Dairyland

Subway

Roan Mtn B&B

Happy's Cafe

Cloudland Market

Redi Mart

Cloudland Dr

Smoky Mtn Bakers

143

↓ 7.5 mi. to Hughes Gap

Dollar Store

Buck Mtn Rd

Roan Mtn Animal Hospital 423-772-4124

Frank & Marty's Pizza

19E

← AT to PO 3.7

3.8 mi

362.1　　Iron Mountain Gap, TN 107, NC 226　**Buladean, NC** (4.1E)

⌂ **Fox Den**

🍴 **Mountain Grill** 828-688-9061 Large meals, cash only, closed Su.

366.2　　Greasy Creek Gap

🛏🛶☂🍴🚲🐾⛺🚗🅿🖥✉ (0.6E) **Greasy Creek Friendly**
828-688-9948　All room prices include tax: $10PP bunkhouse, $15PP/up indoor accommodations, $7.50PP tenting includes shower. Shower without stay $3. Pets okay outside. Open year-round, self serve during the Sabbath (sundown Friday to sundown Saturday). Home cooked meals, including vegetarian options. Limited kitchen privileges, and a well-stocked store including snacks and meals for multi-day resupply, Coleman/alcohol/oz. Shuttles Hot Springs to Damascus. Parking $2/night. Directions: take old jeep road trail east (not compass east), then take first left. You should be going downhill all the way. Free long distance calls within US. Hostel is first house to your right. Maildrops: 1827 Greasy Creek Rd, Bakersville, NC 28705.

391.8　　US 19E

🛏🛶☂⊛☂🛍🚌🚗🅿✉ (0.3W) **Mountain Harbour B&B/Hiker Hostel**
866-772-9494　⟨www.mountainharbour.net⟩　Hostel over barn overlooking creek $25PP, semi-private king bed $55, includes linens, shower, towel, full kitchen, wood burning stove, and video library. Tenting with shower $10, non-guest shower w/towel $4, guest laundry w/soap $6 for guests, telephone w/calling card. Breakfast $12 available during peak hiker season. B&B rooms $100-165 includes breakfast, separate shower & fireplace, A/C, refrigerator, and cable TV/DVD. Free town shuttle at 5pm. Complimentary white gas/denatured alcohol. Sells fuel canisters. Slack pack/long distance shuttles by arrangement. Secured parking $5/day or $2/day with shuttle. Open year round. Maildrops: (non-guests $5) 9151 Hwy 19E, Roan Mountain, TN 37687.

Roan Mountain, TN 37687 (3.5W)

🛏 🚿 ⛺ 📶 🅿 **Roan Mountain B&B** 423-772-3207 ⟨www.roanmtbb.com⟩ Hiker rate $65S, $85D does not include breakfast, but will drop off at local restaurant. Free pickup after 3:30, free return before 7am to trail at Hwy 19E. Longer shuttles for a fee. Pets okay, no smoking inside. Free do-it-yourself laundry. Parking for section hikers.

🍴 **Bob's Dairyland** 423-772-3641
🍴 **Smoky Mountain Bakers** fresh bread, wood-fired pizza
🍴 **Frank & Mary's Pizza** 423-772-3083, closed M & Tu.

🍴 **Cloudland Pizza** 707-304-2770 Wood fired pizza.
🏪 💲 **Redi Mart** 423-772-3032 M-Sa 8-10, Su 10-8
🏪 **Cloudland Market** 423-772-3201

Elk Park, NC 28622 (2.4E, see services on map)

Newland, NC (7E, 19E to NC 194)

🏨 📶 💻 **The Shady Lawn Lodge** 828-733-9006, Thru-hikers get 10% off regular room rates, which are typically approx. $60. Free pickup & return when driver is available. Laundry and restaurants nearby.

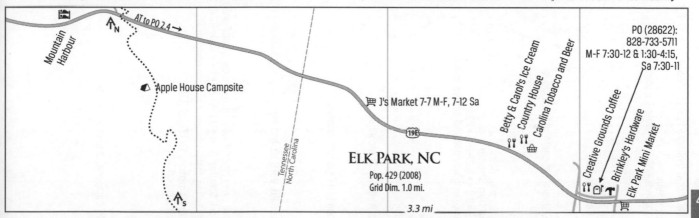

ELK PARK, NC
Pop. 429 (2008)
Grid Dim. 1.0 mi.

3.3 mi

404.4 (0.2W) Side trail to hostel - follow powerline.
405.0 (0.3W) Upper Laurel Fork. Blue-blazed side trail to hostel originates at the hand-railed footbridge. Follow side trail along creek.
🏨🛏⛺📶✉ (0.2W) **Vango/Abby Memorial Hostel**
423-772-3450, vangoabby@gmail.com. Non-profit, donation-based, hostel run by "Scotty," Trekkie, engineer, trail maintainer and 3x AT thru-hiker who has over 14,000 trail miles. Open Feb 1 - Nov 31, cash only. Heated bunkroom with stove, and small library. Sleeps 6.

Suggested donation $9/night, $12 if using heat, includes shower. Upper private room & deck, queen bed w/linens, heat, $15S/$25D. Shower w/o stay $3, wash $3, dryer $3. Resupply basics, beverages, pizza, B&J ice cream, and stove fuels. Hike-in/hike-out only; no yellow-blazers and no parking. No drugs or alcohol. Pets okay. Maildrops must be mailed 2 weeks in advance: PO Box 185, Roan Mtn, TN 37687

SoBo	NoBo	Description	Elev
1780.3	405.0	Upper Laurel Fork, 2 tent sites next to waterfall, side trail to hostel. (pg.43)	3335
1779.6	405.7	Footbridge, stream.	3466
1779.4	405.9	USFS 293 (gravel), campsite, waterfall south on AT.	3475
1778.6	406.7	Spring.	3363
1778.4	406.9	Spring.	3393
1778.0	407.3	Footbridge, stream.	3463
1777.6	407.7	Hardcore Cascades.	3413
1776.8	408.5	Stream.	3648
1776.3	409.0	Campsite, several streams and footbridges	3581
1774.7	410.6	Rock outcropping, views	3945
1774.6	410.7	**Moreland Gap Shelter** 29.5◀27.6◀9.6▶8.2▶16.6▶23.8 Water source long way downhill across from shelter.	3823
1772.5	412.8	Spring.	3839
1772.0	413.3	Forest Service road.	3805
1771.2	414.1	Trail skirts White Rocks Mountain.	4012
1770.0	415.3	Trail to Coon Den Falls 0.8E downhill	3450
1768.9	416.4	Stream.	2919
1768.5	416.8	Barn	2647
1768.3	417.0	Dennis Cove Rd, USFS 50, hostels N36 15.858 W82 7.387 P (pg.46-47)	2550
1767.1	418.2	Laurel Falls. Do not swim close to falls, there is a dangerous whirlpool	2120
1766.4	418.9	**Laurel Fork Shelter** 35.8◀17.8◀8.2▶8.4▶15.6▶22.4	2186
1766.1	419.2	Waycaster Spring, footbridge, and campsite north on AT	2048
1765.6	419.7	Side trail to **Hampton, TN** US 321 (1.0W) (pg.46-47) Hampton is west on 321.	1984
1763.1	422.2	Pond Flats, campsite, stream 0.1N on AT	3706

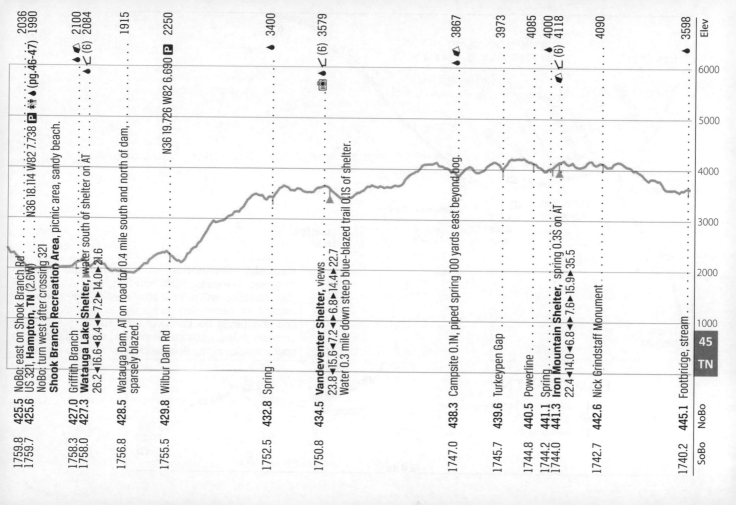

NoBo		SoBo	Elev

NoBo column (mileage) / descriptions / **SoBo** / **Elev**:

- **425.5** NoBo: east on Shook Branch Rd .... N36 18.114 W82 7.738 — SoBo 1759.8 — Elev 2036
- **425.6** US 321, **Hampton, TN** (2.6W) .... (pg.46-47) — SoBo 1759.7 — Elev 1990
  NoBo: turn west after crossing 321
  Shook Branch Recreation Area, picnic area, sandy beach.
- **427.0** Griffith Branch — SoBo 1758.3 — Elev 2100
- **427.3** **Watauga Lake Shelter,** water south of shelter on AT — SoBo 1758.0 — Elev 2084
  26.2◀16.6◀8.4◀▶7.2▶14.0▶21.6
- **428.5** Watauga Dam, AT on road for 0.4 mile south and north of dam, sparsely blazed. — SoBo 1756.8 — Elev 1915
- **429.8** Wilbur Dam Rd — SoBo 1755.5 — Elev 2250

N36 19.726 W82 6.690

- **432.8** Spring — SoBo 1752.5 — Elev 3400
- **434.5** **Vandeventer Shelter,** views — SoBo 1750.8 — Elev 3579
  23.8◀15.6◀7.2◀▶6.8▶14.4▶22.7
  Water 0.3 mile down steep blue-blazed trail 0.1S of shelter.
- **438.3** Campsite 0.1N, piped spring 100 yards east beyond bog. — SoBo 1747.0 — Elev 3867
- **439.6** Turkeypen Gap — SoBo 1745.7 — Elev 3973
- **440.5** Powerline — SoBo 1744.8 — Elev 4085
- **441.1** Spring — SoBo 1744.2 — Elev 4000
- **441.3** **Iron Mountain Shelter,** spring 0.3S on AT — SoBo 1744.0 — Elev 4118
  22.4◀14.0◀6.8◀▶7.6▶15.9▶35.5
- **442.6** Nick Grindstaff Monument — SoBo 1742.7 — Elev 4090
- **445.1** Footbridge, stream — SoBo 1740.2 — Elev 3598

6000 5000 4000 3000 2000 1000

45
TN

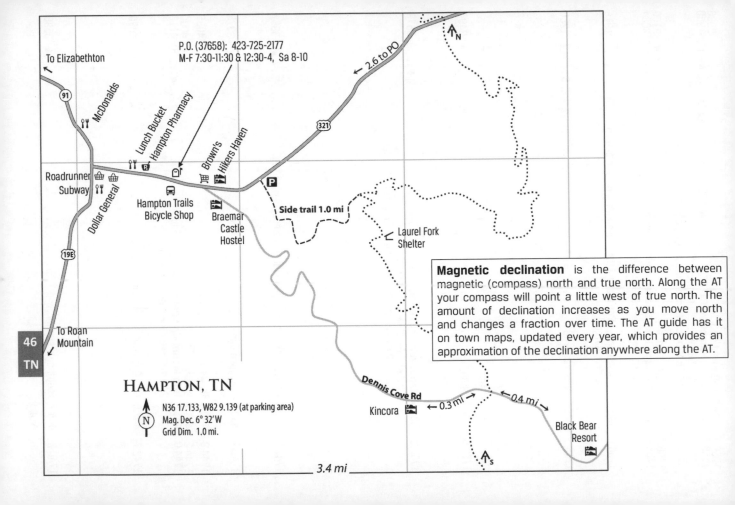

417.0   Dennis Cove Rd, USFS 50

🏨⬛�⬧⛺🚌✉ (0.3W) **Kincora Hiking Hostel** 423-725-4409
Cooking facilities, laundry, $5 per night suggested donation. No
dogs, 3 night limit. Coleman/alcohol/oz, owner Bob Peoples will hold
packages for hikers mailed to 1278 Dennis Cove Rd, Hampton, TN
37658.

🏨⬛⬧🏠⛺🚌🖥✉ (0.4E) **Black Bear Resort**   423-725-5988
⟨www.blackbearresorttn.com⟩ Clean and spacious creekside resort
with bunkroom $15, upper bunkroom $20, tenting $10PP. Four-
person cabin $40/$55, $15EAP, 6-person max. Courtesy phone,
computer, movies (DVD) and free morning coffee for all guests. Camp
store with long-term resupply items, snacks, ice cream and
food that can be prepared on-site with microwave or stove. Laundry
$4. Fuel/oz & canister fuel. Pet friendly, accepts credit cards. Long
and short distance shuttles. Parking free for section-hiking guests,
$2/night for non-guests. Maildrops (non-guest fee $5): 1511 Dennis
Cove Rd, Hampton, TN 37658.

419.7   Side trail to Hampton (1.0W)
425.6   US 321 (2.6W to Hampton)
        Hampton, TN

🏪 🏨🚌 📞 **Brown's Grocery & Braemar Castle Hostel**
423-725-2411, 423-725-2262.   Both operated by Sutton Brown;
check in at grocery to stay at the hostel or for shuttles. Store open
M-Sa 8-6, closed Sunday.

🏨⛺🚌📶🖥🍴 **Hikers Haven** 423-707-7941, 10-10, 7 days. Bunk
& shower $12, tent & shower $8. Shuttles, resupply, ice cream and
Trailburger Cafe on-site. Coin laundry $2, internet access $3/hr.
Maildrops: 703/707 Hwy 321, Hampton, TN 37658.

🚌 **Hampton Trails Bicycle Shop** 423-725-5000
⟨www.hamptontrails.com⟩ hamptontrails@embarqmail.com.

        Elizabethton, TN (services 5 mi. north of Hampton)
🏨📶🖥✉ **Americourt** 423-542-4466 $59.95 plus tax, up to 4

in room, includes hot breakfast. Pets $20. Not available on race
weekends. Maildrops: 1515 Hwy 19 East, Elizabethton,TN 37643.
🍴 **Little Caesars, Arbys, Lone Star Steakhouse**
🏪 **Food City, Big Lots**
🎬 **State Line Drive-in** 423-542-5422 Showings F, Sa & Su
        Bulter, TN

🏨⛺🚌📶🖥✉ **Iron Mountain Inn** 423-768-2446 ⟨www.
creeksidechalet.net⟩ 10 miles from Hampton, but you can call for
pickup or for directions. Fee for pickup/return. B&B room includes
breakfast for $100S/$150D. Log cabin with hot tub under the stars.
Free laundry. Shuttles from Watauga Lake to Damascus. Maildrops:
c/o Woods, 268 Moreland Dr, Butler, TN 37640.

🏨⛺📶 **Appalachian Folk School** 423-341-1843 ⟨www.warrendoyle.
com⟩ Non-profit run by Warren Doyle offers work-for-stay weeknights
(M-Th) only (2-3 hrs/night) for all hikers who have a spiritual/poetic
connection to the trail. Kitchen privileges, shower, wireless, laundry
and rides to/from the AT between Rt. 321 (Hampton) and VA 603 (Fox
Creek).

445.9 TN 91

🏨⬛⛺ (2.0E) **Switchback Creek Campground** 407-484-3388
570 Wallace Rd, Shady Valley, TN 37688. 2-person cabin $40,
campsite $12+tax. Showers, laundry, call for ride. 1.5 miles farther
east to US 421 and Shady Valley (below).

452.4 Low Gap, US 421
        Shady Valley, TN 37688 (2.7E)
🏤 M-F 7:30-11:00 & 12-3:30, Sa 7:30-9:30, 423-739-2173
🏠🍴 **Shady Valley Country Store & Deli** M-Sa 6am-6pm. Short term
resupply, Coleman fuel. Deli serves burgers and sandwiches.
🍴 **Raceway Restaurant** Open 7am-8pm all days except W & Su,
when hours are 7am-2pm.

Elevation profile — page 48, TN

SoBo	NoBo	Description	Elev
1739.9	445.4	Roadbed.	3601
1739.4	445.9	TN 91. N36 28.883 W81 57.619 P (pg.47) Shady Valley, TN (3.5E) South end of handicap-accessible trail.	3525
1738.6	446.7	North end of handicap-accessible trail	3625
1736.4	448.9	Double Springs Shelter 21.6◄14.4◄7.6◄▶8.3▶27.9▶34.3 Spring about 0.1N of shelter. Rich Knob to south, Holston Mtn Trail to north.	4225 ⊏(6)
1734.8	450.5	Locust Knob.	3624
1733.9	451.4	Campsite to west.	3615
1732.9	452.4	Low Gap, US 421 Piped spring on south side of road. Shady Valley, TN (2.7E) N36 32.316 W81 56.933 P (pg.47)	3384
1731.5	453.8	Low stone wall on east side of AT	3575
1731.0	454.3	Double Spring Gap, campsite	3550
1730.6	454.7	Weak, muddy spring east side of AT.	3666
1729.6	455.7	McQueens Knob, disused shelter 0.1N.	3900
1729.2	456.1	McQueens Gap, USFS 69 N36 34.460 W81 55.921 P	3680
1728.1	457.2	Abingdon Gap Shelter 22.7◄15.9◄8.3◄▶19.6▶26.0▶38.2 Piped spring 0.2 mile behind shelter on blue-blazed trail.	3798 ⊏(5)
1724.1	461.2	Campsite, unnamed gap	3731
1723.2	462.1	Campsite to west.	3652
1723.0	462.3	Backbone Rock Trail leads 2.3E to USFS recreation area.	3553
1721.6	463.7	TN-VA border.	3302
1720.0	465.3	Campsite, Spring 0.1E on blue-blazed trail	2825

48
TN

NoBo	Feature	Elev	SoBo
467.1	**Damascus, VA** (south). Mercedes Street and welcome sign. N36 38.162 W81 47.378 P (pg.50-51)	1975	1718.2
467.7	**Damascus, VA** (Laurel and Shady) (pg.50-51)	1962	1717.7
468.5	**Damascus, VA** (north). (pg.50-51)	2019	1716.8
469.0	US 58, AT follows Virginia Creeper Trail for 0.4 mile. Campsite to west	2388	1716.3
469.4	Spring	2548	1715.9
470.9	Iron Mountain Trail to west.	2933	1714.4
472.4	Beech Grove Gap Trail to west, streams and footbridges in area	2313	1712.9
472.9	Feathercamp Trail to west, stream, campsite.	2236	1712.4
473.0	US 58, Feathercamp Branch N36 38.694 W81 44.197 P	2200	1712.3
473.3	Stream.	2179	1712.0
473.8	Stream.	2206	1711.5
474.6	Footbridge, campsite.	2299	1710.7
475.3	Taylors Valley Trail	2429	1710.0
476.8	**Saunders Shelter** (0.2W) 35.5◄27.9◄19.6◄▶6.4▶18.6▶23.7. Reliable spring on right behind shelter and down road.	3378	1708.5
477.2	North shelter side trail	3354	1708.1
479.1	Beartree Gap Trail, 3.0W to Beartree Recreation Area	3050	1706.2
479.2	Pond, campsite.	3012	1706.1
479.8	Stream.	2978	1705.5
480.2	Footbridge, stream	2909	1705.1
480.8	AT + Creeper Trail (south end)	2695	1704.5
481.5	Luther Hassinger Memorial Bridge. AT + Creeper Trail (north end), VA 728. N36 38.965 W81 40.345 P	2786	1703.8
481.8	Stream.	2829	1703.5
482.0	VA 859, Grassy Creek Rd (gravel)	2954	1703.3
482.2	Streams	3043	1703.1
483.2	**Lost Mountain Shelter** 34.3◄26.0◄6.4◄▶12.2▶17.3▶23.2 Water source on trail to left of shelter.	3399	1702.1
484.3	US 58, footbridge, stream N36 38.389 W81 39.926 P	3160	1701.0
484.6	Stream, campsite	3253	1700.7
485.0	Spring	3397	1700.3
485.2	Fence stile	3504	1700.1
485.5	VA 601, Beech Mountain Rd Fence stile, 50 yards north of road is sign for spring to west. N36 38.235 W81 38.425 P	3600	1699.8

49

VA

NoBo SoBo

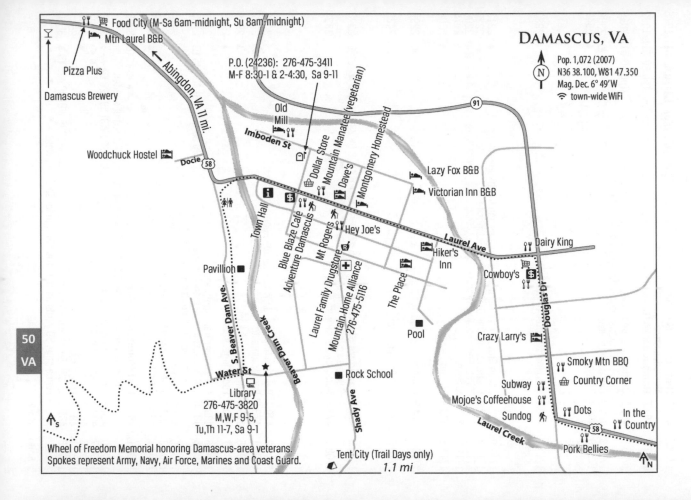

Food City (M-Sa 6am-midnight, Su 8am-midnight)

Mtn Laurel B&B

Pizza Plus

Damascus Brewery

DAMASCUS, VA

Pop. 1,072 (2007)
N36 38.100, W81 47.350
Mag. Dec. 6° 49'W
town-wide WiFi

Abingdon, VA 11 mi.

P.O. (24236): 276-475-3411
M-F 8:30-1 & 2-4:30, Sa 9-11

91

Old
Mill

Imboden St

Woodchuck Hostel

Docie

58

Dollar Store

Mountain Manatee (vegetarian)

Dave's

Montgomery Homestead

Lazy Fox B&B

Victorian Inn B&B

Town Hall

Blue Blaze Cafe

Adventure Damascus

Mt Rogers

Hey Joe's

Laurel Ave

Dairy King

Pavillion

Laurel Family Drugstore

Mountain Home Alliance
276-475-5116

Hiker's
Inn

Cowboy's

The Place

Pool

Crazy Larry's

S. Beaver Dam Ave.

Beaver Dam Creek

Water St

Rock School

Douglas Dr

Smoky Mtn BBQ

Country Corner

Subway

Dots

Mojoe's Coffeehouse

Library
276-475-3820
M,W,F 9-5,
Tu,Th 11-7, Sa 9-1

Shady Ave

Sundog

In the
Country

Laurel Creek

N

Pork Bellies

58

Wheel of Freedom Memorial honoring Damascus-area veterans.
Spokes represent Army, Navy, Air Force, Marines and Coast Guard.

Tent City (Trail Days only)

1.1 mi

50

VA

467.1 Mercedes Street, *Damascus, VA* (more services on map)

467.6 Laurel and Shady

468.5 US 58

Trail Days ⟨www.traildays.us⟩ (May 16-18) is the largest event on the AT. Hiker reunion and talent show, presentations, music, contra dancing, and hiker parade. Many gear reps & retailers on-hand.

Dave's Place $20 per room per night for 1 or 2 persons, maximum stay 2 nights. All rooms private. Shower without stay $3. No alcohol, no pets, no smoking. Check in at Mount Rogers Outfitters.

Hikers Inn 276-475-3788, $25 bunks, hostel private room $45. Rooms in house $65; $55/night for multi-night stays, Laundry $5. Run by Lee and Paul (2010 thru-hiker "Skink"). Open mid-March through October. A/C in all rooms. Smoking allowed outside, dogs allowed in hostel, cash or check.

The Place 276-475-3441, 276-492-3983 Methodist Church-run bunkrooms and tenting. Seasonal caretaker, please help to keep the bunkroom clean. No pets, no alcohol, 2 night max unless sick/injured. Suggested donation $6. No vehicle-assisted hikers (except during Trail Days).

Crazy Larry's 276-274-3637 Bunkroom holds 4 (up to 6 in a crunch), and tenting in yard available by donation, Breakfast & kitchen use included in stay. Drinking in moderation. Laundry for non-guests $5. Guest maildrops: 209 Douglas Drive, Damascus, VA 24236.

Woodchuck Hostel 406-407-1272 Large comfortable common area. Bed w/linens $25, tenting w/shower $10. Laundry $5.00. Dogs welcome. Quiet location with spacious yard near trail and Food City. Open Mar 15 - Oct 15.

Montgomery Homestead Inn 276-475-3053 $65/up. No smoking, no alcohol, no pets. Guest only maildrops: (USPS) PO Box 12, (FedEx/UPS) 103 E. Laurel Ave, Damascus, VA 24236.

Victorian Inn B&B 276-475-5059, $70+tax, includes breakfast. Also, 2 bedroom cottage $120/night for 4 persons, $20EAP up to 7.

Cottage room does not include breakfast. No pets.

Lazy Fox B&B 276-475-5838, $65/up+tax. No pets. Maildrops: PO Box 757, 133 Imboden St, Damascus, VA 24236.

Mountain Laurel B&B 276-475-5956

Food City (0.5W on US 58) 276-475-3653, 7 days.

Mt. Rogers Outfitters 276-475-5416 ⟨www.mtrogersoutfitters.com⟩ Full service backpacking store, fuel/oz. Shuttle service for the Appalachian Trail, parking for section hikers $2/day. Shower only $3. Maildrops: PO Box 546, 110 W Laurel Ave, Damascus, VA 24236.

Adventure Damascus ⟨www.AdventureDamascus.com⟩ 888-595-2453 or 276-475-6262 Catering to thru-hikers with backpacking gear, hiker foods, alcohol/Coleman/oz, other fuels, bike rentals, shuttles to area trailheads by arrangement, $2 showers ($4 includes a towel), open 7 days year-round. USPS and UPS Maildrops: PO Box 1113, 128 W. Laurel Ave. Damascus, VA 24236.

Sundog Outfitter 276-475-6252 ⟨www.sundogoutfitter.com⟩ Backpacking gear and clothing, repairs, hiker food, Coleman/alcohol/oz, other fuels, shuttles to area trailheads by arrangement, open 7 days a week. Maildrops: PO Box 1113 or 331 Douglas Dr, Damascus, VA 24236.

Library 276-475-3820, M,W,F 9-5, T,Th 11-7, Sa 9-1, internet 1 hr.

Gypsy Dave Shuttles 276-492-0873, dstinnard@yahoo.com

497.9 **Grayson Highlands State Park**

276-579-7092 Blue-blazed trail (0.5E) to parking; campground 1.5 mi. farther east on road. Park closed in cold weather; call ahead if possible. Camp store with courtesy phone, tent site w/ shower $21, shower only $5. May 1 - mid Oct.

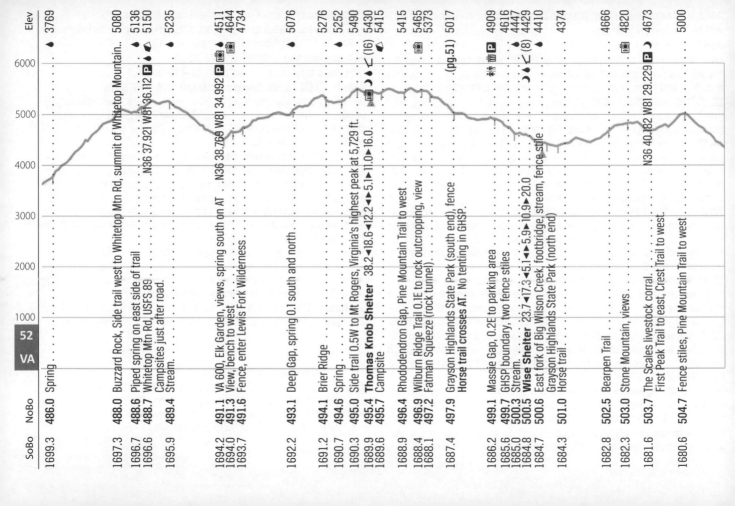

SoBo	NoBo	Description	Elev
1699.3	486.0	Spring	3769
1697.3	488.0	Buzzard Rock, Side trail west to Whitetop Mtn Rd, summit of Whitetop Mountain..	5080
1696.7	488.6	Piped spring on east side of trail	5136
1696.6	488.7	Whitetop Mtn Rd, USFS 89 N36 37.921 W81 36.112	5150
1695.9	489.4	Campsites just after road. Stream.	5235
1694.2	491.1	VA 600, Elk Garden, views, spring south on AT . N36 38.769 W81 34.992	4511
1694.0	491.3	View, bench to west	4644
1693.7	491.6	Fence, enter Lewis Fork Wilderness	4734
1692.2	493.1	Deep Gap, spring 0.1 south and north.	5076
1691.2	494.1	Brier Ridge	5276
1690.7	494.6	Spring	5252
1690.3	495.0	Side trail 0.5W to Mt Rogers, Virginia's highest peak at 5,729 ft.	5490
1689.9	495.4	**Thomas Knob Shelter** 38.2◄18.6◄12.2◄►5.1►11.0►16.0. (16)	5430
1689.6	495.7	Campsite	5415
1688.4	496.4	Rhododendron Gap, Pine Mountain Trail to west	5415
1688.4	496.9	Wilburn Ridge Trail 0.1E to rock outcropping, view	5465
1688.1	497.2	Fatman Squeeze (rock tunnel)	5373
1687.4	497.9	Grayson Highlands State Park (south end), fence (pg.51) **Horse trail crosses AT.** No tenting in GHSP.	5017
1686.2	499.1	Massie Gap, 0.2E to parking area	4909
1685.6	499.7	GHSP boundary, two fence stiles	4616
1685.0	500.3	Stream.	4447
1684.8	500.5	**Wise Shelter** 23.7◄17.3◄5.1◄►5.9►10.9►20.0 (8)	4429
1684.7	500.6	East fork of Big Wilson Creek, footbridge, stream, fence stile	4410
		Grayson Highlands State Park (north end)	
1684.3	501.0	Horse trail	4374
1682.8	502.5	Bearpen Trail	4666
1682.3	503.0	Stone Mountain, views	4820
1681.6	503.7	The Scales livestock corral. N36 40.182 W81 29.229 First Peak Trail to east, Crest Trail to west.	4673
1680.6	504.7	Fence stiles, Pine Mountain Trail to west.	5000

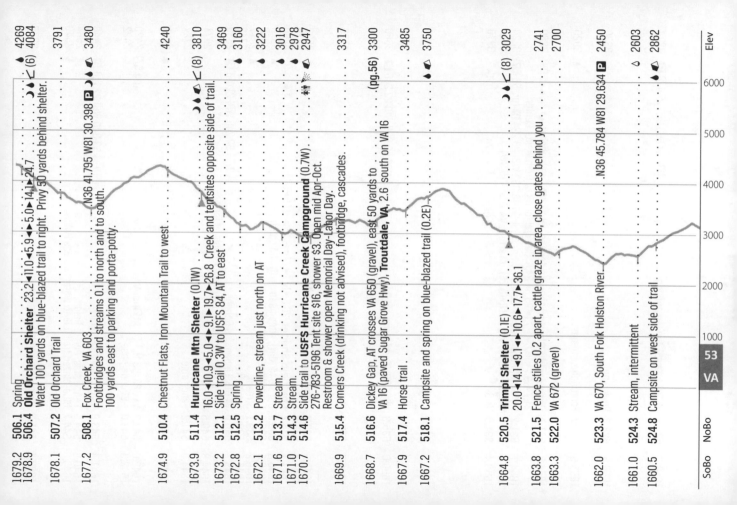

SoBo	NoBo	Description	Elev
1679.2	506.1	Spring	4269
1678.9	506.4	**Old Orchard Shelter** 23.2◀1.0◀5.9▶5.0▶14.1▶24.7 Water 100 yards on blue-blazed trail to right. Privy 50 yards behind shelter.	4084
1678.1	507.2	Old Orchard Trail	3791
1677.2	508.1	Fox Creek, VA 603. N36 41.795 W81 30.398 [P] Footbridges and streams 0.1 to north and to south. 100 yards east to parking and porta-potty.	3480
1674.9	510.4	Chestnut Flats, Iron Mountain Trail to west.	4240
1673.9	511.4	**Hurricane Mtn Shelter** (0.1W) 16.0◀10.9◀5.0▶9.1▶19.7▶26.8 Creek and tentsites opposite side of trail.	3810
1673.2	512.1	Side trail 0.3W to USFS 84, AT to east	3469
1672.8	512.5	Spring	3160
1672.1	513.2	Powerline, stream just north on AT	3222
1671.6	513.7	Stream.	3016
1671.0	514.3	Stream.	2978
1670.7	514.6	Side trail to **USFS Hurricane Creek Campground** (0.7W) 276-783-5196 Tent site $16, shower $3. Open mid Apr-Oct. Restroom & shower open Memorial Day-Labor Day.	2947
1669.9	515.4	Comers Creek (drinking not advised), footbridge, cascades.	3317
1668.7	516.6	Dickey Gap, AT crosses VA 650 (gravel), east 50 yards to VA 16 (paved Sugar Grove Hwy), **Troutdale, VA**, 2.6 south on VA 16 (pg.56)	3300
1667.9	517.4	Horse trail	3485
1667.2	518.1	Campsite and spring on blue-blazed trail (0.2E)	3750
1664.8	520.5	**Trimpi Shelter** (0.1E) 20.0◀14.1◀9.1▶10.6▶17.7▶36.1	3029
1663.8	521.5	Fence stiles 0.2 apart, cattle graze in area, close gates behind you	2741
1663.3	522.0	VA 672 (gravel)	2700
1662.0	523.3	VA 670, South Fork Holston River. N36 45.784 W81 29.634 [P]	2450
1661.0	524.3	Stream, intermittent	2603
1660.5	524.8	Campsite on west side of trail	2862

53

VA

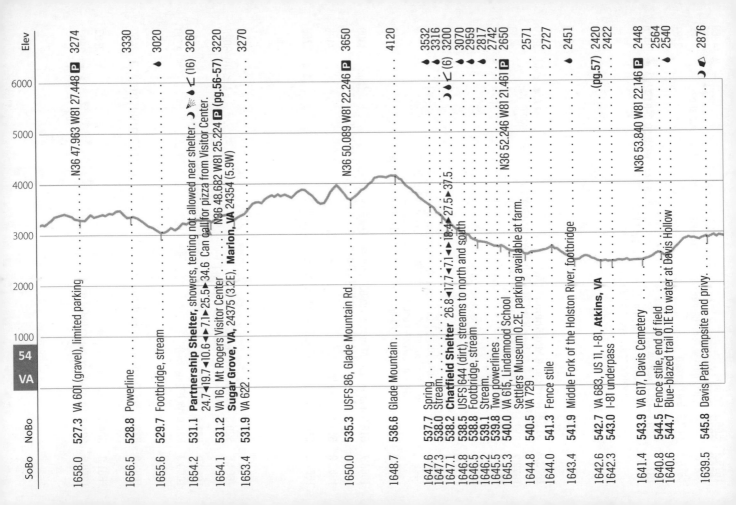

54 VA

SoBo	NoBo	Description	Features	Elev
1658.0	527.3	VA 601 (gravel), limited parking	N36 47.963 W81 27.448 P	3274
1656.5	528.8	Powerline		3330
1655.6	529.7	Footbridge, stream		3020
1654.2	531.1	**Partnership Shelter,** showers, tenting not allowed near shelter. Can call for pizza from Visitor Center. 24.7◄19.7◄10.6►7.1►25.5►34.6	(16)	3260
1654.1	531.2	VA 16, Mt Rogers Visitor Center **(pg.56-57)**		3220
		Sugar Grove, VA, 24375 (3.2E). **Marion, VA** 24354 (5.9W)	N36 48.682 W81 25.224 P	
1653.4	531.9	VA 622		3270
1650.0	535.3	USFS 86, Glade Mountain Rd	N36 50.089 W81 22.246 P	3650
1648.7	536.6	Glade Mountain		4120
1647.6	537.7	Spring		3532
1647.3	538.0	Stream		3316
1647.1	538.2	**Chatfield Shelter** 26.8◄17.7◄7.1►18.4►27.5►37.5	(6)	3200
1646.8	538.5	USFS 644 (dirt), streams to north and south		3070
1646.5	538.8	Footbridge, stream		2959
1646.2	539.1	Stream		2817
1645.5	539.8	Two powerlines		2742
1645.3	540.0	VA 615, Lindamood School Settlers Museum 0.2E, parking available at farm.	N36 52.246 W81 21.461 P	2650
1644.8	540.5	VA 729		2571
1644.0	541.3	Fence stile		2727
1643.4	541.9	Middle Fork of the Holston River, footbridge		2451
1642.6	542.7	VA 683, US 11, I-81, **Atkins, VA** (pg.57)		2420
1642.3	543.0	I-81 underpass		2422
1641.4	543.9	VA 617, Davis Cemetery	N36 53.840 W81 22.146 P	2448
1640.8	544.5	Fence stile, end of field		2564
1640.6	544.7	Blue-blazed trail 0.1E to water at Davis Hollow		2540
1639.5	545.8	Davis Path campsite and privy.		2876

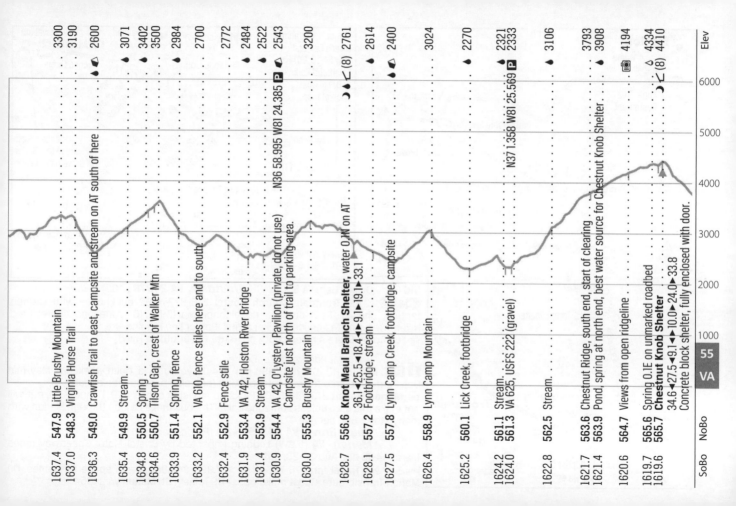

SoBo	NoBo	Feature	Elev
1637.4	547.9	Little Brushy Mountain	3300
1637.0	548.3	Virginia Horse Trail	3190
1636.3	549.0	Crawfish Trail to east, campsite and stream on AT south of here	2600
1635.4	549.9	Stream.	3071
1634.8	550.5	Spring.	3402
1634.6	550.7	Tilson Gap, crest of Walker Mtn	3500
1633.9	551.4	Spring, fence	2984
1633.2	552.1	VA 610, fence stiles here and to south	2700
1632.4	552.9	Fence stile	2772
1631.9	553.4	VA 742, Holston River Bridge	2484
1631.4	553.9	Stream.	2522
1630.9	554.4	VA 42, 0'Lystery Pavilion (private, do not use). Campsite just north of trail to parking area. N36 58.995 W81 24.385 P	2543
1630.0	555.3	Brushy Mountain	3200
1628.7	556.6	**Knot Maul Branch Shelter,** water 0.1N on AT 36.1◄25.5◄18.4◄►9.1►19.1►33.1	2761
1628.1	557.2	Footbridge, stream	2614
1627.5	557.8	Lynn Camp Creek, footbridge, campsite	2400
1626.4	558.9	Lynn Camp Mountain	3024
1625.2	560.1	Lick Creek, footbridge	2270
1624.2	561.1	Stream.	2321
1624.0	561.3	VA 625, USFS 222 (gravel) N37.358 W81 25.569 P	2333
1622.8	562.5	Stream.	3106
1621.7	563.6	Chestnut Ridge, south end, start of clearing	3793
1621.4	563.9	Pond, spring at north end, best water source for Chestnut Knob Shelter.	3908
1620.6	564.7	Views from open ridgeline	4194
1619.7	565.6	Spring 0.1E on unmarked roadbed	4334
1619.6	565.7	**Chestnut Knob Shelter** 34.6◄27.5◄9.1◄►10.0►24.0►33.8 Concrete block shelter, fully enclosed with door.	4410

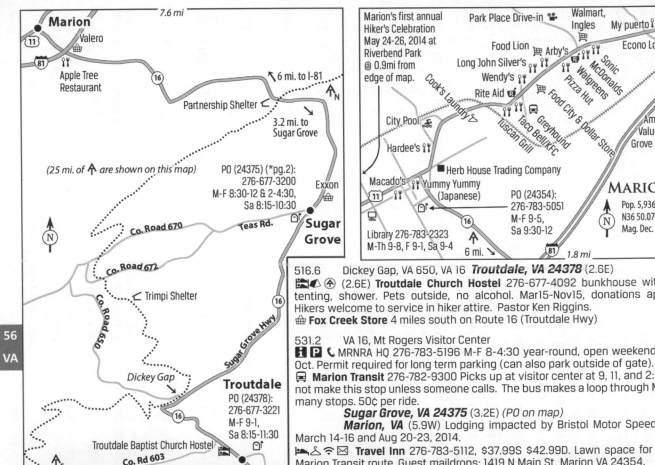

Marion 11, 81
7.6 mi
Valero
Apple Tree Restaurant
16
Partnership Shelter
↑ 6 mi. to I-81
N
3.2 mi. to Sugar Grove

(25 mi. of ↑ are shown on this map)

PO (24375) (*pg.2):
276-677-3200
M-F 8:30-12 & 2-4:30,
Sa 8:15-10:30

Exxon
Co. Road 670
Teas Rd.
Sugar Grove
Co. Road 672
N
Trimpi Shelter
Co. Road 650
Sugar Grove Hwy
16
Dickey Gap
Troutdale
PO (24378):
276-677-3221
M-F 9-1,
Sa 8:15-11:30
16
Troutdale Baptist Church Hostel
Co. Rd 603
↑S

56
VA

Marion's first annual Hiker's Celebration May 24-26, 2014 at Riverbend Park @ 0.9mi from edge of map.

Park Place Drive-in
Walmart, Ingles
Travel Inn
My puerto
Econo Lodge
Food Lion
Arby's
Long John Silver's
Sonic
McDonalds
Wendy's
Walgreens
Pizza Hut
Rite Aid
Cook's Laundry
Food City & Dollar Store
America's Best Value Inn, Sugar Grove Diner inside
City Pool
Taco Bell/KFC
Greyhound
Tuscan Grill
Hardee's
Herb House Trading Company
Macado's
Yummy Yummy (Japanese)
11
PO (24354):
276-783-5051
M-F 9-5,
Sa 9:30-12

MARION, VA
N
Pop. 5,936 (2011)
N36 50.070, W81 31.000
Mag. Dec. 7° 24'W

Library 276-783-2323
M-Th 9-8, F 9-1, Sa 9-4
16
6 mi. ↓
81
1.8 mi

516.6 Dickey Gap, VA 650, VA 16 *Troutdale, VA 24378* (2.6E)
(2.6E) **Troutdale Church Hostel** 276-677-4092 bunkhouse with kitchen, tenting, shower. Pets outside, no alcohol. Mar15-Nov15, donations appreciated. Hikers welcome to service in hiker attire. Pastor Ken Riggins.
Fox Creek Store 4 miles south on Route 16 (Troutdale Hwy)

531.2 VA 16, Mt Rogers Visitor Center
MRNRA HQ 276-783-5196 M-F 8-4:30 year-round, open weekends May-mid Oct. Permit required for long term parking (can also park outside of gate).
Marion Transit 276-782-9300 Picks up at visitor center at 9, 11, and 2:30, but will not make this stop unless someone calls. The bus makes a loop through Marion with many stops. 50¢ per ride.
Sugar Grove, VA 24375 (3.2E) *(PO on map)*
Marion, VA (5.9W) Lodging impacted by Bristol Motor Speedway races March 14-16 and Aug 20-23, 2014.
Travel Inn 276-783-5112, $37.99S $42.99D. Lawn space for games. On Marion Transit route. Guest maildrops: 1419 N Main St, Marion VA 24354.

🛏📶✉ **Econo Lodge** 276-783-6031 $49-$59 cont. B, pets allowed, some smoking rooms. Maildrops: 1420 N. Main St, Marion, VA 24354.

🛏🍴📶 **America's Best Value Inn** 276-378-0481

🍴 **Macado's** beer & wings.

■📶 **Herb House Trading Co.** 276-356-9832 Mural on side of building. Welcomes hikers. Ice cream and local baked goods.

🚌 **Greyhound** 276-783-7114 weekdays only, four buses/day.

🍦 **Park Place Drive-In** 276-781-2222 Walk-ins welcome. Also has mini-golf, arcade, and ice cream shop.

542.7   VA 683, US 11, I-81 ***Atkins, VA 24311*** AT intersects with US 11 between Atkins & Rural Retreat in the township of Groseclose.

🛏⛺🚌 P 📶✉ **Relax Inn** 276-783-5811 $40S $45D, $5EAP, pets $10. Parking $3/day. Call for shuttle availability. Maildrops: (guests only, limit 2 boxes) Relax Inn, 7253 Lee Hwy, Rural Retreat, VA 24368.

🍴 P ✉ **The Barn Restaurant** 276-686-6222 16oz hiker burger, Sunday buffet 11-2, parking for section hikers. Maildrops: 7412 Lee Highway Rural Retreat, VA 24368.

🏪 $ **Shell Convenience Store** 24hr, ATM inside.

■ **Rambunny & Aqua** 276-783-3754 Will help with info & refer shuttles.

🚌 **Skip** 276-783-3604 shuttles by appt, covers Damascus to Pearisburg.

🛏📶🖥✉ **Comfort Inn** (3.7W) 276-783-2144 Get hotel discount book coupon at Exxon or ask for hiker rate, usually approx. $60. Cont. breakfast. Maildrops: 5558 Lee Hwy, Atkins, VA 24311.

580.5   VA 615, Laurel Creek

⚓ **Fort Bastian** 708-207-6725 Nigel "TruBrit" offers place to stay, pickup/return, laundry and breakfast. Call from Jenkins Shelter.

587.6   US 52, North Scenic Hwy, ***Bland, VA 24315*** (3E to PO or Citgo, 4E to hotel & restaurants)

📮 (May be reduced to half-day in 2014, not confirmed) M-F 8:30-11:30 & 12-4, Sa 9 -11, 276-688-3751

🛏📶✉ **Big Walker Motel** 276-688-3331 $57.89 (1 or 2), 62.18 (3 or 4), pets okay. Guest maildrops: 70 Skyview Lane, Bland, VA 24315.

🍴 **Subway**, **Dairy Queen**

🏪🍴☎ $ **Citgo, Bland Square Grill** 276-688-3851 Open 6:30-7 year-round. Groceries, Canister fuel and Heet, Grill serves B/L/D.

🏪 **Dollar General**

➕ **Bland Family Clinic** 276-688-0500 M 10-6, Tu 11-7, Th 9-5, F 10-2.

🖥 **Bland County Library** 276-688-3737 M,W,F,Sa 9:30-4:30, T,Th 9:30-8, 697 Main Street.

🚌 **Bubba's Shuttles** 276-266-6147 barnes.james43@yahoo.com Shuttles from Damascus to Pearisburg & Roanoke Airport.

Bastian, VA 24314 (3W)

📮 M-F 8-12 & 12:30-4, Sa 9:15-11:15, 276-688-4631

🍴 **Pizza Plus** 276-688-3332 Su-Th 11-9, F-Sa 9-10.

🏪 $ **Kangaroo Express** ATM

💊 **Bland Pharmacy** 276-688-4204 M,W,F 9-5, Tu,Th 9-8, Sa 9-12.

➕ **Medical Clinic** 276-688-4331 M,W 8:30-6, Tu,Th 8:30-8, F 8:30-5

Atkins Tank Restaurant
Exxon
Dollar General
PO (24311) 276-783-5551 M-F 8:30-12:30 & 1:45-3:45, Sa 9-10:45
ATKINS, VA
Pop. 1,100 (2007)
Relax Inn
Shell Convenience Store
Comfort Inn
Laundromat
Marathon & Subway
4.3 mi
AT to PO 3.0
The Barn

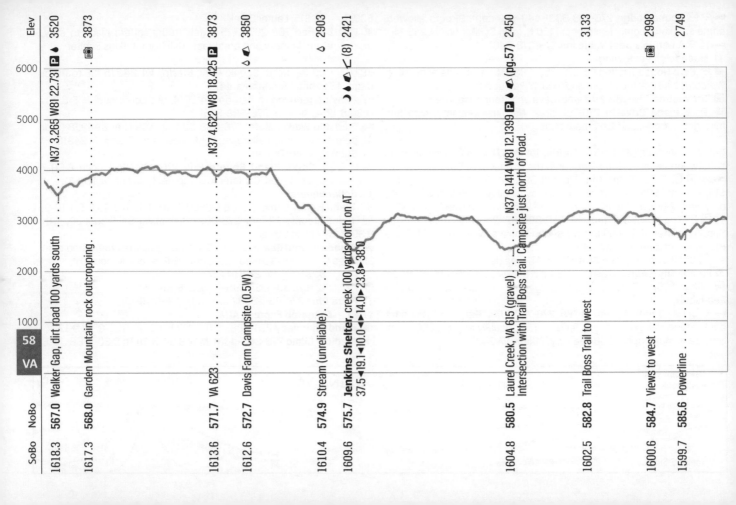

Elev

58
VA

SoBo	NoBo		Elev
1618.3	567.0	Walker Gap, dirt road 100 yards south — N37 3.265 W81 22.731 P	3520
1617.3	568.0	Garden Mountain, rock outcropping	3873
1613.6	571.7	VA 623 — N37 4.622 W81 18.425 P	3873
1612.6	572.7	Davis Farm Campsite (0.5W)	3850
1610.4	574.9	Stream (unreliable)	2903
1609.6	575.7	Jenkins Shelter, creek 100 yards north on AT 37.5◄19.1◄10.0◄▶14.0▶23.8▶38.0 ⊏(8)	2421
1604.8	580.5	Laurel Creek, VA 615 (gravel) Intersection with Trail Boss Trail. Campsite just north of road. — N37 6.1414 W81 12.1399 P (pg.57)	2450
1602.5	582.8	Trail Boss Trail to west	3133
1600.6	584.7	Views to west	2998
1599.7	585.6	Powerline	2749

SoBo	NoBo	Description	Coordinates / Notes	Elev
1598.3	587.0	AT on gravel road from here north to US 52		3101
1597.7	587.6	US 52 (North Scenic Hwy), **Bland, VA** (2.5E), **Bastian, VA** (3W)	(pg.57)	2928
1596.9	588.4	North end of VA 612, road walk over I-77. Water near where the AT enters woods north of road.	N37 8.335 W81 7.595 P ♦	2620
1595.6	589.7	**Helveys Mill Shelter** (0.3E) 33.1◄24.0◄14.0◄▶9.8▶24.0▶33.4 Water source 0.3 mile down switch-backed trail in front of shelter.	☽ ⊏(6)	3139

❀ **Mountain Laurel** – Shrub similar to the rhododendron. Grows five to ten feet high and blossoms with abundant cup-shaped white flowers.

SoBo	NoBo	Description	Coordinates / Notes	Elev
1588.9	596.4	VA 611 (gravel)	N37 8.7155 W81 0.561 P	2820
1588.6	596.7	Stream, unreliable	◁	2685
1587.5	597.8	Brushy Mountain		3101
1585.8	599.5	**Jenny Knob Shelter**, spring near shelter. 33.8◄23.8◄9.8◄▶14.2▶23.6▶38.6	☽ ⊏(6)	2684
1585.1	600.2	Stream, campsite	♦	2333
1584.8	600.5	Stream	♦	2270
1584.6	600.7	Lickskillet Hollow, VA 608, footbridge	N37 9.415 W80 57.682 P	2200
1583.4	601.9	Powerline		2775
1579.4	605.9	Kimberling Creek, suspension bridge		2090
1579.3	606.0	VA 606, parking to east. **Trent's Grocery** (0.5W), **Nature Way** (3.6E)	N37 10.544 W80 54.500 P (pg.62)	2105

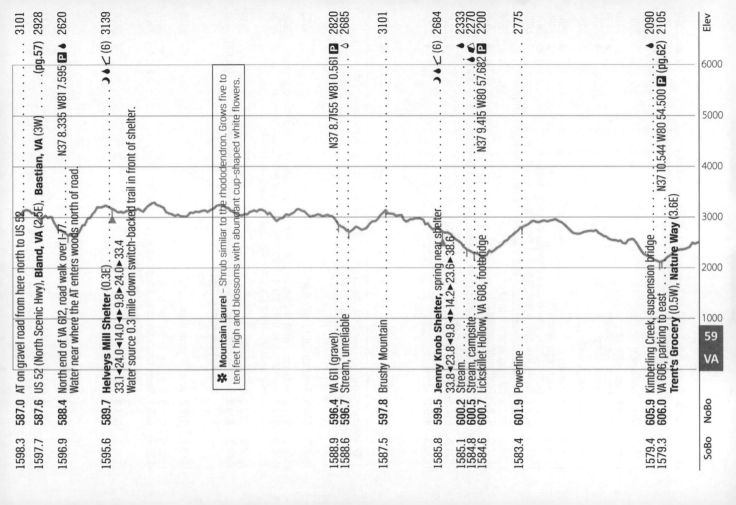

SoBo	NoBo		Elev
1577.5	607.8	Dismal Falls Trail, 0.3W to waterfall, camping on side trail.	2399
1577.2	608.1	Road on other side of falls sometimes brings visitors by car. Stream, campsite	2326
1576.5	608.8	Footbridge	2369
1575.9	609.4	Footbridge	2410
1575.7	609.6	Footbridge, stream	2434
1575.5	609.8	Two streams	2497
1574.9	610.4	Woods road	2620
1574.4	610.9	Streams	2562
1574.0	611.3	Footbridge, stream (2)	2485
1573.8	611.5	Dismal Creek, gravel road, campsite, footbridge to north	2478
1573.6	611.7	Ribble Trail 3.0W connects with AT near Big Horse Gap	2483
1573.0	612.3	Center of one-mile stretch with at-least 6 stream crossings by footbridge.	2505
1572.4	612.9	Clearing, side trail to west	2536
1572.1	613.2	Footbridge, stream (2)	2538
1571.8	613.5	Dirt road	2600
1571.6	613.7	Wapiti Shelter (0.1E) 38.0◀24.0◀14.2◀▶9.4▶24.4▶36.9	2622
1571.4	613.9	Stream.	2668
1571.0	614.3	Stream.	2823
1570.3	615.0	Spring	3359
1569.0	616.3	View	3899

✱ Rhododendron – 10-15 foot tall shrubs with broad waxy leaves. Grows in thick stands that the AT sometimes tunnels through. Flowers grow in large bouquets of ruffled pink flowers.

1566.7	618.6	Side trail 0.1E to radio tower	4023
1566.1	619.2	Ribble Trail west, wide grassy path, reconnects with AT south of Wapiti Shelter.	3800
1566.0	619.3	Big Horse Gap, USFS 103 △ Sometimes confused with Sugar Run Gap, which is 1.5N. There is a short sign south of road, west of AT	3800
1564.8	620.5	Woods road	3549
1564.4	620.9	Sugar Run Gap, Sugar Run Rd (gravel), road fork in view to east ... (pg.62)	3450
		Woods Hole Hostel (0.5E)	
1563.1	622.2	View, 30 yards east.	3940
1562.3	623.0	Roadbed, campsites 0.3W	3576
1562.2	623.1	**Docs Knob Shelter,** reliable spring to left of shelter 33.4◀23.6◀9.4◀▶15.0▶27.5▶31.4	3560
1561.1	624.2	Spring	3416
1559.5	625.8	Spring	3161
1558.9	626.4	Powerline, view	3443

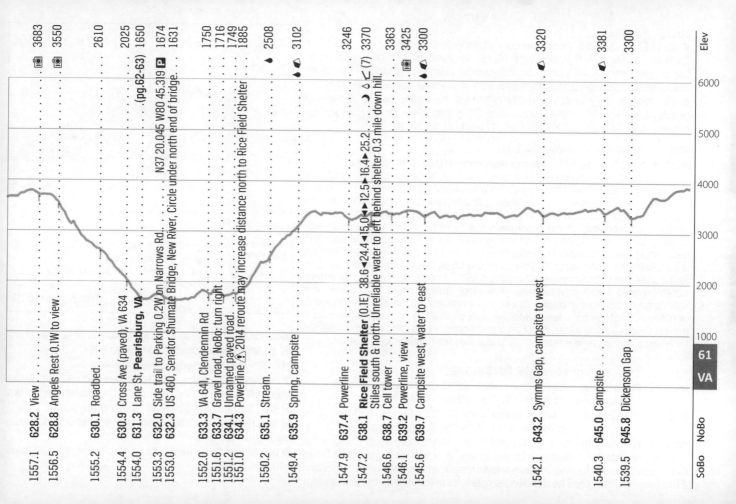

SoBo	NoBo		Elev
1557.1	628.2	View.	3683
1556.5	628.8	Angels Rest 0.1W to view.	3550
1555.2	630.1	Roadbed.	2610
1554.4	630.9	Cross Ave (paved), VA 634	2025
1554.0	631.3	Lane St, **Pearisburg, VA** (pg.62-63)	1650
1553.3	632.0	Side trail to Parking 0.2W on Narrows Rd	1674
1553.0	632.3	US 460, Senator Shumate Bridge, New River, Circle under north end of bridge. N37 20.045 W80 45.319	1631
1552.0	633.3	VA 641, Clendennin Rd	1750
1551.6	633.7	Gravel road, NoBo: turn right.	1716
1551.2	634.1	Unnamed paved road.	1749
1551.0	634.3	Powerline ⚠ 2014 reroute may increase distance north to Rice Field Shelter	1885
1550.2	635.1	Stream.	2508
1549.4	635.9	Spring, campsite	3102
1547.9	637.4	Powerline	3246
1547.2	638.1	**Rice Field Shelter** (0.1E) 38.6◀24.4◀15.0◀▶12.5▶16.4▶25.2 ⌂⊆(7) Stiles south & north. Unreliable water to left behind shelter 0.3 mile down hill.	3370
1546.6	638.7	Cell tower	3363
1546.1	639.2	Powerline, view.	3425
1545.6	639.7	Campsite west, water to east	3300
1542.1	643.2	Symms Gap, campsite to west.	3320
1540.3	645.0	**Campsite**	3381
1539.5	645.8	Dickenson Gap	3300

61
VA

606.0   VA 606

🏕️🏬🍴💲🚿⛺🚌✉ **Trent's Grocery** (0.5W) 276-928-1349
Open M-Sa 7-8, Sun 9-8. Deli with pizza, hamburgers, hot dogs and more. Camping $6, shower $3, laundry $3. Coleman/alcohol/oz and canister fuel. Soda machines outside. Shuttles. Maildrops: 900 Wilderness Rd, Bland, VA 24315.

🛒🍴 **Nature Way** (3.6E) 540-921-1381 M-S 8am-5pm Unique Amish-run grocery with organic, locally grown foods. Dry goods, jerky, candy, produce, ice cream & sandwiches. 106 Nature Lane, Pearisburg, VA 24134

620.9   Sugar Run Gap, Sugar Run Rd

🛏️🏨🍴⛺🚌💻✉ **Woods Hole Hostel** (0.5E) 540-921-3444
〈www.woodsholehostel.com〉 Open year-round. A "Slice of heaven, not to be missed." The 1880's chestnut-log cabin was discovered by Roy & Tillie Wood, who opened the hostel in 1986. Their granddaughter, Neville, continues the legacy with her husband Michael, placing an emphasis on sustainable living through beekeeping, farming, organic gardening, yoga(free), & massage therapy. Directions: NoBo right on dirt road at Sugar Run Gap, SoBo turn left. Bear left at fork, go downhill 0.5 mile to hostel on right. Offers massage, healing arts, & retreats. Bunkhouse $15PP has mattresses, electricity, and hot shower, and coffee/tea in the morning. Camping $10PP. Pet fee $3. Two indoor rooms: $25PP shared / $50 private (thru-hiker rate). Guests often invited to share local/organic communal meals. Dinner $13, breakfast $8. Please call to inquire or reserve. Shuttles for a fee, computer access, laundry, smoothies, snacks & drinks, Coleman/alcohol/oz, fuel canisters. Accepts cash and credit. Maildrops for guests: Woods Hole Hostel, 3696 Sugar Run Rd, Pearisburg, VA 24134.

62

VA

631.3   Lane St, *Pearisburg, VA 24134* (0.9E)

🛏️📶✉ **Plaza Motel** 540-921-2591 $40S $50D plus tax, no pets, accepts credit cards. Maildrops: 415 N. Main St, Pearisburg, VA 24134.

🛏️💲⛺📶💻✉ **Holiday Motor Lodge** 540-921-1551 Rooms $33/up. Game room, pool, pet friendly. Maildrops: 401 N Main Street, Pearisburg, VA 24134.

🏨 **Holy Family Hostel** 540-921-3547 Early May to late Sept; if you arrive later, please call for availability. Please check in or call during daylight hours (8am-6pm). Bunks; tenting in designated areas, toilet, hot shower, refrigerator, 2 microwaves, grill. Keep hostel clean & noise down (church in residential area).

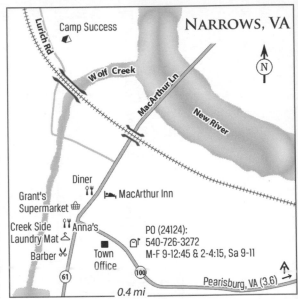

Donation $10PP per night, 2 night max. No pets or alcohol.
⛺ **EZ Way Laundromat** M-Sa 6-9, Su 6-8
💊 **Rite Aid Pharmacy** 540-921-1284
🔧 **Harvey Electronics and Hardware** 540-921-1456 Cell phones & supplies Canister fuel, alcohol/oz, tent repair kits.
🚌 **Don Raines** 540-921-7433 Anytime, anywhere
🚌 **Tom Hoffman** 540-921-1184 〈gopullman@aol.com〉 mid-range shuttles centered in Pearisburg.
■ **Old Towne Shoe Repair** Open Wed & Sat, Warner Baker 540-230-6357

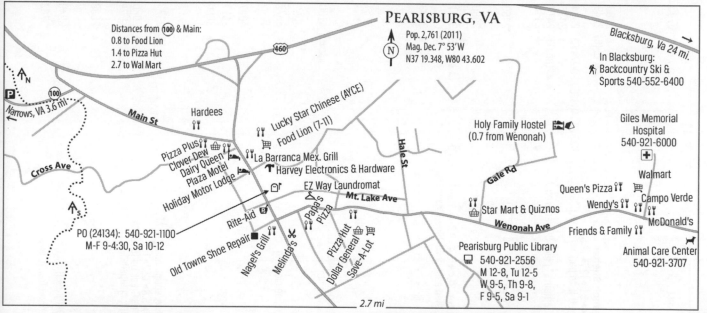

PEARISBURG, VA

Pop. 2,761 (2011)
Mag. Dec. 7° 53'W
N37 19.348, W80 43.602

Distances from (100) & Main:
0.8 to Food Lion
1.4 to Pizza Hut
2.7 to Wal Mart

Blacksburg, Va 24 mi.

In Blacksburg:
Backcountry Ski &
Sports 540-552-6400

Narrows, VA 3.6 mi.

Cross Ave

Main St

Hardees

Pizza Plus
Clover Dew
Dairy Queen
Plaza Motel
Holiday Motor Lodge

Lucky Star Chinese (AYCE)
Food Lion (7-11)
La Barranca Mex. Grill
Harvey Electronics & Hardware

EZ Way Laundromat

Hale St

Mt. Lake Ave

Holy Family Hostel
(0.7 from Wenonah)

Giles Memorial
Hospital
540-921-6000

Gale Rd

Walmart

Queen's Pizza

Campo Verde

Wendy's

McDonald's

Star Mart & Quiznos

Wenonah Ave

Friends & Family

PO (24134): 540-921-1100
M-F 9-4:30, Sa 10-12

Rite-Aid

Old Towne Shoe Repair

Nagel's Grill

Melinda's

Papa's Pizza

Pizza Hut
Dollar General
Save-A-Lot

Animal Care Center
540-921-3707

Pearisburg Public Library
540-921-2556
M 12-8, Tu 12-5
W 9-5, Th 9-8,
F 9-5, Sa 9-1

2.7 mi

Narrows, VA (3.6W on VA 100)

MacArthur Inn 540-726-7510 $45D. Call for ride from Pearisburg area trailheads, ride $5 each way. Longer shuttles and slackpacking can be arranged. Free long distance phone, cable TV and WiFi. In center of town with all services (restaurants, laundry, PO, grocery) in close walking distance. On-site restaurant serves breakfast 6am-11am M-Sa, and dinner when there is group interest. Maildrops: 117 MacArthur Lane, Narrows, VA 24124.

Camp Success Camping $5, no showers. Check in at Town Office 540-726-3020 M-F 9-5. Call ahead if you will arrive on weekend or after hours.

Grants Supermarket 540-726-2303 M–Sa 8–9, Sun 9–8

Blue Moon Diner (B/L)

Anna's Restaurant (L/D)

651.8   **The Captain's**

 Camping available at 4464 Big Stony Creek Rd, about 30 yards from trail. Use zip line to cross the creek. You may camp even when The Captain is not home. Dogs will bark but are friendly and are contained by an invisible electric fence. Hiker Feed two weeks after Trail Days. *This is not a hostel; do not enter the house.* If it rains, you may stay on back porch.

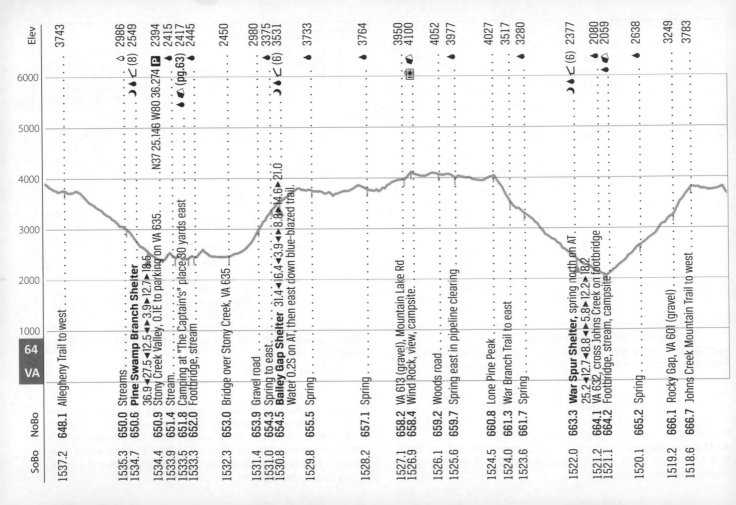

SoBo	NoBo	Description	Elev
1537.2	648.1	Allegheny Trail to west	3743
1535.3	650.0	Streams	2986
1534.7	650.6	**Pine Swamp Branch Shelter** 36.9◄27.5◄12.5◄►3.9►12.7►18.5	2549
1534.4	650.9	Stony Creek Valley, 0.1E to parking on VA 635. N37 25.146 W80 36.274 🅿	2394
1533.9	651.4	Stream.	2415
1533.5	651.8	Camping at "The Captain's" place 30 yards east (pg.63)	2417
1533.3	652.0	Footbridge, stream	2445
1532.3	653.0	Bridge over Stony Creek, VA 635	2450
1531.4	653.9	Gravel road	2980
1531.0	654.3	Spring to east.	3375
1530.8	654.5	**Bailey Gap Shelter** 31.4◄16.4◄3.9◄►8.8►14.6►21.0 Water 0.2S on AT, then east down blue-blazed trail.	3531
1529.8	655.5	Spring	3733
1528.2	657.1	Spring	3764
1527.1	658.2	VA 613 (gravel), Mountain Lake Rd	3950
1526.9	658.4	Wind Rock, view, campsite.	4100
1526.1	659.2	Woods road	4052
1525.6	659.7	Spring east in pipeline clearing	3977
1524.5	660.8	Lone Pine Peak	4027
1524.0	661.3	War Branch Trail to east	3517
1523.6	661.7	Spring	3280
1522.0	663.3	**War Spur Shelter**, spring north on AT. 25.2◄12.7◄8.8◄►5.8►12.2►18.2	2377
1521.2	664.1	VA 632, cross Johns Creek on footbridge	2080
1521.1	664.2	Footbridge, stream, campsite	2059
1520.1	665.2	Spring	2638
1519.2	666.1	Rocky Gap, VA 601 (gravel)	3249
1518.6	666.7	Johns Creek Mountain Trail to west	3783

64

VA

NoBo	SoBo	Description	Elev
667.9	1517.4	Kelly Knob, view.	3743
669.1	1516.2	**Laurel Creek Shelter** 18.5◄14.6◄5.8▼6.4▲12.4▲22.5. Water 60 yards north of shelter junction and west of AT.	2817 ☽⊏(6)
669.3	1516.0	Stream	2786
669.7	1515.6	Piney Ridge, abandoned house to west.	2653
671.1	1514.2	Pasture, several fence stiles	2317
671.5	1513.8	Footbridge, Sinking Creek, VA 42 **Newport, VA** (8.0E) (pg.68) "trail east" (Nobo right, Sobo left) is compass west.	2200
672.4	1512.9	VA 630 (paved), chimney, and footbridge close together	2234
672.8	1512.5	Keffer Oak, largest oak tree on AT in south, over 18' around, over 300 yrs old Dover Oak along AT in NY is slightly larger.	2403
673.2	1512.1	Powerline	2591
674.5	1510.8	Powerline	3259
675.3	1510.0	Bruisers Knob	3435
675.5	1509.8	**Sarver Hollow Shelter** (0.4E) (2002) 21.0◄12.2◄6.4▲6.0▲16.1▲29.7	3418 ☽⊏(6)
677.4	1507.9	View	3375
677.7	1507.6	View	3350
678.8	1506.5	North end of ridge crest on Sinking Creek Mountain West is old route of AT, leading 2.5 miles to Old Hall Rd.	3383
680.4	1504.9	Stream.	2720
681.5	1503.8	**Niday Shelter,** water on opposite side of AT 18.2◄12.4◄6.0▲10.1▲23.7▲24.7	2005 ☽⊏(6)
682.9	1502.4	VA 621, Craig Creek Rd	1558
683.4	1501.9	Many footbridges crossing Craig Creek and feeder streams. within a mile north of road.	1605
685.8	1499.5	Bench at southern crest of Brush Mountain	3064
686.6	1498.7	Audie Murphy Monument Murphy was most decorated American soldier of World War II. Monument on blue-blazed trail to west.	3100

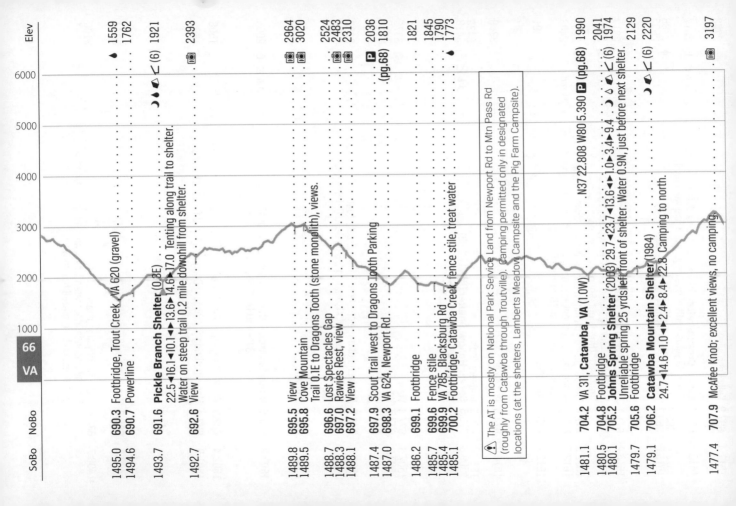

66
VA

SoBo	NoBo	Description	Elev
1495.0	690.3	Footbridge, Trout Creek, VA 620 (gravel)	1559
1494.6	690.7	Powerline	1762
1493.7	691.6	**Pickle Branch Shelter** (0.3E) 22.5◄16.1◄10.1►13.6►14.6►17.0 Tenting along trail to shelter. Water on steep trail 0.2 mile downhill from shelter.	1921
1492.7	692.7	View	2393
1489.8	695.5	View	2964
1489.5	695.8	Cove Mountain. Trail 0.1E to Dragons Tooth (stone monolith), views.	3020
1488.7	696.6	Lost Spectacles Gap	2524
1488.3	697.0	Rawies Rest, view	2483
1488.1	697.2	View	2310
1487.4	697.4	Scout Trail west to Dragons Tooth Parking	2036
1487.0	698.3	VA 624, Newport Rd. (pg.68)	1810
1486.2	699.1	Footbridge	1821
1485.7	699.6	Fence stile	1845
1485.4	699.9	VA 785, Blacksburg Rd	1790
1485.1	700.2	Footbridge, Catawba Creek, fence stile, treat water	1773
1481.1	704.2	VA 311, **Catawba, VA** (1.0W) N37 22.808 W80 5.390 P (pg.68)	1990
1480.5	704.8	Footbridge	2041
1480.1	705.2	**Johns Spring Shelter** (2003) 29.7◄23.7◄13.6►1.0►3.4►9.4 Unreliable spring 25 yrds left front of shelter. Water 0.9N, just before next shelter.	1974
1479.7	705.6	Footbridge	2129
1479.1	706.2	**Catawba Mountain Shelter** (1984) 24.7◄14.6◄1.0►2.4►8.4►22.8 Camping to north.	2220
1477.4	707.9	McAfee Knob; excellent views, no camping.	3197

The AT is mostly on National Park Service Land from Newport Rd to Mtn Pass Rd (roughly from Catawba through Troutville). Camping permitted only in designated locations (at the shelters, Lamberts Meadow Campsite and the Pig Farm Campsite).

NoBo	Feature	Elev
708.4	Powerline	2797
708.5	Water to east, Pig Farm campsite	2696
708.6	**Campbell Shelter** (1989), water behind shelter	2649 (6)
	17.0◀3.4◀2.4◀▶6.0▶20.4▶26.6	
	✿ **Fire Pink** – Scarlet-colored flower with five snake-tongued petals.	
711.7	Brickeys Gap, Lamberts Meadow Trail to east	2250
713.5	Tinker Cliffs, 0.5 mile cliff walk, views back to McAfee Knob	3000
714.0	Scorched Earth Gap, Andy Layne Trail to west	2600
714.6	**Lamberts Meadow Shelter** 9.4◀8.4◀6.0◀▶14.4▶20.6▶27.9	2143 (6)
714.9	Lamberts Meadow Campsite, Sawmill Run	2000
	Footbridge, stream. Trail north of footbridge to east rejoins AT at Brickeys Gap.	
717.1	Blue-blazed trail west to view	2273
718.9	Angels Gap	1800
719.3	Powerline	1900
720.0	Hay Rock, view	1900
721.2	Powerline, view	1915
722.0	Powerline	1982
722.8	Powerline	1440
723.4	Powerline, railroad tracks, bridge	1238
724.0	US 220, **Daleville, VA** (pg.68-69)	1350
725.2	I-81, trail passes under on VA 779	1400
725.5	US 11, RR tracks, **Troutville, VA** (0.8W) . N37 24.269 W79 53.369 🅿 (pg.68-69)	1300
725.8	Fence stile	1497
726.0	VA 652, Mountain Pass Rd	1450
726.3	Fence	1524

SoBo
1476.9
1476.8
1476.7
1473.6
1471.8
1471.3
1470.7
1470.4
1468.2
1466.4
1466.0
1465.3
1464.1
1463.3
1462.5
1461.9
1461.3
1460.1
1459.8
1459.5
1459.3
1459.0

671.5   VA 42, Sinking Creek, Trail "east" here is compass west.

🛏🛰✉ (0.5E) **The Huffman House B&B** 540-544-6942 ⟨www.thehuffmanhousebandb.com⟩, $139–$169 double, $20EAP, reservations required. Owned by 1999 thru-hikers. Maildrops (call first): 16 Huffman Store Dr., Newport, VA 24128.

🛏 (1.0W) **Sublett Place** 540-544-3099 ⟨www.thesublettplace.com⟩ Home and cottage for rent, prices seasonal.

⛺ (1.0W) **Joe's Trees** 540-544-7303 ⟨www.joestrees.com⟩ Limited summer/fall hours (call ahead), 7 days Nov 15-Dec 21, closed Dec 22-Apr. Drinks, jerky, cheese, jams.

Newport, VA 24128 (8E)
Store, post office and restaurant near intersection of 42 and 460.

🏣 M-F 8:15-12:30 & 2:30-4:15, Sa 9-11, 540-544-7415

🛒 **Super Val-U** 540-544-7202

🍴 **Mikie's 7th** 540-544-0007 Tu-Sa 5:30-8:30.

698.3   VA 624, Newport Rd

🏠🚲🚌✉ (0.3E) **Four Pines Hostel** Owner Joe Mitchell cell: 540-309-8615 Hostel is a 3-bay garage with shower; please leave a donation. Pet friendly. Shuttles to/from The Homeplace Restaurant (Thurs-Sun) and to Catawba Grocery. Longer shuttles for a fee. Maildrops: 6164 Newport Rd. Catawba VA 24070

🛒🍴 **Catawba Grocery** 540-384-8050 West 0.3 mile to VA 311 and then left 0.1 mile to store, Su-Th 5am-10pm, F&Sa 5am-11pm. Grill serves breakfast, pizza, burgers, ice cream.

68
VA

704.2   VA 311, *Catawba, VA 24070* (1W)

🏣 (1.0W) M-F 9-12:30 & 2:30-5, Sa 8:30-10:30, 540-384-6011

🍴 (1.4W) **Homeplace Restaurant** 540-384-7252 Th 4-8, F-Sa 3-8, Su 11-6, Popular AYCE family-style meals including drink, dessert, and tax; $14 (two meats) $19 (three meats), $8 (kids 3-11).

724.0   US 220, *Daleville, VA*

725.5   US 11, *Troutville, VA*

Troutville Trail Days June 6-7 at Town Park. Food, vendors, & 5K race.

🔥🌲⛺ **Troutville Park & Fire Station** Free camping at town park, no pets. Free laundry and showers at fire station.

🛏⛺🛰🖥✉💲 **Howard Johnson Express** 540-992-1234 $49.95 hiker rate, cont. breakfast. Game room and pool. Maildrops: 437 Roanoke Road, Daleville, VA 24083.

🛏⛺🛰🖥 **Super 8** 540-992-3000 $59.36 + tax, cont B, pool, accepts major credit cards.

🛏🛰🖥 **Comfort Inn** 540-992-5600 hiker rate $49.99D, $5EAP, continental breakfast.

🛏🛰🖥 **Quality Inn** 540-992-5335 $71/up, pets $25.

🛏⛺✉ **Holiday Inn Express** 540-966-4444 $99-119. Maildrops: 3200 Lee Hwy, Troutville, VA 24175.

🛏 **Red Roof Inn** 540-992-5055

🛏🛰 **Travel Lodge** 540-992-6700 $38.95 $6EAP.

🍴 **Three Li'l Pigs** 540-966-0165 Summer M-Th 11-9:30, F-Sa 11-11, Su 11-9, Hiker friendly, hand-chopped BBQ ribs and wings, large selection of beer, some locally-brewed. Thru-hikers get free banana pudding dessert Mid-April to June 1.

🛒💊 **Kroger Grocery Store and Pharmacy** 540-992-4920 24hr, pharmacy M-F 8-9, Sa 9-6, Su 12-6.

🥾🚌🛰🖥✉ **Outdoor Trails** 540-992-5850 Full service outfitter. White gas, denatured alcohol and Dr. Bronners soap/oz. Computer for internet use, list of shuttlers. Open M-F 9-8, Sat 9-6 during hiking season (Apr 28-Jun 28); open M-F 10-8, Sat 10-6 the rest of the year. Maildrops: Botetourt Commons, 28 Kingston Dr, Daleville, VA 24083.

🚌 **Homer Witcher** 540-266-4849 Trail maintainer & 2002 thru-hiker.

🚌 **Del Schechterly** 540-529-6028 Covers Pearisburg-Waynesboro.

🍺 **Flying Mouse Brewery** Check ⟨www.flyingmousebrewery.com⟩ for beer tasting events. 0.4W to Precast Way, then right 0.1mi.

Roanoke, VA (13E)
✈ A large city with an airport approx 13 miles from the AT.

🥾 (5E) **Gander Mountain** 540-362-3658

🥾 (10E) **Sportsman's Warehouse** 540-366-9700 (3550 Ferncliff Ave NW) Full service outfitter with full line of gear including fuel, freeze dried foods, boots, clothes and trekking poles.

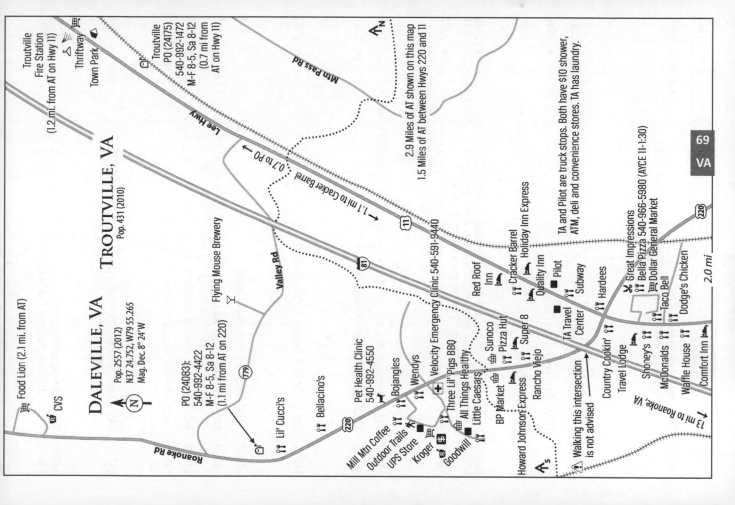

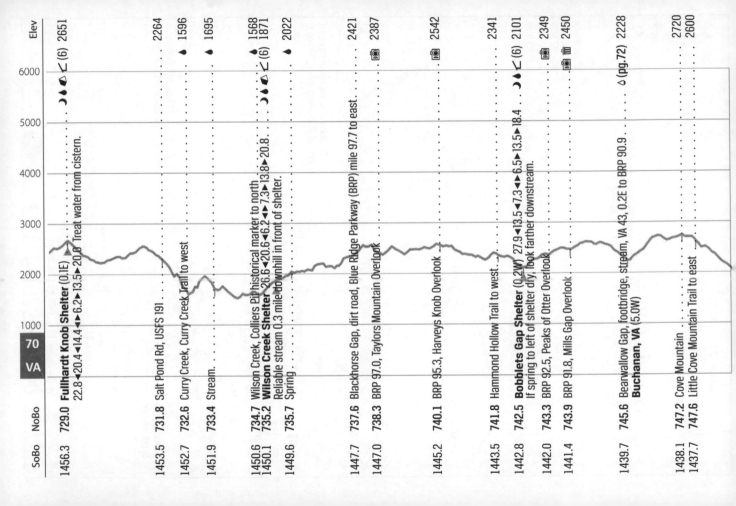

SoBo	NoBo		Elev
			70 VA
1456.3	729.0	**Fullhardt Knob Shelter** (0.1E) 22.8◀20.4◀14.4◀▶6.2▶13.5▶20.0 Treat water from cistern. ☾ ◖ ◐ ⊂ (6) ▲	2651
1453.5	731.8	Salt Pond Rd, USFS 191	2264
1452.7	732.6	Curry Creek, Curry Creek Trail to west ◖	1596
1451.9	733.4	Stream. ◖	1695
1450.6	734.7	Wilson Creek, Colliers Dip historical marker to north	1568
1450.1	735.2	**Wilson Creek Shelter** 26.6◀20.6◀6.2◀▶7.3▶13.8▶20.8. ☾ ◖ ◐ ⊂ (6)	1871
1449.6	735.7	Reliable stream 0.3 mile downhill in front of shelter. Spring ◖	2022
1447.7	737.6	Blackhorse Gap, dirt road, Blue Ridge Parkway (BRP) mile 97.7 to east.	2421
1447.0	738.3	BRP 97.0, Taylors Mountain Overlook 🖼	2387
1445.2	740.1	BRP 95.3, Harveys Knob Overlook 🖼	2542
1443.5	741.8	Hammond Hollow Trail to west	2341
1442.8	742.5	**Bobblets Gap Shelter** (0.2W) 27.9◀13.5◀7.3◀▶6.5▶13.5▶18.4 If spring to left of shelter dry, look farther downstream. ☾ ◖ ◐ ⊂ (6)	2101
1442.0	743.3	BRP 92.5, Peaks of Otter Overlook 🖼	2349
1441.4	743.9	BRP 91.8, Mills Gap Overlook 🖼 🏛	2450
1439.7	745.6	Bearwallow Gap, footbridge, stream, VA 43, 0.2E to BRP 90.9 **Buchanan, VA** (5.0W) △ (pg.72)	2228
1438.1	747.2	Cove Mountain	2720
1437.7	747.6	Little Cove Mountain Trail to east	2600

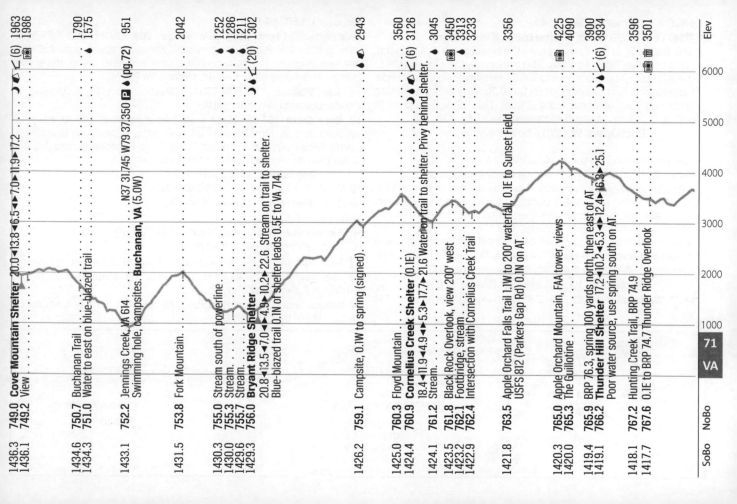

SoBo	NoBo	Description	Elev
1436.3	749.0	**Cove Mountain Shelter** 20.0◄13.8◄6.5◄▶7.0▶11.9▶17.2)△ (6) 📷	1963
1436.1	749.2	View	1986
1434.6	750.7	Buchanan Trail	1790
1434.3	751.0	Water to east on blue-blazed trail	1575
1433.1	752.2	Jennings Creek, VA 614. . . . . N37 31.745 W79 37.350 P ◆ (pg.72) Swimming hole, campsites. **Buchanan, VA** (5.0W)	951
1431.5	753.8	Fork Mountain.	2042
1430.3	755.0	Stream south of powerline	1252
1430.0	755.3	Stream.	1286
1429.6	755.7	Stream.	1211
1429.3	756.0	**Bryant Ridge Shelter** 20.8◄13.5◄7.0◄▶4.9▶10.2▶22.6 Stream on trail to shelter. Blue-blazed trail 0.1N of shelter leads 0.5E to VA 714.)◆ (20)	1302
1426.2	759.1	Campsite, 0.1W to spring (signed).	2943
1425.0	760.3	Floyd Mountain	3560
1424.4	760.9	**Cornelius Creek Shelter** (0.1E) 18.4◄11.9◄4.9◄▶5.3▶17.7▶21.6 Water on trail to shelter.)◆ (6)	3126
1424.1	761.2	Stream.	3045
1423.5	761.8	Black Rock Overlook, view 200' west	3450
1423.2	762.1	Footbridge, stream	3313
1422.9	762.4	Intersection with Cornelius Creek Trail	3233
1421.8	763.5	Apple Orchard Falls Trail 1.1W to 200' waterfall, 0.1E to Sunset Field, USFS 812 (Parkers Gap Rd) 0.1N on AT.	3356
1420.3	765.0	Apple Orchard Mountain, FAA tower, views 📷	4225
1420.0	765.3	The Guillotine	4090
1419.4	765.9	BRP 76.3, spring 100 yards north, then east of AT	3900
1419.1	766.2	**Thunder Hill Shelter** 17.2◄10.2◄5.3◄▶12.4▶16.3▶25.1 Poor water source, use spring south on AT.)◆ (6)	3934
1418.1	767.2	Hunting Creek Trail, BRP 74.9	3596
1417.7	767.6	0.1E to BRP 74.7 Thunder Ridge Overlook 📷 🏛	3501

745.6   Bearwallow Gap, VA 43

🛏🎒🍴🏪 (5.5E) **Peaks of Otter Lodge & Restaurant**
540-586-1081 To get to resort from the trailhead on VA 43, go 0.1E on to the Blue Ridge Parkway (the overpass), then follow BRP to the left 5.0 miles. Motel rooms $126 weekdays, $136 weekends, higher in fall. Restaurant open for B/L/D. Sunday buffet breakfast. Some supplies at camp store. Closes Dec. 15 and reopens in spring. Camping managed separately, 540-586-7321, $16.

        Buchanan, VA (5W) *Also see next entry.*

752.2   Jennings Creek 💧 (0.3E), VA 614

🛏🎒🍴🏪🚿⛺🛜📧 (1.2E) **Middle Creek Campground**
540-254-2550 ⟨www.middlecreekcampground.com⟩ cabins $65-75, $5EAP cabin sleeps 4-6, camping $20 (2 persons), showers $5, snack bar, Ask about shuttles, small amount of resupply, Coleman/alcohol/oz, and canister fuel. Laundry room (around back) is always open. Can also be reached on the northern side of Fork Mountain by taking VA 714 and VA 614 east 1.4 miles. Guest maildrops: 1164 Middle Creek Rd, Buchanan, VA 24066.

        Buchanan, VA (I-81 exit 168) (5W on VA 614)

🛏🛜 **Wattstull Inn** 540-254-1551, $68+tax/up, $5EAP, pets $15 each.

780.8   US 501, VA 130

🛏🎒🏪⛺📧 **Lynchburg/Blue Ridge KOA** (5.0E) 866-883-5228
Hiker special $15PP includes tent site, shower w/towel, pool. $10 day-use including shower. Four-person cabins available. Camp store, coin laundry. Maildrops: 6252 Elon Rd, Monroe ,VA 24574.

🚌 **Ken Wallace** 434-609-2704   Shuttles covering   Daleville to Waynesboro and Lynchburg KOA.

🚌 **Gary Serra** 757-681-2254 Gary has completed the AT twice in sections and is familiar with all trailheads. Pickups at Glasgow & Buena Vista trailheads. Shuttles along AT, to Roanoke, Lynchburg and Charlottesville airports, and to Amtrak station.

        Big Island, VA 24526 (5.6E)

📮 M-F 8-12 & 2-4, Sa 8-10, 434-299-5072

🏪🍴📧 **H&H Food Market** 434-299-5153 7 days 5:30-9, B/L/D, Maildrops: 11619 Lee Jackson Hwy, Big Island, VA 24526.

➕ **Big Island Family Medical Center** 434-299-5951

        Glasgow, VA 24555 (5.9W)

ℹ️ **Town Hall** 540-258-2246 Maintains shelter & Knick Field restrooms

🛒 **Glasgow Grocery Express** 540-258-1818 M-Sa 6-11:30pm, Su 8-1130pm, Coleman/alcohol/oz.

✈️ **Natural Bridge Animal Hospital** 434-291-1444 4.5W of Glasgow on VA 130. M,W,F 8-5:30, T,Th 8-7.

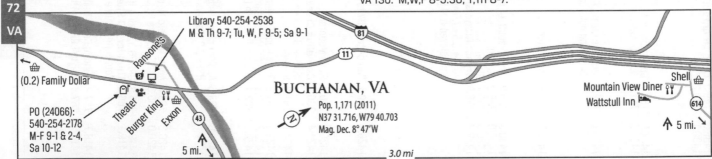

Library 540-254-2538
M & Th 9-7; Tu, W, F 9-5; Sa 9-1

(0.2) Family Dollar

PO (24066):
540-254-2178
M-F 9-1 & 2-4,
Sa 10-12

Ransone's
Theater
Burger King
Exxon

BUCHANAN, VA
Pop. 1,171 (2011)
N37 31.716, W79 40.703
Mag. Dec. 8° 47'W

5 mi.

Mountain View Diner
Wattstull Inn
Shell

🏕 5 mi.

3.0 mi

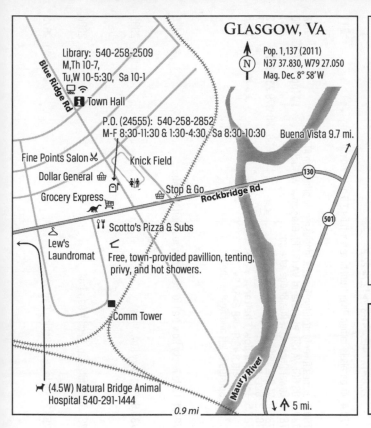

GLASGOW, VA

Pop. 1,137 (2011)
N37 37.830, W79 27.050
Mag. Dec. 8° 58′ W

Library: 540-258-2509
M,Th 10-7,
Tu,W 10-5:30, Sa 10-1

Town Hall

Blue Ridge Rd

P.O. (24555): 540-258-2852
M-F 8:30-11:30 & 1:30-4:30, Sa 8:30-10:30

Buena Vista 9.7 mi.

Fine Points Salon

Knick Field

Dollar General

Grocery Express

Stop & Go

Rockbridge Rd.

130

501

Lew's Laundromat

Scotto's Pizza & Subs

Free, town-provided pavillion, tenting, privy, and hot showers.

Comm Tower

Maury River

(4.5W) Natural Bridge Animal Hospital 540-291-1444

0.9 mi.

5 mi.

Minimize Campfire Impacts

•Use stoves for cooking – if you need a fire, build one only where it's legal and in an existing fire ring. Leave hatchets and saws at home – collect dead and downed wood that you can break by hand. Burn all wood to ash.

•Do not try to burn trash, including foil, plastic, glass, cans, tea bags, food, or anything with food on it. These items do not burn thoroughly. They create noxious fumes, attract wildlife like skunks and bears, and make the area unsightly.

•Where campfires are permitted, leave the fire ring clean by removing others' trash and scattering unused wood, cold coals, and ashes 200 feet away from camp after the fire is cold and completely out.

Read more of the Leave No Trace techniques developed for the A.T.: www.appalachiantrail.org/LNT

Water Sources

Be aware of trail conditions before heading out, and tune in to advice from outfitters and other hikers. The trail gets re-routed, springs dry up, streams alter their course. Be prepared to deal with changes, particularly with respect to water sources. Never plan to carry just enough water to reach the next spring.

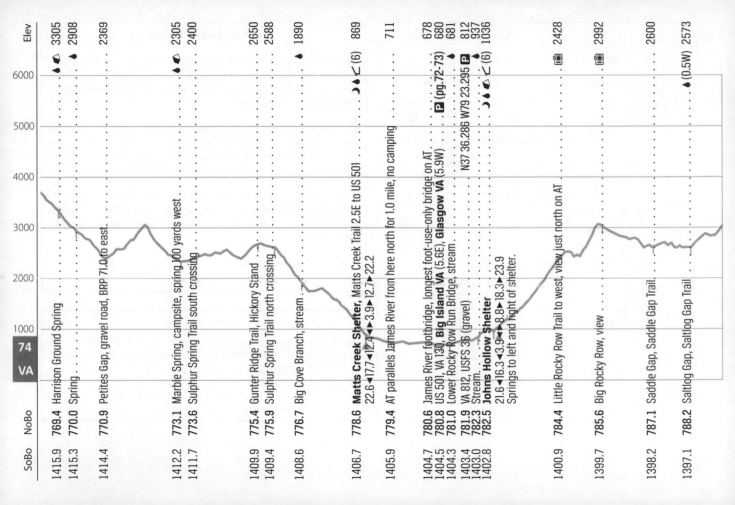

Elev	NoBo	SoBo	Description
3305	769.4	1415.9	Harrison Ground Spring
2908	770.0	1415.3	Spring
2369	770.9	1414.4	Petites Gap, gravel road, BRP 71.0 to east.
2305	773.1	1412.2	Marble Spring, campsite, spring 100 yards west
2400	773.6	1411.7	Sulphur Spring Trail south crossing
2650	775.4	1409.9	Gunter Ridge Trail, Hickory Stand
2588	775.9	1409.4	Sulphur Spring Trail north crossing
1890	776.7	1408.6	Big Cove Branch, stream
869	778.6	1406.7	**Matts Creek Shelter**, Matts Creek Trail 2.5E to US 501 22.6◀17.7◀12.4▶3.9▶12.7▶22.2
711	779.4	1405.9	AT parallels James River from here north for 1.0 mile, no camping
678	780.6	1404.7	James River footbridge, longest foot-use-only bridge on AT
680	780.8	1404.5	US 501, VA 130, **Big Island VA** (5.6E), **Glasgow VA** (5.9W)
681	781.0	1404.3	Lower Rocky Row Run Bridge, stream.
812	781.9	1403.4	VA 812, USFS 36 (gravel) N37 36.286 W79 23.295
937	782.3	1403.0	Stream.
1036	782.5	1402.8	**Johns Hollow Shelter** 21.6◀16.3◀3.9▶8.8▶18.3▶23.9 Springs to left and right of shelter.
2428	784.4	1400.9	Little Rocky Row Trail to west, view just north on AT
2992	785.6	1399.7	Big Rocky Row, view
2600	787.1	1398.2	Saddle Gap, Saddle Gap Trail.
2573	788.2	1397.1	Saltlog Gap, Saltlog Gap Trail (0.5W)

Elev	Feature	NoBo	SoBo
3372	Bluff Mountain, Ottie Cline Powell monument, views.	789.7	1395.6
2850	Punchbowl Mountain.	790.8	1394.5
2504	**Punchbowl Shelter** (0.2W), spring front left of shelter. 25.1◀12.7◀8.8▶9.5▶15.1▶25.3	791.3	1394.0
2170	BRP 51?	791.7	1393.6
2100	VA 607, Robinson Gap Rd (gravel) N37 40.567 W79 19.92 🅿 ◆ Water west 30 yards.	792.0	1393.3
	N37 40.426 W79 20.081 🅿 🏛		
2228	Rice Mountain	793.9	1391.4
1722	Spring.	794.5	1390.8
1358	Dirt road.	794.9	1390.4
1002	Reservoir Rd (gravel), Pedlar River Bridge. N37 40.227 W79 17.067 🅿 ◆ ◁ campsite 0.2S of road.	795.8	1389.5
1207	Spring.	797.5	1387.8
1096	Campsite.	798.0	1387.3
1151	Stream.	798.3	1387.0
1317	Gravel road.	798.8	1386.5
1373	Stream.	799.1	1386.2
1381	**Brown Mountain Creek Shelter**)◆⊏(6) 22.2◀18.3◀9.5▶5.6▶15.8▶22.4 In dry conditions, get water from Brown Mountain Creek south of shelter. Swimming hole.	800.8	1384.5
2065	US 60, **Buena Vista, VA** (9.3W) N37 43.405 W79 15.036 🅿 (pg.78-79)	802.6	1382.7
2662	USFS 507 (dirt)	803.5	1381.8
4059	Bald Knob	805.4	1379.9
3487	Hotel Trail, **Cow Camp Gap Shelter** (0.6E))◆⊏(8) 23.9◀15.1◀5.6▶10.2▶16.8▶24.4 Water source on blue-blazed trail left of shelter before small stream crossing.	806.4	1378.9
4022	Cold Mountain, views. 🄑	807.6	1377.7
3485	Hog Camp Gap, USFS 48 (gravel), Grassy meadow with many campsites. ◆ ◆ ◁ Signed spring just north of road crossing and 0.3 east.	808.9	1376.4
		NoBo	SoBo

75 VA

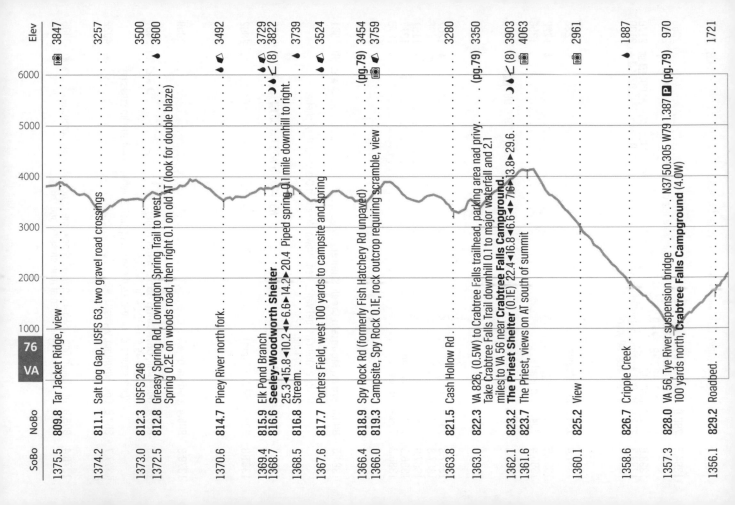

SoBo	NoBo	Feature	Elev
1375.5	**809.8**	Tar Jacket Ridge, view	3847
1374.2	811.1	Salt Log Gap, USFS 63, two gravel road crossings	3257
1373.0	812.3	USFS 246	3500
1372.5	812.8	Greasy Spring Rd, Lovington Spring Trail to west. Spring 0.2E on woods road, then right 0.1 on old AT (look for double blaze)	3600
1370.6	814.7	Piney River north fork.	3492
1369.4	815.9	Elk Pond Branch	3729
1368.7	816.6	**Seeley-Woodworth Shelter** 25.3◄15.8◄10.2◄▶6.6▶14.2▶20.4	3822
1368.5	816.8	Stream. Piped spring 0.1 mile downhill to right.	3739
1367.6	817.7	Porters Field, west 100 yards to campsite and spring	3524
1366.4	818.9	Spy Rock Rd (formerly Fish Hatchery Rd unpaved) (pg.79)	3454
1366.0	819.3	Campsite, Spy Rock 0.1E, rock outcrop requiring scramble, view	3759
1363.8	821.5	Cash Hollow Rd	3280
1363.0	822.3	VA 826, (0.5W) to Crabtree Falls trailhead, parking area nad privy. Take Crabtree Falls Trail downhill 0.1 to major waterfall and 2.1 miles to VA 56 near **Crabtree Falls Campground.** (pg.79)	3350
1362.1	823.2	**The Priest Shelter** (0.1E) 22.4◄16.8◄6.6◄▶7.6▶13.8▶29.6.	3903
1361.6	823.7	The Priest, views on AT south of summit	4063
1360.1	825.2	View	2961
1358.6	826.7	Cripple Creek	1887
1357.3	828.0	VA 56, Tye River suspension bridge N37 50.305 W79 1.387 P (pg.79) 100 yards north, **Crabtree Falls Campground** (4.0W)	970
1356.1	829.2	Roadbed.	1721

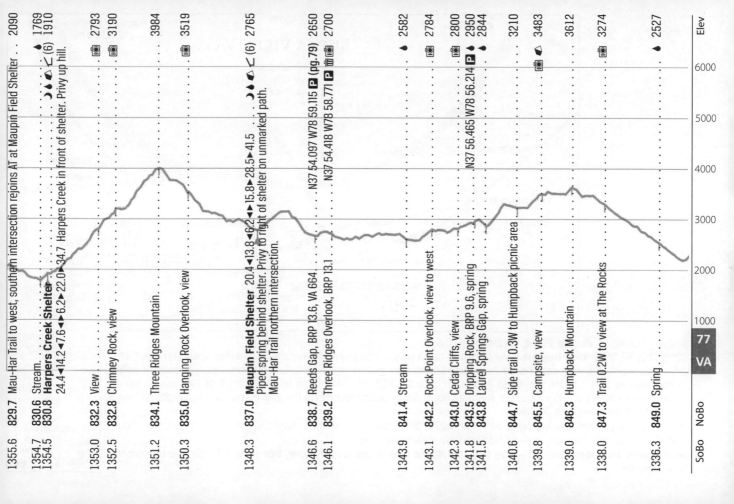

SoBo	NoBo		Elev
1355.6	829.7	Mau-Har Trail to west, southern intersection rejoins AT at Maupin Field Shelter	2090
1354.7	830.6	Stream.	1769
1354.5	830.8	**Harpers Creek Shelter** 24.4◄14.2◄7.6◄▶6.2▶22.0▶34.7 Harpers Creek in front of shelter. Privy up hill.	1910 ◗◆⌂⊏(6)
1353.0	832.3	View	2793
1352.5	832.8	Chimney Rock, view	3190
1351.2	834.1	Three Ridges Mountain	3984
1350.3	835.0	Hanging Rock Overlook, view	3519
1348.3	837.0	**Maupin Field Shelter** 20.4◄13.8◄6.2◄▶15.8▶28.5▶41.5 Piped spring behind shelter. Privy to right of shelter on unmarked path. Mau-Har Trail northern intersection.	2765 ◗◆⌂⊏(6)
1346.6	838.7	Reeds Gap, BRP 13.6, VA 664. N37 54.097 W78 59.115 P (pg.79)	2650
1346.1	839.2	Three Ridges Overlook, BRP 13.1 N37 54.418 W78 58.771 P 🏛	2700
1343.9	841.4	Stream	2582 ◆
1343.1	842.2	Rock Point Overlook, view to west.	2784
1342.3	843.0	Cedar Cliffs, view	2800
1341.8	843.5	Dripping Rock, BRP 9.6, spring N37 56.465 W78 56.214 P	2950
1341.5	843.8	Laurel Springs Gap, spring	2844 ◆
1340.6	844.7	Side trail 0.3W to Humpback picnic area	3210
1339.8	845.5	Campsite, view	3483
1339.0	846.3	Humpback Mountain	3612
1338.0	847.3	Trail 0.2W to view at The Rocks	3274
1336.3	849.0	Spring	2527 ◆

BUENA VISTA, VA

1.5 mi

Pop. 6222 (2009)
N37 44.045, W79 21.222
Mag. Dec. 8° 58'W

Glen Maury Park

Food Lion, Dollar General and CVS 0.9 mi.

6 mi. Lexington, VA

10th

Todd's BBQ
T-N-T's
Nick's Italian

Maury River

Edgewater Animal Hospital

Exxon
Budget Inn
Subway
Ice Cream & More
Burger King

12th

Kenny's Burgers
Buena Vista Coin Laundry

Magnolia Ave

501

Original Italian Pizza
Bluedogart Cafe

Amish Cupboard
Don Tequilas

Family Dollar

Hardees

Lewis Grocery

Canton Chinese Restaurant

Domino's 540-261-1111

29th St.

PO (24416): 540-261-8959
M-F 8:30-4:30

20th 21st

Library 540-261-2715
M-W & F 10-5, Thurs 1-7
Sat 10-1

60

Sheltman's Grocery

Visitor Center

Buena Vista Motel

9.3 mi.

78
VA

802.6   US 60   *Buena Vista, VA 24416* (9.3W)

🏠⚡️🍴⛺🚌📶✉️ **Blue Dog Art Café** 540-460-0933 Hostel $20 per night includes breakfast open Mar-Oct. Call in advance, check-in during cafe hours 7am-6pm. Shuttles for guests at 10:30, 3:30, and 6pm will only come if called. Once-daily resupply run for guests to Food Lion. Laundry $5/load. Alcohol/oz and canister fuel. Restaurant serves healthy meals for B/L/D and includes a menu for dogs! Thru-hikers please sign the wall in the café. Maildrops: 112 West 21st Street, Buena vista, VA. 24416

🏕️🚿 **Glen Maury Park Campground** 540-261-7321 AT hiker special $5 tentsite. Free shower, even without stay, South end of town across river. Maury River Fiddlers Convention mid-June.

🛏️📶 **Buena Vista Motel** 540-261-2138 $39-$79 Rooms have fridge & microwave, free local calls. Shuttle to/from trail for a small fee.

⊨📶⛺ **Budget Inn** 540-261-2156 $49-$89, pets $10 and must use smoking room.

🍴🏪 **Amish Cupboard** 540-264-0215 Deli, Ice Cream, jerky, tons of candy and dried foods. M-F 10-7, Sa 10-6.

🍴🏪 **Lewis Grocery** Short order grill with excellent burger.

🏬 **Food Lion** 540-261-7672, 7 days

🚌 **Maury Express** Area bus makes hourly loop though BV and connects with a Lexington loop bus. 50¢ per board. M-F 8-5, Sa 10-4.

🐕 **Edgewater Animal Hospital** 540-261-4114 M-F 8-7, Sa 10-12

ℹ️ 🚹 🅿️ **Regional Visitor Center** 540-261-8004 Multi-day parking.
Lexington, VA 24450 (15W of Buena Vista)
⊨⛺📶✉️ **Brierley Hill B&B** 540-464-8421 relax@brierleyhill.com Thru-hiker special $75PP for standard double occupancy room. Includes breakfast, free use of laundry facilities, and WiFi. Shuttle to/from the AT (Rt. 60) for additional fee. No Pets. Maildrops: 985 Borden Rd, Lexington, VA 24450.

⊨⛺📶✉️ **502 South Main B&B** 540-460-7353 info@southmain. com. "Thru-hiker special" $75PP for 2 or 3 persons. Round trip to AT (Rt. 60) $10PP, free laundry, hearty breakfast. Restaurants & shops nearby. No pets, No smoking. Maildrops: 502 S. Main St, Lexington VA 24450

🚶 **Walkabout Outfitter** 540-464-4453 Full service outfitter owned by Kirk Miller (Flying Monkey '99). Fuel canisters.

818.9   Spy Rock Rd
Montebello, VA 24464
2.4W to post office, general store. Go downhill on gravel road 1.1W to parking area on Fish Hatchery Rd. Watch for right turn 0.5 from AT, and watch for blue blazes. Follow F.H. Road (turn right at intersection) 0.9mi. to Crabtree Falls Hwy (VA 56). Go left on VA 56 0.4 miles to post office.
🏠 M-F 10-2, Sa 10-1, 540-377-9218

🔥🏪⛺ **Montebello Camping & General Store** 540-377-2650 Store open year-round, camping & laundry Apr 1 - Oct 31. Thru-hiker rate $10 site and $3EAP sometimes has fuel/oz.

*⊨**Dutch Haus B&B** 540-377-2119 Likely to be closed for the 2014 season; call to check availability.

822.3   VA 826 (0.5 on road and 2.1 on falls trail to campground)
828.0   VA 56, Tye River (4W to campground)
⊨🔥🏪🚿⛺✉️ **Crabtree Falls Campground** 540-377-2066 ⟨www.crabtreefallscampground.com⟩ cfcg@ceva.net, cabins $50 four people, camping $26/site(2 tents). Laundry, free shower w/o stay. Trail foods and snacks, ice cream, sodas. fuel/oz. Maildrops (shoebox size or smaller): 11039 Crabtree Falls Hwy, Tyro, VA 22976.

838.7   Reeds Gap, Rte 664 (5.0E to pub)
🔥🍴 **Devils Backbone Brewpub** 434-361-1001 On Rte. 664 at intersection with Patrick Henry Hwy (151). Open 11:30 to 9 seven days, later on weekends. Serves L/D and sometimes hiker-only breakfast for $5. Hikers welcome to camp on-site. Pickup rarely available, but morning return ride often provided.

Red-spotted newt is the slow-moving red lizard that can be seen anywhere along the AT. The newt lives on land for the middle stage of its life, which lasts about two years. During this stage, it's also known as a *red eft*. It is a tadpole in its first stage. In its last stage it returns to water and turns green, but retains its red spots.

SoBo	NoBo	Feature	Elev
1335.3	850.0	Spring	2347
1335.2	850.1	Side trail 0.2W to Humpback Gap, BRP 6.0	2339
1334.3	851.0	Glass Hollow Overlook, view to east.	2267
1333.9	851.4	Side trail 1.3W to Humpback Visitor Center	2303
1333.8	851.5	Albright Loop Trail to west	2239
1332.5	852.8	**Paul C. Wolfe Shelter** 29.6◄22.0◄15.8◄▶12.7▶25.7▶38.9. Mill Creek 50 yards in front of shelter. Waterfall with pool 100 yards.	1594
1331.7	853.6	Small cemetery	1878
1331.0	854.3	Cabin ruins, chimney.	2085
1330.8	854.5	Spring	2058
1329.4	855.9	Stream	1883
1328.6	856.7	Stream	1745
1327.4	857.9	US 250 + Blue Ridge Pkwy . . . N38 1.864 W78 51.545 [P] [H] ⚥ (pg.82-83) Rockfish Gap, **Waynesboro, VA** (3.7W), I-64 overpass, south end of Skyline Dr.	1912
1326.5	858.8	Shenandoah National Park (SNP) (pg.84) Entrance station and self-registration for overnight permits.	2215
1325.0	860.3	"Wrong Way" side trail to east	2572
1323.8	861.5	Skyline 102.1, McCormick Gap	2444
1322.5	862.8	Bears Den Mountain, communication towers.	2885
1322.0	863.3	Skyline 99.5, Beagle Gap, stream	2550
1321.2	864.1	Little Calf Mountain.	2895
1320.5	864.8	Calf Mountain.	2983
1319.8	865.5	**Calf Mountain Shelter** (0.3W) 34.7◄28.5◄12.7▶13.0▶26.2▶34.4. Spring on way to shelter.	2703
1319.4	865.9	Powerline. Bear pole.	2303
1319.3	866.0	Spring	2316
1318.8	866.5	Gravel road 0.1W to Skyline 96.9 Jarman Gap	2270
1318.7	866.6	Spring, just south of woods road	2161
1317.0	868.3	Skyline 95.3, Sawmill Run Overlook	2200
1315.6	869.7	Turk Mountain Trail to west.	2636
1315.4	869.9	Skyline 94.1, Turk Gap.	2600

Additional coordinates shown on profile: N38 4.373 W78 47.607 [P]; N38 7.740 W78 47.092 [P]

NoBo	Features	Elev	SoBo
871.9	Skyline 92.4	3100	1313.4
872.3	Wildcat Ridge Trail east to Skyline 92.1 . . . N38 8.904 W78 46.477 P	3000	1313.0
	✽ **Turks Cap Lily** – Petals of this down-facing large flower curl back to form a bun (Turk's cap) shape. Common color is flame orange and yellow, speckled with brown dots.		
874.9	Skyline 90.0, spur trail to east leads to Riprap parking area. P	2797	1310.4
875.4	Riprap Trail branches to west	3015	1309.9
876.1	Skyline 88.9	2639	1309.2
877.8	Skyline 87.4, Black Rock Gap, Paine Run Trail . . . N38 12.398 W78 44.974 P	2321	1307.5
878.0	Skyline 87.2	2385	1307.3
878.5	**Blackrock Hut** (0.2E) 41.5◀25.7◀13.0◀▶13.2▶21.4▶33.8 ☽ ◑ ⌂ (6)	2758	1306.8
878.9	Trayfoot Mountain Trail to west	3087	1306.4
879.0	Blackrock, views from summit, which is skirted by the AT 📷	3101	1306.3
879.6	Blackrock parking area. . . . N38 13.331 W78 43.992 P	2927	1305.7
880.1	Skyline 84.3.	2800	1305.2
880.2	Jones Run parking . . . N38 13.805 W78 43.577 P	2788	1305.1
880.8	Two trails west to Dundo Campground (primitive, reserved for group use).	2752	1304.5
881.5	Skyline 82.9, Browns Gap . . . N38 14.424 W78 42.653 P	2579	1303.8
882.1	Big Run Loop Trail to west	2826	1303.2
882.4	Skyline 82.2.	2775	1302.9
882.9	West to Doyles River Parking Overlook, Skyline 81.9 N38 14.306 W78 41.686 P 📷	2838	1302.4
883.7	Doyles River Trail, west to Skyline 81.1, east to Doyles River Cabin (locked) and 0.1E to falls N38 15.254 W78 40.982 P ♦	2855	1301.6
884.5	Trail to Loft Mtn amphitheater.	3176	1300.8
884.6	Trail to **Loft Mtn Campground** (go here if camping). ◁(pg.85) ♦	3263	1300.7
885.2	Trail to **Loft Mtn Campground** ◁(pg.85)	3294	1300.1
885.6	Powerline (pg.85)	3237	1299.7
885.8	Trail to **Loft Mtn Store** (in view to west) (pg.85)	3165	1299.5
887.0	Frazier Discovery Trail 0.3W to **Loft Mtn Wayside**	3299	1298.3
887.1	Frazier Discovery Trail to west	3306	1298.2
888.0	Trail to 0.5W to **Loft Mtn Wayside** (flatter than FDT), Ivy Creek spring 0.1W ♦	2985	1297.3
888.6	Cross Ivy Creek ♦	2580	1296.7
889.3	View to west 📷	2961	1296.0
890.1	West to Skyline 77.5, Ivy Creek Overlook 📷	2890	1295.2

NoBo   SoBo   Elev

857.9   Rockfish Gap

ℹ 📞 🅿 Afton Mountain Visitor Center 540-943-5187 Open most days 9-5. Hiker flyers offer current info about town services and trail angels. Many lodging facilities offer free pickup/return from this location. Long-term parking okay; leave contact info and expected return date.

🛏 **Inn at Afton** 540-942-5201 Hiker rate $40+tax, pets allowed, Some restaurants deliver here.

🛏⛺🛰✉ (0.5W on 250) **Colony House Motel** 540-942-4156 $49S, $59D+tax, pets $10, some snacks sold on-site, all rooms have micro and fridge. Maildrops: 494 Three Notched Mtn Hwy, Waynesboro, VA 22980.

🍴 **King's Kettle Corn** Mid-March through Nov. M-F 9am-7pm; Sa,Su 8am-8pm; Dec-Mar open Thurs-Sun. Hot dogs, sodas, ice cream, coffee, kettle corn, and gourmet popcorn.

Waynesboro, VA 22980 (4.5W on I-64)

Home to **Hiker Fest** on June 14, gather at camp area 11am for food and a movie. Camping area (bottom right corner of map) has pavillion, grill, and solar charger; shower at YMCA nearby.

🔌 🚿 **YMCA** 540-942-5107 Free camping and showers. Use of YMCA facilities $10. Check-in at front desk, need photo ID.

🏠🌂🛰🖥 **Grace Hiker Hostel** Supervised hostel at Lutheran Church open May 26-June 22, closed Su nights, 2-night limit. Check-in 5-8pm, check-out 9am; hikers staying over may leave packs. Bunks in air-conditioned Fellowship Hall, showers, internet, big-screen TV with DVD, kitchenette with snacks and breakfast foods in a separate hiker lounge. 20 hiker max. No pets, smoking, drugs, alcohol, firearms or foul language. Donations gratefully accepted. Congregation cooks free dinner Thursday

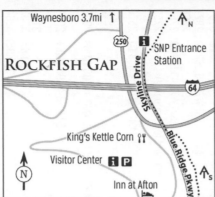

Waynesboro 3.7mi ↑   ↗N
250   SNP Entrance
ROCKFISH GAP   Station
                    64
King's Kettle Corn 🍴
Visitor Center ℹ🅿
                    ↑s
Inn at Afton 🛏

nights followed by optional vespers service.

🏠⛺🚌🛰🖥 **Stanimal's Hostel** 540-290-4002 AdamStanley06@gmail.com $20 hiker-only hostel includes pickup/return, resupply ride & limited errands, mattress with clean linens, shower w/towel, soap, laundry. Large private area including sunroom and finished basement, laptop, WiFi and DVDs. Fridge, freezer & microwave. Snacks, drinks, and ice cream for sale. Optional AYCE dinner and breakfast for small fee depending on group size. Discounted slackpacking for multinight guests. Residential area. Please respect noise level. Hikers are required to call ahead and speak with owner prior to staying. Owned by Adam Stanley AT '04, PCT '10.

🛏🛰✉ **Tree Streets Inn** 540-949-4484, $80S/D, includes breakfast, pool, snacks, no pets. Call from Rockfish Gap for free pickup/return with stay. Maildrops (pre-registered guests only; other packages will be returned): 421 Walnut Avenue, Waynesboro, VA 22980.

🛏🛰 **Belle Hearth B&B** 540-943-1910 ⟨www.bellehearth.com⟩ $75S, $95D, higher on weekends, includes B, pool, pickup/return. No pets, no smoking.

🛏🛰🖥 **Quality Inn** 540-942-1171 Hiker rates $59.49S $63.74 up to 4, pets $10. Includes continental breakfast.

🍴 **Heritage on Main** Hiker-friendly sports bar with variety of beer on tap, burgers, salads, sandwiches. Open 11-11. Live music Wed & Sat, trivia Thurs.

🍴 **Weasie's Kitchen** AYCE pancake challenge $6.39.

🥾✉ **Rockfish Gap Outfitters** 540-943-1461 full service outfitter, Coleman/alcohol/oz, other fuels, shuttle information. Ice cream and freeze-dried foods. Located between town and trail, so ask your ride to stop on the way. Maildrops (please provide ETA): 1461 E. Main St., Waynesboro, VA 22980

🚌 **DuBose Egleston** 540-487-6388 Shuttles Roanoke to Harpers Ferry.

🔧 **Ace Hardware** Coleman/oz.

🛶 **Aquablaze Solutions** 540-910-3566 ⟨www.aquablazesolutions.com⟩ Sells used canoe and gear and buys it back later, enabling hikers to travel the Shenandoah River as far as Harpers Ferry. Return shuttle available for 2000-milers. Please learn the rules for camping on the river.

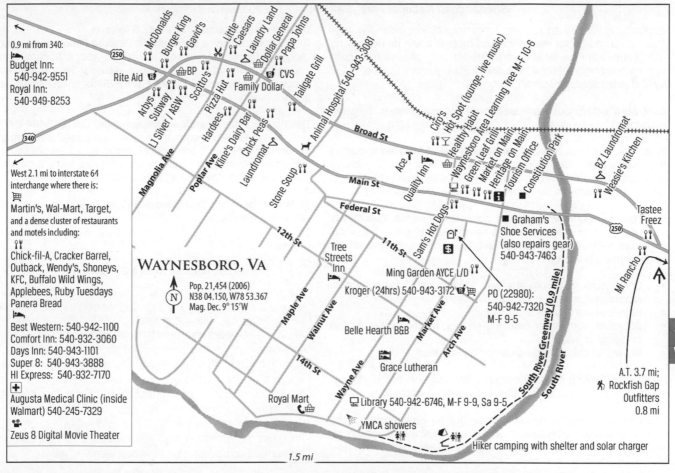

Backcountry Permits are required for overnight hikes within the park. There is no charge for the permit and there is a fine for not having one. Permits are available from self-registration sites at the south and north entrance of the AT into SNP, from any park visitor center, or by mail (see contact information above).

Concrete 4"x4" signposts are used to mark intersections. Information is stamped into an aluminum band at the top of the post.

What is known as a "shelter" on most of the AT is called a "hut" in Shenandoah, and three-sided day-use-only structures are called "shelters." When overnighting in the park, please use the huts or designated campsites, which are usually near the huts.

Backcountry stay is limited to 14 consecutive nights; two at any one location. If you cannot tent in a designated campsite, follow LNT principles of dispersed camping. Tenting at a new location is limited to one night and must be:

- One quarter mile from any park facility (roads, campgrounds, lodges, visitor centers, and picnic areas).
- 10 yards from any water source.
- 50 yards from other camping parties, building ruins, or "no camping" signs.
- Not within designated no camping locations.

Groups are limited to 10. Campfires are only permitted at pre-constructed fire rings at the huts. Pets must be leashed.

Lodges and campgrounds are typically full on weekends. A small number of unreserved walk-in tentsites are available on a first-come, first-served basis at all campgrounds except Lewis Mtn.

Delaware North Companies Parks & Resorts
⟨GoShenandoah.com⟩ operates the Skyland Resort, Big Meadows Lodge and Lewis Mountain Cabins, gift shops & camp stores and restaurants within Shenandoah National Park; many readily accessible from the trail. Call 877-247-9261 for special offers, rates and availability.

The Park Service operates campgrounds. Call 877-444-6777 or visit ⟨www.recreation.gov⟩ to reserve campsites. All campsites accommodate 2 tents and up to 6 persons. All except Mathews Arm have coin operated laundry and showers. Many facilities are closed November-May and all are closed December-March.

Yellow Cab of the Shenandoah 540-692-9200 serves all of SNP (24/7). Pet friendly, accepts CC.

If You Plan to be a 2000-Miler

The ATC recognizes hikers who have completed the trail, all at once or in sections, with a "2000-miler" certificate. Your name will be printed in the March/April issue of ATC's member magazine, *AT Journeys*, and listed on ATC's website. The honor system application states that conditional bypasses and reroutes are acceptable and that "Issues of sequence, direction, speed, length of time or whether one carries a pack are not considered." The number "2,000" is used out of tradition, and does not imply that hiking less than the full mileage qualifies. Feel free to set your own agenda on the AT, but if 2000-miler recognition is important to you keep in mind that the application will ask if you "have made an honest effort to walk the entire Trail."

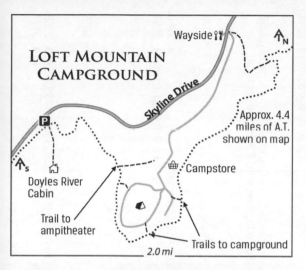

LOFT MOUNTAIN CAMPGROUND

Wayside
Skyline Drive
Approx. 4.4 miles of A.T. shown on map
Campstore
Doyles River Cabin
Trail to ampitheater
Trails to campground
2.0 mi

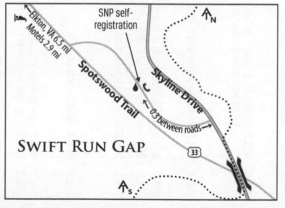

SWIFT RUN GAP

SNP self-registration
Elkton, VA 6.5 mi
Motels 2.9 mi
Spotswood Trail
Skyline Drive
0.3 between roads
33

884.6, 885.2   Loft Mountain Campground
885.8   Loft Mountain Wayside

Loft Mountain Campground Campsites $15. AT skirts the campground, and several short side trails lead to campsites and the camp store. Showers, laundry and long term resupply available from camp store. Open May-Oct.

Loft Mountain Wayside 1.1 miles from camp store, serves B/L/D, short-order menu, 9-5:30, 7 days. Open 4/22 - 11/9.

903.3   US 33, Swift Run Gap. US 33 is also known as Spotswood Trail. The AT crosses over US 33 on the Skyline Drive. North of the bridge, take access road to the west to reach US 33.

(2.9W):

Country View Motel 540-298-0025 $50 most rooms hold 4. shuttle possible back to trail and to Elkton. Pets okay. Maildrops for guests: 19974 Spotswood Trail, Elkton, VA 22827.

(3.2W):

Swift Run Camping 540-298-8086, $20 campsite, laundry, pool, and snack bar.

Bear Mountain Grocery with deli, daily 6am–9pm.

(6.5W): *Elkton, VA 22827*

M-F 8:30-4:30, Sa 9-11, 540-298-7772

Food Lion, O'Dell's Grocery

Pizza Hut, several fast-food restaurants

Rite Aid

911.5, 911.6   Lewis Mountain Campground

Lewis Mountain Campground and Cabins 540-999-2255, campsites $15. Reservations, 877-847-1919, Lewis Mountain Camp store, open 9-7 in summer. May-Oct.

Elev		SoBo	NoBo	Description
2493	☽ ⚬ ◆ ⊂ (6)	1293.6	891.7	**Pinefield Hut** (0.1E), Skyline Dr (0.1W),
				38.9◀26.2◀13.2◀▶8.2▶20.6▶32.1 Spring on trail to shelter and 50 yards
				behind. Both unreliable. Campsites uphill, beyond shelter.
2590	P	1293.4	891.9	N38 17.411 W78 38.511 Skyline 75.2, Pinefield Gap.
2870		1292.6	892.7	Weaver Mountain.
2250	◆	1291.5	893.8	Skyline 73.2, Simmons Gap
				Simmons Gap ranger station on paved road 0.2E from where AT crosses Skyline.
				Water available at pump outside buildings.
2577	📷	1288.7	896.6	View east to Powell Gap Hollow
2294		1288.2	897.1	Skyline 69.9, Powell Gap.
2600		1286.6	898.7	Skyline 68.6, Smith Roach Gap
3200	☽ ◆ ⚬ ⊂ (6)	1285.4	899.9	**Hightop Hut** (0.1W), reliable spring 0.1 from shelter
				34.4◀21.4◀8.2◀▶12.4▶23.9▶34.8
3534	◆	1284.9	900.4	Spring east of AT
3523	📷	1284.7	900.6	View to west from flank of Hightop Mtn.
2650	P	1283.3	902.0	Skyline 66.7 N38 20.691 W78 33.183
2367	◆ (pg.85) ☏	1282.0	903.3	Skyline 65.5, Swift Run Gap, bridge over US 33, **Elkton, VA** (6.4W)
				US 33 access rd north of bridge 0.1W to phone, water & SNP self-registration
3020		1280.4	904.9	Saddleback Mtn Trail to east.
2956	◆	1279.4	905.9	Trail 0.3E to spring at former South River Shelter site
2884	P (0.1W)🚻	1278.9	906.4	South River Picnic Area 0.1W N38 22.904 W78 31.151
2880		1278.5	906.8	Falls Trail to east. South River Fire Road.
3615		1276.9	908.4	Baldface Mountain.
3150	P ◆	1275.7	909.6	Spring, Pocosin Cabin (locked), Parking on Skyline. N38 24.813 W78 29.379
3147	P ◆	1275.6	909.7	Trail west to parking on Skyline

SoBo	NoBo	Description	Elev
1273.8	911.5	West to **Lewis Mtn Campground & Cabins** (pg.85)	3444
1273.7	911.6	West to **Lewis Mtn Campground**. N38 26.234 W78 28.737 🅿 (pg.85)	3392
1273.0	912.3	**Bearfence Mountain Hut** (0.1E), unreliable spring. 🅿 🜄 ◭ ⊏ (6) 33.8◀20.6◀12.4◀▶11.5▶22.4▶26.8	3212
1272.3	913.0	Bearfence Mountain Loop Trail, two intersections 0.2 mile apart, views 0.1E. 📷	3523
1271.8	913.5	Skyline 56.4, Bearfence Mtn Trail, parking 0.1W. N38 27.141 W78 28.015 🅿	3397
1270.4	914.9	Skyline 55.1, Bootens Gap. N38 28.049 W78 27.440 🅿	3243
1269.9	915.4	Laurel Prong Trail to east.	3514
1269.5	915.8	Hazeltop.	3812
1267.6	917.7	Skyline 52.8, Milam Gap, parking to east. N38 29.928 W78 26.741 🅿	3300
1267.0	918.3	Spring, No camping in Big Meadows clearing within sight of Skyline Dr ◆	3266
1266.5	918.8	Tanners Ridge Rd (gravel), cemetery	3325
1265.9	919.4	Lewis Spring & Road, Lewis Falls 0.5W. N38 27.141 W78 28.015 🅿 ◆ (pg. 88)	3332
1265.4	919.9	Gravel road 0.2E to Skyline, then left 0.2 to **Big Meadows Wayside** Rock outcropping, view	3618
1265.0	920.3	Trail to **Big Meadows Lodge**, Lewis Falls 0.5W. (pg.88)	3563
1264.6	920.7	Trail east to **Big Meadows Campground** (pg.88)	3560
1264.4	920.9	David Spring 20 yards west ◆	3490
1264.2	921.1	Stream. ◆	3381
1263.4	921.9	Fishers Gap, Skyline 49.3 to east, maintenance road	3050
1263.2	922.1	Franklin Cliffs, view. 📷	3023
1262.1	923.2	Trail to Spitler Knoll parking, 4 cars N38 32.892 W78 24.828 🅿	3238
1261.5	923.8	**Rock Spring Hut** (0.2W). ◗ ◆ ◭ ⊏ (8) 32.1◀23.9◀11.5◀▶10.9▶15.3▶28.4 Locked cabin in front.	3530
1261.2	924.1	Trail east to Hawksbill Mountain. No camping on summit (anywhere above 3600')	3640
1260.2	925.1	Hawksbill Gap, parking to east. N38 33.776 W78 22.952 🅿	3361
1259.7	925.6	Stream, trail to Crescent Rock Overlook, parking to east. 🅿 📷	3416
1258.9	926.4	Spring	3314
1258.0	927.3	Spring N38 35.201 W78 23.006 🅿	3440
1257.7	927.6	Skyland stables, service road	3550
1257.1	928.2	Trail to **Skyland Resort & Restaurant** (0.1W). 🅿 (pg.88)	3748
1257.0	928.3	Skyland service road north. N38 35.557 W78 22.559 🅿	3697
1256.5	928.8	Trail to Stony Man Summit (0.2W) Highest point on the AT in SNP	3837
1256.0	929.3	Little Stony Man Cliffs, overlook to west. 📷	3554
1255.7	929.6	Passamaquoddy Trail	3414
1255.4	929.9	Spur trail to parking N38 36.354 W78 21.983 🅿	3237
1255.0	930.3	Stony Man Overlook N38 36.735 W78 21.747 🅿 📷	3092
1254.5	930.7	Nicholson Hollow Trail	3120
1254.5	930.8	Crusher Ridge Trail	3202

919.4   Lewis Spring Rd (See map for easiest access.)

920.3   Big Meadows Lodge

🍴🚌 **Big Meadows Wayside** B/L/D, Fuel/oz at gas station. Open 3/17 - 11/30.

🛏🍴💲 **Big Meadows Lodge** Lodge rooms, cabins & suites, reservations required. Some pet-friendly rooms. B: 7:30-10:30, L: 12-2, D: 5:30-9. Open 5/14 - 11/2 (first Sun of Nov).

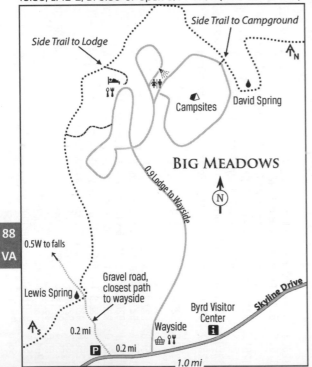

Side Trail to Lodge

Side Trail to Campground

Campsites

David Spring

BIG MEADOWS

N

0.9 Lodge to Wayside

0.5W to falls

Lewis Spring

Gravel road, closest path to wayside

0.2 mi   0.2 mi

Byrd Visitor Center ℹ

Wayside 🏪🍴

Skyline Drive

1.0 mi

88 VA

920.7   Big Meadows Campground

🔥👥🚿⛺ **Big Meadows Campground** 540-999-3231 Tentsites $20 for 2 tents & 6 persons, self-register after-hours. Coin laundry & showers, Open May-Oct.

928.2   Side trail to Skyland

🛏🍴💲👥 **Skyland Resort and Restaurant** 540-999-2212 Rates seasonal, reservations required. Dining room hours B: 7:30-10:30, L: 12-2, D: 5:30-9, nightly entertainment. Snack foods and sodas sold at gift shop and vending machines. Open 3/27 - 11/30 (Sunday following Thanksgiving).

937.9   US 211, Thornton Gap

🛏🍴📶(4.5W on US 211) to **Brookside Cabins & Restaurant** 540-743-5698 $85-$200 cabins open year-round, range in size (2-6 persons). Some have kitchen & hot tub, no TV or phone. Restaurant AYCE L/D buffet daily, weekend breakfast buffet. Open 2/14-Thanksgiving, 7 days 8am-8pm, later in summer.

🛏🔥🍴🏧⛺📶(5.3W) **Yogi Bear's Jellystone Park** 540-743-4002 Cabins $55-$275 hold 6-10, summer weekend 3-night min. Tent sites $35-80, 2-night minimum on weekends. Pets at tentsites only. All stays include free water slide, paddle boat, mini golf & laser tag, Memorial to Labor Day snack shop serving hamburgers, hot dogs, pizza. Coin laundry, camp store, pool.

🛏⛺📶🖥 (6.9W) **Days Inn** 540-743-4521 $80-$300, pool, cont. B, pets $15.

Luray, VA 22835 (9W) Farmer's market held on Saturdays.

🛏📶🖥 **Budget Inn** 540-743-5176 $55D/up, $10EAP, pets $10. Maildrops 320 W. Main St, Luray, VA 22835.

🛏📶 **Luray Caverns Motels** East and West Buildings 540-743-4536, 888-941-4531, Su-Th $73, F-Sa $91. 20% discount coupon on food at Luray Caverns. No pets or maildrops.

🛏📶 **Cardinal Inn** 888-648-4663 Hiker rate: winter $65, summer $75.

🛏📶 **South Court Inn B&B** 540-843-0980 ⟨southcourtinn.com⟩ Discounted rate for hikers $100S/D when rooms available, includes big breakfast. No pets, smoking outside only. Wir sprechen Deutsch.

🛏📶 **Mayne View B&B** 540-743-7921 ⟨mayneview.com⟩ $99-175D, includes full breakfast. 10% discount for single, $10EAP for rooms that hold 4. Outdoor hot tub w/view, movie library.

Best Western 540-743-6511 Call for rates, pet fee $20.

Woodruff House & Victorian Inn B&B 540-743-1494

Mimslyn Inn 540-743-5105 Rooms $169/up, **Speakeasy** on-site, dinner 4-11pm, full bar and W-F entertainment.

Appalachian Outdoors Adventures 540-743-7400 Full-service outfitter, Coleman/alcohol/oz, canisters, freeze-dried foods. M-Th 10-6, F-Sa 10-8, Su 1-5. Maildrops: 2 West Main St., Luray, VA 22835.

Visitor Center 540-743-3915 M-Sa 9-5, Su 12-4. 5mi. north of town on Shenandoah River:

Rock Tavern River Kamp 540-843-4232 Tentsites $35 for 4, Yurt $99 (4 person), luxury cabins hold up to 10. Canoe portage around Shenandoah River Dam and shuttles from Thornton Gap. Please call 24 hrs in advance for shuttles.

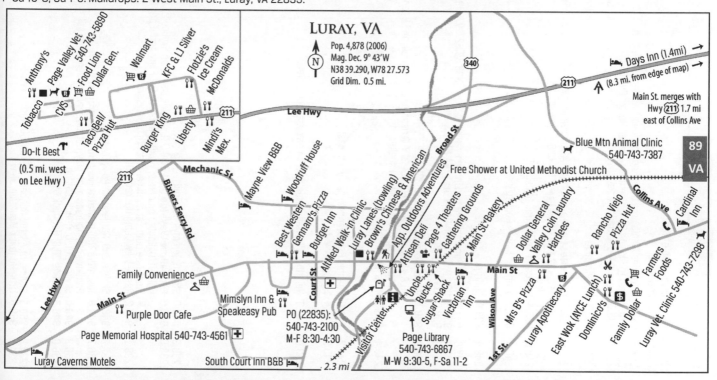

LURAY, VA
Pop. 4,878 (2006)
Mag. Dec. 9° 43'W
N38 39.290, W78 27.573
Grid Dim. 0.5 mi.

89
VA

SoBo	NoBo	Feature	Elev
1253.9	931.4	Corbin Cabin Trail	3149
1253.4	931.9	Powerline	3333
1252.8	932.5	Pinnacles Picnic Area & Parking, restrooms, water from faucet. 🅿️♨	3420
1252.6	932.6	East to Skyline 36.4, side trail to Jewell Hollow Overlook 📷	3335
1252.3	933.0	Leading Ridge Trail to west.	3409
1251.6	933.7	The Pinnacle	3730
1250.6	934.7	Byrds Nest #3 Hut, spring 0.4E on service road. ♦☾⌂(8)	3279
		34.8◀22.4◀10.9▶4.4▶17.5▶28.0	
1250.2	935.1	View	3351
1249.9	935.4	Meadows Spring Trail to east. ♦(0.3E)	3389
1249.3	936.0	Overlook, Mary's Rock to west. 📷	3504
1248.4	936.9	Spring ♦	2917
1247.6	937.7	Trail to Panorama RR parking, powerline N38 39.627 W78 19.326 🅿️♨	2399
1247.4	937.9	US 211, Thornton Gap, **Luray, VA** (9W). (pg.88-89)	2307
1247.3	938.0	Skyline 31.2.	2374
1246.2	939.1	**Pass Mountain Hut** (1939) (0.2E) ♦☾⌂(8)	2812
		26.8◀15.3◀4.4▶13.1▶23.6▶31.7 2-bear poles, 2 privies, and 8 tent sites.	
		Piped spring 15 yards behind shelter.	
1245.4	939.9	Pass Mountain ♦	3052
1244.3	941.0	Beahms Gap Overlook, parking to east 🅿️📷	2490
1243.9	941.4	Spring to west ♦	2436
1243.0	942.3	Neighbor Mtn Trail, Byrds Nest #4 day use picnic area. ♦(0.5E)	2666
1239.3	946.0	Stream, Jeremys Run Trail ♦	2225
1238.8	946.5	**Elkwallow Wayside** (and Gap) 0.1E on side trail or on Skyline 23.9 ♨☾¶	2480
		Grill B/L/D, limited groceries, vending outside, 9-7 Early April-Early Oct.	
		Frost-free pump at picnic area south of wayside.	
1238.1	947.2	Range View Cabin (locked) 0.1E ♦(0.1E)	2971
1237.3	948.0	Skyline 21.9, Rattlesnake Point Overlook 📷	3084
1236.7	948.6	Tuscarora Trail to **Mathews Arm Campground** (0.7W) ⛺	3400
		Primitive campground open May-Oct; no services. Tent sites $14.	
1236.3	949.0	Skyline 21.1, Hogback parking 🅿️	3350
1236.0	949.3	Skyline 20.8, Hogback Overlook 📷	3350
1234.8	950.5	Skyline 19.7, Little Hogback parking 50 yards east 🅿️	3026
1234.7	950.6	Little Hogback Mountain, view. 📷	3050

SoBo	NoBo	Description	Elev
1234.1	951.2	Skyline 18.8	2822
1233.1	952.2	**Gravel Springs Hut** (0.2E), spring en route to shelter. 🅟 ◐ ⌂ ⊂(8)	2658
1232.9	952.4	Skyline 17.7, Gravel Springs Gap. N38 46.068 W78 14.010 🅟 28.4◀17.5◀13.1◀▶10.5▶18.6▶24.1	2666
1232.1	953.2	View west	3063
1231.8	953.5	South Marshall Mountain	3212
1231.3	954.0	Skyline 15.9, parking to west. 🅟	3050
1230.6	954.7	North Marshall Mountain, view	3368
1229.6	955.7	Hogwallow Flat	2952
1229.1	956.2	Skyline 14.2, Hogwallow Gap. N38 47.388 W78 11.319 🅟	2739
1227.4	957.9	Skyline 12.3, Jenkins Gap, parking to east. N38 48.389 W78 10.846 🅟	2400
1226.5	958.8	Compton Springs ◐	2700
1226.1	959.2	Compton Peak	2909
1225.3	960.0	Skyline 10.4, Compton Gap parking. N38 49.414 W78 10.234 🅟	2427
1223.5	961.8	Compton Gap Trail ("Chester Gap" post), **Front Royal Hostel** (0.5E) (pg. 94)	2350
1223.3	962.0	SNP permit self-registration station.	2337
1222.6	962.7	**Tom Floyd Shelter** 28.0◀23.6◀10.5◀▶8.1▶13.6▶18.1 ◐ ⌂ ⊂(6)	1961
1222.5	962.8	Ginger Spring to west ◐	1850
1221.1	964.2	VA 602, stream ◐	1150
1219.7	965.6	US 522, **Front Royal, VA** (3.5W) (pg.94-95). N38 52.682 W78 9.044 🅟 AT parallel to US 522 for 0.2mi between N & S trailheads	950
1218.9	966.4	Bear Hollow Creek ◐	1080
1216.3	969.0	Forest Service Rd	1841
1216.1	969.2	Sealock Spring, Mosby Campsite. Named after Colonel John Mosby. ◐ ⛺ ◓	1760
1215.4	969.9	Powerline	1668
1214.5	970.8	**Jim & Molly Denton Shelter**, Spring on AT 31.7◀18.6◀8.1◀▶5.5▶10.0▶18.4 Excellent shelter, porch, chairs, solar shower. 🌣 ◐ ⌂ ⊂(8)	1343

SoBo	NoBo		Elev
1213.4	971.9	Stream.	1057
1213.3	972.0	VA 638	1081
1211.5	973.8	VA 55, Manassas Gap, RR tracks to south. N38 54.550 W78 3.199 P (pg. 95) AT passes under I-66 on Tuckers Lane.	800
1211.3	974.0	Tuckers Lane parking, Footbridge, stream N38 54.679 W78 3.178 P	819
1210.0	975.3	Stone wall.	1431
1209.0	976.3	**Manassas Gap Shelter** 24.1◄13.6◄5.5◄▶4.5▶12.9▶19.8 (6) Bear Pole. Reliable spring downhill to right of shelter on side trail. Blue-blazed trail south of shelter leads 0.9W to VA 638.	1696
1207.7	977.6	Spring	1736
1207.0	978.3	Trico Tower Trail 0.4W to comm tower, some parking on VA 638.	2102
1204.5	980.8	**Dicks Dome Shelter** (0.2E) 18.1◄10.0◄4.5◄▶4.5▶8.4▶15.3▶29.5 (4) Whiskey Hollow Creek in front of shelter (treat water). Stream on AT 75 yards north of shelter side-trail.	1409
1204.1	981.2	Powerline	1632
1203.5	981.8	Spring	1772
1203.3	982.0	Signal Knob parking on VA 638 / Fire Trail Rd 0.1W. N38 59.112 W77 59.980 P	1851
1202.5	982.8	Boundary to Sky Meadows State Park.	1851
1202.2	983.1	Bench, 1.7E to **Sky Meadows State Park Visitors Center** 800-933-PARK Open W-Su, 8-5, restrooms, soda machine, 12 sites & primitive group camping, $9PP, reservation required, campers must arrive before dusk.	1821
1201.4	983.9	View 0.4E on Ambassador Whitehouse Trail	1598
1199.8	985.5	Two footbridges, streams	914
1199.7	985.6	Ashby Gap, US 50/17	960
1199.5	985.8	Trail 0.1E to parking on VA 601, Blueridge Mtn Rd N39 0.942 W77 57.718 P	1090
1198.3	987.0	Stream.	1142
1197.7	987.6	Stream.	1042
1197.4	987.9	Trail west to Myron Glaser Cabin (locked)	1122
1196.9	988.4	Stream.	1010
1196.5	988.8	Fishers Hill Trail to west	1107
1196.1	989.2	**Rod Hollow Shelter** (0.1W) 18.4◄12.9◄8.4◄▶6.9▶21.1▶36.7 (8) Piped spring left of shelter. Stream on AT south of side trail.	917
1195.7	989.6	Stream, Fishers Hill Trail to west, south end of The Roller Coaster 13.5 miles of tightly packed ascents and descents.	824
1194.4	990.9	Spring at Bolden Hollow	871

SoBo	NoBo	Feature	Elev
1192.8	992.5	Footbridge, Morgan Mill Stream, campsite ◆	800
1192.4	992.9	VA 605, Morgan Mill Rd (gravel) N39 4.327 W77 54.720 **P**	1033
1191.6	993.7	Stream. ◆	1034
1190.7	994.6	Buzzard Hill, AT east of summit	1276
1190.1	995.2	Two streams ◆	836
1189.2	996.1	**Sam Moore Shelter** (1990) 19.8◀15.3▼6.9◀14.2▼29.8▶33.9 ☾ ⊃◀◆⊭ ⊂(6)	931
		Springs in front of shelter and to the left. Several tent sites to left of shelter.	
1188.7	996.6	Campsite ◆	1305
1187.9	997.4	Spout Run Ravine, stream ◆	736
1186.7	998.6	Footbridge, stream, campsite 60 yards north on AT ◆	834
1186.2	999.1	Bears Den Rocks, **Bears Den Hostel** (0.2E), view north on AT ◙ (pg. 95)	1267
1185.6	999.7	Snickers Gap, VA 7 & 679 (Pine Grove Rd) N39 6.919 W77 50.849 **P** (pg. 95)	1000
1184.8	1000.5	Stream. ◆	851
1183.3	1002.0	**VA-WV** border	1057
1183.1	1002.2	Spring ◆	1193
1182.9	1002.4	Raven Rocks, Crescent Rock 0.1E, view	1297
1182.7	1002.6	Campsite, trail east to tower ◆	1427
1182.3	1003.0	The Roller Coaster (north end); 13.5 miles of ascents and descents ◆	1200
		Sand Spring to west, good water source, Devils Racecourse boulder field to north	
1179.4	1005.9	Wilson Gap	1380
1178.2	1007.1	Two trails 0.2E to **Blackburn AT Center** N39 11.259 W77 47.866 **P** (pg. 95)	1650
1176.5	1008.8	Laurel Springs, boardwalk △	1458
1175.5	1009.8	Buzzard Rocks	1532
1175.0	1010.3	**David Lesser Memorial Shelter** (0.1E) ☾◆◀⊂(6)	1438
		29.5◀21.1◀14.2▼15.6◀19.7▶24.7 Overflow camping area below shelter. Spring	
		0.2 mile downhill from shelter.	
1173.7	1011.6	Roadbed.	1334

93
WV

Elev

961.8 Compton Gap Trail (post labeled "VA 610/Chester Gap")

🚏🏠⛺📧✉ **Front Royal Terrapin Station Hostel** (0.5E) 540-539-0509, Go east (straight ahead for NoBo) on Compton Gap Trail 0.5 mi. to paved road. Hostel is first house on the left on paved road. Enter around back through marked gate. Open Apr 27-July 4, 2014, includes bunk w/mattress, shower, soap, shower clothes, laundry, free morning shuttle to town for groceries, PO, etc...Cost $19/night, $35/2nights, $50/3nights. Three night max unless injured. Fuel, snacks, sodas, ice cream & oven pizza on site. Special: bunk, laundry, pizza, soda & ice cream $30. Free slackpacking for overnight guests; shuttles available for all. Hikers only, picture ID required, reservations encouraged. Owned by Mike Evans (AT '95, PCT '98), ⟨gratefulgg@hotmail.com⟩. Guest maildrops: 304 Chester Gap Rd, Chester Gap, VA 22623.

🚐 **Mobile Mike's** 540-539-0509 shuttles and more (Mike Evans).

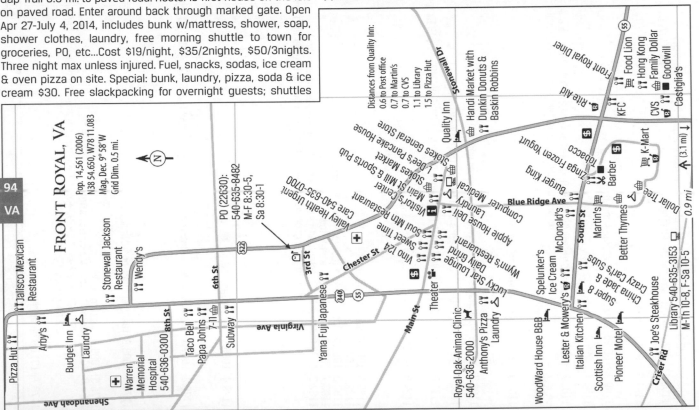

FRONT ROYAL, VA

Pop. 14,561 (2006)
N38 54.650, W78 11.083
Mag. Dec 9° 58'W
Grid Dim. 0.5 mi.

94
VA

Distances from Quality Inn:
0.6 to Post office
0.7 to Martin's
0.7 to CVS
1.1 to Library
1.5 to Pizza Hut

PO (22630):
540-635-8482
M-F 8:30-5,
Sa 8:30-1

Library 540-635-3153
M-Th 10-8, F-Sa 10-5

965.6   US 522 (Remount Road) *Front Royal 22630* (4W)

🏠🅿️✉️ **Mountain Home Cabbin** 540-692-6198
MountainHomeAT@gmail.com. Renovated "cabbin" of historic home at 3471 Remount Rd (US 522). AT parallels 522 for 0.25. From south side trailhead parking lot, home is 100 yards east on 522 (red roof visible). Open year-round. Walk-ins okay Apr-Sept, 4pm Fri - 6pm Sun. Other times, call/email for reservations. Sleeps up to 6, individually or as a group. $20PP includes bed, fresh linens, bath/shower, cont. breakfast & daily town shuttle for laundry & resupply. Pizza, ice cream, and snacks for sale on site. All hikers welcome to get water from faucet on SW corner of the cabbin. Dogs may stay in outdoor kennel with doghouse. Parking $3/day. No alcohol, smoking outside in designated area. Owned by Lisa and Scott ("Possible" AT '12) Jenkins.

ℹ️ 🚻 📶 **Visitor Center** 540-635-5788 7 days, 9-5pm. Often has hiker goodie bags. Restrooms, hiker box, pack storage. Cold drinks for sale.

🛏️⛺📶✉️ **Quality Inn** 540-635-3161 $65 S/D, $10EAP (up to 4) includes continental B. Pets $15. Pool. If you need ride back to AT in the morning, let them know when you check in. 🍴**Thunwa Thai** on-site. Maildrops: 10 Commerce Avenue, Front Royal, VA 22630.

🛏️📶 **Woodward House B&B** 540-635-7010 $110D includes breakfast, pickup and return to trail.

🛏️📶🖥️ **Super 8** 540-636-4888 10% hiker discount, pets $10.

🛏️📶 **Scottish Inn** 540-636-6168 $50/up, pets $10.

🛏️📶 **Budget Inn** 540-635-2196

🛏️📶 **Pioneer Motel** 540-635-4784 $39S+tax

🍴 **Lucky Star Lounge** L/D variety, some vegetarian, live music.

🏪 **Stokes Market** Wonderfully random selction of goods & foods.

🚐 **Alyson Browett** 540-764-0711 Shuttle range Luray-HF and Dulles.

973.8   VA 55, Manassas Gap, *Linden, VA 22642* (1.2W)

📬 M-F 8-12 & 1-5, Sa 8-12, 540-636-9936, packages held only 15 days.

🍴 **Apple House Restaurant** 540-636-6329 Tu-Su 7-8, M 7-5 year-round. Hiker specials, some supplies and rides sometimes available.

🏪 **Monterey Convenience Store**

999.1   Bears Den Rocks

🏠🍴♨️🛏️🚿⛺🅿️🖥️✉️ **Bears Den Hostel and Trail Center** 540-554-8708 ⟨www.bearsdencenter.org⟩ The castle-like stone lodge, ATC owned and PATC operated. Bunk & shower $17, tenting $12PP includes shower with full house privileges. Hiker Special: Bunk, laundry, pizza, soda & a pint of Ben & Jerry's ice cream for $30. All prices include self-serve pancake breakfast. Credit cards accepted. Hiker room, which has TV, shower, Internet and sodas for sale, is accessible all day by entering a mileage code. The upper lodge, kitchen, camp store and office open 5-9pm daily. Checkout is at 9am. Slackpacking available, Shuttles may be available during summer months only. Short-term parking $3/day. Maildrops can be picked up during office hours: Bears Den Hostel, 18393 Blue Ridge Mountain Rd, Bluemont, VA 20135. Hosts the *Northern Ruck* Jan 31-Feb 2, 2014.

999.7   Snickers Gap, VA 7 & 679 (Pine Grove Rd). AT crosses VA 7 at its intersection with Pine Grove Rd. Take Pine Grove Rd. west to anitque shop & restaurants. For PO, take VA 7 0.8E, then right on route 734 for another 0.8 mile.

Bluemont, VA 20135

📬 (1.7E) M-F 10-1 & 2-5, Sa 8:30-12, 540-554-4537

🏪📶💧 (0.2W) **Snickers Gap Antiques** Hiker-friendly store with limited snacks & first aid items, WiFi, free water fill-up.

🍴 (0.3W) **Horseshoe Curve Restaurant** 540-554-8291 Tu-Sa 12-9, Su 12-6. Good pub food.

🍴 (0.9W) **Pine Grove Restaurant** 540-554-8126 M-Sa 6:30-8, Su7-2.

1007.1   Side trails (0.2E) to:

🏠🍴♨️📞💧 **Blackburn AT Center** 540-338-9028. PATC caretaker on-site. Hiker bunks in small cabin with wood-burning stove. On porch of main building: logbook, donation box, pay phone, and electrical outlets (welcome to charge devices). Solar shower on lawn, water from hose, picnic tables. Open year-round.

SoBo	NoBo	Description	Elev
1172.0	1013.3	Keys Gap, WV 9, markets 0.3E or W .... N39 15.694 W77 45.750 P (pg. 98)	926
1170.5	1014.8	Powerline	923
1169.8	1015.5	Campsite	1120
1168.1	1017.2	VA-WV border, Loudoun Heights, Loudoun Heights Trail to east	1134
1167.5	1017.8	WV 32, Chestnut Hill Rd	599
1166.6	1018.7	US 340, north end of Shenandoah River Bridge ⚠ No hitchhiking on 340 (pg.98)	336
1166.3	1019.0	Side trail to Appalachian Trail Conservancy (0.2W) (pg.98)	440
1165.9	1019.4	Jefferson Rock, view north to Potomac and Shenandoah Rivers	450
1165.7	1019.6	Harpers Ferry, WV, High Street ...... N39 18.989 W77 45.350 P (pg.98-99)	297
1165.4	1019.9	Potomac River, Byron Memorial Footbridge, WV-MD border. North of river turn east on C&O Canal Towpath. No camping on AT section of towpath.	275
1164.3	1021.0	Pass under Sandy Hook Bridge (US 340)	289
1162.8	1022.5	C&O Canal Towpath north end, RR tracks, US 340 underpass (pg.100)	266
1162.2	1023.1	From Keep Tryst Rd: Knoxville, MD (1.0W) Brunswick, MD (2.5E) Weverton Rd N39 19.977 W77 40.993 P	392
1161.5	1023.8	Trail east to Weverton Cliffs, view	880

✱ **Poison Ivy** – Vine that can grow as ground cover or that can cling to trees or other brush. Stems redden toward the end and terminate with 3 pointed-oval leaves.

SoBo	NoBo	Description	Elev
1159.4	1025.9	**Ed Garvey Shelter** 36.7◄29.8◄15.6►4.1►9.1►16.6 Water on steep 0.4 mile trail in front of shelter. 2 tent sites north & south of shelter. (12)	1100
1157.6	1027.7	Brownsville Gap, roadbed	1082
1155.7	1029.6	Gapland Rd, Gathland State Park, War Correspondents Monument .... Frost-free spigot by restrooms. No camping, no trash cans.	950
1155.3	1030.0	**Crampton Gap Shelter** (0.3E), intermittent spring 0.1S on AT ...... (6) 33.9◄19.7◄4.1►5.9►12.5►20.7 NoBo: consider bringing water from Gathland SP in dry season.	1185

SoBo	NoBo	Description	Elev
1152.7	1032.6	Spring 0.5E, trail to Bear Spring Cabin (locked)	1458
1152.1	1033.2	White Rock Cliff, view.	1606
1151.9	1033.4	Lambs Knoll 50 yards west to tower, view	1751
1150.8	1034.5	Lambs Knoll tower road (paved)	1374
1150.3	1035.0	**Rocky Run Shelter** (0.2W) 24.7◄9.1◄5.0►7.5►15.7►20.6. Left fork on side trail to better water source & old shelter. Right to new shelter.	1011
1149.3	1036.0	Fox Gap, Reno Monument Rd (paved), **South Mountain Creamery** (2E).	1057
1148.5	1036.8	**Dahlgren Backpack Campground**. Large tenting area, picnic tables, restrooms; no fee. Note proximity to road.	980
1148.2	1037.1	Turners Gap, US At. 40, restaurant 0.1W, **Boonsboro, MD** (2.5W) (pg.100-101)	1086
1146.9	1038.4	Monument Rd.	1350
1146.6	1038.7	Washington Monument State Park, picnic tables, parking and restrooms adjacent to visitor center.	1427
1146.3	1039.0	Washington Monument (0.1W)	1550
1146.0	1039.3	Powerline	1319
1144.2	1041.1	Boonsboro Mountain Rd, residential area	1324
1143.9	1041.4	Bartman Hill Trail 0.6M to Greenbrier SP (pg.100)	1409
1143.4	1041.9	I-70 footbridge, US 40 N39 32.115 W77 36.209 P (pg.100) Parking north end of footbridge 0.1 east.	1267
1142.8	1042.5	**Pine Knob Shelter** (0.1W), south end of loop trail 16.6◄12.5◄7.5►8.2►13.1►22.7 Piped spring next to shelter.	1389
1141.2	1044.1	Annapolis Rocks to west, Campsite (0.2W) (13). Caretaker on site. Tentsites near outstanding overlook.	1820
1140.2	1045.1	Black Rock Cliffs to west	1821
1139.8	1045.5	Black Rock Creek	1591
1139.6	1045.7	**Pogo Memorial Campsite**. Campsite east of AT, spring 100 yards west. Thurston Griggs Trail to west.	1500
1134.8	1050.5	Wolfsville Rd, MD17, **Smithsburg, MD** (1.5W)	1400
1134.6	1050.7	**Ensign Cowall Shelter** 20.7◄15.7◄8.2►4.9►14.5►16.9 (pg.101) (8). Boxed spring, somewhat stagnant, south between shelter & road.	1415
1134.4	1050.9	Powerline	1519
1133.3	1052.0	Foxville Rd, MD 77, **Smithsburg, MD** (1.7W)	1604

1013.3 Keys Gap, WV 9

🏕🍴 (0.3E) **Sweet Springs Country Store** M-Sa 4am-11pm, Su 7am-11pm

⛺🍴 (0.3W veer left at intersection) **Mini-Mart & Torlone's Pizza**

🏨🍴🚿⛺ (2.0E) **Stoneybrook Organic Farm** 703-622-7526 (Matt or Ron) 37091 Charlestown Pike, Hillsboro, VA 20132. Full day WFS includes shower, laundry and meals. *Free pickup/return from Bears Den, Blackburn Trail Center, Keys Gap, or Harpers Ferry.*

1018.7 US 340, Shenandoah River Bridge
Go west on 340 to the Quality Hotel, KOA, or to Charles Town; east to Frederick. NoBos stay on the AT for better access to Harpers Ferry.

🛏⛺🛜🖥 **Econo Lodge** 304-535-6391 $99-$119 (peak rate mid-summer), 10% thru-hiker discount, breakfast bar, no pets.

⛺🛏🍴⛺🚿⛺ (1.2W) **Harpers Ferry KOA** 304-535-6895 Camping $40/up. One room cabin for five $77/up. Shower only $5, coin laundry on-site.

🛏🍴⛺🛜🖥 (1.3W) **Quality Hotel** 304-535-6302 $99/up, 10% hiker discount. Pool, **Vista Tavern** (L/D) on-site.

Charles Town, WV 25414 (6W) All major services.

🏕🛒 **Walmart** with grocery and pharmacy 304-728-2720

➕ **Jefferson Urgent Care** 304-728-8533 M-F 9-7, Sa-Su 9-5

🐾 **Jefferson Animal Hospital** 304-725-0428

Frederick, MD 21701 (20E) All major services.

98
WV

1019.0 Side Trail to ATC HQ (0.2W)

ℹ️⛺✉️ **Appalachian Trail Conservancy HQ** - 304-535-6331 ⟨www.appalachiantrail.org⟩ Open year-round, 7 days a week 9-5, Closed Thanksgiving, Christmas and New Year's Day. If you're thru-hiking or hiking the entire trail in sections, have your photo taken for the album; a postcard version of this photo may be purchased (first one is free for ATC members). Hiker lounge, register, scale, and cold drinks inside, along with hats, shirts, maps, all ATC publications. Coleman/denatured alcohol/oz for donation. There is an information board on the front porch. Maildrops: (USPS) PO Box 807 or (FedEx/UPS) 799 Washington St, Harpers Ferry, WV 25425.

1019.6 *Harpers Ferry, WV 25425* *(more services on map)*

🏨⛺⛺🚌🛜🖥✉️ **Teahorse Hostel** 304-535-6848 0.5W of ATC ⟨www.teahorsehostel.com⟩. $33 per bunk plus tax includes waffle breakfast. Laundry $6. No pets, alcohol or smoking. Shuttle range Thorton Gap to Duncannon and Dulles Airport. Call before sending maildrops in off-season (winter). Maildrops ($2 fee for non-guests): 1312 W. Washington St., Harpers Ferry, WV 25425.

🛏 **Harpers Ferry Hostel** (in Knoxville, see pg. 100)

🛏🍴⛺⛺🚌 **Town's Inn Lodging, Dining, and Sundry Supplies** 304-932-0677 ⟨www.TheTownsInn.com⟩ Three rooms in historic downtown building: Shenandoah sleeps 6, $120, Potomac $120/4, Appalachian Room $140/2. Laundry $5, shuttles $1/mile, no maildrops, Visa/MC accepted. Restaurant and shop downstairs open 6am-10pm every day, stocked specifically for hiker resupply.

🛏🛜 **Laurel Lodge** 304-535-2886 $135-180 for 2 includes big breakfast, view overlooking Potomac.

🥾⛺ **The Outfitter at Harpers Ferry & Harpers Ferry General Store** 888-535-2087 Knowledgeable full service outfitter with good selection of shoes and trail food. Shuttle referrals. Open daily 10-6.

➕ **Foot and Ankle Care** Dr. Warren BeVards, 304-535-3040

ℹ️🅿️ **Harpers Ferry National Historical Park** 304-535-6029 $6 entrance fee, long-term parking. Free shuttle bus to lower town.

🚌 **HostelHiker.com** 202-670-6323 Short route when available centered in HF covering AT from Thorton Gap to Pen-Mar Park. Daily route to/from DC, Dulles and Baltimore. Registered/insured.

🚌 **Mark "Strings" Cusic** 304-433-0028 mdcusic@frontier.com

🚌 **Pan Tran** 304-263-0876 Route to Charles Town (Walmart) M-F 1:35 and 3:05, $2.50 each way.

🚆 **Amtrak** 800-USA-RAIL "Capitol Limited" daily 11:25am-1:10pm HF to Washington, DC Union Station (DC to HF 4:05-5:16pm). $12 each way.

🚆 **Maryland Rail Commuter Service (MARC)** 410-539-5000 ⟨www.mta.maryland.gov/marc-train⟩. "Brunswick Line" M-F to Washington DC Union Station 5:25am, 5:50am and 6:50am, returns 4:25, 5:40 and 6:20pm. $11 each way.

HARPERS FERRY, WV

N

Pop. 318 (2006)
36.82N, 84.49W
Mag. Dec. 6° 18'W

Polk St

Canal House

Anvil

Teahorse Hostel

Washington St

Bolivar-HF Library
304-535-2301
M,Tu,F,Sa 10-5:30
W,Th 10-8

7-11

Country Cafe
7-3, 7 days

Harpers Ferry
Family Medicine
304-535-6343

Econo Lodge

Union St

PO (25425)
304-535-2479:
M-F 8-4, Sa 9-12

Mena's Italian
(closed M)

Laurel Lodge

Potomac St

Potomac River

Fillmore St

ATC → 0.6 to AT

side trail/0.2
to ATC HQ

Shenandoah St

Jefferson Rock

Railroad Station
Amtrak: Chicago ◇ Wash.
MARC: Martinsburg ◇ Wash.

N

340

Shoreline Rd

KOA

Harpers Ferry National
Historic Park - parking
and shuttle

← Charles Town (all major services) 6.7 from AT

← Quality Hotel (1.3 from AT)

Shenandoah River

Chestnut Hill Rd

1.8 mi

Frederick, MD 21 mi
Washington, DC 68 mi

340

99

WV

Origin of town names:
Harpers Ferry - Potomac ferry service operated by Robert Harper.
Charles Town - Founded by Charles Washington, brother of George.
Frederick, MD - Frederick Calvert, 6th Baron Baltimore.

High St

Hannah's BBQ

Potomac St

Church St

Secret Six Tavern

Town's Inn & Sundry Store

Coach House Grill & Bar

Cannonball Deli

Confectionaries

Pvt Quinn's Pub

Scoops Ice Cream

General Store &
Outfitter at HF

Coffee Mill

Lower Town

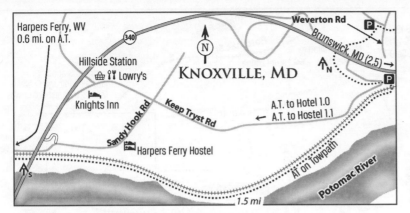

Harpers Ferry, WV
0.6 mi. on A.T.

Hillside Station
Lowry's

KNOXVILLE, MD

Knights Inn

Keep Tryst Rd

Sandy Hook Rd

Harpers Ferry Hostel

A.T. to Hotel 1.0
← A.T. to Hostel 1.1

Weverton Rd

Brunswick, MD (2.5)

A.T. on Towpath

Potomac River

1.5 mi

1022.5   US 340, Keep Tryst Rd, *Knoxville, MD, 21758* (1W)
Harpers Ferry Hostel
301-834-7652 ⟨www.harpersferryhostel.org⟩ Discounted rate for thru-hikers $20.16 includes tax, shower, internet & WiFi, make-your-own AYCE pancakes with coffee & tea. Bunkroom has A/C & heat. Laundry $2 wash (soap provided), $2 dry. Tenting $6PP, pay extra $5 for shower and $3 for breakfast. Campers permitted inside only for shower, laundry or breakfast. WiFi on back porch, porta-potty, fire pits, grill. Service dogs okay inside, otherwise dogs on leash allowed only if tenting. Soda & Gatorade machine, store with hiker snacks, often free leftovers in fridge & hiker cupboard. Movie nights on request. No drinking. Non-guest parking $5/day. *Summer* (Labor - Mem. Day): check-in 3-10pm, check out 11am. *Spring & Fall* (Apr 15 - Labor Day & Mem. Day - Nov. 30): check-in 5-10pm, check out 10am. *Winter* (Dec 1–Apr 14): closed. Maildrops: 19123 Sandy Hook Rd, Knoxville, MD 21758.
    Knights Inn 301-660-3580 Hiker rate $59.99 room can accomodate 4 and includes continental breakfast.
    Hillside Station 301-834-5300 Convenience store with pizza, wings, and more. M-Sa 6am-8:30pm, Su 8-8.

Brunswick, MD 21716 (2.5E from Keep Tryst Rd)
M-F 8:30-1 & 2-4:30, Sa 9-12, 301-834-9944
Wing N' Pizza Shack 301-834-5555 Delivers to HF Hostel

1037.1   Turners Gap, US Alt 40
(0.1W) **Old South Mountain Inn** 301-432-6155 Tu–F 5-9, Sa 4-close, Su brunch 10:30-2, dinner 12-7:30. Men, no sleevless shirts. Please shower first. Dining reservations preferred.

Boonsboro, MD (2.5W)
Vesta Pizzeria 301-432-6166 M-Tu 11-9, W-Su 11-10. Delivers to Turner's Gap (Dahlgren campground).
Mountainside Deli 301-432-6700 M-F 6am-8pm, Sa 8am-8pm, Su 11am-6pm.
Cronise Market Place 301-432-7377 M-Sa 9-7, Su 12-6
Turn the Page Book Store Café 301-432-4588
Crawfords 301-432-2903 M-F 7am-6pm, Sa 7am-3pm

1041.4   Bartman Hill Trail (0.6W) to:
Greenbrier State Park 301-791-4767 Prices listed as MD resident/nonresident. camping 4/5–last full weekend in October. Pets okay. Lunch concession stand open Mem-Labor Day. Entrance fee $5 not charged if camping or if you walk in on Bartman Trail. Tent sites with showers $26-28, higher weekends/holidays. Lake swimming, row boat and paddle boat rentals.

1041.9   I-70, US 40, (1.4W on US 40) to:
Dogpatch Tavern 301-791-2844
Greenbrier State Park (listed above)

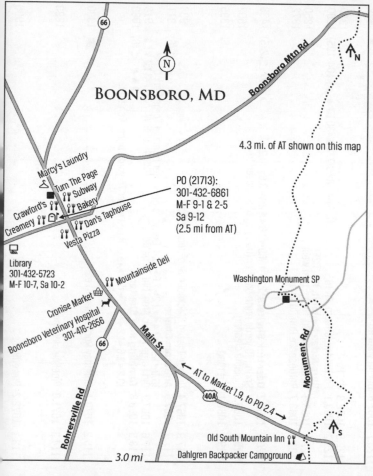

BOONSBORO, MD

4.3 mi. of AT shown on this map

Marcy's Laundry
Turn The Page
Subway
Bakery
Crawford's Creamery
Dan's Taphouse
Vesta Pizza

PO (21713):
301-432-6861
M-F 9-1 & 2-5
Sa 9-12
(2.5 mi from AT)

Library
301-432-5723
M-F 10-7, Sa 10-2

Mountainside Deli

Washington Monument SP

Cronise Market
Boonsboro Veterinary Hospital
301-416-2656

Main St

← AT to Market 1.9, to PO 2.4 →

Rohrersville Rd

Monument Rd

Old South Mountain Inn

3.0 mi

Dahlgren Backpacker Campground

1050.5   Wolfsville Rd, MD 17

💧 (0.3E) If shelter water source is dry, you may get water from ranger's house. Go 0.1 east (compass south) to a gravel road on left, then 0.2 on gravel road to first house on left.

🛏️🧭⌂⚒📞💻✉ (0.3W) **The Free State Hiker Hostel** 301-824-2407 ⟨www.freestatehiker.com⟩ $32 stay includes climate-controlled bunkroom, linens, hot shower, laundry (detergent supplied), internet & free long-distance phone. Open Mar 15-Nov 15, two night limit, check-in between 2-9pm. Credit cards accepted. Pizza and Mexican delivery available. Water available from spigot in front. No alcohol and no pets. Maildrops: (non-guest $2) c/o Free State Hiker, LLC 11626 Wolfsville Road, Smithsburg, Maryland 21783.

Smithsburg, MD 21783 (1.5W)

🏤 M-F 8:30-1 & 2-4:30, Sa 8:30-12, 301-824-2828
🏦 **Dollar General Store** 301-824-6940, 7 days 8-10
🛒 **Food Lion** 301-824-7011, daily 7am-11pm
🍴 **Smithsburg Market** 301-824-2171, M-Sa 8am-8pm, Su 10am-8pm
🍴 **Rocky's Pizzeria** 301-824-2066, 7 days 11am-10pm
🍴 **Vince's New York Pizza** 301-824-3939, daily 11am-11pm
🍴 **Dixie Diner** 301-824-5334, closed M, Tu 7-2, W-F 7-8, Sa-Su 7-2
🍴 **Subway** 301-824-3826, 24 hrs
🍴 **China 88** 301-824-7300
➕ **Smithsburg Emergency Medical** 301-824-3314
🐕 **Smithsburg Veterinary Clinic** 301-416-0888
℞ **Home Care Pharmacy**
℞ **Rite Aid** 301-824-2211, store 8-9, pharmacy 9-6
⚒ **Laundry**
💻 **Library** 301-824-7722 M,W-F 10am-7pm, Tu 12-9pm, Sa 10am-2pm
🔧 **Ace Hardware**

SoBo	NoBo	Description	Elev
1132.1	1053.2	Spring	1348
1131.9	1053.4	Powerline	1369
1131.5	1053.8	Warner Gap Hollow stream, Warner Gap Rd (gravel, AT to west).	1150
1130.8	1054.5	Little Antietam Creek	1094
1130.7	1054.6	Raven Rock Rd, MD 491	1073
1130.4	1054.9	Raven Rock Cliff, view 100 yards east.	1297
1129.7	1055.6	**Raven Rock Shelter** (0.1W), Ritchie Rd (0.6E) (16) ⊂	1682
		20.6◄13.1◄4.9◄▶9.6▶12.0▶13.2 New "two story" shelter. Water on opposite side of AT (0.3E) on steep side trail.	
1127.9	1057.4	Ends of High Rock Loop Trail 0.2 apart 0.1E from either end to view and parking. N39 41.690 W77 31.394 **P**	1822

> ⚠ *Many springs in PA run dry in June, July & August*

SoBo	NoBo	Description	Elev
1125.1	1060.2	Pen Mar County Park N39 42.983 W77 30.433 **P** (pg.104-105)	1280
1124.8	1060.5	**Cascade, MD** (1.4E) **Waynesboro, PA** (2.1W to Walmart, downtown 4.5)	1250
1124.7	1060.6	**MD-PA** border, RR Tracks, Mason-Dixon Line. Pen Mar Rd	1240
1124.2	1061.1	Falls Creek, footbridge, campsite	1050
1123.7	1061.6	Buena Vista Rd	1290
1122.5	1062.8	Old PA 16.	1350
1122.2	1063.1	Footbridge, stream, PA 16. N39 44.482 W77 29.430 **P** (pg.104-105)	1200
1122.0	1063.3	**Blue Ridge Summit, PA** (1.2E) Mentzer Gap Rd, NoBo: turn west	1250
1121.6	1063.7	Rattlesnake Run Rd (gravel)	1372
1120.1	1065.2	**Deer Lick Shelters** (2x5) ⊂	1435
		22.7◄14.5◄9.6◄▶2.4▶3.6▶10.2. Spring 10 yards north on AT or (0.2E) on blue-blazed trail.	
1119.8	1065.5	Pipeline clearing	1502
1119.2	1066.1	Dirt road.	1395
1117.9	1067.4	Orange-blazed Chickadee Snowmobile Trail	938
1117.7	1067.6	**Antietam Shelter** ⊂ (6)	911
		16.9◄12.0◄2.4◄▶1.2▶7.8▶13.4 Better to get water from Old Forge Park 0.1N	
1117.6	1067.7	Old Forge Picnic Area, Old Forge Rd **P** N39 48.089 W77 28.773	916
1116.5	1068.8	**Tumbling Run Shelters.** ⊂ (8)	1089
		13.2◄3.6◄1.2◄▶6.0▶12.2▶19.6 Piped water 75 yards right of shelter.	
1115.2	1070.1	Chimney Rocks, view to east	1900
1114.3	1071.0	Pipeline clearing	1883
1113.1	1072.2	Powerline	1986

SoBo	NoBo	Description	Elev
1112.5	1072.8	Snowy Mountain Rd	1687
1111.9	1073.4	Swamp Rd, **South Mountain, PA** 17261 (1.0E) (pg.105)	1560
1111.6	1073.7	PA 233, **South Mountain, PA** 17261 (1.2E) (pg.105)	1600
1109.9	1075.4	**Rocky Mountain Shelters** (0.2E) ☾ ♦ ⌂ ⌐ (8)	1660
		10.2◀7.8◀6.6◀▶5.6▶13.0▶19.2	
		Piped spring 0.5 mile on trail to road, then right 75 yards.	
1106.9	1078.4	US 30, **Fayetteville, PA** (3.5W) N39 54.352 W77 28.714 ℗ (pg.106)	960
		Overnight parking SW corner of US 30 & Pine Grove Rd, check in at park HQ.	
1106.5	1078.8	Side trail to **Caledonia State Park**, pool area (pg.106)	939
1105.7	1079.6	Locust Gap Rd, Valley Trail to west	1343
1104.3	1081.0	**Quarry Gap Shelters** 13.4◀12.2◀5.6◀▶7.4▶13.6▶24.5 ☾ ♦ ⌂ ⌐ (8)	1473
1104.0	1081.3	Footbridge, stream	1547
1103.6	1081.7	Hosack Run Trail to east	1838
1102.8	1082.5	5-way gravel road intersection	2005
1102.0	1083.3	Powerline	1889
1101.6	1083.7	Woods road	2024
1100.3	1085.0	Middle Ridge Road	2075
1099.7	1085.6	3 Points (intersecting gravel roads), campsite to north	1985
1099.3	1086.0	PATC Milesburn Cabin (locked), spring 100 yards west	1704
1099.0	1086.3	Ridge Rd (gravel), campsite north of road	1918
1098.2	1087.1	Rocky Knob Trail (orange-blazed)	1919
1097.6	1087.7	Powerline, campsite to north	1936
1096.9	1088.4	**Birch Run Shelter**, stream 75 yards north on AT ☾ ♦ ⌂ ⌐ (10)	1811
		19.6◀13.0◀7.4◀▶6.2▶▶25.2	
1096.8	1088.5	Footbridge, stream	1805
1095.6	1089.7	Shippensburg Rd N39 59.834 W77 24.301 ℗	2040
1094.5	1090.8	Service road (gravel)	1952
1093.7	1091.6	Side trail to Michener Cabin (locked) ♦ (0.3E)	1850
1093.1	1092.2	Woods road, **AT Midpoint** (2014) is 0.45mi. north of this road	1852

Elev

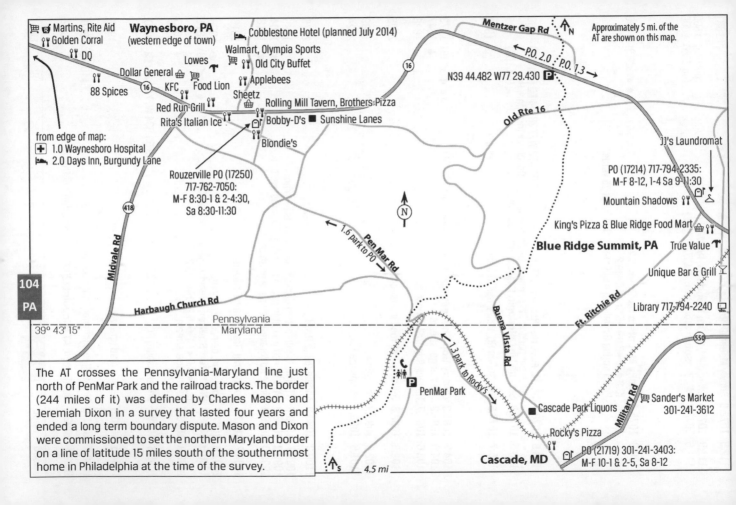

Martins, Rite Aid
Golden Corral
DQ

Waynesboro, PA
(western edge of town)

Cobblestone Hotel (planned July 2014)

Walmart, Olympia Sports
Old City Buffet

Lowes

Dollar General
KFC
Food Lion
88 Spices

Applebees

Sheetz

Red Run Grill
Rita's Italian Ice

Rolling Mill Tavern, Brothers Pizza
Bobby-D's   Sunshine Lanes

Blondie's

from edge of map:
+ 1.0 Waynesboro Hospital
🛏 2.0 Days Inn, Burgundy Lane

Rouzerville PO (17250)
717-762-7050:
M-F 8:30-1 & 2-4:30,
Sa 8:30-11:30

Mentzer Gap Rd

N

Approximately 5 mi. of the AT are shown on this map.

← P.O. 2.0   P.O. 1.3 →

16

N39 44.482 W77 29.430 P

Old Rte 16

JJ's Laundromat

PO (17214) 717-794-2335:
M-F 8-12, 1-4 Sa 9-11:30

Mountain Shadows

King's Pizza & Blue Ridge Food Mart

Blue Ridge Summit, PA   True Value

Unique Bar & Grill

Library 717-794-2240

550

418

Midvale Rd

N

← 1.6 park to PO

Pen Mar Rd

Harbaugh Church Rd

Pennsylvania
Maryland

39° 43' 15"

104
PA

Buena Vista Rd

Ft. Ritchie Rd

1.3 park to Rocky's →

PenMar Park

Cascade Park Liquors

Military Rd

Sander's Market
301-241-3612

Rocky's Pizza

PO (21719) 301-241-3403:
M-F 10-1 & 2-5, Sa 8-12

Cascade, MD

N
s   4.5 mi

The AT crosses the Pennsylvania-Maryland line just north of PenMar Park and the railroad tracks. The border (244 miles of it) was defined by Charles Mason and Jeremiah Dixon in a survey that lasted four years and ended a long term boundary dispute. Mason and Dixon were commissioned to set the northern Maryland border on a line of latitude 15 miles south of the southernmost home in Philadelphia at the time of the survey.

1060.2   Pen Mar County Park

🚶🏕☎ Open first Sunday in May to last Sunday in Oct. Vending machines & water; no camping. Restrooms locked when park closed. Bobby D's & other pizza places deliver. Pen Mar Rd passes in front of park, east of AT. If intending to walk to town, do so from AT/Pen Mar Rd intersection 0.3N of park. Rouzerville PO is nearest to the AT. Just beyond the PO, reach Main St (PA 16), and turn left to reach many services on the western edge of Waynesboro. Hospital, Days Inn, Burgundy Lane and more restaurants approx. 3mi. further west, in downtown Waynesboro.

🚌 **Dennis Sewell** 301-241-3176

Waynesboro, PA 17214 (2.1W)

🏪 **Walmart, Food Lion**

🍴 **Bobby D's Pizza** 717-762-0388

🍴 **Old City Buffet** American, Chinese, Japanese AYCE L/D.

🍴 **Golden Corral, 88 Spices** (both offer buffets)

Also: Olympia Sports large selection of running shoes.

3W of Walmart:

🛏⛺🚌📶🖥✉ **Burgundy Lane B&B** 717-762-8112 $90-105D w/full breakfast, free laundry & shuttle to trailhead or town stop. Longer shuttles for fee. Maildrops: 128 W Main St, Waynesboro, PA 17268.

🛏📶🖥⛺ **Days Inn** 717-762-9113 $59S, $69D, $5EAP. Continental breakfast, $10 pet fee, laundry next door.

➕ **Waynesboro Hospital** 717-765-4000 501 E Main St.

🐾 **Wayne Heights Animal Hospital** 717-765-9636

🎭 **Waynesboro Theater** 717-762-7879

Cascade, MD (1.4E on Pen Mar/High Rock Rd)

🛒 **Sanders Market** M–Sa 8:30–8, open till 9pm Tu and Sa.

1063.1   PA 16   *Blue Ridge Summit, PA 17214* (1.2E)

🍴 **Unique Bar and Grill** 717-794-2565 live music, **Summit Plaza** 717-794-2500 open 7–8, B/L/D.

⛓ **JJ's Laundromat**

🔨 **True Value Hardware**

1073.4   Swamp Rd, dirt road, walk for 0.3 before connecting with paved South Mountain Rd. (1.0E) total to PO.

1073.7   PA 233 - 0.2E of the trailhead, PA 233 veers to the north; stay to right on South Mountain Rd. (1.2E) total to PO.

South Mountain, PA 17261 (1.0E or 1.2E)

🍴 **South Mountain Tavern** 717-749-3845 M-Sa 9am-2am

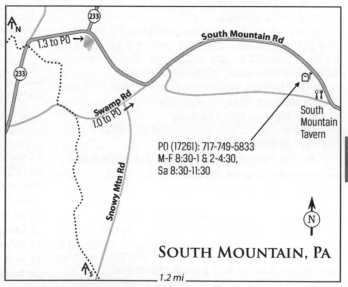

1.3 to PO →

1.0 to PO →

PO (17261): 717-749-5833
M-F 8:30-1 & 2-4:30,
Sa 8:30-11:30

South Mountain Tavern

South Mountain Rd

Swamp Rd

Snowy Mtn Rd

SOUTH MOUNTAIN, PA

— 1.2 mi —

1078.4   US 30
1078.8   Side trail to park
🔌 ♨ 🎒 ☕ **Caledonia State Park** 717-352-2161 Open Mar. 29 - Dec. 9. Pool & snack bar open seven days in summer (Jun. 8 - Labor Day) snack bar 11-7.   Phone and vending next to the pool and near office. Campsites with showers, $21 Su-Th, $25 F-Sa, (2013) $2 more for campsites that allow pets, $2 less for PA residents. $3 shower only.

🍴(1.5E) **Bobby A's Grill & Bar** 717-352-2252

Fayetteville, PA 17222 (spread out to west)
(0.4W)🍴☕ **La Mattina's Italian Restaurant** 717-352-8503 Tu-Th 11-1:30, F&Sa 11-10:30, Su 12-9:30. Pizza, ice cream.
(1.7W)🏪 **Rutter's Market**
(2.3W)🏪 **Dollar General**
(2.6W)🛏🍴🛜✉ **Scottish Inn and Suites** 717-352-2144, 800-251-1962 $59S, $69D, $15 pets. $5 for pickup or return to trail. $10 for ride to Walmart. Guest maildrops: 5651 Lincoln Way East, Fayetteville, PA 17222
(2.6W)🍴 **Flamingo Restaurant** excellent large breakfast.
(3.1W)🍴 **Vince's Pizza** 717-401-0096
(3.1W)🛁 **Squeaky Clean Laundry**
(3.2W)📮 M-F 8-4:30, Sa 8:30-12, 717-352-2022
(3.2W)💊 **Rite Aid**
(7W)🏬🍴💊 **Walmart** 24hrs w/ pharmacy and **Subway**.
🚐 **Freeman's Shuttle Service** 717-352-2513, 717-658-9185. Front Royal to DWG.

1097.9   PA 233, Pine Grove Furnace State Park
🏪 **Pine Grove General Store** 717-731-6700 Open 7 days Memorial Day to Labor Day 9am-7pm; Open F-Su spring & fall. Foods and cold drinks, short-order grill. Soda machine outside. Home of the **half gallon challenge.**

ℹ️ ♨ **A.T. Museum** ⟨www.atmuseum.org⟩ Hikers welcome to bring food to eat outside & relax. Artifacts of pioneering hikers, past thru-hiker photos, signs from Springer & Katahdin. Sells halfway patch. Open Mar 29-May 4 weekends 12-4; May 10-July 6 every day 9-4; July 7-Aug 3 every day 12-4; Aug 6-Nov 2 W-Sun 12-4 **Hiker Festival** June 7.

🏠♨⛺🛜🖥✉ **Ironmasters Mansion Hostel** 717-486-4108. West end of Pine Grove Furnace State Park. English Tudor brick residence (with secret room) built by the Ironmaster for his family in 1829; renovated in 2010 as a hostel. $25/person w/breakfast; $35 Hiker's Package includes 2 meals, shower, laundry, drink, dessert, and AT Halfway souvenir; 5-9pm check-in and 9 am checkout; closed during day 9am – 5pm and Tuesday nights. Season Apr 1- Nov 1. Maildrops: Ironmasters Hostel, 1212 Pine Grove Rd, Gardners, PA 17324.

🔌 🚻 🅿 **Pine Grove Furnace State Park** 717-486-7174 Office and parking west of Museum. Open last week of March - second weekend in Dec. Apr-Oct open 7 days; spring & fall weekdays only. Least expensive campsites $21 weekdays, $25 weekends, $2 off for PA residents.   Some dog-allowed sites. Beach/swimming area. Restrooms throughout park. Check in with the park office before leaving a vehicle overnight; cars can be left for up to one week.

1104.3   Side trail (0.7W) to campground
🛏 🔌 🏪 ⛺ **Mountain Creek Campground** 717-486-7681 Open Apr-Nov, cabins $50D, $5EAP, tent sites $28, heated pool, camp store.

1108.7   PA 94   **Mt. Holly Springs, PA 17065** (2.5W) Services at two intersections 0.5mi apart. 5mi farther to 81 interchange with Walmart and movies at Carlisle Commons.
📮 M-F 8-1 & 2-4:30, Sa 9-12, 717-486-3468
🛏🍴🖥🛜 **Holly Inn, Restaurant and Tavern** 717-486-3823 $55D $10EAP, free ride to/from AT if available, $5 pick up from Pine Grove Furnace SP. Fri live music, Sa karaoke, Sun open mic. Restaurant open 11:30-9.
🏪 **Sheetz, Dollar General**
🍴 **Laura's** breakfast, lunch, and ice cream.
🍴 **Subway**, **Sicilia Pizza**
💊 **Holly Pharmacy** 717-486-5321
🛁 **Dollie's Laundromat**

1117.5   PA 174, *Boiling Springs, PA 17007*

☾☽ Free hiker campsite with privy south of town. Railroad tracks pass very near campsite.

⊨♔♙⌂🅵⚞☂🖥✉ **Allenberry Resort Inn & Playhouse** 717-258-3211, 800-430-5468 ⟨www.allenberry.com⟩ Hiker special $40 double occupancy. Restaurant and bar, no food service on Monday, limited on Tuesday. Buffets sometimes available ($6 breakfast, $10 lunch, $15 dinner). Theater shows $10, $4 laundry, pool open memorial-labor day, accepts credit cards. Gift shop carries snacks, beer and some toiletries. A large variety of 6-packs can be purchased from the bar. $5 fee for maildrops: 1559 Boiling Springs Rd, Boiling Springs, PA 17007

⊨⚞☂✉ **Gelinas Manor** 717-258-6584 ⟨www.gelinasmanor.com⟩ Room w/shared bath for $99D/up. No pets, no packs inside. Full breakfast at 8:30. Laundry $6/load. Credit cards accepted. Maildrops w/reservation: MUST say "in care of Gelinas Manor", 219 Front Street, Boiling Springs, PA 17007.

⊨⚞☂ **Red Cardinal B&B** 717-245-0823 Prices seasonal, queen bed room includes full breakfast & pickup/return from Boiling Springs (2mi away). No pets, no smoking.

♙ **Anile's Ristorante & Pizzeria** 717-258-5070 L/D subs, pizza, entrees. Su-Th 11-10, F-Sa 11-11,

♙ **Caffe 101** B/L/D.

♙ **Boiling Springs Tavern** 717-258-3614 L/D 11:30-2, 5-9:30, closed Su-M.

♔ **Karn's Quality Foods** 717-258-1458 Daily 7–10.

⌂🅵 **Gettys Food Mart** 717-241-6163 ATM inside.

♖ **Yellow Breeches Outfitters** 717-258-6752 Primarily a fishing outfitter; limited hiking selection.

♒ **Boiling Springs Pool** 717-258-4121 Memorial Day-Labor Day, M-Su 11-7, $12 admission, $1 hot shower.

🐕 **Boiling Springs Animal Hospital** 717-258-4575 M-T 8-7:30, W-F 8-6, Sa 8-1, 1.4W on Park Drive.

🚐 **Mike's Shuttle Service** 717-497-6022

ℹ **ATC Mid-Atlantic Regional Office** 717-258-5771 Open wkdays 8-5. Water faucet on south side of building. Staff and bulletin board provide info on trail conditions, water availability and parking. Small shop with guidebooks and maps. White gas/denatured alcohol for small donation.

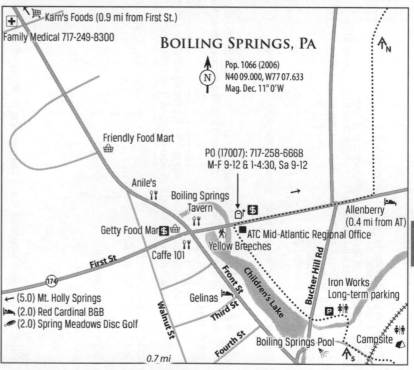

BOILING SPRINGS, PA

Pop. 1066 (2006)
N40 09.000, W77 07.633
Mag. Dec. 11° 0'W

Karn's Foods (0.9 mi from First St.)
Family Medical 717-249-8300

Friendly Food Mart

Anile's

Boiling Springs Tavern

PO (17007): 717-258-6668
M-F 9-12 & 1-4:30, Sa 9-12

Allenberry
(0.4 mi from AT)

ATC Mid-Atlantic Regional Office

Getty Food Mart

Yellow Breeches

Caffe 101

First St

Children's Lake

Bucher Hill Rd

Iron Works
Long-term parking

← (5.0) Mt. Holly Springs
⊨ (2.0) Red Cardinal B&B
⚐ (2.0) Spring Meadows Disc Golf

Gelinas

Walnut St

Third St

Fourth St

Front St

Boiling Springs Pool

Campsite

0.7 mi

107

PA

SoBo	NoBo		Elev
1091.8	1093.5	Woodrow Rd (gravel), campsite 0.1N	1787
1091.3	1094.0	Stream.	1545
1090.8	1094.5	Sunset Rocks Trail to east, rejoins AT to north	1335
1090.7	1094.6	**Toms Run Shelters,** (one shelter burned down late in 2013).	1319
		19.2◄13.6◄6.2▲10.9►19.0►37.2 Water behind shelter	
1090.5	1094.8	Stream.	1291
1090.4	1094.9	Midpoint Sign	1303
1089.5	1095.8	Michaux Rd	1330
1088.6	1096.7	Toms Run, footbridge, stream. Sunset Rocks Trail to east.	1031
1087.4	1097.9	PA 233 (paved), **AT Museum** . . . . N40 01.971 W77 18.291 P (pg.106)	912
		NoBo on road 0.1W, veer right on road into **Pine Grove Furnace State Park.**	
1086.5	1098.8	Fuller Lake	846
		⊘ No camping within one mile of PGF SP; camping within the park only at designated (paid) campsites. No overnight sleeping in pavillions.	
1084.7	1100.6	Campsite	1243
1084.5	1100.8	Pole Steeple Trail to west	1300
1083.5	1101.8	Campsite	1366
1081.3	1104.0	Roadbed	1056
1081.0	1104.3	Trail to **Mountain Creek Campground** (0.7W) signed & steep. (pg.106)	1026
1079.9	1105.4	Spring 50 yards west on marked trail	748
1079.8	1105.5	**James Fry (Tagg Run) Shelter** (0.2E), campsite west of AT	719
		24.5◄17.1◄10.9▲8.1►26.3►33.6 Spring uphill from shelter; water 0.2E farther.	
1079.4	1105.9	Pine Grove Rd (paved)	685
1079.2	1106.1	Stream	660
1078.8	1106.5	⚠ Cross RR tracks; sharp east turn for NoBo.	656
1078.6	1106.7	PA 34, Hunters Run Rd . . . . N40 4.624 W77 11.702 P (0.5S)	632
		Green Mountain Store (0.2E) 7 days	
1076.6	1108.7	PA 94, **Mt Holly Springs, PA** (2.5W) . . . . . . (pg.106)	880
1076.3	1109.0	Sheet Iron Roof Rd, trail to **Deer Run Campground.**	774
		(0.4W) 717-486-8168, tentsite $10 w/shower, cabin $b2.	
1075.9	1109.4	Footbridge, stream, campsite	687
1075.6	1109.7	Footbridge, stream	675
1075.2	1110.1	Old Town Rd (gravel)	745
1074.6	1110.7	Rock maze	1179
1074.2	1111.1	Rock maze	1092
1073.8	1111.5	Whiskey Spring Rd, reliable water from spring	830
		⊘ No camping in Cumberland Valley between Alec Kennedy and Darlington Shelters, except at backpackers campsite south of Boiling Springs.	

SoBo	NoBo	Description	Elev
1071.8	1113.5	Little Dogwood Run, campsite, orange-blazed trail 1.7E to BSA campground ◆ ⛺	884
1071.7	1113.6	**Alec Kennedy Shelter** (0.2E), spring behind shelter is unreliable . . . ◗ ⌂ (7)	966
		25.2◄19.0◄8.1◄▲18.2►25.5►33.8	
1070.8	1114.5	Center Point Knob, original AT midpoint, White Rocks Trail 0.4E to view 📷	1060
1069.4	1115.9	Cornfield, south end	561
1068.9	1116.4	Leidigh Dr	562
1068.3	1117.0	Backpacker's Campsite (nearby railroad tracks can be noisy) ◗ ⛺	514
1068.0	1117.3	Bucher Hill Rd, Iron Works Parking. N40 8.868 W77 7.445 🅿 ◗	501
1067.8	1117.5	PA 174, First Street, ATC Mid-Atlantic Regional Office (pg.107)	500
		Boiling Springs, PA	
1066.3	1119.0	Stone wall	618
1065.7	1119.6	PA 74, York Rd. N40 10.385 W77 7.263 🅿	579
1064.7	1120.6	Lisburn Rd. ◗	555
1064.2	1121.1	Byers Rd.	557
1064.1	1121.2	Footbridge, stream	511
1063.7	1121.6	PA 641, Trindle Rd. N40 11.700 W77 6.500 🅿	540
1062.5	1122.8	Ridge Rd, Biddle Rd. (pg.112)	475
1062.0	1123.3	Old Stonehouse Rd, footbridge, stream ◗	477
1061.3	1124.0	Appalachian Dr.	514
1061.0	1124.3	PA Turnpike (I-76) overpass	497
1060.4	1124.9	Railroad tracks	475
1059.8	1125.5	US 11, **Carlisle, PA** (5.0W) (pg.112)	490
1058.9	1126.4	Pass over I-81 on Bernheisel Rd	485
1058.3	1127.0	Fence stile (two)	517
1057.5	1127.8	Conodoguinet Creek, footbridge adjacent to road . N40 15.589 W77 6.221 🅿 ◗	480
		Scott Farm Trail Work Center Open May–Oct, picnic table, no camping. The AT u-turns, passes under bridge, and heads north.	
1056.4	1128.9	Sherwood Drive, parking to east. N40 16.439 W77 5.967 🅿 ◗	439
		Many footbridges, streams north and south of this road	
1055.5	1129.8	PA 944 tunnel	480
1054.6	1130.7	Piped spring where AT crosses overgrown dirt road ◗	731
		NoBo planning stay at Darlington Shelter consider getting water here.	
1053.9	1131.4	View 📷	1132
1053.6	1131.7	Darlington Trail, Tuscarora Trail	1271
1053.5	1131.8	**Darlington Shelter** (0.1E) 37.2◄26.3◄18.2◄▲7.3►15.6►22.3 ◗ ⌂ (5)	1223
		Unreliable water on blue-blazed trail in front of shelter. Taj Mahal privy.	

SoBo	NoBo	Description	Elev
1052.0	1133.3	Gravel road	750
1051.6	1133.7	Millers Gap Rd (paved) N40 19.359 W77 4.260 P	704
1051.3	1134.0	PA 850	690
1049.9	1135.4	Service road	780
1049.7	1135.6	Footbridge, stream	883
1048.7	1136.6	Pipeline, view, trail very rocky from here north to PA 274 [photo]	1335
1047.1	1138.2	Blue-blazed trail 0.4W to service road	1254
1046.2	1139.1	**Cove Mountain Shelter** (0.2E) ☾ ⌂(8) 33.6◄25.5◄7.3▲8.3▶15.0▶33.0 Spring 0.1 mile on steep side trail.	1268
1044.2	1141.1	Hawk Rock, view [photo]	992
1043.5	1141.8	⚠ Old trail to west, AT turns east (uphill for NoBo) ♦	455
1043.1	1142.2	Inn Rd, trail very rocky from here south to pipeline.	384
1042.6	1142.7	PA 274, pass under US 11/15	385
1042.2	1143.1	**Duncannon, PA**, High St + Broadway (pg.112-113)	398
1040.3	1145.0	Susquehanna River N40 23.759 W77 0.512 P North end of Clarks Ferry Bridge, US 22/322, railroad tracks	402
1039.5	1145.8	View	620
1038.1	1147.2	Susquehanna Trail to west. ☾	1157
1037.9	1147.4	**Clarks Ferry Shelter** (0.1E) 33.8◄15.6◄8.3▲6.7▶24.7▶38.1 ♦ ⌂(8) Reliable piped spring just beyond shelter. [photo]	1258
1037.6	1147.7	Powerline	1346
1035.0	1150.3	Powerline	1242
1034.1	1151.2	PA 225 N40 24.711 W76 55.796 P	1263
1033.5	1151.8	Powerline	1297
1032.1	1153.2	Table Rock, view [photo]	1347

SoBo	NoBo	Feature	Elev
1031.2	1154.1	**Peters Mountain Shelter** 22.3◄15.0◄6.7◄▶18.0▶31.4▶35.5 ... ◗ ⊏(16)	1188
		Weak spring 0.3 mile steeply downhill from shelter (300 rock steps).	
1030.2	1155.1	Victoria Trail. ⌂ See State Game Lands guidelines pg. 113	1202
1029.6	1155.7	Whitetail Trail	1325
1028.5	1156.8	Kinter View	1320
1027.1	1158.2	Shikellimy Trail 0.9E to parking area. N40 26.259 W76 49.185 P	1164
1026.1	1159.2	Campsite	1366
1024.8	1160.5	Spring 100 yards east on side trail	700
1024.5	1160.8	PA 325, Clarks Creek north of road. N40 27.092 W76 46.574 P	550
1024.2	1161.1	Spring	604
1024.1	1161.2	Henry Knauber Trail to east	682
1022.8	1162.5	Spring	1286
1021.2	1164.1	Horse-Shoe Trail to east	1650
1020.5	1164.8	Rattling Run.	1533
1018.0	1167.3	Yellow Springs Trail	1386
1017.8	1167.5	Clearing with trail register, camping; Yellow Springs Village Site, old coal mining settlement (0.7W)	1450
1016.9	1168.4	Spring	1402
1015.7	1169.6	Sand Spring Trail west to "The General"	1382
1015.5	1169.8	Cold Spring Trail to east	1400
1013.3	1172.0	Spring, campsite	1113
1013.2	1172.1	**Rausch Gap Shelter** (0.3E) 33.0◄24.7◄18.0◄▶13.4▶17.5▶32.6 ⊏(6)	1094
1012.7	1172.6	At on gravel road for 0.2 mile, bridge over Rausch Creek	925
1012.4	1172.9	Cemetery to west	877
1012.2	1173.1	Stony Creek, footbridge	842

1122.8   Ridge Rd, Biddle Rd

🛏⛺📶🖥 **Pheasant Field B&B** (0.5W) 717-258-0717 $135/up, free pickup and return with stay, free laundry, behaved pets ok. Go 0.25W to Hickory Town Rd, turn left on road, B&B on right.

1125.5   US 11 (Carlisle Pike), *Carlisle, PA 17013* (0.5W to hotels)
The AT passes over the highway on a footbridge. Side trails are bushwhacked down to the road on either end. Most businesses listed below are on the outskirts of Carlisle to the west in view from the overpass. Hotels run short of rooms (and go up in price) every other weekend when there is a car show.

🛏⛺📶🖥✉ **Super 8 Motel**   717-249-7000 $54.99S, $59.99D, cont. breakfast, $10 pet fee, free WiFi, computer $1/20mins. Guest maildrops: 1800 Harrisburg Pike, Carlisle, PA 17013.

🛏⛺📶 **Days Inn** 717-245-2242 $55/up, cont B, $20 pet fee.

🛏⛺📶🖥✉ **Red Roof Inn** 717-245-2400 call for rates. Maildrops: 1450 Harrisburg Pike, Carlisle, PA 17015.

🛏📶 **Americas Best Value Inn** 717-249-7775 $49.99/up, cont B, $15 pet fee.

🛏📶🖥⛺ **Hotel Carlisle** 717-243-1717 $25 pet fee.

🍴 **Middlesex Diner** 24hrs.

🍴🏧🚿⛺ **Flying J Truckstop** 717-243-6659, 24hrs. Has store, diner, pizza by the slice, showers ($12) and laundry.

Mechanicsburg, PA 17050 (7E)
Large city with many motels, restaurants, and retail.

🛏🍸 **Park Inn** 717-697-0321 Notable due to its two sizeable bars (**Legends Sports Bar & Grille** and **Buck Wild's Roadhouse**) and sand volleyball courts.

1142.5   High St

Duncannon, PA 17020 (more services on map)

🛏⊛🍴🖥✉ **Doyle Hotel** 717-834-6789, $25S, $7.50EAP + tax, bar serves L/D, iso canisters, Coleman/alcohol/oz, accepts Visa/MC/Disc. Maildrops: (USPS/UPS) 7 North Market Street, Duncannon, PA 17020.

🛏⛺ **Motel Stardust** 717-834-3191 Sometimes pickup/return rides available.

🛏📶 **Red Carpet Inn** 717-834-3320 $55S, $65D + tax.

⛵🚌 **Riverfront Campground** 717-834-5252, south of the Clarks Ferry Bridge, sites and shower $5PP, shuttles.

🍴 **Road Hawg BBQ** Th-Su

🍴 **Zeiderelli's Pizza & Subs** 717-834-3331

🍴 **Sorrento Pizza** 717-834-5167

🍴 **Goodies** Breakfast 6am-11am

🍴 **Ranch House Restaurant** B/L/D, near Motel Stardust has dinner buffet F-Sa, breakfast on weekends.

🏪 **Mutzabaugh's Market** 717-834-3121 7 days, pickup/return to Doyle 4pm daily.

🏥 **Rite Aid** next door to market.

🏧🍴🚿⛺ **Pilot Travel Plaza** 717-834-3156, $8 showers.

🐾 **Cove Mountain Animal Hospital** 717-834-5534

📶 **Store 34** M-F 12-7, Sa 10-4. High speed internet $3.00/30 min, $5/hr.

🔧 **Maguire's True Value Hardware** Coleman and Heet.

🚌 **Trail Angel Mary** 717-834-4706 2 Ann St, Duncannon, PA 17020

🥾 **Blue Mountain Outfitters** 717-957-2413 8mi south in Maryville, PA

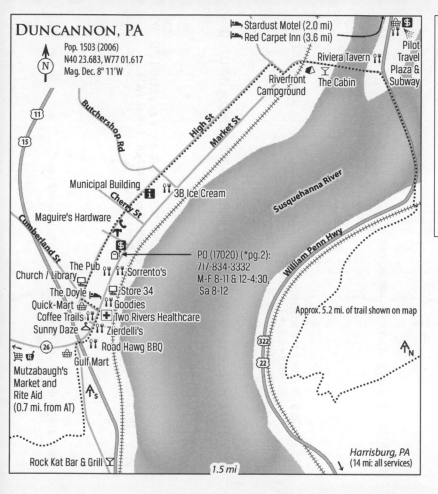

DUNCANNON, PA

Pop. 1503 (2006)
N40 23.683, W77 01.617
Mag. Dec. 8° 11'W

Stardust Motel (2.0 mi)
Red Carpet Inn (3.6 mi)

Riviera Tavern

Pilot Travel Plaza & Subway

Riverfront Campground

The Cabin

Butchershop Rd

High St

Market St

Susquehanna River

Municipal Building

3B Ice Cream

Maguire's Hardware

Cherry St

Cumberland St

PO (17020) (*pg.2):
717-834-3332
M-F 8-11 & 12-4:30,
Sa 8-12

William Penn Hwy

The Pub

Church / Library

Sorrento's

The Doyle

Store 34

Quick-Mart

Goodies

Coffee Trails

Two Rivers Healthcare

Sunny Daze

Zierdelli's

Approx. 5.2 mi. of trail shown on map

Road Hawg BBQ

Gulf Mart

Mutzabaugh's
Market and
Rite Aid
(0.7 mi. from AT)

Rock Kat Bar & Grill

1.5 mi

Harrisburg, PA
(14 mi: all services)

The AT is on **State Game Lands** in PA from north of Peters Mtn Shelter to Wind Gap, with the exception of small patches of land, mostly near major road crossings. Watch for posted regulations.

Primitive one-night camping is allowed:
- Only by hikers starting and ending at different locations.
- Within 200 feet of the AT, and
- 500 feet from water sources, trailheads, road crossings, and parking areas.
- Only small campfires are allowed, and only when the wildfire danger is less than "high."

Rausch Gap Shelter, Bake Oven Knob and George Outerbridge Shelters are on State Game Lands.

113
PA

Elev	
1357	
656	
583	
491	
695	
480	
450	
614	
1382	
1421	
1235	
1286	
1335	
1473	
1450	
1500	

114

PA

SoBo	NoBo	
1011.1	1174.2	Second Mountain
1009.4	1175.9	Field
1009.1	1176.2	Cross two roads: Greenpoint School Rd, then PA 72
1008.5	1176.8	Pass under PA 72 and cross PA 443 N40 28.923 W76 33.038 P
		Stream, campsite south of PA 72
1007.7	1177.6	Campsite
1007.1	1178.2	Swatara Gap, PA 72, **Lickdale, PA** (2.1E) (pg.116)
1006.7	1178.6	I-81, AT passes underneath
1006.4	1178.9	Gravel road
1002.5	1182.8	Abandoned powerline overlook, view
999.8	1185.5	**William Penn Shelter** (0.1E)
		38.1◀31.4◀13.4▶4.1▶19.2▶33.9
		Water and tent sites 0.1W on blue-blazed trail.
997.7	1187.6	PA 645, Waggoners Gap Rd N40 30.396 W76 22.609 P (pg.116-117)
		Pine Grove, PA (3.4W)
996.5	1188.8	Fisher Lookout, view
995.8	1189.5	Kimmel Lookout, view
995.7	1189.6	PA 501, **501 Shelter** (0.1W) N40 30.751 W76 20.664 P **Pine Grove, PA** (4.2W)
		35.5◀17.5◀4.1▶15.1▶29.8▶ 38.9 **Pine Grove, PA** (4.2W)
995.2	1190.1	Trail to Pilger Ruh (Pilgrims Rest), spring to east, **Bethel, PA** (4.1E)
		Applebee Campsite to west.
992.6	1192.7	Round Head, Shower Steps Trail, campsite to south on AT.
		Side trail to view.

SoBo	NoBo		Elev
990.6	1194.7	Overlook, view 📷	1402
990.2	1195.1	⚠ NoBo: AT turns east, Boulderfield Trail to west (straight ahead)	1278
990.1	1195.2	Hertline Campsite and picnic table	1200
989.4	1195.9	Pipeline, road paralleling pipeline, cross twice, then parallel to AT	1505
986.7	1198.6	Fort Dietrich Snyder Monument (0.2W)	1424
986.4	1198.9	PA 183, Rentschler Marker on side trail 30 yards north of road	1375
985.9	1199.4	Game Commission road (gravel) N40 31.636 W76 12.888 P	1429
985.1	1200.2	Black Swatara Spring 0.3E	1510
982.5	1202.8	Eagles Nest Trail to east	1580
981.3	1204.0	Sand Spring Trail 0.2E to spring	1510
980.6	1204.7	Eagles Nest Shelter (0.3W), spring on trail to shelter ⊂(8) 32.6◄19.2◄15.1◄►14.7►23.8►31.2	1593
978.7	1206.6	Shartlesville-Cross Mtn Rd (overgrown dirt road)	1450
976.0	1209.3	Phillips Canyon Spring (unmarked, unreliable)	1500
974.0	1211.3	State Game Land Rd	1415
973.4	1211.9	Pipeline clearing, AT crosses multiple times	1408
971.8	1213.5	Schuylkill Trail 2.4E to Hamburg, parking 0.1N N40 34.774 W76 1.600 P	551
971.6	1213.7	Port Clinton, PA, Broad St + Penn St (pg.118-119)	426
971.3	1214.0	PA 61, Blue Mtn Rd, Hamburg, PA (1.7E) (pg.118-119)	490

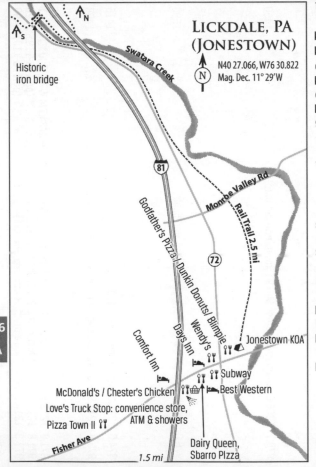

1177.9   Swatara Gap, PA 72
Lickdale, PA (Jonestown) (2.1E)
🛏♿🛜🖥 **Days Inn** 717-865-4064 $55/up, cont B, pets $15, jacuzzi.
🛏♿🛜🖥 **Best Western** 717-865-4234 $89.99/up, cont B. Guests get 10% discount at Sbarro and DQ, indoor heated pool, pet fee $15.
🛏♿🛜🖥 **Comfort Inn** 717-865-8080 Summer rates $75S, $80D plus tax, cont B, pets $10, pool.
🛏🍴🚿♿ **Jonestown KOA** 877-865-6411 Open 7 days. Summer 5am-9pm. Tentsite $31/up, cabin sleeps 4 $60/up. Pets on leash okay.
🍴💲🚿📞 **Love's Truckstop** $10 showers, ATM, 24 Hrs

1187.6   PA 645
Pine Grove, PA (3.4W) *(more services on map)*
🍴**Original Italian Pizza** 570-345-5432 Delivers to 501 shelter.
🍴**Sholls Family Restaurant** 570-345-8715 Open Tu-Su, delivers to 501 shelter.
🍴💲🚿♿ **Pilot Travel Center** 570-345-8800, 24hr, other side of 81, **Subway, Dairy Queen** and **Auntie Anne's Pretzel**, shower $12.
🛒 **Bergers Market** 570-345-3663, open 7 days
🚌 **Carlin's AT Shuttle Service** 570-345-0474. Shuttles anywhere in PA.
      4.8W near intersection of I-81
🛏🛜🖥**Comfort Inn** 570-345-8031 $65 includes hot breakfast. Hiker friendly, honors flat rate all season, pool, $10/pet.
🛏🛜 **Econo Lodge** 570-345-4099 Hiker rate $50 when room available, includes full breakfast. Pets $10 allowed in smoking rooms only.
🛏🛜 **Relax Inn** 570-345-8095 $50-$55, Pets $10. HBO.

1189.6   PA 501
Bethel, PA (4.1E) *(services on map)*
⊏ **501 Shelter** Caretaker house nearby, solar shower, water from hose near shower, no alcohol, no smoking in shelter, pets on leash.
      Pine Grove, PA 17963 (4.2W)

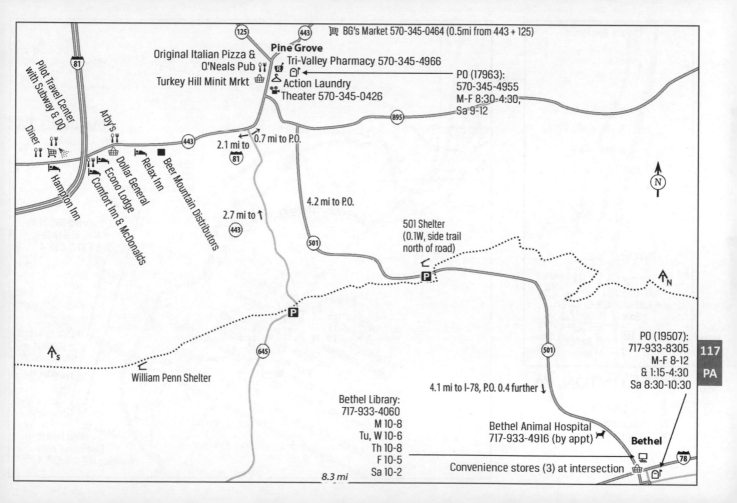

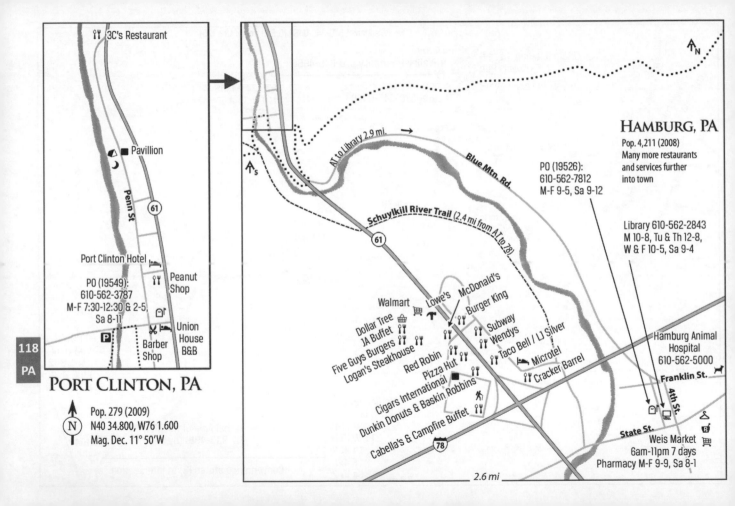

1213.7   Broad St, Penn St
Port Clinton, PA 19549 *(more services on map)*

🛏🍴⚶ **Union House B&B** ⟨www.union-house.com⟩ 610-562-3155 after 5pm 610-562-4076, open Friday-Sunday.

🛏🍴⚶ **Port Clinton Hotel** 610-562-3354, 888-562-2626 ⟨www.portclintonhotel.net⟩ $56.68S, $62.13D, $10 deposit for room key and towel, limited rooms available. Laundry, dining Tu-Th 11-9, F-Sa 11-closing, Su 11-10, closed Monday, Please shower before use of dining room, Visa/MC accepted.

🏪 💲 **The Peanut Shop** soda, candy, dried fruit, trail mixes, ATM.

⚑ 👫 **Pavillion Tenting** sign in at pavillion, no car camping, no drive-ins.

1214.0   PA 61, Blue Mtn Rd
Hamburg, PA 19526 (1.7E) *(Walmart and many restaurants on edge of town nearest to Port Clinton, see map)*

🛏🍴⚶📶 **Microtel Inn** 610-562-4234 ⟨www.microtelinn.com⟩ $84.50S $100.50 up to 4, includes continental breakfast. **Pappy T's** pub & lounge on-site.

🥾 **Cabela's** 610-929-7000, M-Sa 8-9, Su 9-8. Full line of hiking gear, canister fuel. Pickup from trailhead if staff is available.

🍴 **Campfire Restaurant** Inside Cabela's serves B/L/D, closes a little earlier than the store. AYCE meals on weekends.

🏪 **Turkey Hill Market**

💊 **Rite Aid** 610-562-9454, **CVS** 610-562-2454

⚶ **Hamburg Coin Laundry**

🐾 **Hamburg Animal Hospital** 610-562-5000 M-Th 9-7, Sa 9-11.

🚌 **Barta Bus Service** 610-921-0601⟨www.bartabus.com⟩ Routes within Hamburg $1.95 per boarding, stops at Cabellas.

Pottsville, PA 17901 (15W, compass north of AT on PA 61)

🍺 **Yuengling Brewery** 570-628-4890 America's oldest brewery has two tours on weekdays, as-needed on Sat. Closed-toe shoes required.

1220.1   Blue-blazed trail to campground
1222.8   Yellow-blazed trail to campground

🛏⚑🏪🍴⚶ **Blue Rocks Campground** 610-756-6366 Tentsite $32 tentsite, cabin $55/up accommodates 2 adults, 2 children. Coin showers & laundry. Open year-round with limited days Nov-Mar. Camp store closed Dec-Mar.

Leave What You Find

•Leave plants, cultural artifacts and other natural objects where you found them for others to enjoy.

•Don't build structures or dig trenches around tents.

•Do not damage live trees or plants; green wood burns poorly. Collect only firewood that is dead, down, and no larger than your wrist. Leave dead standing trees and dead limbs on standing trees for the wildlife.

•Consider using rubber tips on the bottom of your trekking poles to avoid scratch marks on rocks, "clicking" sounds, and leaving holes along the trail.

•Avoid introducing or transporting non-native species by checking your boots, socks, packs, tents, and clothing for non-native seeds that you could remove before hitting the trail.

Read more of the Leave No Trace techniques developed for the A.T.:   www.appalachiantrail.org/LNT

SoBo	NoBo	Description	Elev
968.8	1216.5	Spring to west, campsite	1199
967.6	1217.7	Minnehaha Spring, frequently dry	1374
966.2	1219.1	Reservoir Rd, stream north on AT . . . . N40 35.374 W75 56.659 ◗	889
965.9	1219.4	Parking 0.3E on AT with permission from Hamburg Borough 610-562-7821 M-F 8-5. **Windsor Furnace Shelter** (0.1W) . . . . ◗⊆(8)	867
965.2	1220.1	33.9◀29.8◀14.7▶9.1▶16.5▶26.5 No swimming, creek south of shelter. Blue-blazed trail to **Blue Rocks Campground** (1.5E) . . . . (pg.119)	1009
964.3	1221.0	Pulpit Rock, 30 yards west to privy at Pulpit Rock Astronomical Park. . . . . . . ☾🏛	1582
962.5	1222.8	Yellow-blazed trail to **Blue Rocks Campground** (1.5E) . . . . (pg.119)	1594
962.1	1223.2	The Pinnacle, 0.1E to panoramic view, no camping or fires . . . . 🏛	1615
960.4	1224.9	Furnace Creek Trail to west	1448
960.2	1225.1	Gold Spring, no camping . . . . ◗	1381
959.5	1225.8	Blue-blazed trail 1.5W reconnects with AT near Windsor Furnace Shelter	1422
959.2	1226.1	Pinnacle Spur Trail to west	1403
958.6	1226.7	Panther Spring, dependable . . . . ◗	1074
957.7	1227.6	Parking lot 0.4E on side trail . . . . N40 37.528 W75 57.208 Ⓟ	838
956.8	1228.5	Hawk Mountain Rd, **Eckville Shelter** (0.2E) Open May-Sep . . . . ☾🚿◗⊆(6) 38.9◀23.8◀9.1▶7.4▶17.4▶24.2 Enclosed bunkroom, tent platforms, flush toilet, spigot at side of caretaker's house. 1.6W to Hawk Mountain Sanctuary.	697
956.3	1229.0	Footbridge, stream, campsite north on AT . . . . ◗▲	587
954.9	1230.4	Hawk Mtn Trail to west	1377
953.8	1231.5	Dans Pulpit, trail register . . . . 🏛	1597
953.2	1232.1	Dans Spring 0.1E . . . . △	1565

SoBo	NoBo			Elev
950.6	1234.7	Tri-County Corner, ⚠ AT to west.		1532
949.4	1235.9	**Allentown Hiking Club Shelter**	☾ 🛖 ⼷(8)	1500
		31.2◀16.5◀7.4◀▶10.0▶16.8▶33.5		
949.1	1236.2	Unreliable spring downhill in front of shelter 0.2 mile, another 0.1 farther. Springs to east; Blue 100 yards, Yellow 0.3 mi	♦	1340
947.5	1237.8	Fort Franklin Rd (gravel)	N40 41.655 W75 50.515 [P]	1350
945.6	1239.7	Trail 0.2W to restaurant (closer to AT + PA 309)		1354
945.3	1240.0	PA 309, Blue Mountain Summit	N40 42.429 W75 48.516 [P] (pg.122)	1360
943.4	1241.9	Powerline, New Tripoli Campsite 0.2W.	♦	1488
942.2	1243.1	Knife Edge, view	📷	1630
941.8	1243.5	Bear Rocks, view	📷	1604
940.4	1244.9	Bake Oven Knob Rd (gravel)	N40 44.677 W75 44.314 [P]	1450
940.0	1245.3	Bake Oven Knob.		1560
939.4	1245.9	**Bake Oven Knob Shelter** 26.5◀17.4◀10.0◀▶6.8▶23.5▶37.3	♦ 🛖 ⼷(6)	1404
		Trail in front leads downhill to multiple water sources, more reliable farther down.		
937.0	1248.3	Lehigh Furnace Gap, Ashfield Rd, Comm tower	N40 46.173 W75 41.649 [P]	1320
935.8	1249.5	South Mountain Trail 0.3E to view	📷	1583
934.2	1251.1	North Trail (scenic route) to west, TV tower, AT is over Lehigh Valley Tunnel		1506
933.8	1251.5	Tower access road		1486
932.8	1252.5	North Trail (scenic route) to west		1085
932.6	1252.7	**George W. Outerbridge Shelter**, reliable piped spring 0.1N.	♦ ⼷(6)	999
		24.2◀16.8◀6.8◀▶16.7▶30.5▶61.7		
932.1	1253.2	Lehigh River, south bank, PA 873, **Slatington, PA** (2.0E)	(pg.122)	437
931.6	1253.7	PA 248/145 traffic light, **Walnutport, PA** (2.0E)	(pg.122)	506
931.4	1253.9	Superfund Trailhead, **Palmerton, PA** (1.5W) N40 46.989 W75 36.247 [P] (pg.123)		515
		Water 0.4W on blue-blazed trail to Palmerton.		

1240.0 PA 309

🛏🏕🍴🚌✉💧 **Blue Mountain Summit B&B** 570-386-2003 ⟨www.bluemountainsummit.com⟩ In view to west. $95–$125D includes breakfast. Open 7 days by appt. No pets. Help yourself to water at outside spigot at southwest corner of building. Please be respectful of non-hiking guests at the B&B and restaurant; okay to hang out in back, but please don't loiter in front or hang clothes to dry. Camping with permission, no fires. Ask about shuttles. Dining (summer) Th 12-9, F 12-10, Sa 11-9, Su 11-8; winter (after Thanksgiving) Th hours 4-9, F-Su same as summer. Live music on Fridays. All major credit cards accepted. Guest maildrops (call first): 2520 W Penn Pike, Andreas, PA 18211.

1253.2 Lehigh River, PA 873
Slatington, PA 18080 (2E) *(more services on map)*
🍴 **Slatington Diner** B/L
💊 **Bechtel's Pharmacy** 610-767-4121
💻 **Slatington Library** 610-767-6461 M,W: 9-7, Tu 9-3, F 9-5, Sa 8-2.
🔧 **AF Boyer Hardware**

1253.7 PA 248/145
Walnutport, PA 18088 (2E)
🛒 **Pathmark Supermarket** 610-760-8008, M-Sa 6-12pm, Su 6-10.
🍴 **Valley Pizza Family Restaurant** 610-767-9000 L/D, delivers.
➕ **St Luke's Family Practice Center** 610-760-8080
💊 **Rite Aid Pharmacy** 610-767-9595
🐕 **Blue Ridge Veterinary Clinic** 610-767-4896 Call before coming.

122
PA

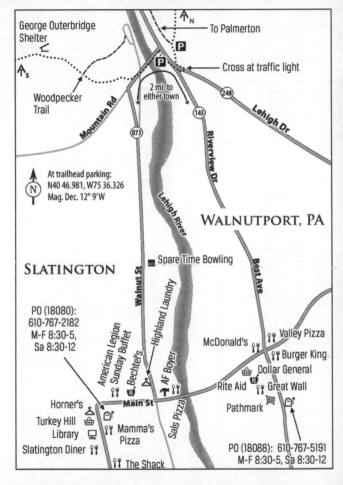

George Outerbridge Shelter

To Palmerton

Cross at traffic light

Woodpecker Trail

Mountain Rd

873

2 mi. to either town

145

248

Lehigh Dr

Riverview Dr

Lehigh River

At trailhead parking:
N40 46.981, W75 36.326
Mag. Dec. 12° 9'W

WALNUTPORT, PA

Spare Time Bowling

SLATINGTON

Walnut St

Best Ave

Highland Laundry

PO (18080):
610-767-2182
M-F 8:30-5,
Sa 8:30-12

American Legion
Sunday Buffet

Bechtel's

AF Boyer

Sals Pizza

McDonald's

Valley Pizza

Burger King

Dollar General

Rite Aid

Great Wall

Pathmark

Horner's
Turkey Hill
Library
Slatington Diner

Main St

Mamma's Pizza

The Shack

PO (18088): 610-767-5191
M-F 8:30-5, Sa 8:30-12

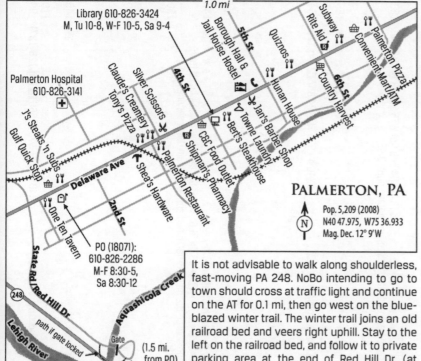

Library 610-826-3424
M, Tu 10-8, W-F 10-5, Sa 9-4

PALMERTON, PA

Pop. 5,209 (2008)
N40 47.975, W75 36.933
Mag. Dec. 12° 9'W

Palmerton Hospital
610-826-3141

PO (18071):
610-826-2286
M-F 8:30-5,
Sa 8:30-12

(1.5 mi.
from PO)

It is not advisable to walk along shoulderless, fast-moving PA 248. NoBo intending to go to town should cross at traffic light and continue on the AT for 0.1 mi, then go west on the blue-blazed winter trail. The winter trail joins an old railroad bed and veers right uphill. Stay to the left on the railroad bed, and follow it to private parking area at the end of Red Hill Dr. (at bottom left of town map). Cross Red Hill bridge and follow the road into town. If the bridge is gated or access is denied, hop the guardrail to PA 248, cautiously cross Aquashicola Creek on the 248 bridge, then hop the guardrail again to retun to Red Hill Drive. The total distance to town is 1.5W miles on level ground.

1253.9   Superfund Trailhead
Palmerton, PA 18071 (1.5W)
Town Ordinance: Pets must be kept on leash.
🏠⊕ **Jail House Hostel** 610-826-2505
443 Delaware Avenue. Basement of the borough hall was never used as a jail. Hikers stay free; showers available. Check in at the borough office before 4pm on weekdays. Check in at police station after hours and on weekends. 10pm curfew. ID is required. One night limit, no vehicle-assisted hikers. No pets inside, but they can be left leashed outside.
🛏🐾 **Sunny Rest Resort** 610-377-2911 *Clothing optional* resort 2 miles outside of town, rides sometimes available. Hotel rooms $84-114 weekdays, day visit $44/couple; prices higher on weekends. Camping $71. Restaurant (B/L/D), nightclub, two heated pools, outdoor bar, volleyball, nature trails, WiFi. 425 Sunny Rest Rd, Palmerton, PA.
🍴 **Palmerton Restaurant** 610-826-5454 Dining M-Th 4-10, F-Su 11-10.
🛒🅂 **Country Harvest** 610-824-3663 8am-9pm 7 days.
🍴🖥 **Bert's Restaurant** B/L/D, has internet access.
🍴 **Tony's Pizzeria** L/D, no delivery.
🍴 **Joe's Place** L/D, deli sandwiches.
✚ **Palmerton Hospital** 610-826-3141
🐾 **Little Gap Animal Hospital** 610-826-2793 (3.5W) from town.
⚠ **Laundromat** 5am-7pm 7 days.
🚌 **Brenda** 484-725-9396 Local shuttles and limited work-for-stay.
🚌 **Jason "SoulFlute"** 484-224-6981 Palmerton-area shuttles, slackpacks Port Clinton-DWG.

123
PA

124
PA

SoBo	NoBo	Description	Elev
930.6	**1254.7**	Superfund Detour south end	1429
		Rocky, steep trail from Lehigh Gap. Deforested ridge due to zinc smelting from 1898-1980. Palmerton Superfund site.	
928.0	1257.3	High metallic content spring 0.1W (unmarked N40 48.305 W75 33.408) emergency water source.	1383
927.8	1257.5	Superfund Detour north, powerline	1360
926.7	**1258.6**	Little Gap Rd, **Danielsville, PA** (1.5E) N40 48.369 W75 32.077 **P** (pg.126)	1100
926.3	1259.0	Tower access road (gavel)	1330
923.1	1262.2	Dirt road, powerline.	1553
921.9	1263.4	Delps Trail to east, Campsite near trail intersection, unreliable spring 0.4E △ (0.4E) N40 48.551 W75 27.073 **P** (0.7E)	1580
920.3	1265.0	Stempa Spring 0.6E	1557
919.4	1265.9	Smith Gap Rd (paved) N40 49.530 W75 24.857 **P** (pg.126)	1540
915.9	**1269.4**	**Leroy A. Smith Shelter** (0.2E). 33.5◄23.5◄16.7◄▶13.8▶45.0▶51.6 Water 0.2 mile down blue-blazed trail; second source 0.2 mile farther. Piped spring 0.5 mile down service road. (8)	1477
915.7	1269.6	Powerline	1500
914.0	1271.3	Pipeline	1501
912.3	1273.0	Hahns Overlook, view.	1450
911.5	1273.8	Powerline	1108
911.3	1274.0	PA 33, **Wind Gap, PA** (1.0E) N40 51.639 W75 17.565 **P** (pg.126-127)	980

SoBo	NoBo	Description		Elev
909.2	1276.1	Private road (gravel)		1585
905.5	1279.8	Campsite		1632
904.9	1280.4	Wolf Rocks bypass trail south end to west. Spring 100 yards west (treat)		1586
904.4	1280.9	Wolf Rocks, view		1616
903.8	1281.5	Wolf Rocks bypass trail north end to west.		1542
902.7	1282.6	Fox Gap, PA 191 (paved)	N40 56.126 W75 11.815 P	1400
902.1	1283.2	**Kirkridge Shelter** 37.3◄30.5◄13.8◄►31.2►37.8►43.6		1467
		Tap 0.1 mile to back left of shelter, off in cold months. ◣ ⌒ ⊂(6)		
901.8	1283.5	Campsite, view		1505
900.2	1285.1	Totts Gap, gravel road, powerline to south		1300
899.9	1285.4	Pipeline		1381
899.6	1285.7	Roadbed.		1402
898.2	1287.1	Mt Minsi		1461
897.2	1288.1	Lookout Rock, view		800
897.0	1288.3	Stream.		837
896.4	1288.9	Council Rock		600
896.3	1289.0	Turn east on gravel road		629
895.7	1289.4	Hiker parking lot	N40 58.788 W75 8.518 P	549
895.5	1289.5	PA 611, **Delaware Water Gap, PA** (pg.128)		425
895.4	1289.6	**PA-NJ border**, I-80, Delaware River Bridge west bank		324
894.4	1290.9	Kittatinny Visitor Center	N40 58.219 W75 7.729 P H	313
		NoBo: cross under I-80 and turn left.		
894.0	1291.3	Parking, water pump (disabled in winter) V.C. is preferred for overnight.	P	321
		parking, Stop "camping for A.T. through hikers" refers to a site 3.0N on AT.		
893.7	1291.6	Dunnfield Trail to east		472
892.5	1292.8	Holly Spring Trail		950
890.4	1294.9	Backpacker Campsite, Douglas Trail to west, water south of camp. No fires, use bear boxes/poles, leash dogs.		1287

1258.6   Little Gap Rd

🍴💧 **Slopeside Grill** 0.2W and 0.5mi up driveway. Hikers welcome to get water from outside spigot. Grill hours: Fri 5-11pm, Sat 2-11pm, Sun 2-9pm.

Danielsville, PA 18038 (1.5E on Blue Mountain Dr, then left on Mountainview Dr to PO and B&B.)
🏤 M-F 8:30-12 & 2-4:30, Sa 8-12, 610-767-6882
🛏⛺🚐📶✉ **Filbert B&B** 610-428-3300 ⟨www.filbertbnb.com⟩ $100S, $150D. Hosted by Kathy in Victorian farmhouse with A/C includes full country breakfast. Will pickup at Little Gap (no charge). Fee for pickup at PA 309, Lehigh Gap, Smith Gap, or Wind Gap. Call ahead for reservations, surcharge for credit cards. Laundry for a fee. Parking for section hikers, ask about shuttles. Italian & Chinese restaurants will deliver. Maildrops: 3740 Filbert Dr, Danielsville, PA 18038.
🍴💲 (0.8E) **Blue Mountain Restaurant & Ice Cream** 610-767-6379.
🏪 (1.0E) **Miller's Market**

1265.9   Smith Gap Rd

💧🚿🚐🅿 (1.0W) Home of John "Mechanical Man" and Linda "Crayon Lady" Stempa, eponym of the spring 0.7 mile south. The Stempas (610-381-4606) welcome you to get water from the spigot at rear of the house (no need to call) and to use the outside shower during daylight hours. Pet friendly. Please sign register. This is a safe place to park your car. For-fee shuttles ranging from Port Clinton to Delaware Water Gap. Sodas $1, ask about stoves and fuel. When they are home and **only with permission**, camp or stay in garage with hot shower, towel and ride to take out food and ATM when available, and ride back to trail for $10; call in advance.

🍴🏪🚿⛺ (2.7W) **Evergreen Lake** 610-837-6401 West 1.7 on Smith Gap Road, then left one mile on Mountain Road. Tenting $28 for up to 2 adults, 2 children. Snack shop, laundry, free showers.

1274.0   PA 33

🛏(0.1W) **Gateway Motel** 610-863-4959, $60S $65D. Sells soda and bottled water. Non-guests: please do not loiter on lawn or use hose.
🐾 (4W) **Creature Comforts** 610-381-2287, 24/7 emergency care.

Wind Gap, PA 18091 (1E)
🏤 M-F 8:30-5, Sa 8:30-12, 610-863-6206
🛏📶 **Travel Inn** 610-863-4146 $59D weekdays, $69D weekends. Room for 4 $69 weekdays, $79 weekends, no pets.
🛏📶 **Red Carpet Inn** 610-863-7782
🛒 **Giant Food Store** 24hr, deli with salad bar.
🛒💊 **K-Mart** with pharmacy
🏪 **Turkey Hill Market**
🍴🍺 **Beer Stein** Hiker friendly, hose outside, ask about camping. Serves L/D wings, seafood.
🍴 **J&R's Smokehouse** L/D
🍴 **Sal's Pizza** 610-863-7565, delivers
🍴 **Hong Kong Chinese** L/D buffet
💊 **CVS** 610-863-5341
➕ **Priority Care** 610-654-5454 Walk-in clinic M-F 8am-8pm, Sa 10am-5pm, Su 10am-4pm.
➕ **Slate Belt Family Practice** 610-863-3019
🎬 **Gap Theatre** 610-863-3094 Movies F-Su.

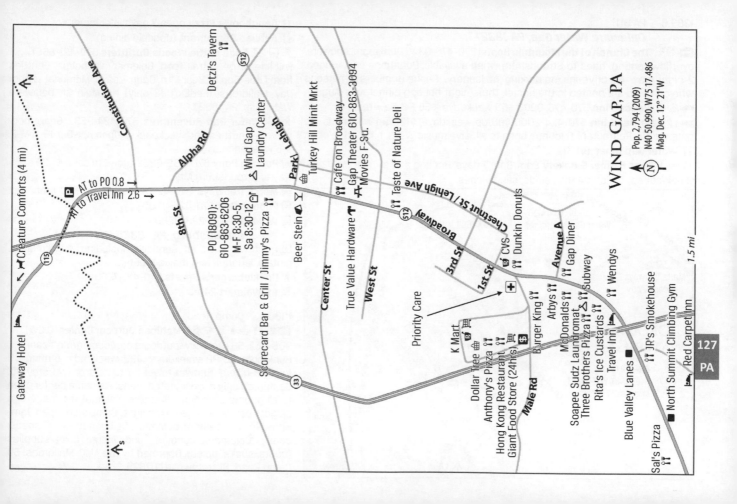

WIND GAP, PA

Pop. 2,794 (2009)
N40 50.990, W75 17.486
Mag. Dec. 12° 21'W

Detzi's Tavern
512

Constitution Ave

Creature Comforts (4 mi)

Alpha Rd

Wind Gap Laundry Center

Lehigh

Turkey Hill Minit Mrkt

Park

Cafe on Broadway

Gap Theater 610-863-3094

Movies F-Su.

AT to PO 0.8 →
AT to Travel Inn 2.6 →

Taste of Nature Deli

8th St

Dunkin Donuts

PO (1809):
610-863-6206
M-F 8:30-5,
Sa 8:30-12

Beer Stein

True Value Hardware

Center St

West St

CVS

(Chestnut St / Lehigh Ave)

512

Broadway

3rd St

1st St

Avenue A

Gap Diner

Subway

Wendys

Scorecard Bar & Grill / Jimmy's Pizza

115

Gateway Hotel

33

Priority Care

K Mart

Dollar Tree

Anthony's Pizza

Hong Kong Restaurant

Giant Food Store (24hrs)

Male Rd

Burger King

McDonalds

Arbys

Soapee Sudz Laundromat

Three Brothers Pizza

Rita's Ice Custards

Travel Inn

JR's Smokehouse

North Summit Climbing Gym

Red Carpet Inn

Blue Valley Lanes

Sal's Pizza

N

1.5 mi

127
PA

Delaware Water Gap, PA 18327

🏠👁🍽 **The Church of the Mountain Hostel** 570-476-0345 Bunkroom, showers, overflow tenting, rides to Stroudsburg when available. Donations encouraged. 2-night max. No drive-ins, no parking, no laundry. Phone numbers of persons who can help are posted in the hostel. Thurs night hot dog dinner June-Aug.

🏠⛺🛜 **Pocono Inn** 570-476-0000 $55 weekdays, $65 F & Sa + tax.

🏠🍽 **Deer Head Inn** 570-424-2000 $90/up weekdays, $120/up weekends. No pets, no TV. Restaurant & lounge open to all. Live music W-Su, hiker attire okay.

🍽 **Water Gap Diner** B/L/D

🍽🏛 **Village Farmer & Bakery** 8am-8pm 7 days. Hot dog and slice of pie $2.49. Breakfast sandwich $4.99, salads, sandwiches.

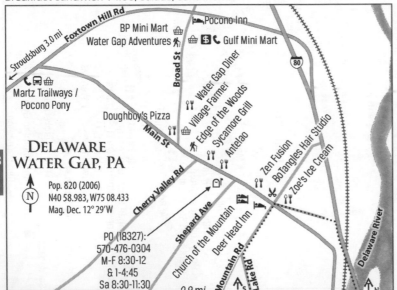

128
PA

🍽 **Doughboy's Pizza** open 7 days in summer.

🍽 **Antelao Restaurant** (upscale dining)

🚶🚌✉ **Edge of the Woods Outfitters** 570-421-6681 Full line of gear, trail food. Coleman/alcohol/oz. Shuttles from Little Gap to Bear Mtn. Open 7 days, Memorial - Labor Day. Maildrops: (FedEx/UPS only) 110 Main St, Delaware Water Gap, PA 18327.

🚶🚌 **Water Gap Adventures** 570-424-8533 Gear, food, fuel/oz, shuttles and slackpacks. Open Apr-Oct 10-5 M-F, 8-6 weekends.

🚌 **Pocono Pony** 570-839-6862 ⟨gomcta.com⟩ $1.25 each way to Stroudsburg Mall.

🚌 **Martz Trailways** 570-421-3040 $56.50 NYC roundtrip.

🚌 **Pocono Cab** 570-424-2800

🚌 **WGM Taxi** 570-223-9289

Stroudsburg, PA 18360 (3.5W)

Large town with all services, including supermarket, motels, laundry, and movie theater.

🚶 **Dunkleberger's Sports** 570-421-7950

🛒 **Walmart** 24hrs

1300.4   Camp Road

🏠🛏🍽🔥💧🍽🛜✉ **Mohican Outdoor Center** (0.3W) 908-362-5670 ⟨www.outdoors.org/lodging/mohican/⟩ Bunkroom $31PP weekdays, $39 weekends, tenting $9 for thru-hikers. Shower/towel for tenters or w/o stay $5. Campfires only in designated areas. Welcome center open to all guests 8am-8pm. Water available at the lodge or a spigot near the garage on the right. Camp store open 9am-5pm (7pm in peak of summer). Deli sandwiches, sodas, candy, Coleman/alcohol/oz, and limited hiker supplies (boots, socks, poles). Operated by the AMC. Maildrops: 50 Camp Road, Blairstown, NJ 07825.

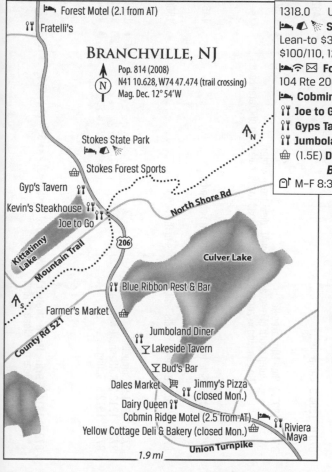

Forest Motel (2.1 from AT)

Fratelli's

BRANCHVILLE, NJ

Pop. 814 (2008)
N41 10.628, W74 47.474 (trail crossing)
Mag. Dec. 12° 54'W

Stokes State Park

Stokes Forest Sports

Gyp's Tavern

Kevin's Steakhouse

Joe to Go

Kittatinny Lake

Mountain Trail

206

North Shore Rd

Culver Lake

Blue Ribbon Rest & Bar

Farmer's Market

County Rd 521

Jumboland Diner

Lakeside Tavern

Bud's Bar

Dales Market

Jimmy's Pizza (closed Mon.)

Dairy Queen

Cobmin Ridge Motel (2.5 from AT)

Yellow Cottage Deli & Bakery (closed Mon.)

Riviera Maya

Union Turnpike

1.9 mi

1318.0   US 206, Culvers Gap *(more services on map)*

Stokes State Park 973-948-3820 Prices listed as NJ resident/nonresident. Lean-to $30/40. Tentsite 1-6 persons $20/25. Cabins: 4-person $55/65, 8-person $100/110, 12-person $140/150. Free showers w/o stay.

Forest Motel 973-948-5456, $45S $55D + tax, pets $20. Guest maildrops: 104 Rte 206 N, Branchville, NJ 07826.

Cobmin Ridge Motel 973-948-3459

Joe to Go ⚠ Watch for posted rules, proprietor will enforce them.

Gyps Tavern ⚠ Packs outside; hikers please eat/drink on patio, not at bar.

Jumboland Diner B/L/D, $2.99 breakfast, Thursday dinner buffet, ice cream.

(1.5E) **Dale's Market** 973-948-3078 M-F 6-9, Sa-Su 7-9

Branchville, NJ 07826 (3.4E)

M-F 8:30-5, Sa 8:30-1, 973-948-3580

1332.3   NJ 23

High Point State Park Headquarters 973-875-4800 Office open year-round 9am-4pm, F & Sa 8-8 in summer. Bathrooms inside, water spigot outside. **Sawmill Lake Camping Area** 2.5 mile from HQ, tentsites $20 NJ resident/$25 non-resident. Maildrops: 1480 State Rte 23, Sussex, NJ 07461.

(1.5E) **High Point Mountain Motel** 973-702-1860 Recently renovated rooms $79.99D, pets $5, no room phone. Laundry $7. Free pickup/return to trail from NJ 23, longer shuttles for a fee. Guest maildrops: 1328 NJ 23, Wantage, NJ 07461.

Port Jervis, NY 12785 (4.4W)

Days Inn 845-856-6611 $65D, $10EAP, cont B, pets $20. Guest maildrops: 2247 Greenville Turnpike, Port Jervis, NY 12771.

Village Pizza 973-293-3364

Shop Rite Market, **Price Chopper**

Rite Aid 845-856-8342, **Medicine Shoppe** 845-856-6681

Bon Secours Community Hospital 845-858-7000

Tri-States Veterinary Medical 845-856-1914

129
NJ

SoBo	NoBo	Feature	Elev
889.6	1295.7	Sunfish Pond south end, no swimming or camping.	1382
889.0	1296.3	Sunfish Pond north end, rock sculptures	1384
888.1	1297.2	Stream.	1452
887.4	1297.9	Powerline	1560
887.3	1298.0	Kittatinny Mountain, rocky summit	1513
886.7	1298.6	Kaiser Trail to west	1410
884.9	1300.4	Camp Rd (gravel), footbridge N41 1.977 W75 0.237 P (pg.128) **Mohican Outdoor Center** (0.3W)	1111
883.7	1301.6	Rattlesnake Swamp Trail, view.	1472
882.8	1302.5	Catfish Lookout Tower, picnic table below the tower	1565
882.2	1303.1	Rattlesnake Spring on dirt road about 17 yards west of AT	1260
881.9	1303.4	Stream.	1248
881.7	1303.6	Millbrook-Blairstown Rd (paved) N41 3.567 W74 57.815 P Millbrook Village (1.1W) historical park with picnic area.	1280
881.4	1303.9	Swamp	1251
881.1	1304.2	Powerline	1392
879.0	1306.3	Campsite	1492
877.9	1307.4	Blue Mtn Lakes Rd Pump south of road and west of AT (disabled in winter). No camping in zone from 0.5 mile of road to one mile north of Crater Lake.	1350
875.8	1309.5	Side trail leads 0.5E to Crater Lake. No camping.	1454
874.8	1310.5	Buttermilk Falls Trail, campsites to the north	1560
873.5	1311.8	Campsite	1306
873.1	1312.2	Rattlesnake Mountain	1492
872.8	1312.5	Spring	1362
870.9	1314.4	**Brink Road Shelter** (0.2W)(2013) 61.7◄45.0◄31.2◄►6.6►12.4►15.3 ⌂(8) Bear box. Close to road.	1234

SoBo	NoBo	Feature	Elev
869.7	1315.6	Jacobs Ladder Trail	1374
867.9	1317.4	Powerline	1239
867.3	1318.0	US 206, Culvers Gap, **Branchville, NJ** (3.4E) (pg.129)	935
867.0	1318.3	Sunrise Mountain Rd (paved) N41 10.780 W74 47.277 [P]	978
865.4	1319.9	Culver Fire Tower	1526
864.4	1320.9	Stony Brook	1348
864.3	1321.0	**Gren Anderson Shelter** (0.1W) ◑●(0.1W)⌇(8) 51.6◄37.8◄6.6◄●5.8►8.7►13.0 Spring to left of shelter and downhill 70 yards.	1341
862.9	1322.4	Tinsley Trail	1454
861.9	1323.4	Sunrise Mountain, no camping at pavilion N41 10.780 W74 47.277 [P]	1653
861.2	1324.1	Roadbed.	1446
860.2	1325.1	Stream (slow outflow from pond), treatment recommended.	1391
858.5	1326.8	**Mashipacong Shelter** 43.6◄12.4◄5.8◄●2.9►7.2►19.6 ⌇(8) Spring (0.6N) on red-blazed Iris Trail. Bear box. Close to road.	1431
858.3	1327.0	Deckertown Turnpike. N41 15.136 W74 41.367 [P]	1336
857.2	1328.1	Three intersections with red-blazed trail	1436
855.6	1329.7	**Rutherford Shelter** (0.4E) 15.3◄8.7◄2.9◄●4.3►16.7►28.2 ◑●⌇(6) Spring 100 yards before shelter on connecting trail. Slow stream. Bear box.	1491
855.4	1329.9	View	1485
854.0	1331.3	Intersection with blue-blazed trail.	1596
853.2	1332.1	Iris Trail 0.2E to parking on NJ 23	1506
853.0	1332.3	NJ 23 N41 18.158 W74 40.065 [P] ● (pg.129) High Point State Park Headquarters, **Port Jervis, NY** (4.4W)	1500
852.0	1333.3	Wooden tower, 0.3W to beach & concessions Mem-Labor Day 12-6	1679
851.8	1333.5	Green-blazed trail 0.3W to 220' tower atop highest point in NJ.	1610
851.3	1334.0	**High Point Shelter** (0.1E) 13.0◄7.2◄4.3◄●12.4►23.9►36.0. ◑●⌇(8) Streams on both sides of shelter. Road to privy to right of shelter. Bear box.	1310
850.0	1335.3	Greenville Rd, County 519 (paved).	1100

Mile	Mile	Description		Elev
849.1	1336.2	Courtwright Rd (gravel), stream on AT 0.1 south of road	◆	966
848.6	1336.7	Streams	◆	951
848.0	1337.3	Fergerson Rd (gravel), east 20 yards on road.		854
847.4	1337.9	Gemmer Rd (paved)		717
847.1	1338.2	Stream.	◆	689
846.7	1338.6	Two footbridges, streams	◆	598
846.4	1338.9	Goodrich Rd (paved)		623
846.2	1339.1	Pond	◆	661
845.9	1339.4	Murray property 0.2W, gravel driveway (pg.135)	◆	655
845.5	1339.8	Goldsmith Lane (gravel)		666
845.1	1340.2	Unionville Rd (paved), County Rd 651 (pg.134)		610
844.9	1340.4	Quarry Rd		607
844.2	1341.1	Lott Rd, **Unionville, NY** (0.7W) (pg.134)		590
843.1	1342.2	NJ 284, **Unionville, NY** (0.7W) N41 17.311 W74 33.141 **P** (pg.134)		429
842.7	1342.6	Lower Rd (Oil City Rd)		511
842.2	1343.1	Carnegie Rd. NoBo: follow road 0.2W		413
841.9	1343.4	State Line Rd, NoBo: follow road 0.5E		420
841.7	1343.6	Wallkill River, parking.		410
841.4	1343.9	AT + State Line Rd north end. NoBo: turn east into Wallkill Reserve		407
840.6	1344.7	90 degree turn on Wallkill perimeter		391
840.2	1345.1	90 degree turn on Wallkill perimeter		407
839.4	1345.9	Liberty Corners Rd (paved)		440
839.3	1346.0	Water to west.	◆	513
838.9	1346.4	**Pochuck Mtn. Shelter** (0.1W) 19.6◄16.7◄12.4◄▶11.5▶23.6▶37.9. ☽ ⌂ ∠ (6)		866
		Bear box. Spigot at vacant house at foot of Pochuck Mountain.		
838.1	1347.2	View.	📷	1092
837.3	1348.0	Pochuck Mountain	📷	1154
836.8	1348.5	Lovemma Lane (gravel)		897
836.6	1348.7	Stream.	◆	822
836.2	1349.1	County Rd 565, **Glenwood, NJ** (1.1W), stream south of road (pg.135)	◆	720
835.5	1349.8	Roadbed.		769
834.7	1350.6	County Rd 517, **Glenwood, NJ** (1.1W) N41 14.142 W74 28.830 **P** (pg.135)		440
834.0	1351.3	Pochuck Creek suspension footbridge.		396
833.3	1352.0	Boardwalk over swamp for (0.6S) and (0.2N) of footbridge. Canal Rd. N41 13.597 W74 28.137 **P**		410
833.1	1352.2	Footbridge, Wawayanda Creek.		403
832.4	1352.9	NJ 94, **Vernon, NJ** (2.4E) N41 13.160 W74 27.306 **P** (pg.135)		450
831.4	1353.9	Spring	◆	963
831.0	1354.3	Pinwheels vista 0.1W, Wawayanda Mountain, side trail 0.8E to views	📷	1340
830.1	1355.2	Footbridge, stream.	◆	1007

SoBo	NoBo		Elev
829.3	1356.0	Barrett Rd (paved), **New Milford, NY** (1.8W). . . . . (pg.135)	1140
828.2	1357.1	Cross stream on Iron Mountain Rd . . . . ♦	1060
827.4	1357.9	**Wawayanda Shelter** (0.1W) . . . . ◖ ⊂(6)	1189
827.2	1358.1	28.2◄23.9◄11.5 ▲12.1►26.4►31.7 Water from park 0.1N and 0.2E. . . . . . . N41 11.883 W74 23.847 **P** ✚◖	1150
826.9	1358.4	Wawayanda State Park (0.2E) . . . . N41 12.085 W74 23.497 **P** (pg.135)	1140
826.4	1358.9	Warwick Turnpike. . . . . ♦	1140
		Footbridge, stream	1113
825.5	1359.8	Long House Dr / Brady Rd . . . . N41 11.732 W74 22.290 **P**	1117

> ▢ Camp only in designated sites; fires only in campsite fire rings. Hitchhiking is illegal in NY.

SoBo	NoBo		Elev
824.4	1360.7	Long House Creek, footbridge . . . . ♦	1085
823.6	1361.7	Ernest Walter Trail (yellow-blazed) to east	1362
823.3	1362.0	**NJ-NY** border, State Line Trail 1.0E to **Lakeside, NJ.**	1385
822.9	1362.4	0.1N on AT is Zig Zag Trail to west / Prospect Rock, highest point on AT in NY. Views of Greenwood Lake to east. . ◙	1433
822.0	1363.3	Furnace Brook . . . . ♦	1161
821.7	1363.6	Ladder	1243

> ⚠ Despite the unimposing profile, rocks, abrupt ups & downs make this section challenging.

SoBo	NoBo		Elev
820.3	1365.0	Cascade Brook . . . . ♦	1184
819.5	1365.8	Village Vista Trail 0.8E to Greenwood Lake	1276
817.9	1367.4	Powerline	1201
817.4	1367.9	NY 17A, **Bellvale, NY** (1.6W) . . . . N41 14.658 W74 17.216 **P** (pg.136-137)	1180
		Greenwood Lake, NY (2.0E)	
816.8	1368.5	Pipeline clearing	1243
816.1	1369.2	Eastern Pinnacles, short bypass trail to west . . . . ◙	1184
815.9	1369.4	Brook	1053
815.6	1369.7	Cat Rocks, view . . . . ◙	1050
815.3	1370.0	**Wildcat Shelter** (0.2W) Water on trail to shelter. . . . . ◖♦ ⊂(8)	1066
		36.0◄23.6◄12.1 ▲14.3►19.6►22.7	
814.0	1371.3	Highlands Trail	774
813.8	1371.5	Lakes Rd (paved), 0.1N powerline, footbridge and stream . . . . ♦♦	680
813.5	1371.8	Fitzgerald Falls . . . . ♦♦	714
812.2	1373.1	Allis Trail, Sterling Fire Tower 5.0E . . . . ◙ ⚐	1251
811.5	1373.8	Mombasha High Point . . . . ◙	1280
810.4	1374.9	Boardwalk, pond	958
810.3	1375.0	West Mombasha Rd, stream just north on AT. . . . . N41 16.159 W74 12.876 **P**	980
809.4	1375.9	Buchanan Mountain	1142

133
NY

SoBo NoBo

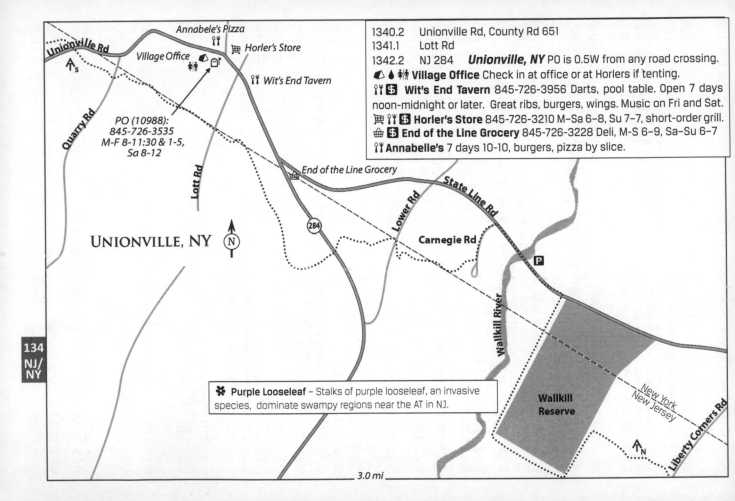

Annabele's Pizza

Unionville Rd

Horler's Store

Village Office

Wit's End Tavern

Quarry Rd

PO (10988):
845-726-3535
M-F 8-11:30 & 1-5,
Sa 8-12

Lott Rd

End of the Line Grocery

UNIONVILLE, NY (N)

284

Lower Rd

State Line Rd

Carnegie Rd

P

Wallkill River

New York
New Jersey

Wallkill
Reserve

Liberty Corners Rd

1340.2	Unionville Rd, County Rd 651
1341.1	Lott Rd
1342.2	NJ 284 **Unionville, NY** PO is 0.5W from any road crossing.

⛺💧🚻 **Village Office** Check in at office or at Horlers if tenting.
🍴💲 **Wit's End Tavern** 845-726-3956 Darts, pool table. Open 7 days noon-midnight or later. Great ribs, burgers, wings. Music on Fri and Sat.
🛒🍴💲 **Horler's Store** 845-726-3210 M–Sa 6–8, Su 7–7, short-order grill.
🏪💲 **End of the Line Grocery** 845-726-3228 Deli, M-S 6–9, Sa–Su 6–7
🍴 **Annabelle's** 7 days 10-10, burgers, pizza by slice.

❉ **Purple Looseleaf** – Stalks of purple looseleaf, an invasive species, dominate swampy regions near the AT in NJ.

3.0 mi

1339.4 Murray property driveway

⌇◐◍♨☾ Private cabin open for the use of long distance hikers as it has been for the last 15 years, tenting, well water, shower & privy. If you feel the need to change your brain chemistry this is probably not your stop but serious hikers welcome. No groups please.

1349.1 County Rd 565

1350.6 County Rd 517 (0.9W to PO and Pochuck Valley Farm)
Glenwood, NJ 07418 (1.1W from either road)
⌂ M-F 7:30–5, Sa 10–2, 973-764-2616

🛏🛰✉ **Apple Valley Inn** 973-764-3735 $145-$160, includes country breakfast, no pets, shuttles to County Roads 517 & 565 with stay. Guest maildrops: PO Box 302, Glenwood, NJ 07418.

⛲🍴◐👫 **Pochuck Valley Farms Market & Deli** 973-764-4732 Open daily M-F 5am–6pm, Sa–Su 5am–5pm. B/L, produce, bakery. Water spigot and restroom.

1352.9 NJ 94

🍴⛲👫 **$** (0.1W) **Heaven Hill Farm & Pitchfork Deli** 973-764-5144 Summer hours 7 days 9–7 (6 on Sundays) ice cream, bakery, seasonal fruit & vegetables. Deli serves B/L. Picnic tables in back.

🛏🛰✉ (1.8E) **Appalachian Motel** 973-764-6070 Weekdays $79D; weekends $99D, $10EAP. Pets $20. Maildrops (guests only): 367 Route 94, Vernon, NJ 07462.

Vernon, NJ 07462 (2.4E)
⌂ M-F 8:30–5, Sa 9:30–12:30, 973-764-9056

🛏◐♨⚒☔⛺🖥 **St. Thomas Episcopal Church Hostel** 973-764-7506 $10PP donation, capacity 12, one night limit. Shower/towel, fridge, micro. Hikers may have to share space with other groups and are expected to help w/cleanup. Pets outside, no alcohol, no smoking. Hikers welcome to Sunday service.

🍴 **Burger King, Paesano Pizza, Little Anthony's** (in A&P plaza), **Mixing Bowl, Dunkin Doughnuts, China Star Restaurant**

🛒🚬**$** **A&P Food Store** M-Sa 7-midnight, Su 7-10, **Starbucks** Inside
🚬 **Rite Aid**
✚ **Vernon Urgent Care** 973-209-2260 1.1 miles beyond hostel, M–F 8-8, Sa–Su 9-5. **Newton Memorial Hospital** 973-383-2121
🐾 **Vernon Veterinary Clinic** 973-764-3630
🖥 **Dorothy Henry Library** M/W/F 9-5, Tu/Th 9-8:30.

1356.0 Barrett Rd
New Milford, NY 10959 (1.8W)
⌂ M-F 8:30-12:30, Sa 9-11:30, 845-986-3557

1358.4 Warwick Turnpike **Warwick, NY 10990**
(See map pg. 136) 2.7W to intersection with NY 94:
🛏◍🚗🅿🛰🖥 **Meadow Lark Farm B&B** 845-651-4286 ⟨www.meadowlarkfarm.com⟩ Weeknight rate $75S/D or $99 for 3-person room, includes breakfast. Rate is higher on Fri-Sa nights. Tenting $15 includes shower & breakfast. All major CC, pets welcome. Shuttles $1 per round-trip mile; free parking for section hikers. Maildrops: 180 Union Corners Rd, Warwick, NY 10990.
🛒 **Shop Rite Supermarket, Price Chopper**
🚬 **Rite Aid**
🍴 **Pronto Pizza, Pennings Farm Market** Harvest Grill, ice cream
🎦 **Warwick Drive-In Theatre** 845-986-4440 Walk-ins welcome. $8 adults, $5 kids and seniors, no credit cards.
       1.5 miles farther north on NY 94 to downtown Warwick, where there are many restaurants and the post office and library.
⌂ M-F 8:30-5, Sa 9-4, 845-986-0271
🐾 **Orchard Grove Animal Hospital** 845-986-9399
✚ **St Anthonys Community Hospital** 845-986-2276
⛺ **South Street Wash & Fold, Warwick Laundry Center**
🖥 **Albert Wisner Public Library** 845-986-1047 M-Th 9-8, F 9-7, Sa 9-5, Su 12-4.

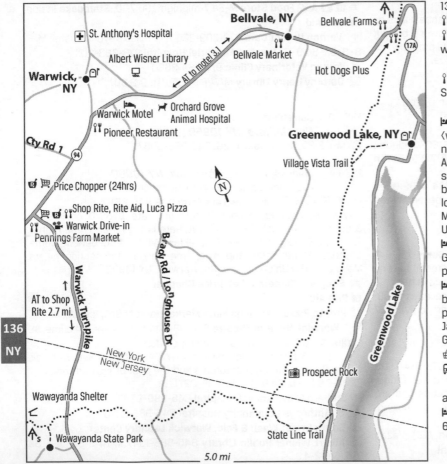

Warwick, NY

St. Anthony's Hospital

Albert Wisner Library

Bellvale, NY

Bellvale Farms

Bellvale Market

AT to motel 3.1

Hot Dogs Plus

Warwick Motel

Orchard Grove Animal Hospital

Pioneer Restaurant

Greenwood Lake, NY

Cty Rd 1

94

Village Vista Trail

Price Chopper (24hrs)

Shop Rite, Rite Aid, Luca Pizza

Warwick Drive-in

Pennings Farm Market

N

Brady Rd / Lighthouse Dr

Warwick Turnpike

AT to Shop Rite 2.7 mi.

Greenwood Lake

New York
New Jersey

Wawayanda Shelter

Prospect Rock

Wawayanda State Park

State Line Trail

5.0 mi

1367.9   NY 17A

Hot Dog Stand Just west of the AT.

 (0.3W) **Bellvale Farms** 845-988-1818 Ice cream, water from hose, can use phone, ask about parking.

Bellvale, NY 10912 (1.6W)

Bellvale Market 845-544-7700, deli M-F 7-7, Sa 8-6, Su 8-5.

Greenwood Lake, NY 10925 (2E)

Anton's on the Lake 845-477-0010 ⟨www.antonsonthelake.com⟩ thru-hiker rate with two-night stay $80S/D Sunday-Thurs, $125/up Friday & Sat. All major CC, rooms with whirlpool available, no pets, no smoking, laundry small loads only, swimming, paddle boats & canoe. Free shuttles and slackpacking w/stay, longer shuttles for a fee. Open year round, hiker friendly. Maildrops for guests: (USPS) PO Box 1505 or (FedEx/UPS) 7 Waterstone Rd, Greenwood Lake, NY 10925.

Lake Lodging 845-477-0700 or 845-705-2005. Good hiker rates, pickup/return when available. No pets, no credit cards.

Breezy Point Inn 845-477-8100 ⟨www.breezypointinn.com⟩ $85 room with 2 double beds, no pets, no smoking, L/D dining 7 days. Closed month of January. Guest maildrops: (UPS/FedEx) 620 Jersey Ave, Greenwood Lake, NY 10925.

Cumberland Farms deli sandwiches, 24/7.

Greenwood Lake Taxi 845-477-0314

Warwick, NY 10990 4.5W to downtown area, see adjacent map & more listings on pg. 135.

Warwick Motel (3.1W from NY 17A) 845-986-6656 $79D/up, continental breakfast.

GREENWOOD LAKE, NY

Pop. 3,419 (2009)
N41 13.360, W74 17.650
Mag. Dec. 13° 4'W
Grid Dim 0.5 mi.

PO (10925):
845-477-7328
M-F 8-5, Sa 9-12

1.8 mi.

17A

3 Corners Cafe

Friendly Beer & Soda

Village Vista Trail
0.8 mi. from park
to

210

17A

Scoops Ice Cream

Subway
CVS
The Grill (B/L)

Frozen Treats

Sunoco

Linden Motel

Sunrise Diner

Lion's Field

Cumberland Farms
(Open 24/7)

Planet Pizza

Walnut St

Lake Lodging

Elm St

Country Kitchen

Irish Whisper

Linden Ave

Ten Eyke Ave

Breezy Point
Inn 0.6 mi.

Mangos

Murphy's

Sing Loong Kitchen

Ashley's Pizza

Jersey Ave

Village Buzz Cafe

True Value Hardware

Country Grocery

NJTransit.com
973-275-5555
(bus to NYC
M-F @ $14)

Library:
845-477-8377
M & F 9-5
Tu-Th 9-9,
Sa 10-4,
Su 11-3

Waterstone Rd.

Windermere Ave

Anton's on
the Lake

0.7 mi

Bridge Inn

137
NY

1379.9   NY 17   *Southfields, NY 10975* (2.1E)
M-F 9–11 & 1–5, Sa 8:30–11:30, 845-351-2628
Tuxedo Motel 845-351-4747 $49.50S, $54.50D, $10EAP, no pets, accepts Visa/MC. Maildrops: 985 Route 17 South, Southfields, NY, 10975
Harriman, NY 10926 (3.7W)
Lodging, groceries, restaurants, and laundromats.

1385.4   Arden Valley Road
Lake Tiorati Cirlce (0.3E) 845-351-2568 Open Mem-Labor Day M-F 10-5, Sa-Su 9-7. Restrooms, free showers, vending machine, swimming.

SoBo	NoBo		Elev
808.6	1376.7	East Mombasha Rd (paved)	840
808.3	1377.0	Little Dam Lake; stepping stones over creek	758
807.2	1378.1	Orange Turnpike . . . . . N41 16.167 W74 10.862 P ♦ (0.5E)	780
806.5	1378.8	Arden Mountain	1180
806.2	1379.1	Sapphire Trail	1140
805.8	1379.5	View . . . . (pg.137)	1042
805.4	1379.9	NY 17, **Southfields, NY** (2.1E), **Harriman, NY** (3.7W)	550
805.0	1380.3	AT on Arden Valley Rd for 0.4 mile. . . N41 15.893 W74 9.261 P	602
		Passes over NY State Thruway 87.	
803.7	1381.6	Island Pond Rd (gravel) 0.1E to pond	1045
803.1	1382.1	Lemon Squeezer, Arden-Surebridge Trail to east	1150
802.8	1382.5	Island Pond Mountain	1349
802.4	1382.9	New York Long Path 52.0E to Manhattan	1091
801.7	1383.6	Surebridge Brook	1113
801.1	1384.2	AT joins Red Dot Trail (south end)	1318
801.0	1384.3	**Fingerboard Shelter** 37.9◀26.4◀14.3◀▶5.3▶8.4▶40.6 . . . . ⌂ C(8)	1348
800.4	1384.9	Fingerboard Mountain	1333
		Spring downhill to left unreliable. Water at Lake Tiorati 0.5E on Hurst Trail.	
799.9	1385.4	Arden Valley Rd (paved), Tiorati Circle (0.3E) . . N41 16.542 W74 5.286 P (pg.137)	1196
799.2	1386.1	Woods road	1039
797.8	1387.5	Footbridge, stream	840
797.7	1387.6	Seven Lakes Dr	850
795.7	1389.6	**William Brien Memorial Shelter** 31.7◀19.6◀5.3◀▶3.1▶35.3▶44.3 . . ⌂ C(8)	1059
		Unreliable spring-fed well 80 yards down blue-blazed trail to right of shelter.	
		Yellow-blazed Menomine Trail to east.	
794.8	1390.5	AT joins Red Dot Trail (north end)	931
794.4	1390.9	Black Mountain, views, can see NY City skyline	1187
793.6	1391.7	Palisades Parkway, busy 4-lane divided hwy. NY City 34E. Visitor.	680
		center in median 0.4W, soda & snack machines. ⚠ Watch blazes next 3mi. north.	
793.3	1392.0	Beechy Bottom Brook, footbridge, parking 0.8W	607
792.6	1392.7	**West Mountain Shelter** (0.6E) 22.7◀8.4◀3.1◀▶32.2▶41.2▶49.0 . . C(8)	1175
		Views of Hudson River & NYC.	
791.9	1393.4	Views from ridge of West Mountain	1111
790.8	1394.5	Seven Lakes Dr	610
790.2	1395.1	Perkins Memorial Dr	805

SoBo	NoBo		Elev
788.4	1396.9	Bear Mountain, Perkins Memorial Tower, Vending machines, view of NYC skyline. N41 18.670 W74 0.434 📷 🎁	1305
787.8	1397.5	Perkins Memorial Dr (south end of 0.3 mi. roadwalk)	1020
		⚠️ NoBo: Upon reaching the park, AT turns left through playground then follows path at edge of lake.	
786.5	1398.8	Bear Mountain Recreation Area, Hessian Lake N41 18.780 W73 59.338 P (pg.140)	175
786.1	1399.2	Tunnel under US 9, Trailside Museum, bear cage is lowest point on AT (pg.140)	163
785.6	1399.7	Bear Mountain Bridge, Hudson River, **Fort Montgomery, NY** (1.8W) (pg.140)	200
785.1	1400.2	NY 9D, Bear Mountain Bridge north end.	218
784.4	1400.9	Camp Smith Trail, 0.6E to Anthonys Nose, views of Hudson River 📷	738
783.4	1401.9	Hemlock Springs Campsite	550
783.2	1402.1	Manitou Rd (gravel). N41 19.776 W73 57.195 P	460
782.2	1403.1	Osborne Loop Trail to west (blue-blazed)	794
781.8	1403.5	Curry Pond Trail to west (yellow-blazed)	864
780.8	1404.5	Osborne Loop Trail to west (blue-blazed)	868
780.3	1405.0	Carriage Connector Trail to west (yellow-blazed)	527
779.8	1405.5	US 9 + NY 403, **Peekskill, NY** (4.5E) (pg.141)	400
779.5	1405.8	Old Highland Turnpike (paved)	451
779.2	1406.1	Franciscan Way (paved), **Graymoor Spiritual Life Center** (0.4E) (pg.141)	530
779.1	1406.2	Two gravel roads	473
777.3	1408.0	Blue-blazed trail 0.1W to Denning Hill 📷	900
776.5	1408.8	Old Albany Post Rd (gravel), Chapman Rd	607
775.5	1409.8	Canopus Hill.	812
774.9	1410.4	Brook (pg.141) 💧	393
774.8	1410.5	Canopus Hill Rd (paved) 💧	420
773.8	1411.5	South Highland Rd (paved), stream north side of road. 💧	570
773.0	1412.3	Stream. 💧	636
772.3	1413.0	Catfish Loop Trail (red-blazed)	926
771.1	1414.2	Dennytown Rd (paved), Three Lake Trail to west N41 25.234 W73 52.135 P 💧 Water on side of pump building, open late-Apr-Oct.	860
770.9	1414.4	Catfish Loop Trail to east (red-blazed)	823
769.5	1415.8	Sunken Mine Rd (gravel), stream to north.	800

1398.8   Bear Mountain Recreation Area, *Bear Mountain, NY 10911*

🏠 M–F 8–10 (8-12 in summer) 845-786-3747 Limited hours not good for maildrop.

🍴 Concessions & vending near Hessian Lake.

🛏🍴💲🛜🖥 **Bear Mountain Inn** 845-786-2731 $149/up+tax, continental breakfast, some pet rooms. Multiple dining options including **1915, Blue Tapas,** and **Hiker Cafe** inside the inn and **Stand 10** seasonal concession lakeside.

🛏🛜 **Overlook Lodge** 845-786-2731 $149/up+tax, continental B, some pet rooms.

1399.2   Trailside Museum and Zoo

Open 10-4:30; no charge for hiking through. No dogs. Lowest elevation on the AT (124') is within the park. If closed, or if you have a dog, use bypass (see map).

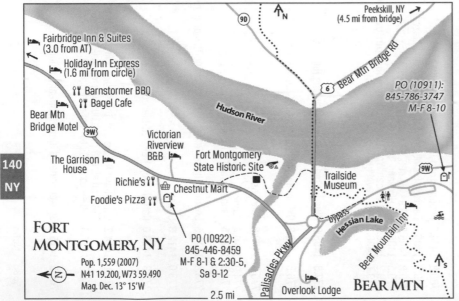

🛏 **Fairbridge Inn & Suites** (3.0 from AT)

🛏 **Holiday Inn Express** (1.6 mi from circle)

🍴 **Barnstormer BBQ**

🛏 🍴 **Bagel Cafe**

🛏 **Bear Mtn Bridge Motel** (9W)

🛏 **The Garrison House**

Victorian Riverview B&B 🛏

Fort Montgomery State Historic Site 🔭⛺

Richie's 🍴

🏛 **Chestnut Mart**

Foodie's Pizza 🍴

🏛 PO (10922): 845-446-8459 M-F 8-1 & 2:30-5, Sa 9-12

FORT MONTGOMERY, NY

Pop. 1,559 (2007)
N41 19.200, W73 59.490
Mag. Dec. 13° 15'W

↖N⃝↗

Hudson River

(9D)

Peekskill, NY → (4.5 mi from bridge)

Bear Mtn Bridge Rd

6

PO (10911): 845-786-3747 M-F 8-10

Palisades Pkwy

Trailside Museum

(9W) 🏠

bypass

Hessian Lake

Bear Mountain Inn

🛏 Overlook Lodge

BEAR MTN ↱S

2.5 mi

1399.7   Bear Mountain Bridge
Fort Montgomery, NY 10922 (1.8W)

🛏🛜✉ **Bear Mountain Bridge Motel** 845-446-2472 $75D, no pets, accepts Visa/MC, pickup/return to trail (zoo) with stay. Wir sprechen Deutsch. Guest maildrops: PO Box 554, Fort Montgomery, NY 10922.

🛏⛺🛜🖥✉ **Holiday Inn Express** 845-446-4277 $110 1-4 persons, full B, indoor pool & sauna, coin laundry, 24-hour business center. Guest maildrops: 1106 Route 9 W, Fort Montgomery, NY 10922-0620.

🛏 **Victorian Riverview Inn** 845-446-5479 $175.

🛏🍴 **The Garrison House** 845-446-2322 $139/up. Ask for hiker rate.

🍴 **Bagel Café** ATM

🍴 **Foodies Pizza** 845-839-0383
Highland Falls, NY (3.8W)

🛏🛜 **Fairbridge Inn & Suites** 845-446-9400 $75D, continental breakfast. Pets $10.

🍴 **Dunkin' Donuts,** and many other restaurants

🏪 **My Town Market**

💊 **Rite Aid**

🖥 **Highland Falls Library** 845-446-3113 M 10-5, Tu 10-7, W-F 10-5, Sa 10-2.

Fort Montgomery State Historic Site Side trail starting from end of bridge guardrail 0.6W passes through Revolutionary War fort for which the town is named. The side trail is roughly the same length as the roadwalk but is more interesting. View the Hudson River bridge down the barrel of a cannon.

1405.5   US 9, NY 403

🍴🚐💲💧 **Appalachian Market** at trailhead. Hiker-friendly, open 24hrs, deli serves B/L/D. Water from spigot on north side of building.

🍴 **Stadium Sports Bar** (0.8E)

    Peekskill, NY 10566 (4.5E) large town

📮 M–F 9–5, Sa 9–4, 914-737-6437

1406.1   Franciscan Way

💧🚿🌙 **Graymoor Spiritual Life Center** (0.4E) 800-338-2620 Hikers permitted to sleep at monastery's ball field picnic shelter which has water, privy, and shower during warm months. Open all season and free. Follow signs and blue-blazes; stay to the left at both forks in the road.

1410.5   Canopus Hill Rd

🍴🏠💲 (1.6E) **Putnam Valley Market** 845-528-8626 Directions: (0.3E) on Canopus Hill Rd, right on Canopus Hollow Rd for 0.1 mile, left on Sunset Hill Road for 1.2 mile. Pizza, hot food from the grill, ATM, open M–Sa 6–9, Su 6–7.

1417.9   NY 301, Canopus Lake (1E to SP)
1419.9   Side trail entry (0.2E to SP beach)

🌙🍴👥🚿 **Clarence Fahnestock State Park** 845-225-7207, 800-456-2267 Open mid-Apr to mid-Dec. Thru-hikers get one free night of camping. Concession at beach open weekends only Memorial Day to June 21. Open every day from June 21 to Labor Day. Hours Su–F 10–4, Sa 10–5.

1424.9   Hortontown RD, **RPH Shelter** (Ralph's Peak Hiker Cabin) Tent spots are evident, but tenting is discouraged. 🍴 Pizza delivered by **Avanti's** 845-896-6500 and **Gian Bruno's** 845-227-9276.

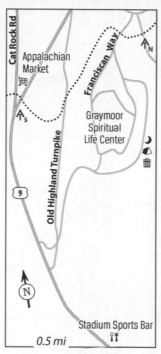

Cat Rock Rd

Appalachian Market

Franciscan Way

Graymoor Spiritual Life Center

Old Highland Turnpike

9

N

Stadium Sports Bar
🍴

0.5 mi

1430.0   NY 52

🏠🍴💲💧📞 (0.4E) **Mountaintop Market Deli** 845-221-0928 Open daily 6–8, ATM and pay phone inside, welcome to water from faucet on side of building.

🍴 **Danny's Pizzeria** pizza by the slice.

    Stormville, NY 12582 (1.9W)

📮 M–F 8:30–5, Sa 9–12, 845-226-2627

1437.2   NY 55

🚐🍴📞 (1.5W) Pleasant Ridge Plaza with **Poughquag Central Market**, **Pleasant Ridge Pizza** L/D.

💊 (1.2W) **Total Care Pharmacy**

🍴 **R's Gulf Quickmart & Deli** 845-452-4040

    Poughquag, NY 12570 (3.1W)

📮 M–F 8:30–5, Sa 8:30–12:30, 845-724-4763

🛏 **Pine Grove Motel** 845-724-5151 Hotel was for sale late in 2013, so call to confirm prices. 2013 prices/policies were $65S $70D, no pets, accepts Visa/MC.

🍴 **Great Wall**, **Clove Valley Deli & Café**

💊 **Total Care Pharmacy**, **Beekman Pharmacy**

🐕 **Beekman Animal Hospital** 845-724-8387

    Pawling, NY (4.0E, see pg. 144)

1442.4   County Rd 20, West Dover Rd
Dover Oak north side of road, largest oak tree on AT. Girth 20' 4" and estimated to be over 300 years old. Spigot on fence post at red house 100 yards east of the trail. Please help yourself, they would prefer that you do not interrupt them to ask permission.

    Pawling, NY 12564 (3.1E, see pg. 144)

SoBo	NoBo	Description	Elev
768.3	1417.0	Three Lakes Trail	1000
767.4	1417.9	NY 301, Canopus Lake, **Clarence Fahnestock SP** (1.0E) (pg.141)	920
766.8	1418.5	Fahnestock Trail to west	1089
765.4	1419.9	Green-blazed trail to lake, **Clarence Fahnestock SP** (0.2E) 📷 ● (pg.141)	974
764.6	1420.7	View of the lake from AT north of this intersection. Stream	1033
763.2	1422.1	Shenandoah Mountain, view, painted 911 Memorial Flag. 📷	1282
762.8	1422.5	Long Hill Rd (gravel)	1100
762.3	1423.0	Powerline	1029
761.7	1423.6	Shenandoah Tenting Area 0.1W, hand pump ● △	900
761.3	1424.0	Brook ●	765
760.5	1424.8	Bridge over brook ●	374
760.4	1424.9	Hortontown Rd, N41 30.843 W73 47.509 🏛 ⊃ ● ⊂ (6) (pg.141)	376
		RPH Shelter (1982) 40.6◀35.3◀32.2▶9.0▶16.8▶25.6 Treat pump water.	
760.1	1425.2	Footbridge, stream, Taconic State Pkwy underpass ●	564
756.9	1428.4	Hosner Mountain Rd, footbridge, stream ●	500
755.3	1430.0	NY 52, **Stormville, NY** (1.9W) N41 32.460 W73 43.969 🅿 (pg.141)	800
754.7	1430.6	Stream ●	839
754.1	1431.2	AT on Old Stormville Mountain Rd for 0.1 mile	970
753.9	1431.4	AT on Stormville Mountain Rd for 0.1 mile, crosses over I-84	950
753.7	1431.6	Grape Hollow Rd	954
752.4	1432.9	Side trail 0.6W to Indian Pass	1167
751.5	1433.8	Mt Egbert	1329
751.4	1433.9	**Morgan Stewart Shelter** ⊃ ● ⊂ (6)	1308
		44.3◀41.2◀9.0▶7.8▶16.6▶20.6	
750.3	1435.0	Depot Hill Rd, parking 0.1W. N41 34.288 W73 40.840 🅿	1230

SoBo	NoBo		Elev
748.5	1436.8	Railroad track, Whakey Lake Stream	680
748.4	1436.9	Old Route 55	696
748.1	1437.2	NY 55, **Poughquag, NY** (3.1W) . . . N41 35.380 W73 39.551 **P** (0.1W) (pg.141)	720
747.8	1437.5	Beekman Uplands Trail to west	755
747.0	1438.3	Footbridge, stream (more streams in this area)	690
746.7	1438.6	Nuclear Lake south end, loop trail to east (yellow-blazed)	738
745.8	1439.5	Nuclear Lake north end, loop trail to east	769
745.4	1439.9	Beekman Uplands Trail to west	861
744.5	1440.8	Footbridge, swampy area	1043
744.2	1441.1	Penny Rd	1128
743.9	1441.4	West Mountain	1200
743.6	1441.7	**Telephone Pioneers Shelter** (0.1E), shelter trail crosses stream	977
742.9	1442.4	49.0◄16.8◄7.8►8.8►12.8►21.2 If dry, get water from residence 0.7N, County Rd 20, West Dover Rd, **Pawling, NY** (3.1E)	650
740.8	1444.5	Footbridge, stream, boardwalk from here north to RR track	505
740.5	1444.8	NY 22, **Appalachian Trail RR Station** . N41 35.629 W73 35.224 **P** (pg.144) **Wingdale** (4W) **Pawling** (2.6E) hot dog stand often here in summer, deli 0.6E	480
740.3	1445.0	Hurd Corners Rd, wooden water tower	480
739.6	1445.7	Stream to west	571
738.8	1446.5	Hammersly Ridge	1032
738.6	1446.7	Red Trail	974
738.2	1447.1	Yellow Trail to east	908
737.8	1447.5	Red Trail to east	951
737.7	1447.6	Green trail west, Red Trail east	966
736.8	1448.5	Pawling Nature Reserve to east	885
735.8	1449.5	Stream	805
735.2	1450.1	Leather Hill Rd (gravel), stream to south	750
734.8	1450.5	**Wiley Shelter** pump 0.1N, treat water 25.6◄16.6◄8.8►4.0►12.4►19.7	735
734.6	1450.7	Duell Hollow Rd	620
734.3	1451.0	Footbridge, stream	472
733.6	1451.7	**NY-CT** border, Hoyt Rd . . . N41 38.508 W73 31.248 **P**	400
733.3	1452.0	Side trail to parking, brook to north	423
733.0	1452.3	CT 55, **Gaylordsville, CT** (2.5E) . N41 38.679 W73 31.155 **P** (pg.144-145) **Wingdale, NY** (3.3W)	431
731.8	1453.5	Ten Mile Hill, Herrick Trail to east	1000
730.8	1454.5	**Ten Mile River Shelter** (0.1E) 20.6◄12.8◄4.0►8.4►15.7►25.7 Water (hand pump) to left. Group campsites across river and up trail to left.	344
730.7	1454.6	Ten Mile River, Ned Anderson Memorial Bridge	335
729.5	1455.8	Bulls Bridge Rd (paved) + Schaghticoke Rd . N41 40.535 W73 30.610 **P** (pg.145) AT on Schaghticoke Rd (gravel) 0.3 mile	410

143
NY

SoBo	NoBo

Pawling, NY (east from NY 55, County Rd 20, or NY 22)
🏕 🚻 **Edward R. Murrow Memorial Park** Town allows hikers to camp in park, one night only. One mile from the center of town, park offers lake swimming, no pets.
🍴 **Vinny's Deli** 845-855-1922, **Gaudino's Pizzeria** 845-855-3200, **Mama Pizza II** 845-855-9270, **Great Wall** 845-855-9750
🍴 **McKeever's Restaurant** L/D
🖥 **Pawling Free Library** Closed Sundays in July and August.
🚐 **Martin and Donna Hunley** 845-505-1671 or 845-546-1832. Shuttle range RPH Shelter to Kent, CT.
🚆 **MTA Metro-North Railroad** (see pg. 145)

1444.8   NY 22, **Appalachian Trail Railroad Station**
🚆 **MTA Metro-North Railroad** (see pg. 145)
🏕 🚻 🚿 ✉ ⚙ **Native Landscapes & Garden Center** 845-855-7050 Open daily 9-5. Owner Pete Muroski is hiker-friendly. Allows camping on site (no fires), use of restrooms, inside shower $5. Some drinks and snacks sold at the office. Maildrops: 991 Route 22, Pawling, NY 12564.
🍴 🍺 🚻 📞 (0.6E) **Tony's Deli** sandwiches, salads, soda machine outside. Open daily 5am–midnight.
   Pawling, NY (2.5E)
   Wingdale, NY 12594 (4W)
🛏 🏕 📶 ✉ **Dutches Motor Lodge** 845-832-6400, 914-525-9276 $73S Ride for a fee. A/C, free long distance, guest laundry $7, one pet room. Maildrops: 1512 Route 22, Wingdale, NY 12594.

1452.3   CT 55, **Gaylordsville, CT 06755** (2.5E to bridge and country store, 0.6 further south to PO and diner)
📮 M-F 8-1 & 2-5, Sa 8-12, 860-354-9727
🍺 💲 📞 **Gaylordsville Country Store** 860-350-3802 deli, grocery M-F 6-7, Sa 6-5, Su 6-3.
🍴 **Burgerittoville Bar & Grill** 860-799-7739 Hamburger burritos, milkshakes. Big Sport bar has Saturday karaoke.
🍴 **Gaylordsville Diner**
🍴 (1.4W) **Wetabuck Tavern** Food, pool table, open noon-9pm.
   Wingdale, NY (3.3W) see map

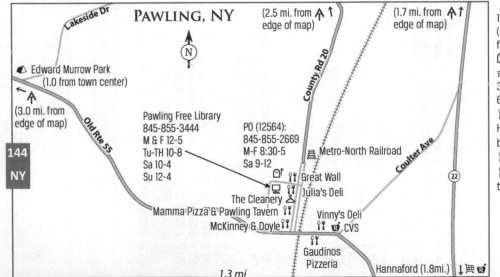

PAWLING, NY

Lakeside Dr

N

(2.5 mi. from 🅰 ↑ edge of map)

(1.7 mi. from 🅰 ↑ edge of map)

County Rd 20

🏕 Edward Murrow Park (1.0 from town center)
← 🅰 ↑ (3.0 mi. from edge of map)

Old Rte 55

Pawling Free Library
845-855-3444
M & F 12-5
Tu-TH 10-8
Sa 10-4
Su 12-4

PO (12564):
845-855-2669
M-F 8:30-5
Sa 9-12

Metro-North Railroad

Coulter Ave

🅿 (22)

Great Wall 🍴
Julia's Deli 🍴
The Cleanery
Mamma Pizza & Pawling Tavern 🍴
McKinney & Doyle 🍴

Vinny's Deli
🍴 🍺 CVS

Gaudinos Pizzeria 🍴

Hannaford (1.8mi.) ↓🛒

1.3 mi

MTA Metro-North Railroad 212-532-4900
⟨www.mta.info/mnr\index.html⟩ Stations on the AT and in Pawling and Wingdale. Trip to NYC Grand Central Station requires a transfer, costs approx. $15 one-way, and takes about two hours. Must pay in cash when boarding at the trailhead; can purchase round trip and pay with credit card if your trip originates at Grand Central Station. Schedule varies by season and summer 2014 schedule not available at time of printing. Also connects to other cities in NY and CT.

1455.8   Bulls Bridge Rd, Schaghticoke Rd
📷 (0.4E) To covered bridge with view of the Housatonic cascading down the backside of a dam. The one-lane bridge was built in 1842. Wooden bridges are covered to protect the wood deck and trusswork from the elements.
          0.2 beyond bridge:
⛪💲 **Country Market** Fruit, ice cream, soda. M-Sa 5:30-7, Sunday 6:30-7
🍴 **Bulls Bridge Inn** 860-927-1000 Dinner $10-20, M-F 5-9:30, Sa 5-10, Su 4-9. Weekend lunch noon-3. American cuisine, casual atmosphere, bar.

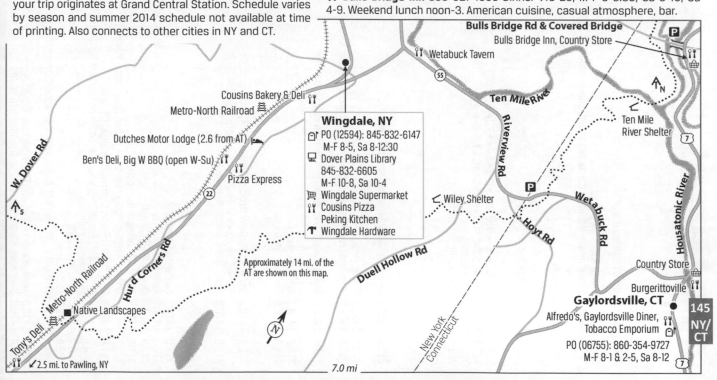

Wingdale, NY
🏤 PO (12594): 845-832-6147
      M-F 8-5, Sa 8-12:30
🖥 Dover Plains Library
      845-832-6605
      M-F 10-8, Sa 10-4
🛒 Wingdale Supermarket
🍴 Cousins Pizza
      Peking Kitchen
🔱 Wingdale Hardware

Metro-North Railroad
Cousins Bakery & Deli
Dutches Motor Lodge (2.6 from AT)
Ben's Deli, Big W BBQ (open W-Su)
Pizza Express
W. Dover Rd
Hurd Corners Rd
Metro-North Railroad
Native Landscapes
Tony's Deli
↙2.5 mi. to Pawling, NY

Approximately 14 mi. of the AT are shown on this map.
Duell Hollow Rd
Wiley Shelter
Hoyt Rd
Riverview Rd
Ten Mile River
Wetabuck Tavern
Bulls Bridge Rd & Covered Bridge
Bulls Bridge Inn, Country Store
Ten Mile River Shelter
Wetabuck Rd
Housatonic River
Country Store
Burgerittoville
Gaylordsville, CT
Alfredo's, Gaylordsville Diner, Tobacco Emporium
PO (06755): 860-354-9727
M-F 8-1 & 2-5, Sa 8-12

New York
Connecticut

7.0 mi

SoBo	NoBo		Feature	Elev
		⊛ Campfires prohibited in CT. Camping only in designated sites.		
728.3	1457.0		CT-NY ⊛	1049
727.7	1457.6		View	1227
726.3	1459.0		NY-CT, stream to north	1218
725.5	1459.8		Indian Rocks, view to east	999
725.3	1460.0		Schaghticoke Mountain Campsite to west, stream on AT	936
724.5	1460.8		Stream	1019
723.4	1461.9		Thayer Brook	980
722.4	1462.9		Mt Algo Shelter 21.2◀12.4◀8.4◀▶7.3▶17.3▶28.7	694
722.1	1463.2		CT 341, Schaghticoke Rd, Kent, CT (0.8E) (pg.148)	350
722.0	1463.3		Macedonia Brook	327
721.5	1463.8		Numeral Rock Trail to east	781
719.3	1466.0		Skiff Mountain Rd (paved), stream to south	850
718.6	1466.7		Calebs Peak	1164
718.3	1467.0		St. Johns Ledges, steep stone steps down to Housatonic River.	943
717.4	1467.9		River Rd south end, NoBo: turn west on road for 0.8 mile	480
716.6	1468.7		Kent Rd to west	443
716.4	1468.9		River Rd north end	407
715.1	1470.2		Stewart Hollow Brook Shelter (0.1W) 19.7◀15.7◀7.3◀▶10.0▶21.4▶28.9 Footbridge over SH Brook.	418
714.5	1470.8		Stony Brook, campsite to west	446
713.0	1472.3		Footbridge, stream	453
712.7	1472.6		River Rd N41 48.342 W73 23.697 P	460
712.5	1472.8		Dawn Hill Rd (paved)	569
711.8	1473.5		Silver Hill Campsite 0.1E, pavillion, water from pump (may take many pumps to get water flowing)	934
711.0	1474.3		CT 4, Guinea Brook, Cornwall Bridge, CT (0.9E) (pg.149)	700
710.8	1474.5		High water Bypass 0.5E on CT 4, then left on unpaved Old Sharon Rd for 0.5 mi.	
710.7	1474.6		Old Sharon Rd (gravel)	758
709.6	1475.7		Breadloaf Trail 0.1E, view	932
709.4	1475.9		Hatch Brook	880
			Pine Knob Loop Trail 1.0E to Housatonic Meadows State Park	967
708.7	1476.6		Another intersection with Pine Knob Loop Trail to east.	1014
708.4	1476.9		Caesar Rd, Caesar Brook Campsite, stream to north	774

Appalachian Trail elevation profile — Connecticut (CT)

SoBo	NoBo	Description	Elev
706.9	1478.4	Stream.	890
706.3	1479.0	Carse Brook, footbridge	810
706.2	1479.1	West Cornwall Rd, **West Cornwall, CT** (2.2E), **Sharon, CT** (4.7W). (pg.149)	852
705.9	1479.4	Pass through cracked boulder similar to Lemon Squeezer.	1126
705.1	1480.2	**Pine Swamp Brook Shelter** 25.7◄17.3◄10.0◄►11.4►18.9►20.1	1100
704.2	1481.1	Sharon Mountain Rd	1150
703.6	1481.7	Woods road	1304
703.4	1481.9	Woods road	1311
702.7	1482.6	Sharon Mountain Campsite 0.1W, stream nearby.	1200
699.8	1485.5	Belters Campsite 0.2W, view.	757
699.5	1485.8	US 7, CT 112	520
698.9	1486.4	US 7 bridge, Housatonic River	539
698.5	1486.8	Mohawk Trail 0.5E to view	543
697.9	1487.4	Warren Turnpike, footbridge, stream to north.	518
697.0	1488.3	Water St parking. **Falls Village, CT** (0.3E) N41 57.352 W73 22.056 (pg.150)	530
696.7	1488.6	Iron Mtn Bridge over Housatonic River	528
696.4	1488.9	Housatonic River Rd, AT crosses road twice 0.2 mi. N41 57.736 W73 22.442	604
		apart. In between are two short trails east to views of great falls.	
695.8	1489.5	Spring	804
694.4	1490.9	Mt Prospect	1475
693.7	1491.6	**Limestone Spring Shelter** (0.5W), road 0.25 farther. 28.7◄21.4◄11.4◄►7.5►8.7►17.5	1339
693.6	1491.7	Rands View (field)	1250
693.2	1492.1	Giants Thumb	1288
692.4	1492.9	Stream.	993
690.3	1495.0	AT on US 44 for 0.2W	700
690.0	1495.3	AT on Cobble Rd 0.2E, **Salisbury, CT** (0.5W). (pg.150-151)	701
689.6	1495.7	Undermountain Rd (paved) N41 59.645 W73 25.615 (pg.150-151)	720
689.3	1496.0	**Salisbury, CT** (0.8W). Stream.	836
688.1	1497.2	Streams (multiple)	1114

147
CT

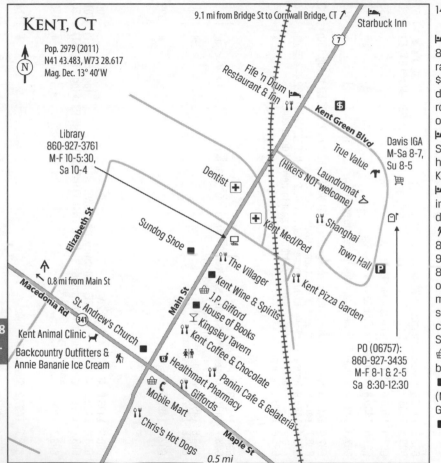

Kent, CT

Pop. 2979 (2011)
N41 43.483, W73 28.617
Mag. Dec. 13° 40'W

9.1 mi from Bridge St to Cornwall Bridge, CT ↗
Starbuck Inn

Fife 'n Drum
Restaurant & Inn

Kent Green Blvd

Davis IGA
M-Sa 8-7,
Su 8-5

True Value

Laundromat
(Hikers NOT welcome)

Library
860-927-3761
M-F 10-5:30,
Sa 10-4

Dentist

Sundog Shoe

Kent Med/Ped

Shanghai

Town Hall

The Villager

Kent Wine & Spirits

J.P. Gifford

House of Books

Kingsley Tavern

Kent Coffee & Chocolate

Kent Pizza Garden

0.8 mi from Main St

Macedonia Rd

St. Andrew's Church

Kent Animal Clinic

Backcountry Outfitters &
Annie Bananie Ice Cream

Elizabeth St

Main St

Healthmart Pharmacy

Panini Cafe & Gelateria

Giffords

Mobile Mart

Chris's Hot Dogs

Maple St

PO (06757):
860-927-3435
M-F 8-1 & 2-5
Sa 8:30-12:30

0.5 mi

1463.2   CT 341, Schaghticoke Rd
Kent, CT 06757 (0.8E)

🛏️🍴📶✉️ Fife 'n Drum Inn & Restaurant
860-927-3509 ⟨www.fifendrum.com⟩ hiker room rates $116D+tax wkdays, $140D+tax wkends, $25EAP+tax, no pets. Call for reservations, front desk closed Tu (can make prior arrangements for room access). Guest maildrops: (USPS) PO Box 188 or (FedEx/UPS) 53 N Main Street, Kent, CT 06757.

🛏️🚗📶 Cooper Creek B&B 860-927-4334 Hiker rate Su-Th $95D. Weekend rates seasonal & considerably higher. 2.5mi. north of town on US 7. Shuttles to/from Kent w/stay, longer shuttles for a fee.

🛏️📶 Starbuck Inn 860-927-1788 $207D/up + tax, includes full breakfast & afternoon tea. Sometimes discounted mid-week, accepts credit cards, no pets.

🚶🍴🚌💲📶✉️ Backcountry Outfitters
860-927-3377⟨www.bcoutfitters.com⟩   M–Sa 9-6, Su 10-4. In summer hours extended 6am till 8pm weekdays, 9pm Fri & Sat, 6pm Sunday. Fuel/oz, isobutane, lmited selection of gear. Farmer's market F 4-7. **Annie Bananie** ice cream & grill inside serving hot dogs, coffee, snacks, barrels of candy, chocolates. Shuttles anywhere. Maildrops: 5 Bridge Street, Kent, CT 06757.

🏠🍴 JP Gifford Breakfast sandwiches, salads, bakery, coffee and supplies.

■ Sundog Shoe 10% hiker discount on footwear (Merrell, High-Tech, Keen), socks (Darn Tough), Dirty Girl Gaiters and footbeds (Superfeet, Power Step).

■ House of Books UPS services, open daily 10-5:30.

1474.3   CT 4, *Cornwall Bridge, CT 06754* (0.9E)

🛏🚶🚐📶✉ **Hitching Post Motel** 860-672-6219 $65/up weekdays, $85/up weekends. Pets $10, laundry $5, shuttles $1.50/mi. Maildrops: 45 Kent Road, Cornwall Bridge, CT 06754.

🛏🚶📶✉ **The Amselhaus** 860-248-3155 $75S, $100 for couple, $50 EAP. Two and three bedroom apartments includes laundry, sat. TV, local and long-distance phone. Rides available. Located behind carpet store, check in at grey house next door to apartments. Maildrops: C/O Tyler, 7 River Road South, Cornwall Bridge, CT 06754.

🛏🚿 **Housatonic Meadows State Park** Camping and Cabins 1.3 mi. north of town on US 7. Campsite $17 for CT residents, $27 non-residents, $3 walk-in fee for first night. Cabins $50 with 2 night minimum. No hammocks. Open mid-Apr to Sep, registration at main cabin by gate, no alcohol.

🛏📶 **Cornwall Inn** 860-672-6884 Su-Th $109D + tax, includes continental breakfast. Weekends %10 hiker discount. 2.2 miles south on US 7. Pickup/return to trailhead for a fee. Pet friendly. Maildrops with reservation.

🛒♩ **Cornwall Country Market** M-F 6am-7pm, Sa-Su 7am-7pm.

🧍 **Housatonic River Outfitters** 860-672-1010 〈www.dryflies.com〉 Some hiker gear, Aquamira, white gas/alcohol/oz (no canisters).

◼ **Cornwall Package Store** 860-672-6645 closed Su, water spigot outside. Stopping to sign their register can be refreshing.

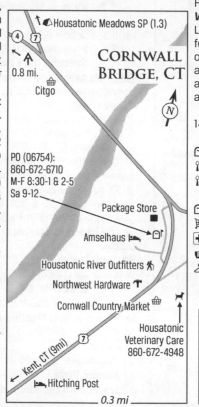

↑ 🛶 Housatonic Meadows SP (1.3)

④ ⑦

CORNWALL BRIDGE, CT

0.8 mi.

Citgo

N

PO (06754):
860-672-6710
M-F 8:30-1 & 2-5
Sa 9-12

Package Store ◼

Amselhaus 🛏 🏧

Housatonic River Outfitters 🧍

Northwest Hardware ⬒

Cornwall Country Market 🛒

Housatonic Veterinary Care 860-672-4948

← Kent, CT (9mi) ⑦

🛏 Hitching Post

── 0.3 mi ──

🏠🕙🏡🚶🚐📶 **Bearded Woods One-of-a-Kind Bunk & Dine** 860-480-2966 Hudson and BIG Lu offer accommodations in their home to hikers $50PP includes: bunk with linens, shower & laundry with amenities, shuttle to/from trail and post office. Cash only. Call or text Hudson for *pickup from West Cornwall, Falls Village or Salisbury*. Last call and shuttle at 5:30. Longer shuttles for a fee. All guests are invited for a family-style dinner and breakfast. Smoking outside. Resupplies available, including stove fuel and Aquamira. Slackpacking and bagged lunches available. Open Memorial weekend to Sept. 1. Relax and let your AT experience be fulfilled.

1479.1   West Cornwall Rd
     West Cornwall, CT 06796 (2.2E)
🏤 M-F 8:30-12 & 2-4:30, Sa 9-12, 860-672-6791
🍴 **Wandering Moose Café** 860-672-0178
🍴 **Buck's Ice Cream**
     Sharon, CT 06069 (4.7W)
🏤 M-F 9:30-4:30, Sa 9:30-12:30, 860-364-5306
🛒 **Sharon Farm Market**
➕ **Sharon Hospital** 860-364-4141
💊 **Sharon Pharmacy**
△ **Queen B Cleaner** 7 days 7-9.

149
CT

About the Author

David Miller (Awol) thru-hiked the AT in 2003, and is the author of *Awol on the Appalachian Trail.* David is a life member of the Appalachian Trail Conservancy.

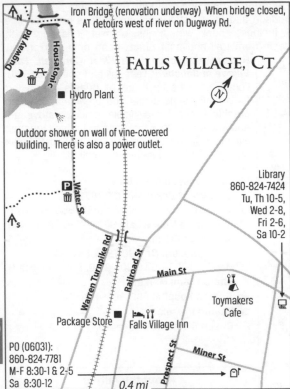

Iron Bridge (renovation underway) When bridge closed, AT detours west of river on Dugway Rd.

FALLS VILLAGE, CT

Dugway Rd

Housatonic

■ Hydro Plant

Outdoor shower on wall of vine-covered building. There is also a power outlet.

Library
860-824-7424
Tu, Th 10-5,
Wed 2-8,
Fri 2-6,
Sa 10-2

Water St

Warren Turnpike Rd

Railroad St

Main St

Toymakers Cafe

Package Store

Falls Village Inn

Prospect St

Miner St

PO (06031):
860-824-7781
M-F 8:30-1 & 2-5
Sa 8:30-12

0.4 mi

🛏 **Bearded Woods One-of-a-Kind Bunk & Dine** Will pick up from Falls Village or Salisbury. See details on pg. 149.

1488.3   Water Street Parking Area
   Falls Village, CT 06031 (*more services on map*)
🍴🚿 **Toymakers Café** 860-824-8168 B/L Thursday-Sunday (Th-F 7-2, Sa-Su 7-4) free tent sites, hiker friendly, knock on upstairs door if closed. Cash only.
🛏🍴 **Falls Village Inn** 860-824-0033 $199/up, also has restaurant & bar.

1495.3   Cobble Rd (0.5W)
1495.7   Undermountain Rd (0.8W)
   Salisbury, CT 06068 (*more services on map*)
🏠✉ **Maria McCabe** offers rooms in her home, 860-435-0593, $35PP, includes shower, use of living room, shuttle to coin laundry, cash only. Guest maildrops 4 Grove Street.
🏠⛺✉ **Vanessa Breton** offers rooms in her home, 860-435-9577, cell 860-671-1457 four beds $40PP, pets $5, laundry $5. Guest maildrops: 7 The Lock Up Rd, Salisbury, CT 06068.
🍴 **Chaiwalla** 860-435-9758 W-Su 10-6. Hiker friendly tea room. Closed in Mar, open weekends only in winter.
🏃✉ **Peter Becks Village Store** 860-596-4217 ⟨www.peterbecks.com⟩ M-Sa 10-6, Su 10-4, full line of gear, denatured alcohol/oz and canisters. Maildrops: 19 Main Street, Salisbury, CT 06068.
🛒🍴 **LaBonne's Market** M-Sa 8-7, Sunday until 6pm. Grocery, deli, bakery, pizza by the slice.
ℹ **Town Hall** 860-435-5170 M-F 8:30-4 Hikers welcome to use bathrooms and phone (local calls only).
   Lakeville, CT
   (*2.0 mi. south of Salisbury*)
🛏📶 **Inn at Iron Masters** 860-435-9844 On US 44 1.0 south of of Town Hall. $159/up Apr - midNov, $131 midNov-Mar, cont B, all non-smoking, 2 pet rooms available.
🍴 **Boathouse** 860-435-2111 Sports bar/restaurant
🍴 **Mizza's Pizza** 860-435-6266
⛭ **Washboard Laundromat** Behind Mizza's

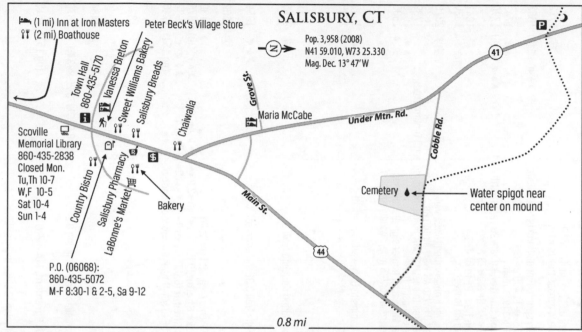

SALISBURY, CT

Pop. 3,958 (2008)
N41 59.010, W73 25.330
Mag. Dec. 13° 47'W

(1 mi) Inn at Iron Masters
(2 mi) Boathouse

Peter Beck's Village Store

Town Hall
860-435-5170

Vanessa Breton

Sweet Williams Bakery

Salisbury Breads

Chaiwalla

Grove St.

Maria McCabe

Under Mtn. Rd.

Cobble Rd.

Scoville
Memorial Library
860-435-2838
Closed Mon.
Tu,Th 10-7
W,F 10-5
Sat 10-4
Sun 1-4

Country Bistro

Salisbury Pharmacy

LaBonne's Market

Bakery

Cemetery

Water spigot near
center on mound

Main St.

44

41

P.O. (06068):
860-435-5072
M-F 8:30-1 & 2-5, Sa 9-12

0.8 mi

1509.8   Elbow Trailhead on MA 41

Racebrook Lodge 413-229-2916 ⟨www.
rblodge.com⟩ Rates lowest off-season (Nov-May). M-Th
$105-$170, F-Su $115-245. Stay includes breakfast. Pets
$15/night. **Stagecoach Tavern** on-site open Th-Su for
dinner. Accepts Visa/MC/Disc, open year-round. Guest
maildrops: 864 S Undermountain Rd, Sheffield, MA 01257.

1513.5   MA 41   *South Egremont, MA 01258* (1.2W)

M-F 8:15-12 & 12:30-4, Sa 9-11:30, 413-528-1571

(0.1W) **ATC New England Regional Office** 413-528-8002 in Kellogg
Conservation Center.

Egremont Market 413-528-0075 Market and deli 6:30am-7pm 7 days.
Ice cream, trail mix, sodas.

Mom's Country Cafe 413-528-2414 Breakfast/Lunch restaurant open
6:30-3 every day and 5-9pm F-Su. Breakfast all day, free refills on coffee,
outdoor water spigot, hikers welcome.

151

CT

152 MA

SoBo	NoBo	Feature	Elev
687.3	1498.0	Lions Head Trail 0.5W to Bunker Hill Rd	1493
687.0	1498.3	Lions Head, view, bypass trail to west	1712
686.2	1499.1	**Riga Shelter,** spring, Tent platform behind shelter	1653
		28.9◀18.9◀7.5◀▶1.2▶10.0▶10.1	
685.6	1499.7	Ball Brook Campsite, stream	1743
685.0	1500.3	**Brassie Brook Shelter,** stream 20 yards north on AT	1770
		20.1◀8.7◀1.2◀▶8.8▶8.9▶23.2	
684.5	1500.8	Undermountain Trail 1.9E to CT 4	1841
684.3	1501.0	Bear Mountain Rd to west	1920
683.6	1501.7	Bear Mountain, rock observation tower, view.	2316
683.2	1502.1	Unmarked trail 0.6W to Mt Washington Rd	1828
683.0	1502.3	Paradise Lane Trail to east, **CT-MA** border 50 yards north (not marked)	1739
682.8	1502.5	Sages Ravine Campsite to west.	1576
682.4	1502.9	Sages Ravine, Misplaced border sign at footbridge.	1535
		AT parallel to stream for 0.3 mile, swimming holes.	
681.1	1504.2	Laurel Ridge Campsite 0.1W, spring to south.	1649
680.9	1504.4	Stream.	1685
679.1	1506.2	Mt Race, views along ridgeline for 0.6S	2365
678.0	1507.3	Race Brook Falls Trail 0.3E to Campsite	1950
677.3	1508.0	Mt Everett	2602
676.6	1508.7	Guilder Pond Picnic Area, Mt Everett Rd.	2130
676.2	1509.1	**The Hemlocks Shelter** (0.1E) 17.5◀10.0◀8.8◀▶0.1▶14.4▶19.7	1975
676.1	1509.2	**Glen Brook Shelter** (0.1E) 10.1◀8.9◀0.1◀▶14.3▶19.6▶21.4	1932
675.5	1509.8	Elbow Trail 1.5E to MA 41 near **Racebrook Lodge**	1746
		(pg.151)	
674.5	1510.8	Mt Bushnell	1822
673.4	1511.9	Jug End, view	1464
672.7	1512.6	Jug End Rd, unreliable piped spring 0.2E N42 8.665 W73 25.893 **P**	876
671.8	1513.5	MA 41, **South Egremont, MA** (1.2W) (pg.151)	810
670.8	1514.5	Footbridge, stream (2 close together).	707
670.2	1515.1	Footbridge, stream	702
670.0	1515.3	Sheffield Egremont Rd, Shays Rebellion Monument N42 8.828 W73 23.200 **P**	700
669.2	1516.1	Gravel road	750
668.9	1516.4	West Rd (paved)	714
668.2	1517.1	US 7, RR to south, soda vending 0.2E at repair shop. **Sheffield, MA** (3.0E), **Great Barrington, MA** (3.0W) (pg.154-155)	694
668.0	1517.3	Footbridge, stream	682

NoBo	Description	Elev
1518.0	Housatonic River, cross on Kellogg Rd Bridge . . . . N42 8.637 W73 21.572 P	720
1518.4	Boardman St	728
1519.8	June Mtn	1238
1520.0	Homes Rd (paved)	1150
1520.8	Footbridge, spring at bottom of cleft	1577
1521.4	East Mountain, view	1800
1521.8	Woods road	1829
1523.5	Ice Gulch, **Tom Leonard Shelter** . . . . ◖ ◗ ⊏ (10)	1617
	23.2◄14.4◄14.3▶5.3▶7.1▶21.1 Campsite overlooking ravine north of shelter.	
	Stream 0.2 on path to left or 0.3 on path to right.	
1524.6	Lake Buel Rd (paved), parking area with kiosk. N42 10.471 W73 17.639 P	1150
1525.5	MA 23 (paved) **East Mountain Retreat Center** (1.0W) N42 11.065 W73 17.444 P (pg.155)	1050
1526.7	Blue Hill Rd (paved), Stony Brook Rd	1550
1527.4	Beartown Mtn Rd, Benedict Pond, 0.5W on blue-blazed trail to	1621
1527.6	**Beartown State Forest**, beach, picnic area, phone, tent sites $10.	1641
	Benedict Pond Loop Trail to west, footbridge and stream east of AT	
1528.1	The Ledges	1820
1528.5	Stream.	1683
1528.8	**Mt Wilcox South Shelters** ◖ ◗ (5) ⊏ (6/12)	1852
	19.7◄19.6◄5.3▶1.8▶15.8▶24.6 Old shelter 0.1E (6), newer shelter 0.2E (12).	
1529.7	Stream (several)	1839
1529.8	Pond, Swann Brook outlet at south end.	1844
1530.6	**Mt Wilcox North Shelter** (0.3E) ⊏ (10)	2136
	21.4◄7.1◄1.8▶14.0▶22.8▶31.6	
1531.3	Motorcycle path	1879
1531.5	Beartown Mountain Rd, NoBo: turn east	1839
1531.8	East Brook, footbridge, more streams north and south	1755
1534.4	Fernside Rd / Jerusalem Rd (gravel).	1200
1534.7	Shaker Campsite to east; platforms, bear box, water north on AT	910
1536.4	Cobble Hill	1233
1536.6	Jerusalem Rd (paved) **Tyringham, MA 01264** (0.6W) (pg.155)	1106
	Water 0.1W on left side of road, water also outside of P.O. 0.6W.	
1537.1	Three streams crossed by footbridges	995
1537.7	Main Rd (paved) **Tyringham, MA** (0.9W) N42 14.125 W73 11.667 P (pg.155)	987
	Water, parking to west.	

SoBo: 667.3, 666.9, 665.5, 665.3, 664.5, 663.9, 663.5, 661.8, 660.7, 659.8, 658.6, 657.9, 657.7, 657.2, 656.8, 656.5, 655.6, 655.5, 654.7, 654.0, 653.8, 653.5, 650.9, 650.6, 648.9, 648.7, 648.2, 647.6

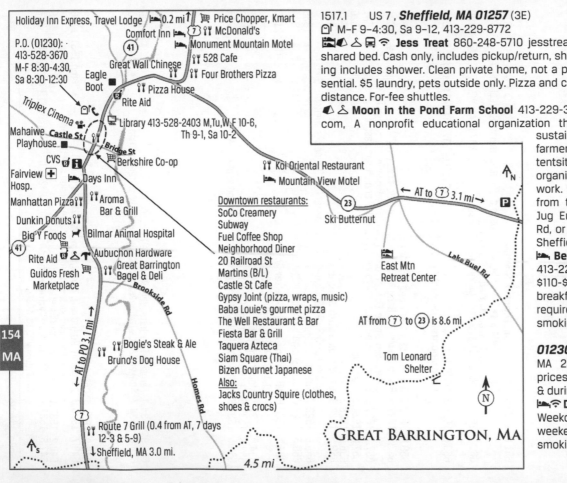

154 MA

Holiday Inn Express, Travel Lodge ⌂ 0.2 mi

Comfort Inn ⌂ ⍾ McDonald's

P.O. (01230):
413-528-3670
M-F 8:30-4:30,
Sa 8:30-12:30

(41)

Eagle Boot

Great Wall Chinese

⍾ Pizza House

Rite Aid

Triplex Cinema ⌂

Mahaiwe Playhouse

Castle St

CVS

Fairview Hosp.

⍾ Days Inn

Manhattan Pizza ⍾

⍾ Aroma Bar & Grill

Dunkin Donuts ⍾

Big Y Foods

(41)

Rite Aid

Aubuchon Hardware

Guidos Fresh Marketplace

⍾ Great Barrington Bagel & Deli

Brookside Rd

⍾ Bogie's Steak & Ale

Bruno's Dog House

AT to PO 3.1 mi

Homes Rd

(7)

⍾ Route 7 Grill (0.4 from AT, 7 days 12-3 & 5-9)

↓ Sheffield, MA 3.0 mi.

↑ S

4.5 mi

⍾ Price Chopper, Kmart

(7) ⍾ McDonald's

⍾ Monument Mountain Motel

⍾ 528 Cafe

⍾ Four Brothers Pizza

Library 413-528-2403 M,Tu,W,F 10-6, Th 9-1, Sa 10-2

Bridge St

⍾ Berkshire Co-op

⍾ Koi Oriental Restaurant

⍾ Mountain View Motel

Downtown restaurants:
SoCo Creamery
Subway
Fuel Coffee Shop
Neighborhood Diner
20 Railroad St
Martins (B/L)
Castle St Cafe
Gypsy Joint (pizza, wraps, music)
Baba Louie's gourmet pizza
The Well Restaurant & Bar
Fiesta Bar & Grill
Taquera Azteca
Siam Square (Thai)
Bizen Gourmet Japanese
Also:
Jacks Country Squire (clothes, shoes & crocs)

(23)

Ski Butternut

← AT to (7) 3.1 mi →

↑ N

P

East Mtn Retreat Center

Lake Buel Rd

AT from (7) to (23) is 8.6 mi

Tom Leonard Shelter

N

GREAT BARRINGTON, MA

1517.1   US 7 , *Sheffield, MA 01257* (3E)
⌂ M-F 9-4:30, Sa 9-12, 413-229-8772

⍾⌂⍾⍾⍾ **Jess Treat** 860-248-5710 jesstrea@gmail.com $35PP or $50 shared bed. Cash only, includes pickup/return, shower, breakfast. $15PP tenting includes shower. Clean private home, not a party place, reservations essential. $5 laundry, pets outside only. Pizza and convenience store in walking distance. For-fee shuttles.

⍾⍾ **Moon in the Pond Farm School** 413-229-3092 dom@moninthepond.com, A nonprofit educational organization that teaches the value of sustainable farming. Organic farmer Dominic Palumbo offers tentsites, shower, $2 laundry, and organic meals in exchange for farm work. Transportation arranged to/from the AT. Can also pickup at Jug End Rd, MA 41, S. Egremont Rd, or Homes Rd. 816 Barnum St., Sheffield, MA 01257

⍾ **Berkshire 1802 House** 413-229-2612 Summer prices $110-$165 for double, includes full breakfast. Multi-night reservation required on weekends, no pets, no smoking.

Great Barrington, MA 01230 (3W from US 7, 4W from MA 23) *Resort town; Lodging prices will be steep on weekends & during special events.

⍾⍾ **Days Inn** 413-528-3150 Weekdays $79, higher on weekends, cont B, no pets, all non-smoking rooms.

🐾🛜✉ **Monument Mountain Motel** 413-528-3272 weekdays $65S $85D. Pickup sometimes avail. Maildrops w/reservation: 247 Stockbridge Rd, Rt 7, Great Barrington, MA 01230

🐾🛜 **Mountain View Motel** 413-528-0250 Weekdays $65S $75D, $20EAP, no pets. Rides sometimes available.

🐾⛺🛜💻✉ **Comfort Inn**
413-644-3200 Prices seasonal. Full B, indoor heated pool & hot tub, no pets. Maildrops with advance reservation: 249 Stockbridge Rd, Rt 7, Great Barrington, MA 01230.

🐾⛺🛜 **Travel Lodge** 413-528-2340 Su-Th $50-89D + tax, $10EAP, cont B, coin laundry.

🏪 **Guido's** Organic produce, cold juices, and more.

➕ **Fairview Hospital** 413-528-0790

1525.5   MA 23

🏨✉ (1W) **East Mountain Retreat Center** 413-528-6617 ⟨www.eastretreat.org⟩ left 1.0 mile, blue sign on left and 0.5 mile on driveway, $10PP donation suggested, shower, use of dryer (no washer), pizzeria delivers to hostel, 10pm curfew and 8:30am checkout. Be aware that other retreat guests practice a vow of silence. Cash only. Maildrops: 8 Lake Buel Rd, Great Barrington, MA 01230.

1536.6   Jerusalem Rd (0.6W to town)
1537.7   Main Rd (0.9W to town)
            Tyringham, MA 01264

🏠 M–F 9-12:30 & 4-5:30, Sa 8:30-12:30, 413-243-1225
🛜💻 **Library** 413-243-1373 Adjacent to P.O. Tu 3-5, Saturday 10-12
🐾**Cobble View B&B** 413-243-2463 Mid-week discounts,includes cont B, no pets, no smoking, Visa/MC accepted.

1544.6   **Upper Goose Pond Cabin** (0.5W)
⛺(14)🔥🚰🌙 On side trail north of pond. Fireplace, covered porch, bunks with mattresses. Swimming and canoeing. The cabin is open daily Memorial Day-Labor Day & weekends through Columbus Day. When caretaker not in residence, hikers may camp on porch (no cooking) or tent platforms. Please store food in bear box. During summer, caretaker brings water; otherwise, pond is water source. Donations requested.

1546.2   US 20
🐾🛜💻✉🚰 (0.1E) **Berkshire Lakeside Lodge** 413-243-9907 Summer rates: weekdays $60-90, weekends $145-160 4-person room w/cont. breakfast. No pets. Hikers welcome to get water. Soda machine. No services nearby but you can get pizza and Chinese food delivered. Maildrops with reservation: 3949 Jacob's Ladder Rd, Rt 10, Becket, MA 01223

        Lee, MA 01238 (5W) Lodging busy and expensive on weekends and during Tanglewood Music Festival.
🏠 M-F 8:30-4:30, Sa 9-12, 413-243-1392
🐾🛜 **Americas Best Value Inn** 413-243-0501 Apr-May $52-55 Su-Th, $65-75 F-Sa, Jun-Oct $60-79 Su-Th, $110-195 F-Sa, cont B.
🐾🛜 **Roadway Inn** 413-243-0813 Jul-Aug $79 weekdays $159-169 weekends, other months $42/up. Cont B.
🐾⛺🛜 **Pilgrim Inn** 413-243-1328 Peak rates Jun 15-Aug; Su-Th $95D, F-Sa $225D. Non-peak rates $85D-$110D. Cont B.
🐾 **Super 8** 413-243-0143
🍴 **Dunkin Donuts, Athena's Pizza House**, **Friendly's**, **Joe's Diner, McDonalds**, and many more.
🏪 **Price Chopper Supermarket** 413-528-2408
💊 **Rite Aid**
🐾 **Valley Veterinary Clinic** 413-243-2414
⛺ **Lee Coin-Op Laundry**

🚌 **BRTA** 800-292-2782 Commuter bus connects *Great Barrington*, *Dalton*, *Cheshire*, *North Adams*, *Adams*, *Williamstown*, *Pittsfield*, *Lee* and **Berkshire Mall**. Buses run M-F 5:45am-7:20pm, Sa 7:15pm-7pm. Fares $1.25/town up to $5 (fare structure may change in 2014), drivers cannot make change. Flag bus anywhere on route.

SoBo	NoBo	Feature	Elev
646.0	1539.3	Baldy Mtn	1901
645.8	1539.5	Webster Rd (gravel)	1800
645.2	1540.1	Knee-Deep Pond to west	1687
644.2	1541.1	Spring on side trail 0.1W	1780
643.4	1541.9	Goose Pond Rd (gravel) N42 16.459 W73 11.025 **P** (0.1E)	1650
643.0	1542.3	Cooper Brook, footbridge	1566
642.5	1542.8	Signed trail junction	1733
		⚠ NoBo: this is not the side trail to Upper Goose Pond Cabin.	
641.4	1543.9	Higley Brook, footbridge, Upper Goose Pond to west	1510
640.8	1544.5	Old chimney	1499
640.7	1544.6	**Upper Goose Pond Cabin** (0.5W) (pg.155)	1570
		21.1◀15.8◀14.0▶8.8▶17.6▶ 34.5	
639.5	1545.8	MA Turnpike I-90	1400
639.2	1546.1	Greenwater Brook, footbridge	1356
639.1	1546.2	US 20, **Lee, MA** (5.0W) hotel 0.1E N42 17.577 W73 9.684 **P** (0.1W) (pg.155)	1400
638.7	1546.6	Powerline, Stream to north	1584
638.3	1547.0	Tyne Rd / Becket Rd, stream to south	1797
637.8	1547.5	Becket Mountain	2180
636.8	1548.5	Walling Mountain	2215
636.2	1549.1	Finerty Pond	1942
634.4	1550.9	Washington Mountain Brook	1762
633.8	1551.5	County Rd (gravel)	1853
633.5	1551.8	Bald Top	2040
631.9	1553.4	**October Mountain Shelter**, intermittent stream, cables ☽ ⌂ ◭ ⌂ (12)	1923
		24.6◀22.8◀8.8▶8.8▶25.7▶ 32.3	
631.2	1554.1	West Branch Rd (gravel)	1960
629.6	1555.7	At joins dirt road and crosses N42 22.618 W73 9.044 **P** (pg.158)	2001
		Washington Mtn Rd (paved), **Becket, MA** 01223 (5.0E)	
627.6	1557.7	Streams	1837

NoBo		Elev
626.5	Blotz Rd (paved), small parking lot on north side ... N42 24.561 W73 9.017 P	1850
625.8	Warner Hill	2050
624.2	Tully Mountain	2092
623.4	Powerline	1944
623.1	**Kay Wood Shelter** (0.2E) 31.6◄17.6◄8.8◄▶16.9▶23.5▶33.4	1775 (10)
622.8	Grange Hall Rd	1655
622.6	Barton Brook, footbridge	1572
621.2	Woods road	1392
620.6	Railroad tracks, Housatonic St + Depot St	1273
620.1	MA 8 & 9, **Dalton, MA** (pg.158)	1200
619.1	AT on Gulf Rd / High St for 1.0 mile ... N42 28.909 W73 10.695 P	1180
616.9	Spring	1915
616.0	Powerlines	1900
615.9	Crystal Mountain Campsite 0.2E, water on AT just north of side trail	1953 (5)
615.1	Gore Brook, outlet of Gore Pond	2028
614.0	Stream	1978
613.6	Stream	1834
612.9	The Cobbles, outcroppings of marble with view of Hoosic River Valley, Mt Greylock, and the town of Cheshire.	1812
611.8	Furnace Hill Rd (south end)	1045
611.3	Main St + School St, **Cheshire, MA** (pg.159)	980
610.8	MA 8, **Cheshire, MA, Adams, MA** (4.0E) (pg.159)	1002
609.7	Outlook Ave (paved), stream and powerline to north	1326
607.1	Old Adams Rd (dirt)	2364

SoBo   NoBo

Elev

✽ **Touch-Me-Not** – Also known as "Jewelweed". Trumpet-shaped flowers with a short curled tail hang horizontally like a bug in flight. Yellow with splotches of orange. Salve from crushed stems is a folk remedy for poison ivy's itch.

1555.7 Washington Mtn Rd

🍂 💧 🚌 ✉ Home of the **"Cookie Lady"** 100 yards east

413-623-5859 Water spigot near the garage door, please sign register on the steps. Homemade cookies often available. Soda, ice cream, boiled eggs & pick your own blueberries. Camping allowed, ask permission first. Shuttle range from Hoyt Rd. in NY to Manchester Center, VT. Maildrops: Roy & Marilyn Wiley, 47 Washington Mountain Road, Becket, MA 01223.

Becket, MA 01223 (5E) 🏠 M–F 8–4, Sa 9–11:30, 413-623-8845

🛏⛺📶(6E) **Becket Motel** 413-623-8888 $95-139+tax, includes shuttle from/to US 20 or Wash Mtn Rd). Tavern next door. Guest maildrops: 29 Chester Road, Becket, MA 01223.

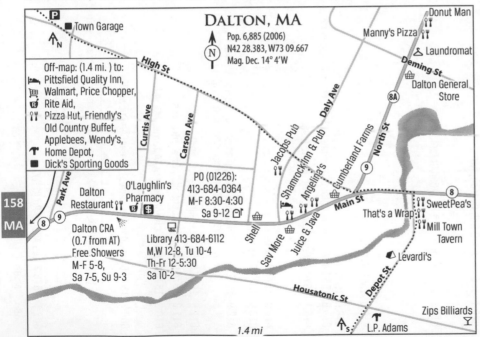

DALTON, MA
Pop. 6,885 (2006)
N42 28.383, W73 09.667
Mag. Dec. 14° 4'W

■ Town Garage

Off-map: (1.4 mi.) to:
🛏 Pittsfield Quality Inn,
🛒 Walmart, Price Chopper,
💊 Rite Aid,
🍴 Pizza Hut, Friendly's Old Country Buffet, Applebees, Wendy's,
🔧 Home Depot,
■ Dick's Sporting Goods

High St

Curtis Ave

Carson Ave

Park Ave

Dalton Restaurant 🍴

O'Laughlin's Pharmacy 💊 💲

PO (01226):
413-684-0364
M–F 8:30–4:30
Sa 9–12 🏠

Dalton CRA
(0.7 from AT)
Free Showers
M–F 5-8,
Sa 7-5, Su 9-3

Library 413-684-6112
M,W 12-8, Tu 10-4
Th-Fr 12-5:30
Sa 10-2

Shell

Sav More

Juice & Java

Jacobs Pub

Shamrock Inn & Pub

Angelina's

Cumberland Farms

Daly Ave

North St

Main St

That's a Wrap

Donut Man

Manny's Pizza 🍴

⛓ Laundromat

Deming St

Dalton General Store

8A

9

8

🍴 SweetPea's

🍴 Mill Town Tavern

▲ Levardi's

Housatonic St

Depot St

Zips Billiards

🔧 L.P. Adams

1.4 mi

Berkshire Mall on SR 8, 4 mi. north of Dalton & 7 mi. south of Cheshire has:

🏃 **EMS** 413-445-4967

🎬 **Regal Cinema 10** 413-445-4967

1565.2   MA 8 & 9   **Dalton, MA 01227**

🍂⚕💧 **Thomas Levardi** 413-684-3359, 413-212-9691. 83 Depot Street, allows hikers to use water spigot outside and, with permission, provides the hospitality of his front porch and back yard for tenting. Space is limited.

🛏⛺📶💻 **Shamrock Village Inn** 413-684-0860 Tax included hiker rates Su-Th are $70.17 for room with a double bed or $72.67 for a room with 2 doubles or 1 queen bed. Fri&Sat $91.53/$100.68 respectively. Well-behaved pets allowed with $75 deposit. Coin laundry, free use of computer and WiFi.

🍴 **That's a Wrap** sandwiches, **Angelina's Subs** with veggie burgers, **Dalton Restaurant** serves D Th–Sa with live entertainment.

🍴 **SweetPea's** Ice cream, summer hours M-Th 12-9, F-Sa 12-10, Su 1-8

⛺ **Dalton Laundry** M-F 9-6, Sa 10-4, Su 10-2.

🔧 **LP Adams** Coleman/denatured alcohol.

Pittsfield, MA Many stores & restaurants approx. 2.0W from Dalton, see map.

🛏⛺📶 **Pittsfield Quality Inn** 413-443-5661 prices seasonal.

| 1574.0 | Main St, School St |
| 1575.5 | MA 8 (4.0E) |

Cheshire, MA 01225

🏠⊕⊗✉ **St. Mary of the Assumption Church** Check in with Father David Raymond (west side door near the mailbox). Use of restrooms and outside cooking area. No laundry or showers. No smoking, alcohol or drugs on church property. Welcome to attend service in hiker attire. Please donate. Maildrops: 159 Church Street, Cheshire, MA 01225.

🏠🛏⚿📶🖥✉ **Harbour House Inn Bed & Breakfast** 413-743-8959 (Eva) ⟨www.harbourhouseinn.com⟩ $85D hiker rate Su-Th, sometimes available on weekends. Includes breakfast, no pets, no smoking, shuttle w/stay often available. Guest maildrops: 725 North State Rd, Cheshire, MA 01225.

🔧 **AT Bicycle Works & Outfitters** 413-822-5357 ⟨www.atbicycleworks.com⟩ Some hiker supplies, Coleman/alcohol by ounce and canisters, owner is 2005 thru-hiker Larry "Draggin" Dragon. No regular hours, call and he will open shop for you.

🍴 **Cobble View Pub & Pizzeria** T–Su 11-10

🍴 **Diane's Twist** Limited hours, deli sandwiches, soda, ice cream.

🏪 **HD Reynolds** a general store, hiker snacks and Coleman fuel.

🚌 **BRTA** stops across the street from the post office.

East from MA 8:

🔧 (2.2E) **Berkshire Outfitters** 413-743-5900 ⟨www.berkshireoutfitters.com⟩ M-F 10-6, Sa 10-5, Su 11-4, Full service outfitter, Coleman/alcohol/oz, freeze-dried foods, minor equipment repairs.

Adams, MA 01220 (4.2E)

🏤 M–F 8:30–4:30, Sa 10–12, 413-743-5177

🏠🛏⚿ **Mount Greylock Inn** 413-743-2665 ⟨www.mountgreylockinn.com⟩ Accepts major CC, open year round.

🛒 **Big Y Foods Supermarket**

💊 **Rite Aid**, **Medicine Shop**

🐾 **Adams Veterinary Clinic** 413-743-4000

🧺⚡ **Thrifty Bundle Laundromat**, **Waterworks**, fast-food outlets.

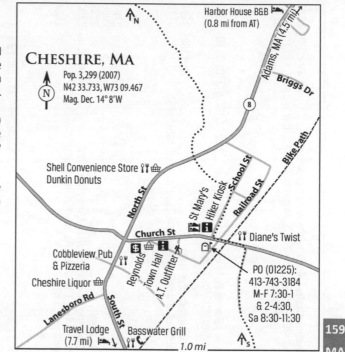

CHESHIRE, MA
Pop. 3,299 (2007)
N42 33.733, W73 09.467
Mag. Dec. 14° 8'W

Harbor House B&B
(0.8 mi from AT)

Adams, MA (4.5 mi)

Briggs Dr

Bike Path

Shell Convenience Store
Dunkin Donuts

North St

School St

Railroad St

St Mary's
Hiker Kiosk

Diane's Twist

Church St

Cobbleview Pub
& Pizzeria

Reynolds
Town Hall

A.T. Outfitter

Cheshire Liquor

Lanesboro Rd

South St

Travel Lodge
(7.7 mi)

Basswater Grill

PO (01225):
413-743-3184
M-F 7:30-1
& 2-4:30,
Sa 8:30-11:30

1.0 mi

159
MA

SoBo	NoBo	Description	Elev
606.2	1579.1	**Mark Noepel Shelter** (0.2E), spring to right of shelter . . . ☾ ● ◀ ⊏ (10)	2843
		34.5◀25.7◀16.9▶6.6▶16.5▶23.7 Spring stronger the farther you go.	
605.7	1579.6	Jones Nose Trail to west	3249
603.9	1581.4	Rockwell Rd / Summit Rd to west. N42 37.864 W73 10.696 P	3026
603.5	1581.8	Cross Rockwell Rd twice, side trails to east	3146
602.9	1582.4	Mt Greylock, highest peak in MA. 🏠(pg.162)	3491
602.5	1582.8	Thunderbolt Trail and Bellows Pipe Trail, 75 yards apart, both to east.	3112
600.9	1584.4	Bernard Farm Trail	2793
600.6	1584.7	Mt Williams	2966
599.8	1585.5	Notch Rd (paved)	2335
599.6	1585.7	**Wilbur Clearing Shelter** (0.3W) On Money Brook Trail . . . ☾ ◊ ● ⊏ (8)	2300
		32.3◀23.5◀6.6▶9.9▶17.1▶23.0 Intermittent stream.	
599.3	1586.0	Mt Prospect Trail to west.	2524
597.7	1587.6	Pattison Rd (paved) . . . N42 41.256 W73 9.586 P	1035
597.1	1588.2	Phelps Ave (south end), on road 0.5 mile	743
596.6	1588.7	MA 2, Hoosic River. . . . N42 41.941 W73 9.208 P (0.1E) (pg.162-163) **North Adams, MA** (east)	660
		footbridge and RR tracks, **Williamstown, MA** (west), 0.1 mile	
596.5	1588.8	Massachusetts Ave, NoBo: east on road for 0.1 mile	678
596.2	1589.1	Footbridge, stream.	759
595.0	1590.3	Petes Spring. Sherman Brook Campsite 0.1W . . . ☾ ●	1354
594.3	1591.0	Bad weather bypass trail.	1808
593.9	1591.4	Pine Cobble Trail to west.	2112
593.8	1591.5	'98 Trail to west.	2132
592.5	1592.8	**MA-VT** border, southern end of Long Trail (LT) . . . ●	2330
592.1	1593.2	The AT and LT are concurrent northbound for the next 105.2 miles. Spring, stream to north.	2172
590.0	1595.3	Stream.	2089
589.7	1595.6	**Seth Warner Shelter** (0.2W) . . . ☾ ◊ ● ⊏ (8)	2243
		33.4◀16.5◀9.9▶7.2▶13.1▶21.6 Brook 0.1 left of shelter, known to dry up.	
589.4	1595.9	Country Rd, Powerline	2290
587.7	1597.6	Powerline . . . ●	2872
586.8	1598.5	Roaring Branch, pond . . . ●	2478

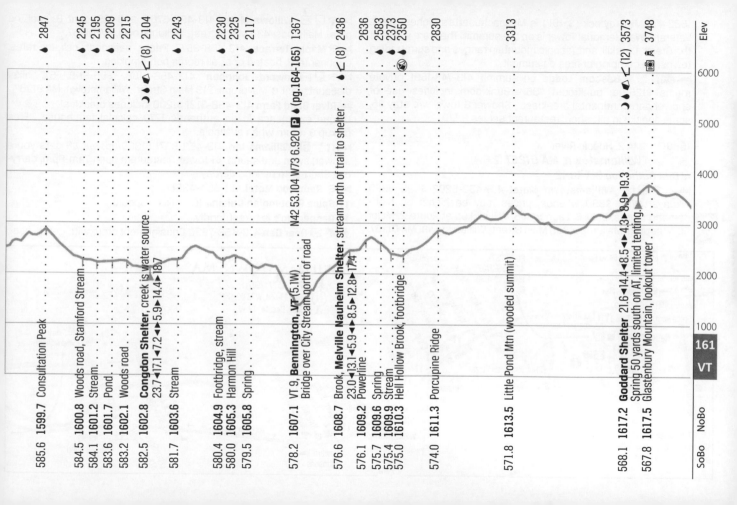

SoBo	NoBo	Feature	Elev
585.6	1599.7	Consultation Peak	2847
584.5	1600.8	Woods road, Stamford Stream	2245
584.1	1601.2	Stream.	2195
583.6	1601.7	Pond.	2209
583.2	1602.1	Woods road	2215
582.5	1602.8	**Congdon Shelter**, creek is water source 23.7◄17.1◄7.2◄▶5.9▶14.4▶18.7	⊂(8) 2104
581.7	1603.6	Stream	2243
580.4	1604.9	Footbridge, stream	2230
580.0	1605.3	Harmon Hill	2325
579.5	1605.8	Spring	2117
578.2	1607.1	VT 9, **Bennington, VT** (5.1W) Bridge over City Stream north of road N42 53.104 W73 6.920 P (pg.164-165)	1367
576.6	1608.7	Brook, **Melville Nauheim Shelter**, stream north of trail to shelter 23.0◄13.1◄5.9◄▶8.5▶12.8▶17.4	⊂(8) 2436
576.1	1609.2	Powerline	2636
575.7	1609.6	Spring	2583
575.4	1609.9	Stream	2373
575.0	1610.3	Hell Hollow Brook, footbridge	2350
574.0	1611.3	Porcupine Ridge	2830
571.8	1613.5	Little Pond Mtn (wooded summit)	3313
568.1	1617.2	**Goddard Shelter** 21.6◄14.4◄8.5◄▶4.3▶8.9▶19.3 Spring 50 yards south on AT, limited tenting.	⊂(12) 3573
567.8	1617.5	Glastenbury Mountain, lookout tower	3748

Elev

1582.4   Mt Greylock (3,491') is Massachusetts's highest peak. Veterans War Memorial Tower is on the summit. There are views of the Green, Catskill, and Taconic mountain ranges and surrounding towns. No camping or fires on summit.

🛏️🛏️🍴🚿📶 **Bascom Lodge** on summit 413-743-1591 private rooms $125/up, bunkroom $36.   Bunkroom includes use of shower and continental breakfast.   Shower & towel w/o stay $5, some snacks in gift shop, restaurant serves B/L/D.

1588.7   MA 2, Hoosic River
Williamstown, MA 01267 (2.6W)
ALDHA Gathering Oct. 10-12

🛏️🚶📶🖥️✉️ **Williamstown Motel** 413-458-5202 $59S $69D wkdays; $79S $89D wkends; prices may be higher on high-demand nights. Cont B. Laundry $8. Will pickup at Route 2. Major CC accepted. Maildrops: 295 Main Street, Williamstown, MA 01267.

🛏️📶🖥️✉️ **Willows Motel** 413-458-5768, $69-129, cont B, pool, no pets. Maildrops: 480 Main Street, Williamstown, MA 01267.

🛏️📶 **Maple Terrace** 413-458-9677 Prices seasonal, call for rates. Continental B, heated pool, all rooms non-smoking.

🛏️📶🖥️✉️ **Howard Johnson** 413-458-8158, $55-$119, 5% hiker discount, cont B. Maildrops: 213 Main Street, Williamstown, MA 01267.

🛏️ **River Bend Farm** 413-458-3121 $120D includes breakfast. Unique experience in an authentic 1770 colonial farmhouse.   Free pickup & return when available.

🛏️🍴🚿Ⓟ **Williams Inn** 413-458-9371 $180D/up, but $6 gets you a shower, swim and sauna, $1 towel. Restaurant open 7am-9pm, carry-out. Short term parking $2/day.

🛏️📶 **Redwood Motel** 413-664-4351

🍴 **Spice Root Indian Cuisine** 10% hiker discount.

🍴 **Desperado's** is hiker friendly.

🚶🔧✉️ **Gear Den** 413-458-7990 Consignment store with gently used

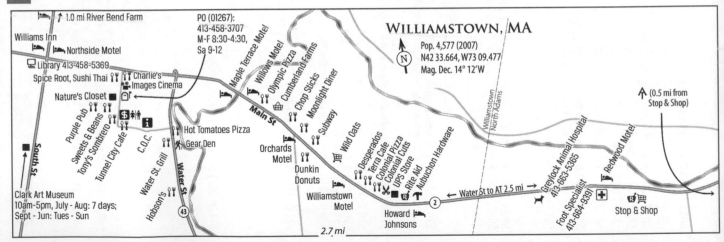

outdoor clothing & gear. Small inventory of new backpacking supplies including books, maps & clothes. Fuel/oz and canister fuel. Camping allowed in back of the store next to river. Maildrops: 130 Water St. Williamstown, MA 01267.

✉ **Nature's Closet** Apparel & footwear. Maildrops: 61 Spring St, Williamstown, MA 01267.

💻 **Milne Public Library** M-F 10-5:30, W 10-8, Sa 10-4

🚌 **Greyhound Bus Service**

North Adams, MA 01247 (services spread out east of AT)

🛏🍴⛺🛜💻 **Holiday Inn** 413-663-6500 Summer rates $169.99/up. Pool, hot tub. **Richmond Grill** on-site.

🍴 **Oriental Buffet**, AYCE L/D buffet

➕ **North Adams Regional Hospital** 413-664-5000

✈ **Greylock Animal Hospital** 413-663-5365, M-Th 8-7, F 8-5, Sa 8-3, Su 9-3, M-F doctor on call until 11pm.

🚌 **David Ackerson** 413-346-1033, 413-652-9573 daveackerson@yahoo.com Shuttles to trailheads ranging from Bear Mtn Bridge to Hanover, and to/from area airports.

Red-spotted newt *is the slow-moving red salamander that can be seen anywhere along the AT. The newt lives on land for the middle stage of its life, which lasts about two years. During this stage, it's also known as a **red eft**. It is a tadpole in its first stage. In its last stage it returns to water and turns green, but retains its red spots.*

163

MA

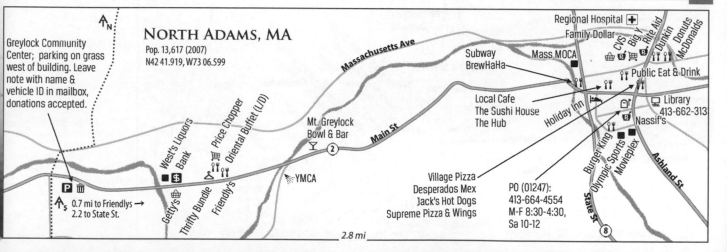

NORTH ADAMS, MA

Pop. 13,617 (2007)
N42 41.919, W73 06.599

Greylock Community Center; parking on grass west of building. Leave note with name & vehicle ID in mailbox, donations accepted.

0.7 mi to Friendlys →
2.2 to State St.

West's Liquors
Bank
Price Chopper
Oriental Buffet (L/D)
Getty's
Thrifty Bundle
Friendly's
YMCA

Mt. Greylock
Bowl & Bar
(2)
Main St

Massachusetts Ave

Subway
BrewHaHa

Local Cafe
The Sushi House
The Hub

Village Pizza
Desperados Mex
Jack's Hot Dogs
Supreme Pizza & Wings

PO (01247):
413-664-4554
M-F 8:30-4:30,
Sa 10-12

Regional Hospital ➕
Family Dollar
Mass MOCA

CVS Big Y Rite Aid
Dunkin
Donuts
McDonalds

Public Eat & Drink

Holiday Inn

Library
413-662-313

Nassif's

Burger King
Olympic Sports
Moviplex

Ashland St
State St
(8)

2.8 mi

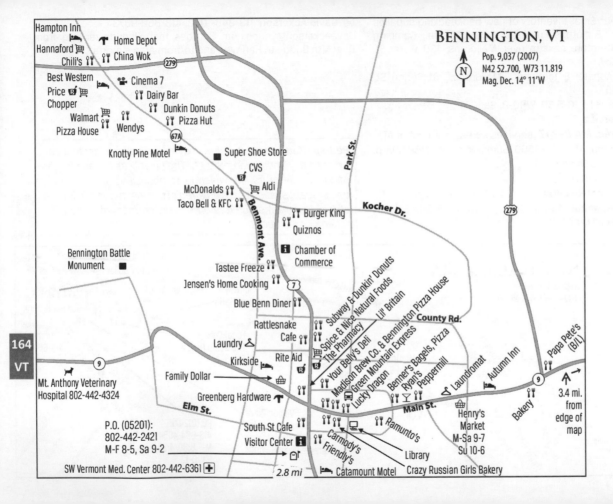

BENNINGTON, VT

Pop. 9,037 (2007)
N42 52.700, W73 11.819
Mag. Dec. 14° 11'W

Hampton Inn
Home Depot
Hannaford
China Wok
Chili's

Best Western
Cinema 7
Price Chopper
Dairy Bar
Walmart
Dunkin Donuts
Pizza House
Pizza Hut
Wendys

Knotty Pine Motel

Super Shoe Store
CVS
Aldi
McDonalds
Taco Bell & KFC

Burger King
Quiznos

Chamber of Commerce

Bennington Battle Monument

Tastee Freeze
Jensen's Home Cooking

Blue Benn Diner

Park St.

Kocher Dr.

279

Subway & Dunkin' Donuts
Nice Natural Foods
Spice
Lil' Britain

The Pharmacy

County Rd.

Rattlesnake Cafe

Laundry

Kirkside
Rite Aid

Family Dollar

Greenberg Hardware

Mt. Anthony Veterinary Hospital 802-442-4324

Elm St.

P.O. (05201):
802-442-2421
M-F 8-5, Sa 9-2

South St Cafe

Visitor Center

SW Vermont Med. Center 802-442-6361

2.8 mi

Your Belly's Deli
Madison Brew Co.
Green Mountain Express
Lucky Dragon
Bennington Pizza House

Benner's Bagels, Pizza
Ryan's
Peppermill

Autumn Inn

Papa Pete's (B/L)

Laundromat

Bakery

3.4 mi. from edge of map

Main St.

Ramunto's

Library

Henry's Market
M-Sa 9-7
Su 10-6

Carmody's
Friendly's

Crazy Russian Girls Bakery

Catamount Motel

164
VT

Bennington, VT 05201 (5.1W)

🛏🏕🚐🛜🖥📧 **Autumn Inn Motel** 802-447-7625 $60S $69D, $10 (each way) for pickup or return to trail. Guest maildrops: 924 Main Street, Bennington, VT 05201.

🛏🛜 **Kirkside Motor Lodge** 802-447-7596, $79/up, reduced rates for hikers, prices seasonal.

🛏🛜🖥📧 **Knotty Pine Motel** 802-442-5487 ⟨www.knottypinemotel.com⟩ 6.5 miles from the AT on VT 9, $80/up, includes cont B, pets free, pool. Maildrops (guests only): 130 Northside Drive, Bennington, VT 05201.

🛏🛜 **Catamount Motel** 802-442-5977, $50S, $10EAP (up to 4 in a room for $80) + tax, Pets okay, accepts credit cards.

🛏🛜 **Best Western** 802-442-6311

🛏🏕🛜🖥 **Hampton Inn** 802-440-9862 rates seasonal, cont bfast.

🍴 **Lil' Britain** Fish & chips.

🚐 **Green Mountain Express** 802-447-0477 ⟨www.greenmtncn.org⟩ 215 Pleasant St. Free bus route "Emerald Line" passes between Bennington and Wilmington (17E) 3 times a day M-F. Board at town bus station, or flag the bus down at the trailhead. You may also request an unscheduled ride from town to trail for $3.

🚐 **Bennington Taxi** 802-442-9052

🎞 **Cinema 7**

■ **Marra's Shoe Service** 802-442-8464 Shoe & clothing repairs.

■ **Bennington Battle Monument** Contains statue of Seth Warner, Revolutionary War leader of the Green Mountain Boys, for whom the shelter is named.

        (3.0E) Prospect Mountain Ski Area

🏠🔥🛜 **Greenwood Lodge & Campsites** 802-442-2547 bunk prices approx. $30.

Green Mountain Club (GMC) ⟨www.greenmountainclub.org⟩ Maintains the AT in Vermont. There is an overnight fee of $5PP at Stratton Pond Shelter, North Shore Tenting Area, and Little Rock Pond Shelter and Tenting Area, and anyone camping within 0.5 mile of these sites. Hikers who pay the $5 fee in cash at Stratton Pond or Little Rock Pond will receive a dated receipt that they can use within 7 days for one free night at the other fee site.

⚠ There are muddy sections of trail in Vermont. Please walk through the mud; do not trample vegetation bordering the trail.

Travel and Camp on Durable Surfaces

• Stay on the trail; never shortcut switchbacks. Take breaks off-trail on durable surfaces, such as rock or grass.

• Restrict activities to areas where vegetation is already absent.

• Avoid expanding existing trails and campsites by walking in the middle of the trail, and using the already-impacted core areas of campsites.

• If tree branches block the trail, move them off if possible, rather than going around and creating new trails.

• Wear gaiters and waterproof boots, so you may walk through puddles instead of walking around them and creating a wide spot in the trail.

Read more of the Leave No Trace techniques developed for the A.T.:   www.appalachiantrail.org/LNT

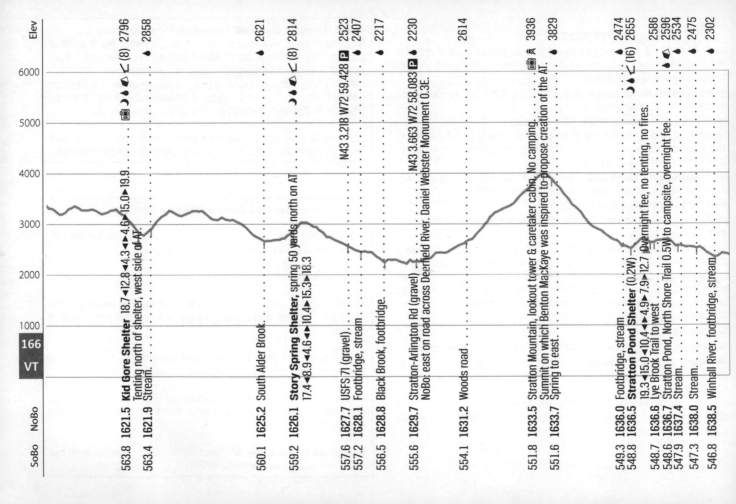

Elev		

SoBo	NoBo	
		Elev
563.8	1621.5	**Kid Gore Shelter** 18.7◀12.8◀4.3◀▶15.0▶19.9 ◎ ⌣ ◑ ◣ ⊏ (8) 2796
		Tenting north of shelter, west side of AT. ◣ 2858
563.4	1621.9	Stream.
560.1	1625.2	South Alder Brook. ◣ 2621
559.2	1626.1	**Story Spring Shelter**, spring 50 yards north on AT ⌣ ◑ ◣ ⊏ (8) 2814
		17.4◀8.9◀4.6◀▶10.4▶15.3▶18.3
557.6	1627.7	USFS 71 (gravel). N43 3.218 W72 59.428 🅿 ◣ 2523
557.2	1628.1	Footbridge, stream. ◣ 2407
556.5	1628.8	Black Brook, footbridge. ◣ 2217
555.6	1629.7	Stratton-Arlington Rd (gravel) N43 3.663 W72 58.083 🅿 ◣ 2230
		NoBo: east on road across Deerfield River. Daniel Webster Monument 0.3E.
554.1	1631.2	Woods road. 2614
551.8	1633.5	Stratton Mountain, lookout tower & caretaker cabin. No camping. ◎ 🏛 3936
		Summit on which Benton MacKaye was inspired to propose creation of the AT.
551.6	1633.7	Spring to east. ◣ 3829
549.3	1636.0	Footbridge, stream. ⌣ ◣ ⊏ (16) 2474
548.8	1636.5	**Stratton Pond Shelter** (0.2W) ◣ 2655
		19.3◀15.0◀10.4◀▶4.9▶7.9▶12.7 Overnight fee, no tenting, no fires.
548.7	1636.6	Lye Brook Trail to west. 2586
548.6	1636.7	Stratton Pond, North Shore Trail 0.5W to campsite, overnight fee. ⌂ 2596
547.9	1637.4	Stream. ◣ 2534
547.3	1638.0	Stream. ◣ 2475
546.8	1638.5	Winhall River, footbridge, stream. ◣ 2302

166

VT

SoBo	NoBo	Description	Elev
545.3	1640.0	Stream.	2246
543.9	1641.4	**William B. Douglas Shelter** (0.5W) 19.9◄15.3◄4.9◄▶3.0▶7.8▶15.9 Spring to left of shelter.	2304
543.0	1642.3	Prospect Rock to west, view. ⚠ NoBo: At turns east off gravel road.	2150
540.9	1644.4	**Spruce Peak Shelter** (0.1W) 18.3◄7.9◄3.0◄▶4.8▶12.9▶17.6.	2247
540.5	1644.8	Spruce Peak 0.1W	2040
540.1	1645.2	Stream, powerline	1833
539.9	1645.4	Stream.	1887
538.6	1646.7	Powerline, footbridge, stream	1704
538.1	1647.2	VT 11 & 30 N43 12.409 W72 58.243 **P** (pg.168-169) **Manchester Center, VT** (5.4W)	1840
537.2	1648.1	Footbridge, stream	2140
536.1	1649.2	**Bromley Shelter** 12.7◄7.8◄4.8◄▶8.1▶12.8▶14.3.	2605
535.5	1649.8	Ski slope	3088
535.1	1650.2	Bromley Mountain, no tenting or fires	3260
532.6	1652.7	Mad Tom Notch, USFS 21 (gravel), water from pump	2446
531.0	1654.3	Styles Peak	3394
529.3	1656.0	Peru Peak	3429
528.4	1656.9	Spring	2819
528.0	1657.3	**Peru Peak Shelter** 15.9◄12.9◄8.1◄▶4.7▶6.2▶6.4	2616
527.7	1657.6	Footbridge, stream (two)	2581
527.5	1657.8	Griffith Lake Tenting Area. Camping only at designated sites within 0.5 mile of Griffith Lake.	2600

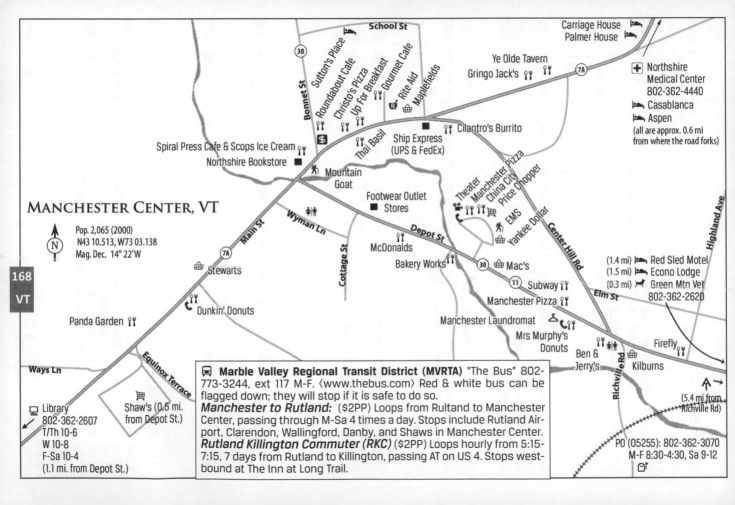

Manchester Center, VT

Pop. 2,065 (2000)
N43 10.513, W73 03.138
Mag. Dec. 14° 22'W

School St

Sutton's Place
Roundabout Cafe
Christo's Pizza
Up For Breakfast
Gourmet Cafe
Rite Aid
Maplefields

Bonnet St

Ye Olde Tavern
Gringo Jack's

Carriage House
Palmer House

+ Northshire
Medical Center
802-362-4440

Casablanca
Aspen
(all are approx. 0.6 mi
from where the road forks)

Cilantro's Burrito

Spiral Press Cafe & Scops Ice Cream
Northshire Bookstore

Thai Basil

Ship Express
(UPS & FedEx)

Mountain
Goat

Theater
Manchester Pizza
China City
Price Chopper

Footwear Outlet
Stores

EMS

Yankee Dollar

(1.4 mi) Red Sled Motel
(1.5 mi) Econo Lodge
(0.3 mi) Green Mtn Vet
802-362-2620

Elm St

Wyman Ln

Depot St

Main St

Cottage St

McDonalds

Bakery Works

Mac's

Subway

Manchester Pizza

Manchester Laundromat

Firefly

Stewarts

Dunkin' Donuts

Panda Garden

Mrs Murphy's
Donuts

Ben &
Jerry's

Kilburns

Richville Rd

(5.4 mi from
Richville Rd)

Ways Ln

Equinox Terrace

Library
802-362-2607
T/Th 10-6
W 10-8
F-Sa 10-4
(1.1 mi. from Depot St.)

Shaw's (0.5 mi.
from Depot St.)

168
VT

Highland Ave

Center Hill Rd

PO (05255): 802-362-3070
M-F 8:30-4:30, Sa 9-12

Marble Valley Regional Transit District (MVRTA) "The Bus" 802-773-3244, ext 117 M-F. ⟨www.thebus.com⟩ Red & white bus can be flagged down; they will stop if it is safe to do so.
Manchester to Rutland: ($2PP) Loops from Rutland to Manchester Center, passing through M-Sa 4 times a day. Stops include Rutland Airport, Clarendon, Wallingford, Danby, and Shaws in Manchester Center.
Rutland Killington Commuter (RKC) ($2PP) Loops hourly from 5:15-7:15, 7 days from Rutland to Killington, passing AT on US 4. Stops westbound at The Inn at Long Trail.

🍴 **Scoopy's** (0.5E) Ice cream, burgers, sodas & more. 11-8, 7 days.

Manchester Center, VT (5.4W)

🛏🌲⛺ **Red Sled Motel** (3.6W) 802-362-2161. Hiker rate $70 per room includes tax. Ride to trail when available. Laundry for a fee, swimming pool, trout pond. Motel is 1.5E of town. There is some resupply on-site. Maildrops: 2066 Depot Street Manchester Center, VT, 05255.

🛏🌲🚌✉ **Econo Lodge** (3.4W) 802-362-3333, $79-$109 includes cont. B. Pets $15. Maildrops: 2187 Depot St, Manchester Center, VT 05255.

🏪 **Dutton Farm Stand** (3.5W) 802-362-3083 Produce stand across from Red Sled Motel, 7 days 9am-7pm. Sodas, baked goods, ice cream.

🛏⛺⚡⛺🌲🖥 **Green Mountain House** 330-388-6478 ⟨www.greenmountainhouse.net⟩ Jeff & Regina Taussig host hikers at their residence. Open Jun 15 - Sep 1. Space is limited so reservations are essential. They offer a clean bed with linens, shower, free laundry, internet/WiFi, phone & well equipped hiker kitchen. Breakfast supplies available. Private room for couples. Not a party place, no alcohol. Check in from 1pm to 8pm. Free shuttles back to the trail in the morning for guests. Credit cards accepted. $25 per person.

🛏🌲✉ **Sutton's Place** 802-362-1165, $65S, $74D, $90(room for 3), pets can stay on porch. Open year-round. Accepts MC/Visa. USPS Maildrops: (USPS) PO Box 142 or (UPS) 55 School St, Manchester Center, VT 05255.

🛏🌲 **Carriage House** 802-362-1706 $68D and up, no pets.

🛏🌲 **Palmer House** 802-362-3600 Hiker friendly, ask for hiker discount, $2.50 for cont B, no pets, indoor and outdoor pool.

🥾 **EMS** 802-366-8082, 7 days 10-6, full service outfitter, Coleman/alcohol/oz, list of shuttlers and places to stay.

🥾✉ **Mountain Goat Outfitter** 802-362-5159, M-Sa 10-6, Su 11-5, ⟨www.mountaingoat.com⟩ full-service outfitter has information about lodging choices for hikers. White Gas/alcohol/oz. Maildrops: 4886 Main St, Manchester, VT 05255.

Peru, VT (Buinesses below are to the east, toward Peru)

🛏⛺🌲✉ **Bromley Sun Lodge** (2.1E) 800-722-2159 $80/up, no pets, tavern, indoor pool, game room, ride to/from trail w/stay. Maildrops: (non-guests $5) 4216 VT 11, Peru, VT 05152.

🛏🍴🚌🌲✉ **Johnny Seesaw's Lodge** (2.5E) 802-824-5533 Wkdays $50S, $75D, wkends higher. Pets $20, restaurant B/D, lounge. Rides sometimes avail. Maildrops: 3574 VT 11, Peru, VT 05152.

🍴🏪 **Bromley Market** (2.5E) 802-824-4444 7 days 7am-7pm

🛏🚌🌲✉ **Bromley View Inn** (3.6E) on VA 30, 877-633-0308 ⟨www.bromleyviewinn.com⟩ $85D/up, includes hot breakfast, call for shuttle to and from VT 11/30 trailhead with stay. Maildrops: 522 VT 30, Bondville, VT 05340.

🍴🏪 **Hapgood General Store & Eatery** (4.2E) 802-824-9824 On Main St. in Peru. Wood-fired pizza, beer and resupply.

📮 M-F 7:15-10:15 & 1-4, Sa 7:15-10:30, 802-293-5105

🛏🍴⛺🌲 **Silas Griffith Inn B&B** 802-293-5567 ⟨www.silasgriffith.com⟩ Starting at $99D midweek, 2 night min weekends & holidays. Includes full breakfast. Check-in starts at 2pm. Laundry $20/load, pets $25. Dinner with advance reservation; vegetarian/gluten free can be arranged. Hiker friendly, family friendly, pet friendly, no smoking. Seasonal hot tub & pool. Maildrops with paid reservation: 178 South Main St, Danby, VT 05739.

🛶🏪🌿🚌🅿✉ **Otter Creek Campground** 802-293-5041 2mi. north of USFS 10 in Danby on US 7, tent sites $18PP, pets on leash, Small selection of food & camping supplies, shuttles & long-term parking for fee. USPS/UPS Maildrops: 1136 US 7, Danby, VT 05739.

🏪 **Mt. Tabor Country Store** 802-293-5641 M-Sa 5-8, Su 5-7

🏪 **Nichols Store & Deli**

🖥 **Silas Griffith Library** 802-293-5106

🔧 **Crosby Hardware** 802-293-5111

📮 M-F 8-4:30, Sa 9-12, 802-446-2140

🍴 **Mom's Country Kitchen** 802-446-2606 B/L, Tu 8-11, W-Sa 6:30-2, Su 7-1.

🍴 **Sal's Italian Restaurant & Pizza**

🏪 **Wallingford Country Store & Deli**, **Cumberland Farms**

🔧 **Nail It Down Hardware**

🖥 **Gilbert Library** 802-446-2685 Tu,Th,F 10-5, W 10-8, Sa 9-12.

🚌 **MVRTA** Stops near Cumberland Farms 4 times daily.

SoBo	NoBo	Description	Elev
527.2	1658.1	Old Job Trail to east, Griffith Lake Trail to west	2614
525.4	1659.9	Baker Peak, Baker Peak Trail to west	2649
523.3	1662.0	**Lost Pond Shelter** 17.6◄12.8◄4.7◄▶1.5▶1.7▶5.0	2210
522.8	1662.5	Spring	1975
521.8	1663.5	Old Job Trail to **Old Job Shelter** (1.0E), Lake Brook is water source	1544
521.6	1663.7	**Big Branch Shelter** 14.3◄6.2◄1.5◄▶0.2▶3.5▶8.3	1512
		Close to road; heavy weekend use. Water source is Big Branch. Privy uphill.	
520.5	1664.8	Danby-Landgrove Rd., N43 22.362 W72 57.764 **P** (pg.169)	1539
		Big Black Branch Bridge, **Danby, VT** (3.5W)	
519.9	1665.4	Footbridge, stream	1667
518.4	1666.9	Homer Stone Brook Trail to west.	1880
518.3	1667.0	**Little Rock Pond Shelter & Tenting Area**	1852
		5.0◄3.5◄3.3◄▶4.8▶9.9▶13.6 Water source is at the caretaker's platform.	
		Overnight fee. Tenting restricted to designated sites.	
517.2	1668.1	Footbridge, stream	1955
514.0	1671.3	Trail to White Rocks Cliff 0.2W	2294
513.5	1671.8	**Greenwall Shelter** (0.2E) 8.3◄8.1◄4.8◄▶5.1▶8.8▶14.6.	2114
		Spring 0.1 mile on side trail behind shelter, prone to fail in dry seasons.	
512.8	1672.5	Bully Brook, Keewaydin Trail to west.	1456
512.1	1673.2	Sugar Hill Rd (gravel)	1270
512.0	1673.3	VT 140, footbridge, stream. N43 27.404 W72 55.972 (0.2E) **P** (pg.169)	1160
		Wallingford, VT (2.8W)	
511.0	1674.3	View on short side trail to west	1715
510.3	1675.0	Bear Mountain	2263
509.4	1675.9	Patch Hollow	1787
509.0	1676.3	Footbridge, stream (3)	1672
508.8	1676.5	Lake Trail loop to west (yellow blazed), 100 yards north, red-blazed tr to east	1673
508.4	1676.9	**Minerva Hinchey Shelter** 13.2◄9.9◄5.1◄▶3.7▶9.5▶13.8	1631
		spring 75 yards in front of shelter.	
506.5	1678.8	View to Rutland Airport.	1371
505.8	1679.5	Clarendon Gorge, suspension bridge, swimming holes in Mill River	815

SoBo	NoBo	Description	Elev
505.7	1679.6	VT 103, restaurant 0.5W N43 31.286 W72 55.550 P ♦ (pg.172) **North Clarendon, VT** (4.2W) **Rutland, VT** (8.0W)	860
505.2	1680.1	View, north end of rock scramble	1326
504.7	1680.6	**Clarendon Shelter** (0.1E) 13.6◄8.8◄3.7►5.8►10.1►12.6 ⊞ ♪♦♠⌐(10)	1264
504.2	1681.1	Beacon Hill	1740
503.9	1681.4	Lottery Rd (gravel), powerline	1658
503.4	1681.9	Hermit Spring to east (unreliable) △	1794
502.3	1683.0	Stream. ♠	1586
502.1	1683.2	Keiffer Rd (gravel) ♠	1523
501.8	1683.5	Cold River Rd / Lower Rd (paved) Nobo east on road 75 yards ⊕	1390
501.0	1684.3	**W.E. Pierce Groceries** in North Shrewsbury (2.4E) Gould Brook to west, AT parallel for 0.5 miles ♠	1480
500.3	1685.0	Upper Cold River Rd (gravel)	1630
499.6	1685.7	Gravel road, Robinson Brook ♠	1742
498.9	1686.4	**Governor Clement Shelter** 14.6◄9.5◄5.8►4.3►6.8►8.7 ♪♦♠⌐(12)	1920
498.6	1686.7	At on gravel road 0.3 miles north of shelter.	2069
497.6	1687.7	Ski trail, blue diamond blazes	2582
496.2	1689.1	Shrewsbury Peak Trail to east, signed.	3512
494.6	1690.7	**Cooper Lodge Shelter** 13.8◄10.1◄4.3►2.5►4.4►7.3 ⊞ ♦♠⌐(16) Spring 60 yards north on AT. Trail behind shelter 0.2 to Killington peak & view. ♪♦♠ view	3928
494.3	1691.0	Bucklin Trail to west	3806

> ❋ **Clintonia** – Foot-tall plant with plastic-looking blue berries atop long stems.

SoBo	NoBo	Description	Elev
492.1	1693.2	**Pico Camp** (0.5E) 12.6◄6.8◄2.5►1.9►4.8►13.8 ♪♦⌐(4) Shelter on Sherburne Pass Tr where it leaves the Long Tr/AT south of Pico summit.	3482
490.9	1694.4	Spring ♠	3153
490.2	1695.1	**Churchill Scott Shelter** (0.1W) 8.7◄4.4◄1.9►2.9►11.9►21.8 ♪△♦⌐ Composting privy, unreliable water at southern spur from shelter, no fires.	2620
490.0	1695.3	Stream. △	2434
489.2	1696.1	Stream. ♠	2062
488.3	1697.0	US 4, **Rutland, VT** (8.5W) N43 39.996 W72 50.997 P (pg.172)	1880
488.2	1697.1	Stream. ♪♦♠⌐(8)	1889
487.3	1698.0	Maine Junction, **Tucker-Johnson Shelter** (0.4W) (planned 2014) 7.3◄4.8◄2.9►9.0►18.9►30.5 ⚠ White-blazed trail to west is the Long Trail	2259
487.1	1698.2	Spring, Deer Leap Trail to east. ♠	2304
486.5	1698.8	Deer Leap Trail 0.3E to view △	2438
486.4	1698.9	Sherburne Pass Trail 0.5E to **Inn at Long Trail** ⊞	2440
485.6	1699.7	Spring ♠	1854

Elev

1679.6   VT 103

🍴 (0.5W) ***Whistle Stop Restaurant** 802-747-7070 Closed for remodeling late in 2013; call before making the walk.

🐾 (0.5W) **Cold River Veterinary Center** 802-747-4076

🏪 (1W) **Loretta's Deli** (formerly "East Clarendon General") 802-772-7638, M–Sa 7–7, Su 8–4.

🚌 **MVRTA** Stops near deli 4/day.

North Clarendon, VT 05759 (4.2W)
🏤 M–F 8–1 & 2–4:30, Sa 8–10, 802-773-7893

🏪 **Mike's Country Store**
Rutland, VT (8W of VT 103)

1697.0   US 4, Rutland, VT (8.5W), **Killington, VT 05751** (1.8E, pg.173)

🛏️🍴🚿⛺🛜✉ (0.8E) **The Inn at Long Trail** 802-775-7181 or 800-325-2540 ⟨www.innatlongtrail.com⟩ Hiker rates on rooms that include full breakfast. Limited pet rooms, reservations recommended on weekends. Overflow camping across street with no facilities. Coin laundry, outside water spigot. Closed mid-April through Mem Day. **McGrath's Irish Pub** L/D 11:30-9pm, live music Fri & Sat. Maildrops: (FedEx/UPS) 709 US 4, Killington, VT 05751.

172 VT

🛏️🛜✉ (1.4W) **Mendon Mountian View Lodge** 802-773-4311 Hiker rate $59S $79D includes breakfast. No pets. Heated pool & suana, bus stops here. Maildrops: 5654 Route 4, Mendon, VT 05701.

🚶🛏️🍴🚿⛺🛜✉ **Hikers Hostel at the Yellow Deli** 802-775-9800 ⟨www.hikershostel.org⟩ $20 Suggested donation, WFS when available. Kitchenette, coin laundry, hiking supplies at **Simon the Tanner**. No pets, no alcohol, no smoking. Free showers even w/o stay. Maildrops: Hiker Hostel, 23 Center Street, Rutland, VT 05701.

🚶 **Mountain Travelers Outdoor Shop** 802-775-0814, M–F 10–6, Sa 10–4. Full line of gear, Coleman/alcohol/oz.

🏪 **Rutland Area Food Co-op** 802-773-0737 7 days

🐾 **Rutland Veterinary** 802-773-2779

🚆 **Amtrak** 800-872-7245 Daily routes Rutland to many NE cities.

🚌 **Rutland Taxi** 802-236-3133

✈ **Rutland Airport** South of Rutland on US 7

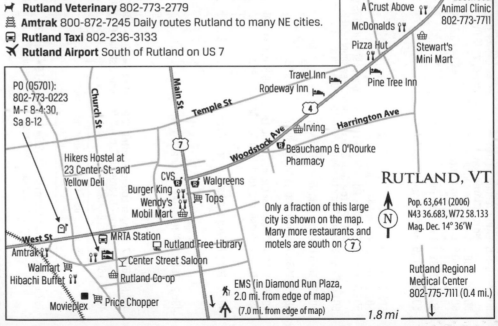

PO (05701):
802-773-0223
M–F 8-4:30,
Sa 8-12

Home Depot
Dunkin Donuts
Mtn Traveler
Little Ceasars
Applebees
(6.7 mi. from edge of map)

Eastwood Animal Clinic 802-773-7711

A Crust Above
McDonalds
Pizza Hut

Stewart's Mini Mart

Travel Inn
Rodeway Inn
Pine Tree Inn

Church St
Main St
Temple St
Woodstock Ave
Harrington Ave
Irving
Beauchamp & O'Rourke Pharmacy

Hikers Hostel at 23 Center St. and Yellow Deli

CVS
Burger King
Wendy's
Mobil Mart
Walgreens
Tops

West St
Amtrak
Walmart
Hibachi Buffet
Movieplex
MRTA Station
Rutland Free Library
Center Street Saloon
Rutland Co-op
Price Chopper

Only a fraction of this large city is shown on the map. Many more restaurants and motels are south on (7)

RUTLAND, VT

Pop. 63,641 (2006)
N43 36.683, W72 58.133
Mag. Dec. 14° 36'W

EMS (in Diamond Run Plaza, 2.0 mi. from edge of map)
(7.0 mi. from edge of map)

Rutland Regional Medical Center 802-775-7111 (0.4 mi.)

1.8 mi

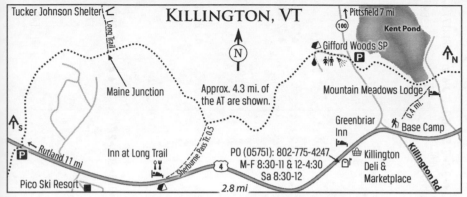

KILLINGTON, VT

Tucker Johnson Shelter ←
Long Trail
Maine Junction
↑ Pittsfield 7 mi
Kent Pond
Gifford Woods SP
Approx. 4.3 mi. of the AT are shown.
Mountain Meadows Lodge
↑ N S
Greenbriar Inn
Base Camp
Rutland 11 mi ←
Inn at Long Trail
Sherburne Pass Tr. 0.5
PO (05751): 802-775-4247
M-F 8:30-11 & 12-4:30
Sa 8:30-12
Killington Deli & Marketplace
Killington Rd
Pico Ski Resort
2.8 mi

1700.1 🏕 🚻 🚿 🚽 The AT passes thru **Gifford Woods State Park** 802-775-5354 Shelters, discounted tent sites for AT hikers in special hiker section, coin-op showers, water spigot. Open Mem Day-Columbus Day. Fills quickly in fall.

1700.3 VT 100 **Killington, VT 05751** (0.6E from VT 100, 1.8E from US 4 trailhead)
🥾 ✉ 🛒 **Base Camp Outfitters** 802-775-0166, Summer hours: 9-6 every day. Full service outfitter, alcohol/oz and canister fuel. Disc golf. Maildrops: 2363 Route 4, Killington VT 05751.
🛏 🛜 **Greenbrier Inn** 802-775-1575 15% discount for hikers, no pets.
🚌 **Apex Shuttle Service** 603-252-8294 AThikershuttle@gmail.com Inn-to-Inn hiking packages between Killington, VT and Franconia Notch, NH with shuttle, lodging and lunches provided, for hikers who want the AT day hiking experience with the comforts of B&Bs and lodges at the end of the day.
🍴 🍸 ⛲ **Scrub a Dub Pub** 802-422-5335 Eat/drink while-u-wash 0.8S of US4 on Killington Rd.
Pittsfield, VT 05762 (7W) 📮 M-F 8-12, 2-4:30, Sa 8:30-11:30, 802-746-8953
🏪 🍴 💲 **Original General Store** B/L/D

1700.9 Kent Pond
🛏 🏕 🌧 🍴 ⛲ 🅿 🛜 🖥 ✉ **Mountain Meadows Lodge** 802-775-1010
⟨www.mountainmeadowslodge.com⟩ AT crosses property. Room $69D, tent/hammock site $10/PP. Lunch or dinner $10. No pets inside; barn & woodshed available. Outdoor pool, hot tub, and sauna. Parking for section hikers. Open year round. Lodging not available most weekends & events. Maildrops: 285 Thundering Brook Rd, Killington, VT 05751. 0.4E side trail to **Base Camp Outfitters**

1720.3 VT 12, Barnard Gulf Rd
🏪 **On The Edge Farm** (0.2W) 802-457-4510 Summer M-F 10-5:30, Sunday 10-5. Fall Th-M 10-5. Pies, fruit, ice cream, smoked meats and cheese, cold drinks.
Woodstock, VT 05091 (4.2E)
📮 M-F 8:30-5, Sa 9-12, 802-457-1323 Pricey resort town, several motels & restaurants, movie theater, bookstore.
🛏 🛜 **Shire River View Motel** 802-457-2211 $138/up
🛏 🛜 **Braeside Motel** 802-457-1366
🍴 **Bentley's**, **Pizza Chef**
🏪 **Cumberland Farms**, **Gillingham FH & Sons**
💊 **Woodstock Pharmacy**
🐾 **Woodstock Vet. Hospital** 802-457-2229
🖥 **Library** 802-457-2295 M-F 10-5

173
VT

1722.2 Woodstock Stage Rd
South Pomfret, VT 05067 (1E)
📮 M-F 8-1 & 2-4:45, Sa 8:30-11:30 802-457-1147 located inside of Teago's
🏪 **Teago's General Store** 802-457-1626 M-Sa 7-6, Su 8-4, B&J ice cream, beer, sandwiches and salads.

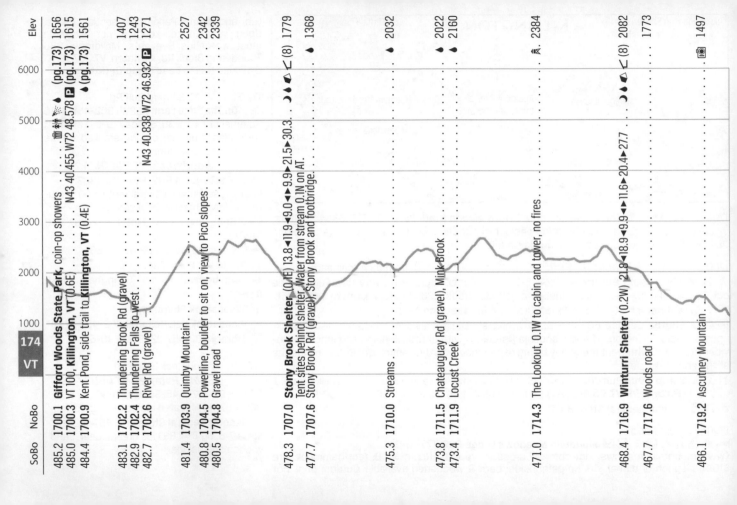

174
VT

SoBo	NoBo	Description	Elev
485.2	1700.1	**Gifford Woods State Park**, coin-op showers ⌖ 🖾 🛁 ♦ (pg.173)	1656
485.0	1700.3	VT 100, **Killington, VT** (0.6E) ⌖ N43 40.455 W72 48.578 P (pg.173)	1615
484.4	1700.9	Kent Pond, side trail to **Killington, VT** (0.4E) ♦ (pg.173)	1561
483.1	1702.2	Thundering Brook Rd (gravel)	1407
482.9	1702.4	Thundering Falls to west.	1243
482.7	1702.6	River Rd (gravel) N43 40.838 W72 46.932 P	1271
481.4	1703.9	Quimby Mountain	2527
480.8	1704.5	Powerline, boulder to sit on, view to Pico slopes	2342
480.5	1704.8	Gravel road	2339
478.3	1707.0	**Stony Brook Shelter** (0.1E) 13.8◀11.9◀9.0◀▶9.9▶21.5▶30.3. Tent sites behind shelter. Water from stream 0.1N on AT. ⌣♦⛺⌂ ⊂(8)	1779
477.7	1707.6	Stony Brook Rd (gravel), Stony Brook and footbridge. ♦	1368
475.3	1710.0	Streams ♦	2032
473.8	1711.5	Chateauguay Rd (gravel), Mink Brook ♦	2022
473.4	1711.9	Locust Creek ♦	2160
471.0	1714.3	The Lookout, 0.1W to cabin and tower, no fires 🅰	2384
468.4	1716.9	**Winturri Shelter** (0.2W) 21.8◀18.9◀9.9◀▶11.6▶20.4▶27.7 ⌣♦⛺⌂ ⊂(8)	2082
467.7	1717.6	Woods road	1773
466.1	1719.2	Ascutney Mountain 📷	1497

SoBo	NoBo	Feature	Elev
465.0	1720.3	VT 12, Barnard Gulf Rd (paved). N43 39.309 W72 33.972 P ♦ (pg.173) Gulf Stream south of road crossing. **Woodstock, VT** (4.2E)	891 / 1551
464.3	1721.0	Dana Hill.	1551
463.1	1722.2	Woodstock Stage Rd, Barnard Brook, **South Pomfret, VT** (1E). (pg.173)	820
462.8	1722.5	Stream	1049
462.3	1723.0	Totman Hill Rd, footbridge, stream.	1038
461.5	1723.8	Bartlett Brook Rd (gravel), footbridge, stream	1055
460.9	1724.4	Pomfret Rd (paved), Pomfret Brook south of road crossing, powerline.	980
460.5	1724.8	View	1588
459.7	1725.6	View	1729
459.1	1726.2	Cloudland Rd (gravel), **Cloudland Market** (0.2W) closed M & Su	1370
458.6	1726.7	Previous AT shelter (Cloudland, 0.5W) now on private land. Owners also own Cloudland Market and hikers are welcome to stay at the shelter.	1614
457.3	1728.0	Thistle Hill.	1954
456.8	1728.5	**Thistle Hill Shelter** (0.2E), stream 0.1 further 30.5◀21.5◀11.6◀▶8.8▶16.1▶25.6	1774
456.5	1728.8	Dimick Brook	1520
455.5	1729.8	Joe Ranger Rd (gravel)	1310
454.9	1730.4	Bunker Hill Rd (dirt)	1418

❋ Queen Anne's Lace – White flower cluster in disk shaped doily 3-5" wide on hairy stem.

SoBo	NoBo	Feature	Elev
452.5	1732.8	Stream	543
452.3	1733.0	Quechee West Hartford Rd, ⚠ NoBo west on road 0.4 mi, cross White River.	481
452.0	1733.3	VT 14, White River, **West Hartford, VT**. (pg.176-177) NoBo: turn west, on road 0.3 mile.	397
451.6	1733.7	Tigertown Rd, NoBo: turn east, on road 0.4 mile	400
451.3	1734.0	I-89 underpass. N43 43.250 W72 24.793 P	560
450.6	1734.7	Podunk Rd (gravel), Podunk Brook N43 43.006 W72 24.013 P	860
450.1	1735.2	Woods road	1052
449.7	1735.6	Woods road, stream	1006
448.0	1737.3	**Happy Hill Shelter** (0.E) 30.3◀20.4◀8.8◀▶7.3▶16.8▶22.5 Brook near shelter, known to run dry.	1426
447.7	1737.6	Tucker Trail 3.1W to Norwich	1336
446.4	1738.9	Woods road	1140
445.2	1740.1	Powerline	1174

SoBo NoBo

Plan Ahead and Prepare

•Check Appalachian Trail (A.T.) guidebooks and maps for guidance and note that camping regulations vary considerably along the Trail. Travel in groups of 10 or fewer. If you are traveling in a group of more than 5, avoid using shelters, leaving them for lone hikers and smaller groups.

•Bring a lightweight trowel or wide tent stake to dig a hole for burying human waste.

•Bring a piece of screening to filter food scraps from your dishwater and pack them out with you.

•Bring a waterproof bag and at least 50 feet of rope to hang food and other scented articles. Or, carry a bear-resistant food container ("bear canister") to store these items.

•Repackage food in resealable bags to minimize waste.

•Prepare for extreme weather, hazards, and emergencies – especially the cold – to avoid impacts from searches, rescues, and campfires.

•Learn when areas are most crowded and try to avoid those times. If you are planning a northbound thru-hike, avoid starting on March 1, March 15, the first day of spring, or April 1.

Read more of the Leave No Trace techniques developed for the A.T.: www.appalachiantrail.org/LNT

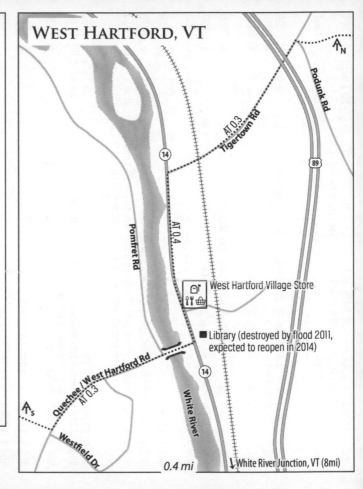

WEST HARTFORD, VT

Podunk Rd

AT 0.3

Tigertown Rd

14

89

Pomfret Rd

AT 0.4

West Hartford Village Store

Library (destroyed by flood 2011, expected to reopen in 2014)

14

Quechee / West Hartford Rd

AT 0.3

White River

Westfield Dr

0.4 mi

White River Junction, VT (8mi)

1733.9   VT 14, White River
West Hartford, VT 05084
⌂ 🏕 🍴 💲 📶 **West Hartford Village Store, Full Belly Deli, Village Post Office** 802-280-1713, winter: M-Sa 8-7, Su 8-5, summer (Mem-Day-LaborDay): M-Sa 7-8, Su 8-7. Thru-hiker specials, big breakfast, groceries catering to hiker resupply. Water from spigot outside. Approved postal provider, so you can ship USPS mail from this location, and receive maildrops: 5187 Rte. 14 North, West Hartford, VT 05084.
🚌 **Big Yellow Taxi** 802-281-8294

1741.7   Main St
Norwich, VT 05055 (more services on map)
🛏 🍴 📶 🖥 ✉ **Norwich Inn** 802-649-1143 ⟨www.norwichinn.com⟩ $99D includes a free beer, rooms for pets, no smoking, reservations recommended. **Jasper Murdocks Ale House** Tu-Su B/L/D, serves dinner 7 days, microbrewery. Maildrops for guests: PO Box 908, Norwich, VT 04055, or FedEx to 325 Main St.
🛒 🖥 **Dan & Whits General Store** 802-649-1602, 7 days 7-9, 0.1W on Main St. Hikers get free day old sandwiches when available. Small gear items, canister fuel, batteries, ponchos, hardware and grocery.
🖥 📶 **Norwich Library** 802-649-1184, M 1-8, Tu-W-F 10-5:30, Th 10-8, Sa 10-3.

┌───┐
🚌 **Advance Transit** ⟨www.advancetransit.com⟩ M-F 6-6, offers FREE bus service connecting Hanover area towns. Detailed schedule and stops are available on-line and at libraries. The routes are indicated on maps, pg. 177 & 178, and primary bus stops are:
Norwich - Dan & Whits (Brown).
Hanover - Dartmouth Book Store (Orange/Blue), Hanover Inn (Brown). White River Junction - Amtrak.
West Lebanon - Main St. (Orange/Red), grocery stores, outfitters.
Lebanon - City Hall (Blue/Red).
└───┘

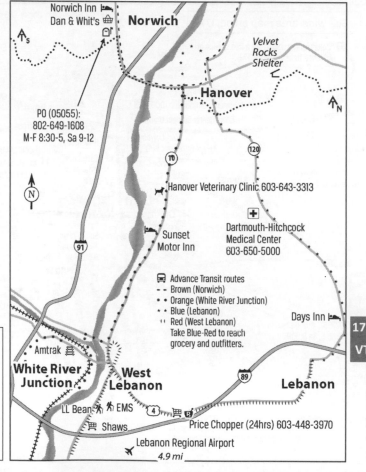

PO (05055):
802-649-1608
M-F 8:30-5, Sa 9-12

Hanover Veterinary Clinic 603-643-3313

Dartmouth-Hitchcock
Medical Center
603-650-5000

Sunset
Motor Inn

🚌 Advance Transit routes
- - Brown (Norwich)
• • Orange (White River Junction)
• • Blue (Lebanon)
'' Red (West Lebanon)
Take Blue-Red to reach
grocery and outfitters.

Days Inn 🛏

Amtrak 🚉

White River
Junction

West
Lebanon

LL Bean 🏃 EMS

Shaws

Lebanon

Price Chopper (24hrs) 603-448-3970

Lebanon Regional Airport
✈
4.9 mi

Norwich Inn 🛏
Dan & Whit's ⛪   Norwich
⌂

Velvet
Rocks
Shelter

Hanover

177

VT

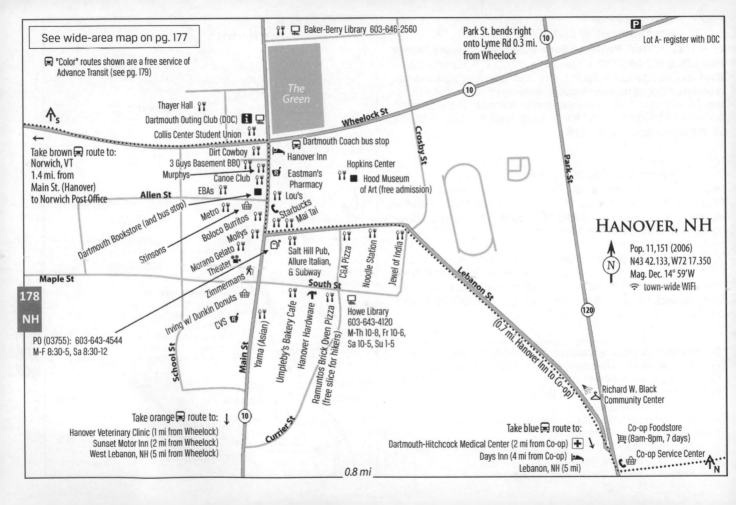

1743.2   Dartmouth College *Hanover, NH 03755*

🆘 **Hanover Friends of the AT** produce a brochure with complete list of hiker services, available at the DOC, PO, libraries, Co-op.

🆘 🛜 🖥 **Dartmouth Outing Club (DOC)** 603-646-2428 In Robinson Hall. Not available during Dartmouth orientation (last week of Aug and first two weeks of Sept). Unsecured room in basement for hikers to store gear while in town, cannot be left overnight. Computers for free internet use. There are no hiker accommodations on campus.

🅿 Overnight parking on Wheelock Street (Lot A), register with DOC. No parking near Connecticut River Bridge.

🛏🍴🏕🚌🛜✉ **Stray Cat's AT Hilton** 603-252-8294 AThikershuttle@gmail.com. Located in Canaan; $45 includes Hanover pickup/return, bunkroom bed w/ fresh linens, shower, use of cable TV, picnic table & grill. Laundry done for you $4. Hearty meat & vegetable dinner with salad and dessert $10; full country breakfast $7.50. Hostel pickup/return from Rte. 112 in Woodstock, VT to Rte 25A in Wentworth, NH for an additonal fee. No alcohol, no pets. Maildrops with reservation: (your name) c/o Steve Lake, 365 Choate Rd, Canaan, NH 03741.

🛏🏕🛜✉ **Sunset Motor Inn** 603-298-8721, open 8-11, Call ahead for availability; discount for hikers. Will shuttle when bus is not running, free laundry before 6pm, quiet after 10pm, $15 pet fee. Maildrops: 305 N Main Street, West Lebanon, NH 03874.

🛏🍴 **Hanover Inn** 603-643-4300 Pricey, discount sometimes avail.

🍴 **EBA's** Full menu and beer, daily specials. Pizza buffet Tuesday night $7.95, Su brunch $11.95.

🍴 **Metro** One free bagel for thru-hikers

🍴 **Jewel of India** buffet Su 11:30-2:30

🏪🍴 **Stinson's** Convenience store with $5 hiker lunch special: deli sandwich, soda & small bag of chips. Good selection of beer & tobacco.

🛒 **Hanover Food Co-op** open daily, large selection. Please use member #7000 at checkout to help fund AT related initiatives.

🚿🏕 **Richard W. Black Recreation Center** 603-643-5315 M-F 9am-5pm, also open Saturdays Sept-June. Shower w/soap $3, laundry w/ soap $2, last call for either 4:30pm.

🏃 **Zimmerman's** Canister fuel, Aquamira, socks & outdoor clothes.

🔨 **Hanover Hardware** Coleman/alcohol/oz

🚌 **Advance Transit** (see pg. 177).

🚌 **Dartmouth Coach** 603-448-2800 No office at stop next to Hanover Inn; you may board bus and buy ticket when it stops in Lebanon. Route goes to Boston and to Logan Airport.

🚌 **Apex Shuttle Service** 603-252-8294 (Steve "Stray Cat" Lake) To/ from anywhere if originating or ending in the Hanover area.

🚌 **Big Yellow Taxi** 603-643-8294

🐾 **Hanover Veterinary** 603-643-3313

White River Junction, VT

🚆 **Amtrak** 800-872-7245 Vermonter line travels north as far as St. Albans, VT, and south through New York, Philadelphia, Baltimore and Washington, DC. There is no ticket office at this station, but you can reserve on the phone and pay when you board.

Lebanon & West Lebanon, NH (see map pg. 177)

🛏🛜🖥 **Days Inn** 603-448-5070, 4 mi. south of the Co-op on Rte 120 on free bus route, cont. B, pets $20.

🏃 **EMS** 603-298-7716, **LL Bean** 603-298-6975

🛒 **Shaw's** 603-298-0388 7am-10pm, 7-9 Sunday

179

NH

1749.6   Etna-Hanover Center Rd, *Etna, NH 03750* (0.8E)

🛏🌐🏕 **Tiggers Tree House** 603-643-9213 Private home; not a party place. No drive-ins. Advance notice ensures a place to stay. Call from trailhead, Etna General Store (will let you use phone) or Dartmouth Outing Club for pickup. Pets allowed, donations accepted or buy laundry soap or work for stay. Rides to grocery store, Walmart, EMS.

🏪🍴 (0.8E) **Etna General Store** 603-643-1655, M-F 6-7, Sa, Su 8-7. Deli, hot meals, open 7 days. Denatured alcohol/oz.

180
NH

SoBo	NoBo		Elev
444.7	1740.6	Stream	835
444.6	1740.7	Elm Street, NoBo: turn east, on road 1.0 mile	839
443.6	1741.7	Main St, **Norwich, VT**, NoBo: turn east, on road 1.4 miles (pg.177)	516
442.7	1742.6	**VT-NH** border, Connecticut River	380
442.1	1743.2	**Hanover, NH**, Dartmouth College N43 42.391 W72 16.656 P (pg.178-179) NoBo: turn east on SR 10.	527
441.4	1743.9	NH 120, trailhead near convenience store.	520
440.7	1744.6	**Velvet Rocks Shelter** (0.2W) 27.7◀16.1◀7.3◀▶9.5▶15.2▶21.9 ⊃ ⊆ (6) Spring on northern access to shelter.	925
440.1	1745.2	North shelter loop trail ▲(0.2W)	974
438.4	1746.9	Pond, boardwalk	809
437.7	1747.6	Trescott Rd (paved)	940
436.4	1748.9	Footbridge, stream (2)	852
436.3	1749.0	Etna-Hanover Center Rd (paved), **Etna, NH** (0.8E). (pg.179) Cell phone reception at cemetery to west	845
433.8	1751.5	Three Mile Rd (gravel) N43 43.077 W72 10.559 P	1416
433.6	1751.7	Mink Brook, footbridge	1347
432.0	1753.3	Moose Mountain south peak	2290
431.2	1754.1	**Moose Mountain Shelter** (0.1E) ⊃ ▲ ⊆ (8) 25.6◀16.8◀9.5◀▶5.7▶12.4▶7.7 Loop trail to shelter, water at AT and northern leg intersection, tenting on northern leg of loop.	2131
429.9	1755.4	Moose Mountain north peak	2315
428.4	1756.9	South fork of Hewes Brook	1059
428.2	1757.1	Goose Pond Rd (paved)	963
426.1	1759.2	Holts Ledge, precipitous drop-off, views	1937
425.5	1759.8	**Trapper John Shelter** (0.2W), privy behind shelter 0.1 mile ⊃ ▲ ⊆ (6) 22.5◀15.2◀5.7◀▶6.7▶12.0▶27.7	1517

✽ **Cattail** – A tall (head-high) plant that grows in swampy areas. Characteristic part of the plant looks like a fuzzy cigar impaled lengthwise on a spear.

SoBo	NoBo	Feature	Elev
424.6	1760.7	Grafton Turnpike(paved), Dorchester Rd . . . N43 47.400 W72 6.000 [P] ◆ (pg.182)	880
		Lyme Center, NH (1.3W), **Lyme, NH** (3.2W) ⚠ Nobo east on wedge of land between fork in road, side trail to Bill Ackerly home 0.1 north of intersection.	
423.2	1762.1	Grant Brook	1212
422.9	1762.4	Concrete milepost	1128
422.6	1762.7	Lyme-Dorchester Rd (gravel) . . . N43 47.400 W72 6.176 [P]	1110
420.9	1764.4	Lamberts Ridge	2361
419.4	1765.9	Smarts Ranger Trail to east	2729
418.9	1766.4	Campsite, weak spring to east, fire tower north of camp, west of AT	3246
418.8	1766.5	Smarts Mountain, **Fire Wardens Cabin** (12)	3237
		21.9◄12.4◄6.7◄►5.3►21.0►27.9 Shelter is cabin north of summit, west of AT. Spring 0.2 in front of cabin. Clark Pond Loop Trail to east.	
414.9	1770.4	South Jacobs Brook	1450
414.3	1771.0	Eastman Ledges	1899
413.9	1771.4	North Jacobs Brook	1936
413.5	1771.8	**Hexacuba Shelter** (0.3E) (2) (8)	2071
		17.7◄12.0◄5.3◄►15.7►22.6►31.6 Shelter on steep side trail, unreliable stream at intersection with side trail.	
411.9	1773.4	Mt Cube south peak, cross Rivendell Trail to west	2911
411.8	1773.5	Side trail 0.3W to Mt Cube north peak	2881
410.2	1775.1	Brackett Brook	1472
409.3	1776.0	Stream	1298
409.1	1776.2	Woods road	1197
408.5	1776.8	NH 25A (paved) Nobo east on road 300 yards N43 54.078 W71 59.029 [P] (pg.186)	915
		Wentworth, NH (4.8E)	
406.7	1778.6	Cape Moonshine Rd (gravel) . . . N43 54.950 W71 57.876 [P] (pg.186)	1432
		AT northbound joins Ore Hill Trail.	
406.0	1779.3	Ore Hill Campsite (shelter destroyed by fire in 2011)	1883
		Muddy spring 100 yards downhill from tentsites.	

1760.7   Grafton Turnpike, Dorchester Rd, Dartmouth Skiway

Bill Ackerly Welcomes hiker visits. Help yourself to water, rest, chat and play a game of croquet.

Lyme Center, NH 03769 (1.3W)

⌂ M–F 8–10, Sa 8–11:30, 603-795-2688

Lyme, NH 03768 (3.2W)

⌂ M–F 7:45–12 & 1:30–5:15, Sa 7:45–12, 603-795-4421

🍴 ☎ **Stella's Italian Kitchen & Market** 603-795-4302 ⟨www.stellaslyme.com⟩, M-Th 10-9, F-Sa 10-10, Su closed.

🛏 📶 🖥 **Dowd's Country Inn B&B** 603-795-4712 ⟨www.dowdscountryinn.com⟩ starting at $85S $100D mid week through Sep, breakfast and afternoon tea included. Pets allowed in some rooms. Call in advance; pickup sometimes available.

🏠 🍴 ☎ **Lyme Country Store** (3.3W) ice cream, produce, deli, 7 days.

🐾 **Lyme Veterinary Hospital** (2.8W) bear right onto High St and hospital is 50 yards up on the left, 603-795-2747.

Appalachian Mountain Club (AMC) 603-466-2727 Maintains the AT from Kinsman Notch, NH to Grafton Notch, ME. AMC operates 8 huts with bunk space for 30-90 people. There is no road access, heat, or showers. Huts use alternative energy sources and composting toilets. Huts are closed in the winter. In the spring and fall huts are open to "self-serve" use for $25. See White Mtn map for dates. Stays during the "full serve" season includes bunk, dinner & breakfast, starting at $125PP for non-members. Reservations recommended and can be made by phone or with any AMC caretaker. Work-for-stay is available to the first 2 thru-hikers to arrive, no reservations. WFS hikers get floor space for sleeping, feast on leftovers, and are typically asked to work 2 hours after breakfast. Lakes of the Clouds Hut has 4 WFS spots and a $10 thru-hiker only bunkroom called "The Dungeon". Don't count on hut stays without reservations, and camping is not allowed near any hut, except at Nauman Tentsite. No pets inside any huts. Limit your WFS to 3 nights in the Whites to give other hikers the opportunity.

🚌 **AMC Hiker Shuttle** (see pg. 187)

White Mountain National Forest (the "Whites")

Passage through the Whites should be planned carefully. It is one of the more heavily visited sections of the AT, and campsites are limited. The trail is rugged, so your pace may be slowed. Weather is dynamic, adding to the dangers of hiking on stretches of trail above treeline.

Take adequate cold-weather gear, check weather reports, carry maps, and know your options for overnighting. The AMC and Randolf Mountain Club (RMC) maintain camps, which are detailed in the following pages. Most have fees. Have cash on hand even if you do not plan to use them; your plans may change.

There are many trails in the Whites. The AT is the only white-blazed trail, but blazes are scant. There are no blazes in the Great Gulf Wilderness Area. The AT is always coincident with another named trail, and the other trail name may be the one you see on signs. Wherever the AT changes from one trail to another, this book uses the notation: "AT: Town Line Tr◄►Glencliff Tr." This means that the AT to the south of this point is coincident with the Town Line Trail; to the north, the AT joins the Glencliff Trail.

The area within a quarter mile of all AMC and RMC facilities and everything above treeline (trees 8' or less) are part of the Forest Protection Area (FPA). Trails are often marked where they enter or leave the FPA. Do not camp within a FPA, and camp at least 200' from water and trails. Rocks aligned to form a trail boundary (scree walls) are an indication that you should not leave the treadway. Doing so damages fragile plant life.

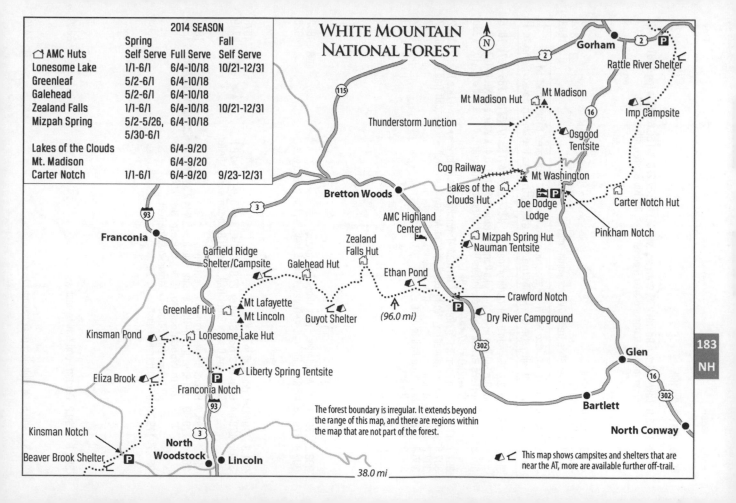

Elev		
1828		

SoBo	NoBo		Elev
404.0	1781.3	Ore Hill.	1828
403.3	1782.0	Lake Tarleton Rd, NH 25C, **Warren, NH** (4E) N43 57.220 W71 56.690 **P** (pg.186) ♦	1543
		AT on road past parking area & power lines, Ore Hill Brook north of road.	
401.3	1784.0	Mt Mist	2200
400.9	1784.4	View	1874
400.7	1784.6	Webster Slide Trail 0.7W to summit, view	1683

⚠ The notation "AT: Ore Hill Tr ▲ Wachipauka Pond Tr" indicates that the AT to the south is coincident with the Ore Hill Tr; the AT to the north joins the Wachipauka Pond Tr.

SoBo	NoBo		Elev
398.7	1786.6	NH 25, Oliverian Brook north of road. N43 59.395 W71 53.971 **P** (pg.186-187)	1055
		AT: Ore Hill Tr ▲ Wachipauka Pond Tr ▼ **Glencliff, NH** (0.4E) **Warren, NH** (5.0E) ☾♦ ⊏ (10)	
397.8	1787.5	**Jeffers Brook Shelter**, Jeffers Brook, footbridge 0.1 south	1330
		27.7◀21.0◀15.7▶6.9▶15.9▶19.9	
397.7	1787.6	Long Pond Rd ⚠ NoBo 0.1E on road AT: Wachipauka Pond Tr ▲ Town Line Tr.	1352
397.5	1787.8	High St (paved) ⚠ NoBo: 0.2W on road. AT: Town Line Trail ▼ Glencliff Trail	1367
397.2	1788.1	Stream.	1527
396.9	1788.4	Hurricane Trail to east	1692
396.0	1789.3	Stream.	2529
395.5	1789.8	Spring	3056
393.2	1792.1	Mt Moosilauke, Gorge Brook Trail to east	4802
392.8	1792.5	AT: Glencliff Trail ▲ Beaver Brook Trail, Benton Trail to west	4628
391.3	1794.0	Ridge Trail to east	4075
390.9	1794.4	**Beaver Brook Shelter** 27.9◀22.6◀6.9▶9.0▶13.0▶28.1 ☾♦ ⊏ (10)	3749
		Shelter on Beaver Brook trail. Beaver Brook on way to shelter.	
389.6	1795.7	Beaver Brook, footbridges, streams	1884
389.4	1795.9	Lost River Rd, NH 112, Kinsman Notch. N44 2.389 W71 47.525 **P** (pg.187-188)	1870
		North Woodstock, NH (5.0E), **Lincoln, NH** (6.0E)	
388.7	1796.6	AT: Beaver Brook Trail ▲ Kinsman Ridge Trail	2664
		Dilly Cliff Trail to east	
386.1	1799.2	Gordon Pond Trail to east	2689
384.8	1800.5	Mt Wolf east peak, summit to west	3478

SoBo	NoBo	Feature	Elev
382.9	1802.4	Reel Brook Trail to west.	2640
382.5	1802.8	Powerline	2616
381.9	1803.4	**Eliza Brook Shelter** 31.6◄15.8◄9.0◄▶4.0▶19.1▶24.6 ☾ ◣ (8) ⊏	2408
381.1	1804.2	3 single tentpads, one double. Water source is brook. Eliza Brook, parallel to AT for 0.8 mi ◣	2880
380.5	1804.8	Harrington Pond ◣	3430
379.4	1805.9	South Kinsman Mountain 📷	4358
378.5	1806.8	North Kinsman Mountain	4293
378.0	1807.3	Mt Kinsman Trail to west.	3856
377.9	1807.4	**Kinsman Pond Shelter** 19.9◄13.0◄4.0◄▶16.6▶20.6▶29.6 ☾ ◣ ◣ (16) ⊏	3763
		Caretaker, fee $8PP. Treat pond water. Kinsman Ridge Tr to west, Kinsman Pond Tr to east. AT: Kinsman Ridge Trail ▲▼ Fishin' Jimmy Trail	
377.0	1808.3	Stream. ◣	2838
376.1	1809.2	Lonesome Lake Hut. ☾ ◣ ☚ **(see AMC notes, pg.182-183)**	2764
		AT: Fishin' Jimmy Tr ▲▶ Cascade Brook Tr (east), many other trail intersections	
375.1	1810.2	Kinsman Pond Trail to east.	2328
374.6	1810.7	Cascade Brook ◣	2116
373.6	1811.7	Whitehouse Brook ◣	1658
373.3	1812.0	US 3, I-93, AT underpass. Town east on US 3; better to take side trail (next entry)	1487
373.1	1812.2	Franconia Notch N44 6.014 W71 40.952 [P] (pg.188-189) **North Woodstock, NH**	1443
		Paved trail (1.0E) to Liberty Springs trailhead parking. **Lincoln, NH** (1.0E) of North Woodstock. (4.8S) left from parking area on US 3. **Liberty Springs Trail** AT: Cascade Brook Trail ▲▶	
372.4	1812.9	Flume side trail to east.	1852
371.9	1813.4	Streams ☾	2082
370.4	1814.9	Liberty Spring Campsite ☾ ◣	3910
		Overnight fee $8PP, caretaker, 7S and 3D platforms.	
370.2	1815.1	AT: Liberty Springs Tr ▲▶ Franconia Ridge Tr to west	4291
368.4	1816.9	Little Haystack Mountain, Falling Waters Trail to west 📷	4800
		NoBo: AT above treeline for next 2.0 miles.	
367.7	1817.6	Mt Lincoln, Franconia Ridge 📷	5089
366.7	1818.6	Mt Lafayette, Greenleaf Hut (1.1W) ☾ ◣ (0.2W) ☚ 📷	5291
		Greenleaf Hut visible from summit of Mt Lafayette. Located down steep Greenleaf Trail. AT: Franconia Ridge Trail ▲▶ Garfield Ridge Trail	
365.9	1819.4	Skookumchuck Trail to west.	4779

185

NH

SoBo   NoBo

1776.8   NH 25A, Gov. Meldrim Thomson Scenic Hwy

⚲ **Mt Cube Sugar Farm** (1.9W) 603-353-4709 Owned by the Thomson family, for whom the road is named. Store is not manned, but caretaker makes frequent stops. Hikers may tent outside or may be allowed to stay in the sugar house. Sometimes more is offered.

   Wentworth, NH 03282 (4.3E on NH 25A, then right 0.5 on NH 25)

⌂♂ M–F 7-11 & 2:45–4:45, Sa 7:15–12, 603-764-9444

🛒☎ **Shawnee's General Store** 603-764-5553.

1778.6   Cape Moonshine Rd

⚲🚿 **Dancing Bones Intentional Community** (1.4E) Hot outdoor showers, open-air kitchen, tenting, composting toilets and good conversation.   This is a residential community, so please be respectful when using shared facilities.   Smoking is permitted in designated areas. Pets are welcome on a case by case basis.

1782.0   Lake Tarleton Rd, NH 25C

   Warren, NH 03279 (4E)

⌂♂ M–F 7:30-9:30 & 3-5, Sa 7:30-12, 603-764-5733

🍴 **Calamity Jane's Restaurant** 603-764-5288, B/L Tu-Th, B/L/D F-Sa

🍴 **Greenhouse Food & Spirits** 603-764-5708 Th,F 3-11pm, Sa 3-10, Su 3-8pm. Open mic Thursdays, band on Fridays.

🛒 **Tedeschi Food Shop** 603-764-9002 5am-11pm, deli closes 9pm. Grocery with produce, deli with sandwiches and pizza.

⚲ **Laundry** M-Su 8:30-8:30

🖥🛜 **Library** 603-764-9072 M-Tu 10-2, W 3-7, Sa 10-1. No WiFi password so you can use it after hours.

🔧 **Burning Bush Hardware**

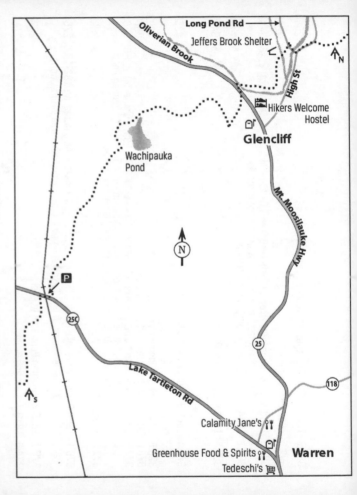

1786.6   NH 25   *Glencliff, NH 03238* (0.4E)

🏤 M-F 7-10 & 2-5, Sa 7-1, 603-989-5154 ⚠ Expects to be reduced to 2 hours/day in 2014.

🛏🛖⚡🚿🏕🚌🍴📶🖥📧 **Hikers Welcome Hostel** 603-989-0040
Bunk ($20) and camping ($15) includes shower. Shower only w/towel $2.50, laundry $2.50 wash, $2.50 dry. Snacks, sodas, and ice cream. All hikers (even non-guests) are welcome to hang out and enjoy huge DVD library. Slackpacking & shuttles (5 miles to resupply in Warren). Free phone calls. Coleman/alcohol/oz. Tools to help with gear repair, and selection of used gear available, particularly winter wear. Both guests and non-guests are welcome to send maildrops (USPS/FedEx/UPS): c/o Hikers Welcome Hostel, 1396 NH Rt 25, PO Box 25, Glencliff, NH 03238

   Warren, NH (5E) see entry pg. 186

1796.9   Lost River Rd, NH 112, Kinsman Notch

🍴📞 **Lost River Gorge** (0.5E) 603-745-8031 A tourist attraction featuring a boulder jumble similar to Mahoosuc Notch. Has gift store with microwavable food (and microwave), snacks, coffee, soda. Open early May - late-Oct.

🏕💲🚿🏕📞📧 **Lost River Valley Campground** (3.0E)
603-745-8321, 800-370-5678 ⟨www.lostriver.com⟩ cabin $59S, 69D, camping primitive sites $20, pets allowed but not in cabins. Showers, coin laundry, pay phone, open mid-May to Columbus Day 8-9, quiet 10pm-8am, owner Jim Kelly. Maildrops: 951 Lost River Rd, North Woodstock, NH 03262.

🛏 (16E) **Wise Way Wellness Center** 603-726-7600 $65 for up to three persons in cabin, includes light breakfast. $10 for pickup and return from Franconia Notch, Kinsman Notch, North Woodstock, or Lincoln. Cabin is 10 miles south of Lincoln in Thornton, NH. This is a serene rustic cabin with no TV or phone. Bathroom and shower inside adjacent building and outdoor bathtub. Amenities include WiFi, pool, sauna, mini-fridge and grill. Epson salt bath available.Licensed Massage Therapist on-site $35/30 min.

   North Woodstock, NH (5E), ***Lincoln, NH*** (6E)
   (See pg. 188-189)

Randolph Mountain Club (RMC)

Maintains the section of the AT from Edmands Col to Madison Hut and four shelters in the Northern Presidentials. Per-person fees for non-members: Gray Knob or Crag Camp $20, The Perch or Log Cabin $10. Fees must be paid in cash for stays at Gray Knob, Crag Camp and The Perch. Persons without cash can stay at the Log Cabin and will receive a receipt to mail in their fee. There is a caretaker year-round at Gray Knob if you need assistance or have questions. During the summer months, a second caretaker is in residence at Crag Camp. A caretaker visits Crag Camp and The Perch every evening throughout the year.

Shelter use is first-come, first-served; no reservations. Weekends are busy. If space is not available, be prepared to camp. Camping is not permitted within a quarter mile of RMC shelters.

There is no trash disposal. Carry in, carry out. Please keep noise to a minimum after 10pm. The use of cell phones and portable TVs is not permitted. Group size is limited to ten. There is no smoking inside RMC facilities. When a camp is full, all guests are asked to limit their stay to two consecutive nights. Outdoor wood campfires are not allowed at any of the camps. Dogs are allowed at RMC's facilities, but they should be under voice control at all times.

🚌 **AMC Hiker Shuttle** 603-466-2727 Schedule on-line: ⟨www.outdoors.org/lodging/lodging-shuttle.cfm⟩   Operates June - Mid Sept daily, and weekends and holidays through Mid-Oct. Stops at Lincoln, Franconia Notch (Liberty Springs Trailhead), Crawford Notch (Webster Cliff Trailhead), Highland Center, Pinkham Notch, and Gorham; $23 for non-members. Walk-ons if space available.

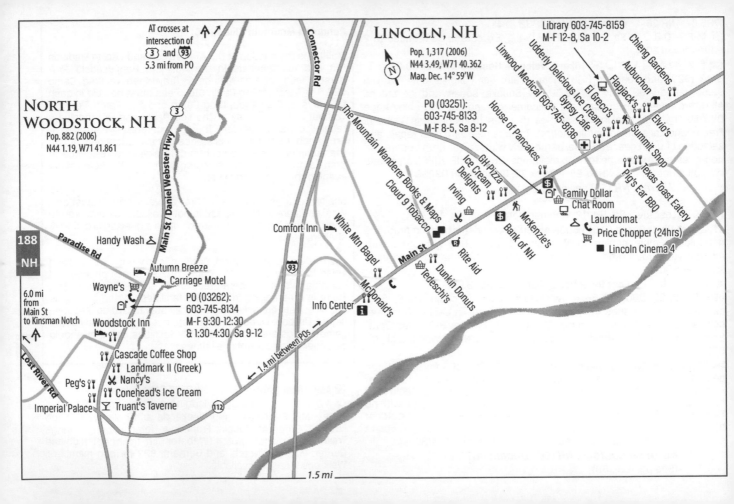

LINCOLN, NH

Pop. 1,317 (2006)
N44 3.49, W71 40.362
Mag. Dec. 14° 59'W

PO (03251):
603-745-8133
M-F 8-5, Sa 8-12

Library 603-745-8159
M-F 12-8, Sa 10-2

Chieng Gardens
Aubuchon
El Greco's
Flapjack's
Elvio's
Udderly Delicious Ice Cream
Gypsy Cafe
Summit Shop
Linwood Medical 603-745-8136
House of Pancakes

Texas Toast Eatery
Pig's Ear BBQ

GH Pizza
Ice Cream
Delights
Irving

Family Dollar
Chat Room

Laundromat
Price Chopper (24hrs)
Lincoln Cinema 4

McKenzie's
Bank of NH

AT crosses at
intersection of
3 and 93
5.3 mi from PO

Connector Rd

The Mountain Wanderer Books & Maps
Cloud 9 Tobacco

Comfort Inn
White Mtn Bagel
Main St

Rite Aid
Dunkin Donuts
Tedeschi's

McDonald's
Info Center

188
NH

NORTH
WOODSTOCK, NH

Pop. 882 (2006)
N44 1.19, W71 41.861

Main St / Daniel Webster Hwy

Paradise Rd
Handy Wash

Autumn Breeze
Carriage Motel

Wayne's

PO (03262):
603-745-8134
M-F 9:30-12:30
& 1:30-4:30, Sa 9-12

6.0 mi
from
Main St
to Kinsman Notch

Woodstock Inn

Lost River Rd

Cascade Coffee Shop
Landmark II (Greek)
Peg's
Nancy's
Conehead's Ice Cream
Imperial Palace
Truant's Taverne

112

1.4 mi between POs

1.5 mi

🍴📞✉ (0.7E) **Flume Visitor Center** 603-745-8391 with cafeteria open daily early May – late Oct, 9–5, serves pastries at breakfast, hamburgers/hot dogs/pizza remainder of the day. Maildrops: Flume Gorge, Rte 3, Franconia Notch State Park, Lincoln, NH 03251.

⛺🏠🚿📞✉ (2.1W) **Lafayette Campground** 603-823-9513, tent sites $25D, limited store, no pets, quiet 10pm. Open mid-May-Columbus Day. Maildrops: Franconia State Park, Lafayette Campground, Franconia, NH 03580.

🛏📶✉ (1.2E) **Profile Motel & Cottages** 603-745-2759 〈www.profilemotel.com〉 $49-$89, fridge and microwave in room, grills and tables outside, open 7am-10pm. Closed Nov-Mar. Maildrops: 391 US 3, Lincoln, NH 03251.

🛏📶✉ (3.0E) **Mt. Liberty Motel** 603-745-3600 〈MtLibertyMotel. com〉 $85 or less includes pickup/return when available and town shuttle. No pets. Closed Nov-Apr. Maildrops: 10 Liberty Road, PO Box 422, Lincoln, NH 03251.

🚌 **AMC Hiker Shuttle** (pg. 187)

🚌 **The Shuttle Connection** 603-745-3140 〈www.shuttleconnection. com〉 Shuttles between town and trail or to bus terminals and airports ranging from Portland, ME to NY. Can handle large groups.

🚌 **Notch Taxi Service** 603-991-8777, Reservations recommended, runs 7 days.

North Woodstock, NH (4.8S of Franconia Notch)

🛏🍴📶🖥 **Woodstock Inn** 603-745-3951, 800-321-3985 〈www.woodstockinnnh.com〉 10% discount for thru-hikers, prices seasonal, stay includes full breakfast, no pets.   Two restaurants, outdoor bar, and a micro-brewery on-site.

🛏📶 **Autumn Breeze** 603-745-8549 〈www.autumnbreezemotel. com〉 summer rates $75-90, rooms have kitchenettes, no pets.

🛏📶✉ **The Carriage Motel** 603-745-2416 〈www.carriagemotel. com〉 $72/up, no pets, game room, pool, gas grills. Closed in winter. Maildrops: 180 Main Street, North Woodstock, NH 03262.

🍴🍴💲 **Wayne's Market** Deli, ATM, 99¢ sandwiches, large beer selection.

🏠 **Fadden's General Store** ice cream, fudge and more.

Lincoln, NH (5.8S of Franconia Notch)

🛏 **Wise Way Wellness Center** 10S of Lincoln, see listing pg. 187.

🚶 **Lahout's Summit Shop** 〈www.lahouts.com〉 603-745-2882 M-F 9:30-5:30, Sa 9-5:30, Su 9-5, full service outfitter, packs, Coleman/alcohol/oz, canister fuel, freeze-dried foods.

🖥 **Chat Room/Books** M-Th 10-6, F-Sa 10-8.

■ **Mountain Wanderer** 603-745-2594 Book and map store has everything you need to navigate the Whites.

Franconia, NH 03580 (11W of Franconia notch)

🏤 M-F 8:30-1 & 2-5, Sa 9-12, 603-823-5611

🛏⛺🚌📶🖥✉ **Gale River Motel** 603-823-5655, 800-255-7989 〈www.galerivermotel.com〉 $50–$200, pets with approval, laundry wash $1, dry $1, Coleman/oz. Free pickup/return to trail with stay, longer shuttles for a fee, open year-round. Maildrops (fee for non-guest): 1 Main Street, Franconia, NH 03580.

🍴 **Mac's Market**

🏠 🍴 **Franconia Village Store** deli

🖥 **Abbie Greenleaf Library**

Littleton, NH (17W)

🚶📶 **Badass Outdoors Gear Shop** 603-444-9445 Full service outfitter 17 miles west (compass north) from Franconia Notch. Thru-hiker discount. Snacks, canister fuel. During spring and summer open M-W 11-5, Th-Su 10-6. Sometimes rides are available.

SoBo	NoBo	Description	Elev
363.6	1821.7	Garfield Pond	3995
363.2	1822.1	Mt Garfield	4500
363.0	1822.3	Garfield Trail to west	4317
362.8	1822.5	**Garfield Ridge Shelter/Campsite** (0.2W), reliable water ⊂ (12)	3951
		28.1◄19.1◄15.1◄●5.5►14.5►56.5 Overnight fee $8PP, caretaker.	
362.3	1823.0	Franconia Brook Trail to east goes steeply down 2.2mi to 13 Falls Campsite.	3451
360.7	1824.6	Gale River Trail to west	3425
360.1	1825.2	Frost Trail to Galehead Hut. ▶ Twinway Trail	3800
357.2	1825.2	AT: Garfield Ridge Trail ◄ ▶ Twinway Trail	
359.3	1826.0	South Twin Mountain, North Twin Spur Trail to west	4902
357.3	1828.0	**Guyot Shelter** 0.7E on Bondcliff Tr, plus 0.3 left on spur trail. ⊂ (14)	4534
		24.6◄20.6◄5.5►9.0►51.0►57.1 Overnight fee $8PP, caretaker,	
357.2	1828.1	Mt. Guyot, view to east.	4597
356.2	1829.1	Trail west to summit of Zeacliff Ridge	4056
354.9	1830.4	Zeacliff Pond to east	3807
354.5	1830.5	Zeacliff, Zeacliff Trail to east	3774
354.3	1831.0	View to east.	3681
353.8	1831.5	Whitewall Brook, many streams leading to falls	3213
353.4	1831.9	Lend-A-Hand Trail to west	2686
353.3	1832.0	Zealand Falls Hut, next to falls	2635
353.0	1832.3	Ethan Pond Trail to west, AT: Twinway Trail ◄ ▶ Ethan Pond Trail	2481
351.6	1833.7	Zeacliff Trail to east.	2461
350.8	1834.5	Stream, Thoreau Falls to east	2483
350.6	1834.7	Footbridge, stream	2483
350.3	1835.0	Stream, Shoal Pond Trail to east	2528
349.6	1835.7	Footbridge, stream	2644
348.3	1837.0	**Ethan Pond Campsite** (0.2W), Ethan Pond, inlet brook to pond ⊂ (8)	2874
		29.6◄14.5◄9.0►42.0►48.1►61.8	
		Overnight fee $8PP, caretaker, 3S and 2D platforms.	
347.2	1838.1	Willey Range Trail to west, stream north on AT	2632
347.0	1838.3	Kedron Flume Trail to west.	2465
345.9	1839.4	Ripley Falls 0.5E	1561
345.7	1839.6	RR tracks, parking, AT: Ethan Pond Trail ▶ road walk. N44 10.627 W71 23.167 P	1438
		AT follows paved parking driveway 0.3 to US 302. (pg.192)	
345.4	1839.9	Crawford Notch, US 302. AT: road walk ◄ ▶ Webster Cliff Trail	1277
345.3	1840.0	Saco River (treat), Saco River Trail to east, Sam Willey Trail to west.	1263
344.6	1840.7	Stream.	1949

190

NH

SoBo	NoBo	Feature	Elev
343.0	1842.3	Webster Cliffs, views from many spots along 0.5 mile traverse	3345
342.1	1843.2	Mt Webster, Webster Jackson Trail to west, NoBo: AT to east	3910
340.7	1844.6	Mt Jackson, Webster Jackson Trail to west	4052
339.0	1846.3	Mizpah cutoff to west, Mizpah Spring Hut to east, Nauman Campsite Tent site next to hut, overnight fee $8PP.	3800
338.2	1847.1	Mt Pierce (Mt Clinton)	4312
338.1	1847.2	AT: Webster Cliff Trail ◀▶ Crawford Path	4262
336.8	1848.5	Mt Eisenhower Loop Trail west to summit	4506
336.2	1849.1	Mt Eisenhower Loop Trail west to summit	4541
336.0	1849.3	Mt Eisenhower Trail to east	4582
335.4	1849.9	Mt Franklin	5004
334.9	1850.4	Mt Monroe Loop Trail west to summit	5163
334.3	1851.0	Mt Monroe Loop Trail west to summit	5157
334.2	1851.1	Lakes of the Clouds Hut (pg.192)	5106
		Four trails intersect near hut. AT stays on Crawford Path.	
333.5	1851.8	Davis Path to east, Westside Trail to west see map pg.193	5617
333.0	1852.3	AT: Crawford Path ◀▶ Trinity Heights Connector	6216
332.9	1852.4	Mt Washington (pg.192-193)	6288
332.7	1852.6	AT: Trinity Heights Connector ◀▶ Gulfside Trail	6100
332.5	1852.8	Cross Cog Railroad, stay west on Gulfside Trail	5921
332.0	1853.3	Westside Trail to west	5476
331.7	1853.6	Mt Clay Loop Trail to east.	5402
331.2	1854.1	Mt Clay Loop Trail to east, Sphinx Trail to east	5189
330.2	1855.1	Mt Jefferson Loop Trail, summit 0.3W	5315
329.8	1855.5	Six Husband Trail 0.4W to Mt Jefferson	5232
329.4	1855.9	Edmands Col, Gulfside Spring 50 yards east. Edmands Col cutoff to east, Randolph Path & Mt Jefferson loop to west.	4938
328.7	1856.6	Israel Ridge Path to RMC Perch Shelter (0.9W), $7 fee	5222
328.1	1857.2	Thunderstorm Junction, RMC cabins to west (pg.192)	5500
327.5	1857.8	Airline Trail, King Ravine Trail to west	5149
327.2	1858.1	Madison Spring Hut, Valley Way Trail 0.6W to VW Tent Site, no fee AT: Gulfside Trail ◀▶ Osgood Trail	4800
326.7	1858.6	Mt Madison, Watson Path to west.	5366
326.4	1858.9	Howker Ridge Trail to east.	5116
326.1	1859.2	Parapet Trail to east, Daniel Webster Trail to west	4877
		There are no blazes in the Great Gulf Wilderness area, approx. Mt. Madison to Auto Rd.	
324.1	1861.2	Osgood Tent Site to west, no fee. AT: Osgood Trail ◀▶ Osgood Cutoff.	2554
323.9	1861.4	Stream.	2540
SoBo	NoBo		Elev

191

NH

1839.9   Crawford Notch, US 302

🍴🔦 (1W) **Willey House** 603-374-0999 Snack bar open 9:30-5, 7 days, weekend before Memorial Day - weekend after Columbus Day.

🔺🚿⛺🔦 (1.8E) **Dry River Campground** 603-374-2272 〈www.nhstateparks.com/crawford.html〉 Tent sites $25 for 2 adults and up to 4 children. Pets allowed, coin laundry & showers, ask about shuttles, quiet 10pm-8am. Open May-3rd week of Oct.

🛏️🏨🍴⛲🚿🚌📶✉️ (3.5W) **AMC's Highland Center** 603-278-4453 〈www.outdoors.org〉 Lodge $103PP/up includes dinner & breakfast. Shapleigh Bunkhouse $78 with dinner and breakfast, $52 with B only. Rates lower for AMC members. No pets, no smoking. Coin shower for non-guests. AMC Shuttle stops daily mid-Jun to Columbus Day, afterwards only weekends and holidays. Restaurant open to all for B/L/D. Store sells snacks, sodas, some clothing and canister fuel. Maildrops ($5 fee): Route 302, Bretton Woods, NH 03574.

🛏️🔺⛲ (E3.3) **Crawford Notch General Store & Campground** 603-374-2779 〈www.crawfordnotch.com〉 Cabins $75-95, tent sites (hold 2 tents) $30. 9% lodging tax. Store carries hiker foods, ice cream and beer. Open mid-May - mid-Oct.

🚌 **Notch Taxi Service** 603-991-8777 Covers northern NH

🚌 **AMC Hiker Shuttle** (pg. 187)

Bretton Woods, NH (8.0W)

🛏️📶✉️ **Above the Notch Motor Inn** 603-846-5156 〈www.abovethenotch.com〉 $73-$88 Open year-round. 8.0W of Crawford Notch or 5 miles from Cog Railway base. Convenience store & laundry within walking distance. Non-smoking, pets $10. Accepts CC. Maildrops: PO Box 429, Twin Mountain, NH 03595.

🍴 **Faybans Station**

⛲ **Bretton Woods Station** convenience store

🧗 **Drummonds Mountain Shop** 603-278-7547 Boots, packs, rain gear, hiking foods, stoves and fuel.

Bartlett, NH (13.0E from Crawford Notch)
Resort town has unique mountain roller coaster and water slide at **Attitash Resort** 800-223-7669 〈www.attitash.com〉.

1851.1   Lakes of the Clouds Hut

🛏️🏨🔵🌙 Lodging and WFS (see AMC notes, pg. 182). Also "The Dungeon," a bunkroom available to 6 thru-hikers for $10PP with access to hut restroom and the common area. When the hut is closed The Dungeon serves as an emergency shelter.

1852.4   Mt Washington, NH

📬(03589) M-S 10-4 For outgoing mail; please do not send maildrops. 🍴⛲🚻🔦 Second highest peak on the AT. **Summit House** open 8am-8pm Memorial Day-Columbus Day. Snack bar open 9am-6pm.

🚂 **Cog Railway** 603-278-5404 〈www.thecog.com〉 Runs hourly. One-way tickets $45 (if space-available) sold at summit station. Base station 3 miles away near Bretton Woods, NH.

1857.2   Thunderstorm Junction

🏨 **Crag Camp Cabin** (1.1W) on Spur Trail, **Gray Knob Cabin** (1.2W) on Lowe Path; $20 fee for either. If you camp along these side trails, it must be at least 0.25mi. from either cabin.

1861.8 - 1863.0 Map of trail intersections

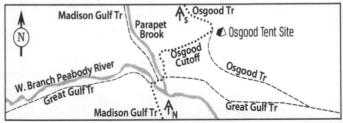

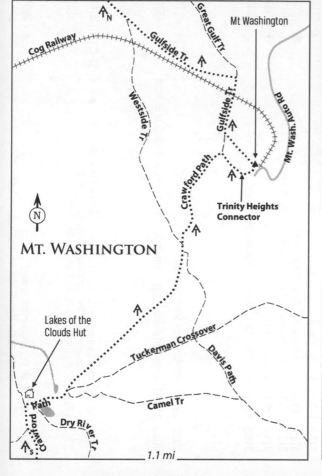

MT. WASHINGTON

Cog Railway
Gulfside Tr.
Great Gulf Tr.
Mt Washington
Gulfside Tr.
Westside Tr.
Mt. Wash. Auto Rd.
Crawford Path
Trinity Heights Connector
Lakes of the Clouds Hut
Tuckerman Crossover
Davis Path
Path
Camel Tr.
Dry River Tr.
Crawford
1.1 mi

American Hiking Society

Founded in 1976, American Hiking Society is the only national organization dedicated to promoting and protecting America's hiking trails, their surrounding natural areas and the hiking experience.

To learn more about American Hiking Society and our programs such as National Trails Day, National Trails Fund, and Volunteer Vacations, visit AmericanHiking.org or call (800) 972-8608.

National Weather Service Wind Chill Chart

		Temperature (°F)												
		35	30	25	20	15	10	5	0	-5	-10	-15	-20	-25
Wind (mph)	5	31	25	19	13	7	1	-5	-11	-16	-22	-28	-34	-40
	10	27	21	15	9	3	-4	-10	-16	-22	-28	-35	-41	-47
	15	25	19	13	6	0	-7	-13	-19	-26	-32	-39	-45	-51
	20	24	17	11	4	-2	-9	-15	-22	-29	-35	-42	-48	-55
	25	23	16	9	3	-4	-11	-17	-24	-31	-37	-44	-51	-58
	30	22	15	8	1	-5	-12	-19	-26	-33	-39	-46	-53	-60
	35	21	14	7	0	-7	-14	-21	-27	-34	-41	-48	-55	-62
	40	20	13	6	-1	-8	-15	-22	-29	-36	-43	-50	-57	-64

SoBo	NoBo		Elev
323.5	1861.8	AT: Osgood Cutoff ◆► Great Gulf Trail to east. (see map pg.192)	2341
323.5	1861.8	⚠ Parapet Brook, AT: Great Gulf Trail ◆► Madison Gulf Trail to west.	2337
323.4	1861.9	⚠ West branch of Peabody River suspension bridge. Great Gulf Tr to east	2300
322.9	1862.4	Stream.	2410
322.0	1863.3	Stream.	2580
321.5	1863.8	Lowes Bald Spot 0.1W	2841
321.4	1863.9	Mt Washington Auto Rd N44 16.892 W71 15.203 P	2731
321.2	1864.1	AT: Madison Gulf Trail ◆► Old Jackson Rd	2673
320.4	1864.9	Nelson Crag Trail and Raymond Path to east	2571
320.1	1865.2	George's Gorge Trail to west	2266
319.4	1865.9	Peabody River, four other trails cross the AT from here to Pinkham Notch ◆	2050
		NH 16, Pinkham Notch N44 15.416 W71 15.158 P (pg.196-197)	
		Gorham, NH (10.7W), AT: Old Jackson Rd ◆► Lost Pond Trail	
318.4	1866.9	AT: Lost Pond Trail ◆► Wildcat Ridge Trail	2016
318.0	1867.3	View	2851
317.4	1867.9	Rocky crevasse, stairs	3259
316.7	1868.6	Wildcat Mountain peak E.	4065
316.4	1868.9	Wildcat Mountain peak D, observation tower, ski gondola 0.1 north	3990
		Gondola rides to/from the AT, $12 round trip, restaurant at base, open Jul-Oct.	
315.3	1870.0	Wildcat Mountain peak C.	4274
314.4	1870.9	Wildcat Mountain peak A.	4422
313.9	1871.4	Spring	3680
313.7	1871.6	AT: Wildcat Ridge Trail ◆► Nineteen Mile Brook Trail to east.	3407
313.5	1871.8	AT: Nineteen Mile Brook Trail ◆► Carter Notch Hut (0.1E).	3308
312.8	1872.5	Spring to west	4311
312.3	1873.0	Carter Dome, Rainbow Trail to east	4832
311.9	1873.4	Black Angel Trail to east, Carter Dome Trail to west.	4616
311.4	1873.9	Mt Hight, view.	4652
310.9	1874.4	Zeta Pass, two Carter Dome trailheads to west	3890
308.8	1876.5	Middle Carter Mountain, view.	4610
308.2	1877.1	North Carter Mountain, North Carter Trail to west, just south of summit	4539
306.3	1879.0	**Imp Campsite** (0.2W) 56.5◄51.0◄42.0◄►6.1►19.8►25.0 ⦗(10)⦘	3344
		Overnight fee $8PP, caretaker, composting privy.	
305.6	1879.7	Stony Brook Trail to west, Moriah Brook Trail to east	3143
304.2	1881.1	Mt Moriah, summit to west.	3991
		AT: Carter Moriah Trail ◆► Kenduskeag Trail	

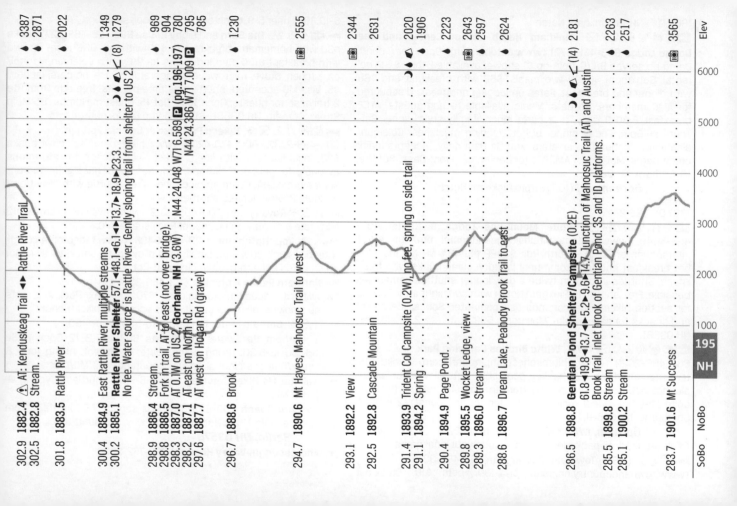

SoBo	NoBo		Elev
302.9	1882.4	AT: Kenduskeag Trail ◄► Rattle River Trail	◆ 3387
302.5	1882.8	Stream.	◆ 2871
301.8	1883.5	Rattle River	◆ 2022
300.4	1884.9	East Rattle River, multiple streams	◆ 1349
300.2	1885.1	**Rattle River Shelter** 57.1◄48.1◄6.1►13.7►18.9►23.3	⊂ (8) 1279
		No fee. Water source is Rattle River. Gently sloping trail from shelter to US 2	
298.9	1886.4	Stream.	◆ 969
298.5	1886.5	Fork in trail, AT to east (not over bridge).	904
298.3	1887.0	AT 0.1W on US 2, **Gorham, NH** (3.6W)	780
298.2	1887.1	AT east on North Rd.	795
297.6	1887.7	AT west on Hogan Rd (gravel)	785
		N44 24.048 W71 6.589 **P** (pg.196-197)	
		N44 24.386 W71 7.009 **P**	
296.7	1888.6	Brook	◆ 1230
294.7	1890.6	**Mt Hayes**, Mahoosuc Trail to west	📷 2555
293.1	1892.2	View	📷 2344
292.5	1892.8	Cascade Mountain	2631
291.4	1893.9	**Trident Col Campsite** (0.2W), no fee, spring on side trail	◖ 2020
291.1	1894.2	Spring	◖ 1906
290.4	1894.9	Page Pond.	◆ 2223
289.8	1895.5	Wocket Ledge, view.	📷 2643
289.3	1896.0	Stream.	◆ 2597
288.6	1896.7	Dream Lake, Peabody Brook Trail to east	◆ 2624
286.5	1898.8	**Gentian Pond Shelter/Campsite** (0.2E)	⊂ (14) 2181
		61.8◄19.8◄13.7►5.2►9.6►14.7 Junction of Mahoosuc Trail (AT) and Austin	
		Brook Trail, inlet brook of Gentian Pond. 3S and ID platforms.	
285.5	1899.8	Stream	◆ 2263
285.1	1900.2	Stream	◆ 2517
283.7	1901.6	**Mt Success**	📷 3565

195
NH

1865.9   NH 16, Pinkham Notch

🛏🍴🚻🚿🚌📞📶✉ **Pinkham Notch Visitor Center and Joe Dodge Lodge** 603-466-2721 ⟨www.outdoors.org⟩ Open year round. Cafeteria serves B/L/D. Coin-op $1 shower available 24hrs, $2 towel rental. Bunkroom $62PP w/o meals, $68 with breakfast and $88 with dinner and breakfast. Rates on lodging and meals discounted for AMC members. No pets. Meals available to non-guests; AYCE breakfast 6:30-9 daily, a la carte lunch, family-style dinner Sat-Thurs at 6pm, Friday dinner buffet. Vending machines, Coleman/alcohol/oz, isobutane canisters. Shuttle 8am daily. Accepts major credit cards. Maildrops: AMC Visitor Center, c/o Front Desk, 361 Rte. 16, Gorham, NH 03581.

> ***Gorham, NH*** (10.7W from Pinkham Notch)

1887.0   US 2

🛏⚙🍴⛺🚌🅿💻✉ **White Mountains Lodge & Hostel** 603-466-5049 ⟨www.whitemountainslodgeandhostel.com⟩ On AT at intersection of Rte 2 + North Rd. $33PP plus 9% NH tax includes hot breakfast and free communal laundry. Clean bunks with fresh linens. Shuttles into town twice a day, longer shuttles sometimes possible. Free shuttle to Pinkham Notch with two night stay. Parking for section hikers. One common-use computer. Sodas, ice cream and snacks for sale on-site. Maildrops: 592 State Rte 2, Shelburne, NH 03581.

🛏🚿⛺⚙🔥🛀📞✉ (1.7W) **White Birches Camping Park** 603-466-2022 ⟨www.whitebirchescampingpark.com⟩ bunks $15, tent sites $13PP, pool, air hockey, pool table, pets allowed, Coleman/alcohol/isobutane, free shuttle from/to trail and town with stay, open May-Oct. Guest maildrops ($5 fee for non-guest): 218 US 2, Shelburne, NH 03581.

> ***Gorham, NH 03581*** (3.6W from US 2)

🏠 ID required; all packages should include your legal name.

🛏🍴📶💻 (2.6W) **Town and Country Inn** 603-466-3315 ⟨www.townandcountryinn.com⟩ $64-130, pets $10. Breakfast 6-10:30, dinner 5-9, cocktails. Indoor pool, sauna.

🛏🛏⚙⛺✉ **The Barn** and **Libby House B&B** 603-466-2271 Bunks $30 with homemade breakfast or $20 without. B&B room for two with breakfast $100. Serving hikers for 29 years. Coleman/alcohol/oz, kitchen, stove, microwave, refrigerator for use, no pets, laundry $5, Visa MC accepted, shuttles as time permits, free ride from Rte 2 trailhead for guests. Open June-Oct 15. Guest maildrops: 55 Main Street, Gorham, NH 03581. $15 maildrop for non-guests.

🛏🛏⚙🍴⛺🚌📶 **Hiker's Paradise** at Colonial Fort Inn 603-466-2732, 800-470-4224 ⟨www.hikersparadise.com⟩ bunks $22 (includes tax) with linen, tub/shower, kitchen. Private rooms available. No pets or maildrops. Coin laundry for guests. Restaurant serves breakfast. Coleman/alcohol/oz. Free shuttle with stay from/to Route 2, other limited shuttles.

🛏🍴⛺📶 **Royalty Inn** 603-466-3312 ⟨www.royaltyinn.com⟩ 2013 hiker rate $79, may go up. Indoor Pool, suana, A/C.

🛏⛺📶 **Top Notch Inn** 603-466-5496 ⟨www.topnotchinn.com⟩ Hiker discount, pool, A/C, small dogs allowed, no smoking, all major credit cards accepted. Open May-mid-Oct.

🛏 **Northern Peaks Motor Inn** 603-466-3374 ⟨www.northernpeaksmotorinn.com⟩ $70/up + tax. Pool, A/C, pets $5, no smoking, all major credit cards accepted, hiker friendly.

🛏🍴⛺📶 **Gorham Motor Inn** 603-466-3381 $58-$158.

🥾⚒ **Gorham Hardware and Sports** 603-466-2312 Open M-Sa 8-5:30, Su 12-5:30. Hiking poles, Water treatment, hiking food & clothes, White gas/alcohol/oz and isobutane. Visa/MC/Disc.

🚌 **Trail Angels Hiker Services** 978-855-9227 Shuttles covering all of NH and ME.

🚌 **Concord Coach** 800-639-3317 Bus service 7:50am daily from Irving store to Pinkham Notch. $6 one-way, $11 round-trip.

> ***Berlin, NH 03570***

➕ **Androscoggin Valley Hospital** 603-752-2200

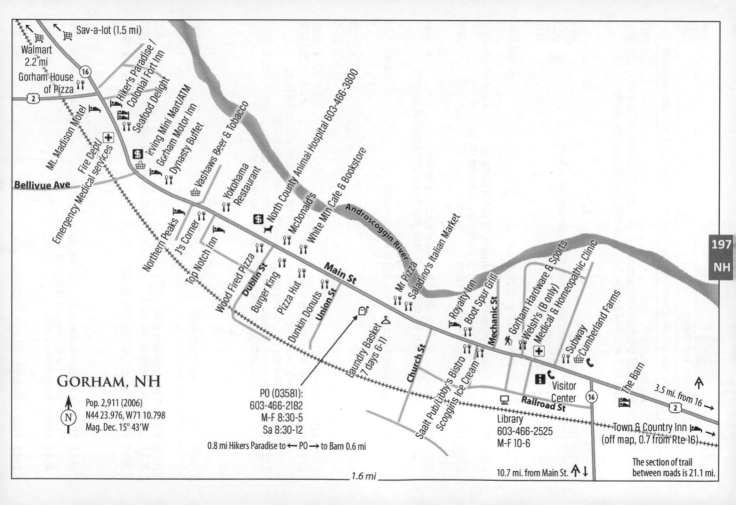

GORHAM, NH

Sav-a-lot (1.5 mi)

Walmart 2.2 mi

Gorham House of Pizza

16

2

Hiker's Paradise / Colonial Fort Inn

Seafood Delight

Irving Mini Mart/ATM

Gorham Motor Inn

Dynasty Buffet

Mt. Madison Motel

Fire Dept /
Emergency Medical services

Bellivue Ave

Vashaws Beer & Tobacco

Yokohama Restaurant

Northern Peaks

North County Animal Hospital 603-466-3800

McDonald's

White Mtn Cafe & Bookstore

Androscoggin River

J's Corner

Top Notch Inn

Wood Fired Pizza

Dublin St

Burger King

Pizza Hut

Dunkin Donuts

Union St

Main St

197
NH

Mr Pizza

Saladino's Italian Market

Royalty Inn

Boot Spur Grill

Mechanic St

Gorham Hardware & Sports

Welsh's (B only)
Medical & Homeopathic Clinic

Subway

Cumberland Farms

The Barn

3.5 mi. from 16

Laundry Basket
7 days 6-11

Saalt Pub/Libby's Bistro

Scoggins Ice Cream

Church St

Visitor Center

16

2

Railroad St

Library
603-466-2525
M-F 10-6

Town & Country Inn
(off map, 0.7 from Rte 16)

Pop. 2,911 (2006)
N44 23.976, W71 10.798
Mag. Dec. 15° 43'W

N

PO (03581):
603-466-2182
M-F 8:30-5
Sa 8:30-12

0.8 mi Hikers Paradise to ← PO → to Barn 0.6 mi

10.7 mi. from Main St. ↑↓

The section of trail
between roads is 21.1 mi.

1.6 mi

Appalachian Trail elevation profile, miles 1902.2–1922.1 (NoBo) / 283.1–263.2 (SoBo), Maine.

SoBo	NoBo	Feature	Elev
283.1	1902.2	Success Trail to west.	3174
		⚠ Camp fires are only allowed along the AT in ME within fireplaces at designated campsites.	
281.8	1903.5	**NH-ME** border	2972
281.3	1904.0	**Carlo Col Shelter and Campsite** (0.3W), on Carlo Col Trail ☽ ♦ ▲ ⊏ (16) 25.0◄18.9◄5.2◄►4.4►9.5►16.4 Platforms 3S and 2D, bear box, no fee.	3210
280.9	1904.4	Mt Carlo	3565
279.5	1905.8	Goose Eye Mountain west peak, Goose Eye Mtn Trail to west 🖼	3804
279.1	1906.2	Goose Eye Mountain east peak 🖼	3790
278.8	1906.5	Wright Trail to east 🖼	3479
277.9	1907.4	Goose Eye Mountain north peak. 🖼	3686
276.9	1908.4	**Full Goose Shelter and Campsite** 3S and 1D platforms ☽ ♦ ▲ ⊏ (12) 23.3◄9.6◄4.4◄►5.1►12.0►15.5 No fee, stream behind shelter.	2966
276.4	1908.9	Fulling Mill Mountain south peak	3395
275.4	1909.9	Mahoosuc Notch south end, Mahoosuc Notch Trail to west. ♦ Most difficult or fun mile of the AT. Make way through jumbled pit of boulders.	2494
274.2	1911.1	Mahoosuc Notch north end, Bull Branch, campsite ♦ ▲	2163
273.2	1912.1	Spring ♦	3291
272.7	1912.6	Mahoosuc Arm	3770
272.0	1913.3	Speck Pond brook ♦	3426
271.8	1913.5	**Speck Pond Shelter & Campsite** ☽ ♦ ▲ ⊏ (8) 14.7◄9.5◄5.1◄►6.9►10.4►20.9 Overnight fee $8PP, caretaker. Spring down Speck Pond Trail just beyond caretaker's yurt. 3S and 3D platforms	3438
270.7	1914.6	Intersection, AT north on Old Speck Tr., south on Mahoosuc Tr. 🖼 ⚑ Side Trail 0.3E to Old Speck summit and observation tower.	4033
268.4	1916.9	Eyebrow Trail to west ♦	2512
268.1	1917.2	Stream. ♦	2391
267.3	1918.0	Eyebrow Trail to west	1521
267.2	1918.1	Grafton Notch, ME 26 N44 35.382 W70 56.803 P 🏛 ☽ (pg.202)	1495
266.4	1918.9	Stream, Table Rock Trail to east ♦	2113
264.9	1920.4	**Baldpate Lean-to** (0.1E), stream next to lean-to ☽ ♦ ▲ ⊏ (8) 16.4◄12.0◄6.9◄►3.5►14.0►26.8	2683
264.1	1921.2	Baldpate west peak 🖼	3662
263.2	1922.1	Baldpate east peak, Grafton Loop Trail 🖼	3810

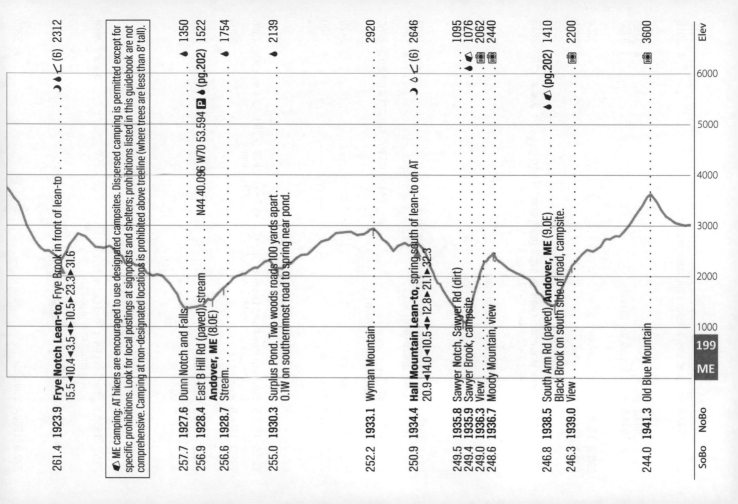

SoBo	NoBo		Elev

261.4 **1923.9** **Frye Notch Lean-to,** Frye Brook in front of lean-to . . . . ☽ ♦ ⊂ (6) 2312
15.5◄10.4◄3.5◄▶10.5▶23.3▶31.6

◆ ME camping: AT hikers are encouraged to use designated campsites. Dispersed camping is permitted except for specific prohibitions. Look for local postings at signposts and shelters; proh bitions listed in this guidebook are not comprehensive. Camping at non-designated locations is prohibited above treeline (where trees are less than 8' tall).

257.7 **1927.6** Dunn Notch and Falls . . . . ♦ 1350
256.9 **1928.4** East B Hill Rd (paved), stream . . . . N44 40.096 W70 53.594 🅿 ♦ (pg.202) 1522
256.6 **1928.7** **Andover, ME (8.0E)** —
Stream. . . . . ♦ 1754

255.0 **1930.3** Surplus Pond. Two woods roads 100 yards apart. . . . . ♦ 2139
0.1W on southernmost road to spring near pond.

252.2 **1933.1** Wyman Mountain 2920

250.9 **1934.4** **Hall Mountain Lean-to,** spring south of lean-to on AT . . . . ☽ △ ⊂ (6) 2646
20.9◄14.0◄10.5◄▶12.8▶21.1▶32.3

249.5 **1935.8** Sawyer Notch, Sawyer Rd (dirt) 1095
249.4 **1935.9** Sawyer Brook, campsite . . . . ♦ 1076
249.0 **1936.3** View . . . . ◎ 2062
248.6 **1936.7** Moody Mountain, view . . . . ◎ 2440

246.8 **1938.5** South Arm Rd (paved) **Andover, ME (9.0E)** . . . . ♦ ◀ (pg.202) 1410
Black Brook on south side of road, campsite.
246.3 **1939.0** View . . . . ◎ 2200

244.0 **1941.3** Old Blue Mountain . . . . ◎ 3600

199
ME

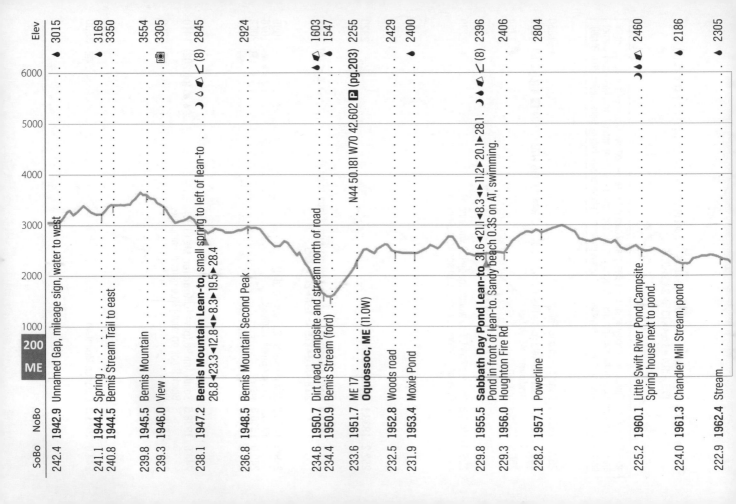

200
ME

SoBo	NoBo		Elev
242.4	1942.9	Unnamed Gap, mileage sign, water to west	3015
241.1	1944.2	Spring	3169
240.8	1944.5	Bemis Stream Trail to east	3350
239.8	1945.5	Bemis Mountain	3554
239.3	1946.0	View	3305
238.1	1947.2	**Bemis Mountain Lean-to,** small spring to left of lean-to 26.8◄23.3◄12.8◄▶8.3▶19.5▶28.4	2845
236.8	1948.5	Bemis Mountain Second Peak	2924
234.6	1950.7	Dirt road, campsite and stream north of road	1603
234.4	1950.9	Bemis Stream (ford)	1547
233.6	1951.7	ME17 N44 50.181 W70 42.602 **P** (pg.203) **Oquossoc, ME** (11.0W)	2255
232.5	1952.8	Woods road	2429
231.9	1953.4	Moxie Pond	2400
229.8	1955.5	**Sabbath Day Pond Lean-to,** 31.6◄21.1◄8.3◄▶11.2▶20.1▶28.1. Pond in front of lean-to. Sandy beach 0.3S on AT, swimming.	2396
229.3	1956.0	Houghton Fire Rd	2406
228.2	1957.1	Powerline	2804
225.2	1960.1	Little Swift River Pond Campsite. Spring house next to pond.	2460
224.0	1961.3	Chandler Mill Stream, pond	2186
222.9	1962.4	Stream.	2305

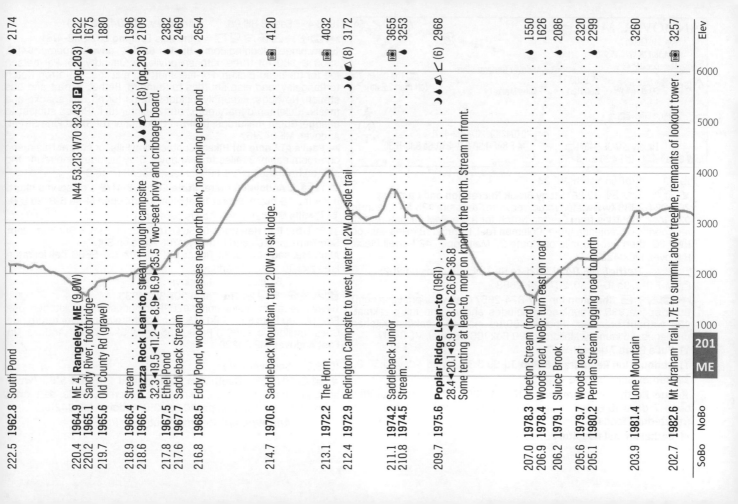

		Elev
222.5	South Pond	● 2174
220.4	**ME 4, Rangeley, ME (9.0W)** N44 53.213 W70 32.431 **P** (pg.203)	1622
220.2	Sandy River, footbridge	● 1675
219.7	Old County Rd (gravel)	1880
218.9	Stream	1996
218.6	**Piazza Rock Lean-to,** stream through campsite 🌙 ● ⌂ ◁ (8) (pg.203)	2109
	32.3◄19.5◄11.2◄▲8.9►16.9►35.5 Two-seat privy and cribbage board.	
217.8	Ethel Pond	● 2382
217.6	Saddleback Stream	● 2469
216.8	Eddy Pond, woods road passes near north bank, no camping near pond	● 2654
214.7	Saddleback Mountain, trail 2.0W to ski lodge.	📷 4120
213.1	The Horn.	📷 4032
212.4	Redington Campsite to west, water 0.2W on side trail 🌙 ● ⌂ (8)	3172
211.1	Saddleback Junior 🌙 ● ◁ ⌂	📷 3655
210.8	Stream.	3253
209.7	**Poplar Ridge Lean-to** (1961) 🌙 ● ◁ ⌂ (6)	2968
	28.4◄20.1◄8.9►8.0►26.6►36.8	
	Some tenting at lean-to, more on knoll to the north. Stream in front.	
207.0	Orbeton Stream (ford)	● 1550
206.9	Woods road, NoBo: turn east on road	1626
206.2	Sluice Brook.	● 2086
205.6	Woods road	● 2320
205.1	Perham Stream, logging road to north	● 2299
203.9	Lone Mountain	3260
202.7	**Mt Abraham Trail,** 1.7E to summit above treeline, remnants of lookout tower	📷 3257

201
ME

SoBo   NoBo

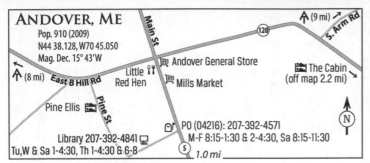

ANDOVER, ME
Pop. 910 (2009)
N44 38.128, W70 45.050
Mag. Dec. 15°43'W

↑ (8 mi) East B Hill Rd

Pine Ellis

Little Red Hen

Main St

↑ (9 mi) ↗ S. Arm Rd
120

Andover General Store
Mills Market

The Cabin (off map 2.2 mi)

PO (04216): 207-392-4571
M-F 8:15-1:30 & 2-4:30, Sa 8:15-11:30

Library 207-392-4841
Tu,W & Sa 1-4:30, Th 1-4:30 & 6-8

Pine St

N

1.0 mi

1918.1   Grafton Notch, ME 26

◐ ⌂ ⚒ ⛺ ➚ ✉ (12.8E) **Stony Brook Recreation and Camping** 207-824-2836 ⟨www.stonybrookrec.com⟩ tent site $25 for 4, lean-to $30 for 4. Shuttles from Grafton Notch for a fee. Pool, miniature golf, rec room, convenience store, Coleman fuel. Located 12 miles east on Hwy 26, then left 0.8 mile on Route 2. Maildrops: 42 Powell Place, Hanover, ME 04237.

Bethel, ME 04217 (12E to Rt 2, right 5 miles on Rt 2)

⌂ M-F 9-4, Sa 10-12:30, 207-824-2668

► 🏠⛺➚✉ **Chapman Inn** 207-824-2657 ⟨www.chapmaninn.com⟩ Bunk space $35 in bunkroom includes shower and full breakfast, $25 without breakfast. Rooms $69/up include breakfast. Kitchen privileges, $5 laundry. Maildrops: PO Box 1067, Bethel, ME 04217.

♟ **Pat's Pizza** 7 days 11-9

♟ **Sudbury Inn Restaurant & Pub**, Tu-Su 5:30-9, pub 7 days 4:30-9.

🛒 **Bethel Shop 'n Save**

🏃 **True North Adventurewear** 207-824-2201 Full service outfitter, open 7 days 10-6. Leki repair, Coleman/alcohol/oz and isobutane, freeze-dried foods.

🐾 **Bethel Animal Hospital** 207-824-2212

1928.4   East B Hill Rd   *Andover, ME 04216* (8E)

► 🏠⌂⛺⛵🚌➚💻✉ **Pine Ellis Lodging** 207-392-4161 ⟨www.pineellislodging.com⟩ Bunks $20PP, private rooms $40S, $50D & $60 for three. Kitchen privileges, laundry $5. Per-person fee for trailhead pickup. For-fee shuttles; slackpack Grafton Notch to Rangeley, and also shuttles to Rumford, Bethel, airport and bus station. No dogs. Resupply includes items for on-trail snacks and meals. Coleman/denatured/oz and canister fuel. Prices subject to change. Guest maildrops: (USPS) PO Box 12 or (UPS) 20 Pine Street, Andover, ME 04216.

► **Paul's AT Camp for Hikers** Contact Pine Ellis for stay at this rustic one-room cabin, 3 miles from Andover. Stay includes one round trip shuttle from the hostel. $60 for four, $15EAP up to 6.

🛒♟💲🔔 **Andover General Store** 207-392-4172 Deli serves short-order food & pizza, **Sweet Treats** ice cream. Open M-Sa 5-8, Su 6-8.

🛒♟ **Mills Market** Open 7 days 5am-9pm.

♟➚ **Little Red Hen** Open Tu-Su (T-Th 6:30am-2pm, F-Sat 6am-8pm, Sun 7am-2pm) closed Monday. AYCE Pizza on Sat.

Also: Massage therapist, Donna Gifford, 207-357-5686, call for rates. Free pickup/return to Andover.

2.8 miles east of Andover:

🏠⛺⛵🚌➚💻✉ **The Cabin** 207-392-1333 ⟨www.thecabininmaine.com⟩ $20PP includes linens, kitchen use. Free pickup from East B Rd or S. Arm Rd; there is a fee for return ride. Guest maildrops: (USPS) PO Box 55 or (UPS) 497 East Andover Rd, East Andover, ME 04226.

1938.5   South Arm Rd

◐ ⌂ ⛺ ✉ (3.5W) **South Arm Campground** 207-364-5155 ⟨www.southarm.com⟩ Tent sites, camp store, no credit cards, pets okay, open May 1–Oct 1. Maildrops: PO Box 310, Andover, ME 04216.

Andover, ME (9E from South Arm Rd)

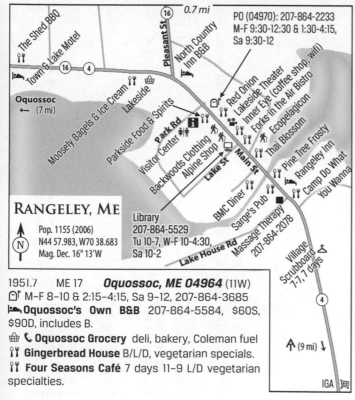

PO (04970): 207-864-2233
M-F 9:30-12:30 & 1:30-4:15,
Sa 9:30-12

RANGELEY, ME

Pop. 1155 (2006)
N44 57.983, W70 38.683
Mag. Dec. 16° 13'W

Library
207-864-5529
Tu 10-7, W-F 10-4:30,
Sa 10-2

0.7 mi

The Shed BBQ
Town & Lake Motel
Oquossoc (7 mi) ←
Moosely Bagels & Ice Cream
Lakeside
Parkside Food & Spirits
Park Rd
Visitor Center
Backwoods Clothing
Alpine Shop
Lake St
Main St
BMC Diner
Sarge's Pub
Massage Therapy 207-864-2078
Lake House Rd
Red Onion
Lakeside Theater
Inner Eye (coffee shop, wifi)
Forks in the Air Bistro
Ecopelagicon
Thai Blossom
Pine Tree Frosty
Rangeley Inn
Camp Do What You Wanna
North Country Inn B&B
Pleasant St
Village Scrubboard 7-7, 7 days
(9 mi)
IGA

1951.7 ME 17 **Oquossoc, ME 04964** (11W)
M-F 8-10 & 2:15-4:15, Sa 9-12, 207-864-3685
Oquossoc's Own B&B 207-864-5584, $60S, $90D, includes B.
Oquossoc Grocery deli, bakery, Coleman fuel
Gingerbread House B/L/D, vegetarian specials.
Four Seasons Café 7 days 11-9 L/D vegetarian specialties.

1964.9 ME 4 **Rangeley, ME** (9W) Safest place to hitch is from end of guardrail 0.3W, in front of Hiker Hut. Rangeley is halfway between the equator and the north pole (3107 miles from either).

Hiker Hut at 2 Pine Road (0.3W of AT) 978-210-3782 hikerhut@gmail.com. $20PP includes bunk w/mattress and pillow, healthy home-cooked meal and shuttle into Rangeley. Private hut for couples $40. Beautiful off-grid setting along the Sandy River with swimming hole, hummingbird watching, and local jewelry artist on-site. Dogs welcome. Maildrops: C/O Steve Lynch, 2 Pine Rd, Sandy River Plantation, ME 04970.

Town & Lake Motel 207-864-3755 Call for hiker rate. Pets $5. Canoes for guest use. Maildrops: PO Box 47, Rangeley, ME 04970.

Saddleback Motor Inn 207-864-3434 $95, pets $10, pool.

Rangeley Inn & Tavern 207-864-3341 ⟨www.rangeleyinn.com⟩ Mid-week rate as low as $99.

North Country Inn B&B 207-864-2440 ⟨www.northcountrybb.com⟩ $99-149, includes full breakfast, specials in mid-week, and off season. Multi-night discount.

Camp Do What You Wanna 207-864-3000 B/L pastries, soups, and sandwiches.

Sarge's Sports Pub & Grub L/D and bar, 7 days 11-1, house bands on Friday and Saturday.

IGA Supermarket 207-864-5089 ATM 7 days 7-8.

Ecopelagicon 207-864-2771 Hiker friendly nature store has white gas/alcohol/oz, canister fuel, freeze-dried foods, water filters, clothes, Leki poles and does warranty work. Ask about shuttles.

Alpine Shop ⟨www.alpineshoprangeley.com⟩ 207-864-3741 M-S 9-7, Su 10-6, some hiking gear, Coleman/alcohol/oz.

Back Woods 207-864-2335 Gear, clothes.

Rangeley Health & Wellness Center On Dallas Hill Rd south of IGA. Medical 207-864-3303. Fitness Center 207-864-3055 $5 shower, towel provided. M-Th 5am-8pm, F 5am-7:30pm, Sa-Su 8-2.

ME

1966.7 **Piazza Rock Lean-to** Two side trails north of shelter; 100 yards north: west to Piazza Rock; 0.1 north: To "The Caves", blue-blazed route through a labyrinth of boulders and caves.

204
ME

Elev	SoBo	NoBo	
3139	201.7	1983.6	**Spaulding Mountain Lean-to**, spring on north shelter loop trail 28.1◄16.9◄8.0◄▶18.6▶28.8▶36.5
4000	200.9	1984.4	Crest NW shoulder of Spaulding Mountain Side trail 0.1E to summit.
3643	200.2	1985.1	Bronze plaque Completion of the last section of the AT from GA-ME.
3645	199.0	1986.3	View to east.
3727	198.7	1986.6	Sugarloaf Mountain, stream 0.2E, Sugarloaf Mountain Trail 0.6E to summit
2195	196.6	1988.7	South Branch Carrabassett River (ford), tenting on north side of river
2264	196.5	1988.8	Caribou Valley Rd (gravel)
2475	196.1	1989.2	Spring
2757	195.5	1989.8	Crocker Cirque Campsite (0.2E), stream
4040	194.4	1990.9	South Crocker Mountain, summit 50 yards west
4228	193.4	1991.9	North Crocker Mountain
3369	192.3	1993.0	Spring
1450	188.2	1997.1	ME 27 (paved), **Stratton, ME** (5.0W). N45 6.201 W70 21.413 **P** (pg.208)
1250	187.4	1997.9	Stratton Brook Pond Rd
1201	187.3	1998.0	Stratton Brook, footbridge
1279	186.5	1998.8	Footbridge, stream
1323	186.4	1998.9	Cranberry Stream Campsite
2400	185.0	2000.3	Bigelow Range Trail 0.2W to Cranberry Pond
3379	183.9	2001.4	View to east
3200	183.3	2002.0	Horns Pond Trail
3183	183.1	2002.2	**Horns Pond Lean-tos** 35.5◄26.6◄18.6◄▶10.2▶17.9▶27.9
3720	182.7	2002.6	Trail 0.2W to North Horn, small boxed spring just south of this intersection
3831	182.6	2002.7	South Horn

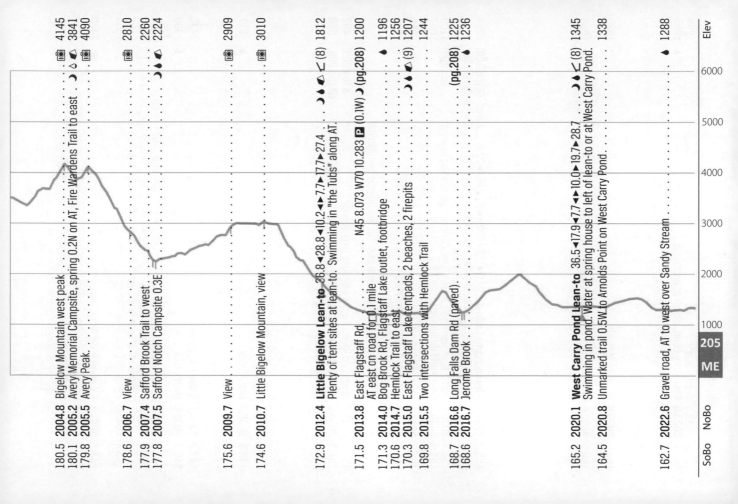

NoBo	Description	Elev
180.5	Bigelow Mountain west peak	4145
180.1	Avery Memorial Campsite, spring 0.2N on AT, Fire Wardens Trail to east	3841
179.8	Avery Peak.	4090
178.6	View	2810
177.9	Safford Brook Trail to west.	2260
177.8	Safford Notch Campsite 0.3E	2224
175.6	View	2909
174.6	Little Bigelow Mountain, view	3010
172.9	**Little Bigelow Lean-to**. 36.8◀28.8◀10.2◀▶7.7▶17.7▶27.4. Plenty of tent sites at lean-to. Swimming in "the Tubs" along AT.	➤●◣⊂(8) 1812
171.5	East Flagstaff Rd, N45 8.073 W70 10.283 **P** (0.1W) ➤ (pg.208) AT east on road for 0.1 mile	1200
171.3	Bog Brook Rd, Flagstaff Lake outlet, footbridge	● 1196
170.6	Hemlock Trail to east.	1256
170.3	East Flagstaff Lake tentpads, 2 beaches, 2 firepits	➤●◣(9) 1207
169.8	Two intersections with Hemlock Trail	1244
168.7	Long Falls Dam Rd (paved). (pg.208)	1225
168.6	Jerome Brook	● 1236
165.2	**West Carry Pond Lean-to**. 36.5◀17.9◀7.7◀▶10.0▶19.7▶28.7. Water at spring house to left of lean-to or at West Carry Pond. Swimming in pond.	➤●⊂(8) 1345
164.5	Unmarked trail 0.5W to Arnolds Point on West Carry Pond.	● 1338
162.7	Gravel road, AT to west over Sandy Stream	● 1288

205
ME

SoBo   NoBo

206
ME

SoBo	NoBo		Elev
161.8	2023.5	Gravel road	1299
161.5	2023.8	East Carry Pond, beach at north end	1269
159.5	2025.8	Scott Rd (gravel)	1339
158.7	2026.6	North branch of Carrying Place Stream	1200
155.2	2030.1	**Pierce Pond Lean-to,** 27.9◀17.7◀10.0◀▶9.7▶18.7▶22.8 ⌒⌐(6) (pg.208)	1224
		Blue-blazed loop trail west to lean-to. From north end of loop, Harrison's is 0.3E.	
155.1	2030.2	Wooden dam, outlet of Pierce Pond	1152
154.8	2030.5	Trail 0.1E to Harrison's Pierce Pond Camps, boat landing to west. (pg.208)	1100
154.6	2030.7	Otter Pond Rd (gravel)	1057
154.1	2031.2	Pierce Pond Stream Falls 0.1E	979
154.0	2031.3	Waterfall 0.1E	953
153.5	2031.8	Otter Pond Stream, footbridge	866
		Camping on either shore of Kennebec River is prohibited.	
151.6	2033.7	Kennebec River. Do not ford. Use ferry service. (pg.209)	492
151.2	2034.1	US 201, **Caratunk, ME** (0.3E) N45 14.302 W69 59.777 P (pg.209)	520
150.9	2034.4	Woods road	673
148.6	2036.7	Holly Brook	911
147.2	2038.1	Grove Rd (gravel)	1233
146.7	2038.6	Holly Brook	1309
146.0	2039.3	Boise-Cascade Logging Rd to west (gravel), Pleasant Pond Rd to east.	1447
145.5	2039.8	**Pleasant Pond Lean-to** 27.4◀19.7◀9.7◀▶9.0▶13.1▶22.0 ⌒◀⌐(6)	1391
		Stream left of lean-to. Beach 0.2 on side trail beyond lean-to.	
145.3	2040.0	Pleasant Pond Beach to east	1355
144.2	2041.1	Pleasant Pond Mountain	2470

Blueberries – Abundant on open summits like Pleasant Pond Mountain and north peak of Moxie Bald.

SoBo	NoBo	Feature	Elev
139.7	2045.6	Stream.	1034
139.3	2046.0	Moxie Pond south end (ford), road, powerlines. N45 14.984 W69 49.857 [P]	970
139.1	2046.2	Baker Stream.	970
138.8	2046.5	Powerline.	1014
136.5	2048.8	**Bald Mountain Brook Lean-to** (0.1E) 28.7◄18.7◄9.0◄▲4.1►13.0►25.0 Bald Mountain Brook in front of lean-to. "AT Road" (gravel) 75 yards north of shelter.	1329
135.1	2050.2	Summit bypass trail to west	2156
134.5	2050.8	Moxie Bald Mountain	2629
134.2	2051.1	Summit bypass trail to west	2418
133.5	2051.8	Trail to Moxie Bald north peak (0.5W)	2221
132.4	2052.9	**Moxie Bald Mountain Lean-to** 22.8◄13.1◄4.1◄▲8.9►20.9►28.3 Bald Mountain Pond in front of lean-to.	1242
131.3	2054.0	Gravel road	1278
130.8	2054.5	Gravel road	1251
130.4	2054.9	Bald Mountain Stream (ford)	1234
128.5	2056.8	Bald Mountain Rd (gravel) bridge and stream to west N45 16.570 W69 41.311 [P]	1136
126.9	2058.4	Marble Brook	1003
126.5	2058.8	West Branch of Piscataquis River (ford) River normally knee-deep. During heavy rain periods, fording can be dangerous.	982
123.5	2061.8	**Horseshoe Canyon Lean-to** 22.0◄13.0◄8.9◄▲12.0►19.4►24.1... On blue-blazed trail. Stream at northern AT junction or river in front and below.	794
123.1	2062.2	Stream.	769

🏪 (2E) **Mountainside Grocers** 207-237-2248, open 7:30–8pm.

Stratton, ME 04982 (5W)

🛏️🖼️☕🚌🛜🖥️✉️ **Stratton Motel** 207-246-4171 〈www.thestrattonmotel.com〉 $25 bunk, $55 private room, credit cards accepted. Shuttle range Gorham to Monson, and also to Bangor or Portland. Canister fuel. Maildrops: PO Box 284, Stratton, ME 04982.

🛏️🍴🛜✉️ **White Wolf Inn** 207-246-2922 $50S/D, $10EAP + tax, pets $10. $60 on weekends. Does not accept Amex. Restaurant (closed Tues) serves L/D. Breakfast on weekends. Home of the 8oz Wolf Burger; Fish Fry Friday; **Wolf Den Bar** on-site. Maildrops: Main Street, PO Box 590, Stratton, ME 04982.

🛏️✉️🛜 **Spillover Motel** 207-246-6571 $69S, $89D. Senior (55+) discount $5. Pets $10, cont B. Full kitchen for use by guests. Maildrops: PO Box 427, Stratton, ME 04982.

🛏️🍷🍴 **Stratton Plaza Hotel** 207-246-2000 $90 room with 2 queen beds. L/D Tu-Sa 11-10. Karaoke, music on weekends.

🏪💲 **Fotter's Market** 207-246-2401 M-Th 8-7, F-Sa 8-8, Su 9-5. Coleman/alcohol/oz.

🔥🏪💲✉️ **Northland Cash Supply** 207-246-2376 Open 7 days 5–10, groceries, beer, tobacco, pizza, hiker box, Coleman/alcohol by ounce. Hiker friendly owner (Mark) provides rides back to the trail for free when he's available. Tenting with permission behind store. Maildrops (no FedEx): 152 Main Street, Stratton, ME 04982.

⛽💲 **Flagstaff Fuel** 207-246-2300 Deli, sodas, protein bars, beer, canister fuel.

2013.8   East Flagstaff Rd
2016.6   Long Falls Dam Rd

Kingfield, ME (18E from either Rd)

🛏️🚌🛜🖥️✉️ **Mountain Village Farm B&B** 207-265-2030 Hiker rate of $40 per person for room with fridge, microwave and private bath. Includes breakfast. Round-trip shuttle $40 for up to 4 persons from either trailhead. Pets welcome. Bed & Breakfast on an organic farm; inquire about work-for-stay. Town center within walking distance has grocery, laundry, and restaurants. Slackpack the Bigelows (Stratton to East Flagstaff Rd, either direction) $30/carload. Maildrops: PO Box 216, Kingfield, ME 04947.

2030.1, 2030.5   Trails to camp

🛏️🍴 **Harrison's Pierce Pond Camps** 207-672-3625, 207-612-8184 May-Nov, 7 days. Bed, shower, and 12-pancake breakfast $40. If you only want breakfast ($9-12 served 7-7:30am), reserve a seat the day before. Cash only. Okay to get water at camp and dispose of trash. Shortest route to camp is west along the north blue-blaze shelter loop trail.

STRATTON, ME

Pop. 368 (2006)
N45 8.450, W70 26.617
Mag. Dec. 16° 20'W

🧭 N

Stratton Diner
Fotter's Market
Stratton Plaza
Stratton Motel & Hostel
Northland General Store
White Wolf Inn, Restaurant & Bar

🛣️ 27
🛣️ 16

Main St
🛣️ 16   🛣️ 27
School St

Old Mill Laundry

PO (04982):
207-246-6461
M-F 8:30-1 & 1:30-4,
Sa 8:30-11

💲

(5.0 mi from PO)

Flagstaff Fuel ⛽
Library M,W,F 10-5; Tu,Th 1-5; Sa 9-1 🖥️🛜
Spillover Motel (0.6 mi from PO) 🛏️→

0.5 mi

2033.7 Kennebec River - The ferry is the official AT route (do not ford); the current is strong and unpredictable due to an upstream dam. Ferry holds 1 or 2.

Before May 1	No service
May 1 - May 23	on-call service $50 time & weather permitting
May 24 - July 10	9am-11am, 7 days
July 11 - Sept 30	9am-11am and 2pm-4pm, 7 days
Oct 1 - Oct 13	9am-11am, 7 days
Oct 14 - Oct 31	on-call service $50 time & weather permitting
After Oct 31	No service

🚐 **Fletcher Mountain Outfitters** 207-672-4879 David Corrigan provides ferry service and shuttles when not operating ferry. Some resupply on-hand.

2034.1 US 201 *Caratunk, ME 04925* (0.3E)
⌂ ☎ M–F 7:30–11:30 & 12–4, Sa 7:30–11:15, 207-672-3416
Accepts debit cards with limited cash back. Phone at town hall behind PO.

🛏️🏠⊕⊕ 🦮 ⚲ 🛜 ✉ (1.3E) **The Sterling Inn** 207-672-3333 ⟨www.mainesterlinginn.com⟩ $40S, $55D, $80/4, bunk room $25. All include continental breakfast. Multi-night discount, credit/debit cards accepted. Ample supplies including fuel/oz, canister fuel, Lipton Sides, batteries & candy bars. Resupply, showers ($2.50) and laundry ($5) available even if you are not staying. Free pickup from trailhead or from PO, return ride $5. Address: 1041 Route 201. Maildrops: PO Box 129, Caratunk Maine 04925.

🛏️🏠⊘🍴💲 🦮 ⚲ 🛜🖥️✉ (2W) **Northern Outdoors** 800-765-7238 ⟨www.northernoutdoors.com⟩ Hikers are welcome to ride free shuttle and use shower and pool with or without stay. Shuttle makes three trips a day coinciding with ferry schedule. Hikers get 25% discount on lodge rooms; prices vary by season and on weekends; peak season is July 12-Sept 1. Weekends in August are often booked. Cabin tents $17-25PP/up, tenting $11-13PP. Coin laundry, hot tub, ATM. No pets. Rafting trips (class IV) require reservation. Food and ale in **Kennebec River Pub & Brewery**. Maildrops: 1771 US 201, The Forks, ME 04985.

⊕ **Berry's General Store** (7.5W) 207-663-4461 Food, and some hardware. 5am-7pm 7 days, year-round. Open till 8 in summer.

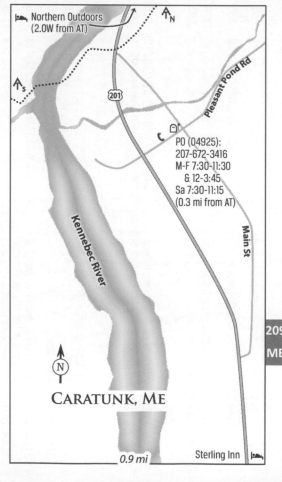

Northern Outdoors (2.0W from AT)

🅝 AT N

AT S

201

PO (04925):
207-672-3416
M-F 7:30-11:30
& 12-3:45
Sa 7:30-11:15
(0.3 mi from AT)

Pleasant Pond Rd

Main St

Kennebec River

🅝

CARATUNK, ME

0.9 mi

Sterling Inn

SoBo	NoBo		Elev
121.2	2064.1	East Branch of Piscataquis River (ford)	650
120.9	2064.4	Gravel road	765
120.8	2064.5	Shirley-Blanchard Rd (paved)	850
		N45 17.072 W69 35.223 P	
119.7	2065.6	AT on woods road for 0.5 mile	976
119.3	2066.0	Gravel road	893
117.8	2067.5	Historic AT route near Lake Hebron.	900
		N45 17.442 W69 31.995 P (pg.212)	
		0.2E on woods road to Pleasant St & parking, then left 1.6 mi to **Monson, ME.**	
117.4	2067.9	Dirt road.	1032
115.9	2069.4	Side trail to Doughty Ponds (0.1W)	1229
115.8	2069.5	Stream.	1251
115.2	2070.1	Gravel road	1386
114.5	2070.8	ME 15 (paved), **Monson, ME** (3.6E)	1215
		N45 19.856 W69 32.122 P (pg.212-213)	
		South end of 100-Mile Wilderness.	
114.4	2070.9	Spectacle Pond outlet	1179
113.6	2071.7	Old Stage Rd (dirt) Once a stagecoach road and part of the original AT	1291
113.3	2072.0	Bell Pond	1278
112.6	2072.7	Lily Pond	1130
111.5	2073.8	**Leeman Brook Lean-to**	1077
		25.0◄20.9◄12.0◄▶7.4▶12.1▶16.1 Stream in front of lean-to.	
110.7	2074.6	North Pond outlet	1023
110.4	2074.9	North Pond Tote Rd	1094
109.3	2076.0	Mud Pond	1026
108.9	2076.4	Bear Pond Ledge	1190
108.5	2076.8	James Brook	935
108.1	2077.2	Woods road	927
108.0	2077.3	Little Wilson Falls, west 30 yards	822
107.7	2077.6	Little Wilson Stream (ford), campsite	750
107.3	2078.0	Follow gravel road for 100 yards, pond	906
105.4	2079.9	Big Wilson Tote Rd	561
105.2	2080.1	Thompson Brook	561
104.8	2080.5	Big Wilson Stream (ford)	600
104.5	2080.8	Railroad tracks	889
104.1	2081.2	**Wilson Valley Lean-to** (1993).	972
		28.3◄19.4◄7.4◄▶4.7▶8.7▶15.6 Spring on opposite side of AT.	
103.4	2081.9	Woods road	1198
102.1	2083.2	Stream	942
101.8	2083.5	Stream	941

210
ME

SoBo	NoBo	Feature	Elev
100.9	2084.4	Wilber Brook	614
100.8	2084.5	Vaughn Stream	633
100.2	2085.1	Bodfish Farm/Long Pond Tote Rd (gravel), ford Long Pond Stream north of road	659
99.4	2085.9	**Long Pond Stream Lean-to** 24.1◀12.1◀4.7▼4.0▶10.9▶20.8 ☽◆ (8)	950
99.2	2086.1	Trail 0.8E to Otter Pond parking P	1075
98.3	2087.0	Barren Slide to east, view	1986
98.1	2087.2	Barren Ledges	2019
96.3	2089.0	Barren Mountain, remnants of tower	2660
95.4	2089.9	Side trail to **Cloud Pond Lean-to** (0.4E) ☽◆ (6)	2501
		16.1◀8.7◀4.0▼6.9▶16.8▶24.0 Cloud Pond is water source.	
93.9	2091.4	Fourth Mountain Bog	1955
93.3	2092.0	Fourth Mountain	2380
92.1	2093.2	Mt Three and a Half	1970
91.7	2093.6	Third Mountain Trail to west	1812
90.8	2094.5	Third Mountain, Monument Cliff 🏕	2087
90.2	2095.1	Trail 0.1E to West Chairback Pond, stream crosses AT north of side trail ◆	1770
89.3	2096.0	View 🏕	2148
89.2	2096.1	Spring ◆	2234
88.9	2096.4	Columbus Mountain	2325
88.5	2096.8	**Chairback Gap Lean-to** 15.6◀10.9◀6.9▼9.9▶17.1▶20.7 ☽ △◆ (6)	1979
		Spring on AT north of shelter.	
88.0	2097.3	Chairback Mountain 🏕	2180
85.9	2099.4	0.2W to East Chairback Pond ◆ (0.2W) ⬦	1722
85.3	2100.0	Spring ◆	1498
84.7	2100.6	Katahdin Ironworks Rd (gravel) N45 28.632 W69 17.107 P (0.4E) ⬦	830
84.2	2101.1	West Branch Pleasant River (ford). ⬦	718
		Wide ford with slick rocky bottom. Campsites to south; no camping/fires for 2.0N.	
83.3	2102.0	Stream. ◆	821
82.8	2102.5	Gulf Hagas Trail to west, 5.2 mile loop trail whose ends intersect the AT ◆	950
		0.7 mile apart. Features narrow, deep gorge with many waterfalls.	
82.1	2103.2	Gulf Hagas Trail to west ◆	1050

211
ME

2067.5 Historic AT route, side trail 0.2E to Pleasant St., left 0.1 to hostel, 1.6 further to **Monson**

◐ ⌂ 🚐 ✉ **100 Mile Wilderness Adventures and Outfitters**
207-991-7030 ⟨www.100milewilderness.info⟩ Camping open mid-May to mid-October, semi-private accommodations available. Laundry, camp store and fuel/oz. Slackpacking, shuttles, and mid-wilderness resupply. Parking for section hikers. Pets welcome. Maildrops for guests: 349 Pleasant St, PO Box 47, Monson, ME 04464.

2070.8   ME 15   **Monson, ME 04464** (3.6E)
Strictly enforced: No stealth camping in town
🛏🏠◐🍴⌂🚿⛺🚐🛜🖥✉💲🅿 **Lakeshore House Lodging & Pub**
207-997-7069, 207-343-5033 ⟨www.thelakeshorehouse.com⟩ Bunkroom $30PP, private rooms (limited availability) $45S/$60D w/shared bath. Well-behaved dogs okay. Reservations appreciated, packs out of rooms by 10am; full check out/vacate by 11:00 AM. Accepts credit cards, ATM on-site. Free for guests: trailhead pickup & return (only till 11:00 AM for return), loaner laptop, WiFi, kayaks, paddleboats, water trampoline. No charge for vehicle parking. Laundry ($5) & shower ($5) available to non-guests. Hiker store with long-term resupply (food and fuel). Statewide shuttles/slackpack/food drops, call for prices. Pub hours: Tu-Sa 12-9, Su 12-8, bar open later, closed M. Live music Su 3-6pm. Please drink responsibly; House quiet by 10:00 PM and NO BINGE DRINKING. Guests welcome at Shaws for breakfast. Maildrops for guests (non-guests $5): PO Box 215, C/O Lakeshore House, Monson, ME 04464 or UPS/FedEx (no Sat delivery): 9 Tenney Hill Rd.

🛏🏠◐◐🍴⌂🍴🚿⛺🚐🛜🖥✉ **Shaw's Lodging** 207-997-3597
shawslodging@gmail.com ⟨www.shawslodging.com⟩ Mid-May-mid-Oct. $25 bunks, $35 private room, $28 semi-private, $12 tenting. Free pickup/return with stay. $8 breakfast, $5 laundry, $5 shower and towel (w/o stay), internet available. Food drops, slackpacking and shuttles all over Maine, Coleman/alcohol/oz, canister fuel & Aquamira. No credit cards. Maildrops (non-guests $5): PO Box 72 or 17 Pleasant St, Monson, ME 04464.

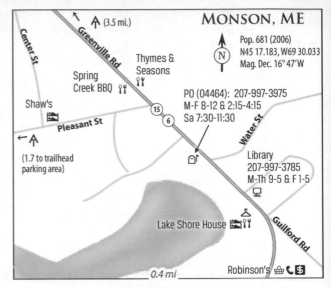

MONSON, ME
Pop. 681 (2006)
N45 17.183, W69 30.033
Mag. Dec. 16° 47'W

PO (04464): 207-997-3975
M-F 8-12 & 2:15-4:15
Sa 7:30-11:30

Library
207-997-3785
M-Th 9-5 & F 1-5

Lake Shore House

Robinson's

0.4 mi

🚐 **Sydney Pratt** 207-997-3221 pielady13@myfairpoint.net known as "The Pie Lady", will shuttle from Stratton to Katahdin.
⌂ 💲 **A.E. Robinson's** 5am-10pm 7 days. ATM fee $2.
🍴 **Spring Creek Bar-B-Q** 207-997-7025 Th-Sa 10am-8pm, Sunday 9am-5pm. Expanded in 2014 to include pub, may be open later.
🍴🛜 **Thymes & Seasons** 207-997-3495 Coffee, tea, paninis, organic food.

212
ME

Greenville, ME 04485 (10W from ME 15)

🛏📶 **Kineo View Motor Lodge** 207-695-4470 $79, $10EAP includes continental breakfast. Clean, quiet motel with a nice view, 7.5 mi. from trailhead.

🛏📶 **Indian Hill Motel** 207-695-2623 $69 weekdays, $79 weekends up to 3 persons.

🍴 **Kelly's Landing** 207-695-4438 7 days 7-9, Su AYCE breakfast.

🍴 **The Black Frog** 207-695-1100 Restaurant, pub, pizza.

🍴 **Dairy Bar** 207-695-2921 ice cream

🛒🍴 **Harris Drug Store** dining counter inside.

🚶🏪 **Indian Hill Trading Post & Supermarket** 800-675-4487

🏠 **Jamieson's Store** supplies, pizza and subs.

🚶🍴📶🖥 **Northwoods Outfitters** 207-695-3288 ⟨www.maineoutfitter.com⟩ Full service outfitter with fuel/ oz and canister fuel. Expresso bar, pastries, internet. 7 days, 8-5.

➕ **Charles Dean Memorial Hospital** 207-695-5200

Also: two banks with ATMs

Guilford, ME (14E from ME 15)

🛏🍴⛺📶🖥 **Salmon's** 828-215-0834, 37 Hudson Ave, Guilford, ME 04443. Bunkroom $25, private room (1 or 2) $50, includes AYCE breakfast, evening pickup from Monson or from trailhead and return after breakfast. Please call for group pickup (up to 5) if possible. Laundry $5/load. Limited capacity in a quiet atmosphere; first-come, first serve, max 2 nights, cash only. Bikes for around-town use; grocery, restaurants, pubs, drugstore, library and post office all within a mile.

Suggestions for Providing Trail Magic. These suggestions incorporate Leave No Trace practices (www.LNT.org) to help those providing trail magic to have the most positive impact on hikers, the Trail, its plants, wildlife, and the volunteers who maintain and preserve it. The ATC and ALDHA endorse these suggestions.

Help conserve and maintain the Trail. The most essential service you can perform is to volunteer to maintain the Trail and overnight sites, or to monitor boundaries and resource conditions. To find out how or where you may assist, visit www.appalachiantrail.org or check with your local trail-maintaining club.

Locate events in developed areas on durable surfaces. Large gatherings in the backcountry can lead to the disturbance of wildlife habitat. Trail towns and local parks are better locations. Keep events small. Consider whether your event may be contributing to an overabundance of trail feeds in the local area or region.

Prepare and serve food safely. If you will be cooking or preparing food, check with the landowner to find an appropriate area and learn what food-safety or other regulations apply. Permits may be required. Charging a fee or asking for donations may not be allowed.

Be present if you provide food or drink. Unattended items and their packaging can harm wildlife that consume them. Unattended items are considered litter and they detract from the wildland character of backcountry environments. .

Restore the site. Leave the site as you found it—don't create a burden for Trail volunteers.

Advertise off-trail. Advertising—even noncommercial—is prohibited on the A.T.

Forgo alcoholic beverages. Don't risk the legality and liability associated with serving minors, over-serving adults, or the safety issues associated with intoxicated hikers.

Be hospitable to all. Be sure to make all trail users and volunteers feel welcome.

Visit ATC's Web site at www.appalachiantrail.org/trailmagic.

SoBo   NoBo

⚠ Roads in the 100 M.W. are ambiguously named on maps and in "local use". Roads that pass near Logan Brook and Cooper Brook Shelters both may be referred to as "B Pond Road". When getting shuttles or supply drops be clear about the destination. All roads are privately owned, gated, and there are fees for using them.

SoBo	NoBo		Elev
78.6	2106.7	**Carl A. Newhall Lean-to** 20.8◄16.8◄9.9◄▶7.2▶10.8▶18.9. ☽ ● ⌂ ⊏(6)	1938
		Gulf Hagas Brook, south of shelter, is water source.	
77.6	2107.7	Gulf Hagas Mountain	2713
76.8	2108.5	Sidney Tappan Campsite, water 0.1E. ● ⌂	2478
76.1	2109.2	West Peak	3178
74.5	2110.8	Hay Mountain	3244
73.7	2111.6	White Brook Trail to east.	3004
72.8	2112.5	White Cap Mountain	3650
71.9	2113.4	View of Katahdin from north side of mountain 24.0◄17.1◄7.2◄▶3.6▶11.7▶23.1	2740
71.4	2113.9	**Logan Brook Lean-to** ☽ ● ⌂ ⊏(6)	2406
		Some tent sites; better sites 0.1N on AT. Logan Brook in front of lean-to; cascades upstream.	
69.8	2115.5	Logan Brook Rd (dirt). Piped spring 50 yards south of road, west of AT. ◆	1620
67.8	2117.5	**East Branch Lean-to,** Pleasant River in front ☽ ● ⊏(6)	1261
		20.7◄10.8◄3.6◄▶8.1▶19.5▶29.6	
67.5	2117.8	East branch of Pleasant River (ford). ◆	1224
65.9	2119.4	Mountain View Pond outlet ◆	1585
65.6	2119.7	Spring to east ◆	1570
64.3	2121.0	Side trail 100 yards to Little Boardman Mountain.	1980
63.0	2122.3	Cooper Brook Rd, a.k.a. Kokadjo-B Pond Rd (gravel)	1230
62.7	2122.6	West to beach on Crawford Pond (no camping) ◆	1253
62.1	2123.2	Cooper Brook ◆	1218

SoBo	NoBo			Elev
60.2	2125.1	Stream	◆	1019
59.7	2125.6	**Cooper Brook Falls Lean-to** 18.9◄11.7◄8.1◄▶11.4▶21.5▶29.6 ⊂(6) ◢◣◢		946
		Brook, falls, swimming hole in front of lean-to. Privy across trail and up hill.	◆	835
59.1	2126.2	Large tributary to Cooper Brook		

❋ **Indian pipe** – A plant without chlorophyll that grows in moist duff. Translucent white candy cane shape 3-4" tall grows in clusters. Scale-like leaves/petals.

SoBo	NoBo			Elev
56.0	2129.3	Jo-Mary Rd N45 39.087 W69 1.900 **P** ◆(pg.216)		625
54.6	2130.7	Footbridge, snowmobile trail	◆	584
53.5	2131.8	Side trail 0.2E to north shore of Cooper Pond	◆	520
53.1	2132.2	Mud Pond to west, footbridge over Mud Brook	◆	508
51.8	2133.5	Antlers Campsite	◢◣◆◢	500
		Campsites on edge of Jo-Mary Lake. Fort Relief two seat privy.		
50.3	2135.0	Potaywadjo Ridge Trail 1.0W	◆	587
50.1	2135.2	East to sandy beach on lower Jo-Mary Lake	◆	580
48.3	2137.0	**Potaywadjo Spring Lean-to** (1995) ◢◣◆◢ ⊂(8)		655
		23.1◄19.5◄11.4◄▶10.1▶18.2▶29.7 Potaywadjo Spring to right.		
48.0	2137.3	Tirio Access Rd (gravel)	◢◣◆	579
47.7	2137.6	Twitchell Brook, footbridge, east to Pemadumcook Lake, view of Katahdin.	◉◆	521
46.5	2138.8	Deer Brook	◆	548
45.8	2139.5	Woods road	◆	565
45.7	2139.6	Mahar Tote Rd (dirt)		566
45.6	2139.7	Tumbledown Dick Stream (ford)	◆	558
45.1	2140.2	High water trail to west	◢◣◆	561
44.5	2140.8	Ford branch of the Nahmakanta Stream	◆◢	584
44.0	2141.3	Nahmakanta Stream Campsite		600
42.0	2143.3	Stream.	◆	676
41.1	2144.2	Gravel Road near south end of Nahmakanta Lake N45 44.162 W69 06.208 **P**		687
		Camping on shore of Nahmakanta Lake is prohibited.		

2129.3   Jo-Mary Rd. (little traffic on road) 12.0E to ME 11.

◢ ⁓ ⅄ (9.0E) **Jo-Mary Campground** 207-723-8117 Campsites $17 per person for ME residents, $22 non-residents; 2-person minimum (camping for one non-resident would cost $44). Pets welcome, coin operated showers and laundry. Open 5/10-9/15/2014.

Manufacturers and Retailers

AntiGravityGear	910-794-3308	Garmont	800-943-4453	Outdoor Research	888-467-4327
Arc'Teryx	866-458-2473	GoLite	888-546-5483	Patagonia	800-638-6464
Asolo/Lowe Alpine	603-448-8827	Gossamer Gear	512-374-0133	Peak 1/Coleman	800-835-3278
Backcountry.com	800-409-4502	Granite Gear	218-834-6157	Petzl	877-807-3805
Big Agnes	877-554-8975	Gregory	877-477-4292	Photon	877-584-6898
Black Diamond	801-278-5552	Hi-Tec	800-521-1698	Primus	307-857-4700
CamelBak	800-767-8725	Hyperlite Mountain Gear	800-464-9208	Princeton Tec	800-257-9080
Campmor	888-226-7667	Jacks 'R' Better	757-643-8908	REI	800-426-4840
Camp Trails	800-345-7622	JanSport	800-552-6776	Royal Robbins	800-587-9044
Cascade Designs	800-531-9531	Katadyn/PUR	800-755-6701	Salomon	800-654-2668
(MSR/Therm-a-Rest/Platypus)		Keen	866-676-5336	Sierra Designs	800-736-8592
Cedar Tree (Packa)	276-780-2354	Kelty	866-349-7225	Sierra Trading Post	800-713-4534
Columbia	800-547-8066	Leki	800-255-9982	Six Moon Designs	503-430-2303
Dana Designs	888-357-3262	Limmer	603-694-2668	Slumberjack	800-233-6283
Danner	877-432-6637	LL Bean	800-441-5713	SOTO Outdoors	503-314-5119
Eagle Creek	800-874-1048	Marmont	888-357-3262	Speer Hammocks	252-619-8292
Eastern Mountain Sports	888-463-6367	Merrell	800-288-3124	Suunto	800-543-9124
Etowah Outfitters	770-975-7829	Montbell	877-666-8235	Tarptent / Henry Shires	650-587-1548
Eureka!	800-572-8822	Montrail	800-826-1598	Tecnica	800-258-3897
Ex Officio	800-644-7303	Mountain Hardwear	800-953-8398	Teva	800-367-8382
Feathered Friends	206-292-2210	Mountainsmith	800-551-5889	The Underwear Guys	570-573-0209
First Need	800-441-8166	Mystery Ranch	406-585-1428	ULA	435-753-5191
Frogg Toggs	800-349-1835	NEMO	800-997-9301	Vasque	800-224-4453
Garmin	800-800-1020	North Face	866-715-3223	Warmstuff/Adventurelite	570-573-0209
		Osprey	866-314-3130	Western Mountaineering	408-287-8944
				Zip Stove	800-594-9046

Baxter State Park

ℹ For information and reservations call 207-723-5140 8am-4pm, 7 days, between Memorial and Columbus Day. When driving, even as far as Medway, tune to AM 1610 for recent reports. On the web: ⟨http://www.baxterstateparkauthority.com/hiking/thru-hiking.html⟩

The hiking season is approximately May 15 through October 15. Dates vary based on weather, and the park can be closed any day of the year due to weather. Weather reports are posted at **Katahdin Stream Campground** (KSC) at 7:00am every morning, along with "Trail Status and Alerts."

Katahdin ascents may be disallowed even when the park is open. Consequences for hiking when the trail is closed include fines, equipment seizure and loss of park visitation privileges.

All hikers intending to climb Katahdin must sign in at KSC and sign out when leaving. Recommended cut-off times for starting hikes to Baxter Peak are noon in June and July, 11am in August, 10am in September, and 9am in October. Overnite camping above treeline is against park regulations and can damage rare alpine plants. Hikers are welcome to leave their backpack at KSC. Loaner daypacks are available at no charge from the KSC ranger's station. Northbound thru-hikers completing their hike in late summer or early fall usually have an easy time hitching from KSC into Millinocket.

There are fees for nonresidents entering the park by car and fees for use of campsites by residents and nonresidents. Fees must be paid in cash; no credit cards and no work-for-stay.

◆ ⊏ **The Birches** near KSC has 2 shelters and one tentsite, open to northbound long distance hikers who have hiked a minimum of "the 100 mile wilderness" immediately prior to entering the Park.

Stay is limited to a single night, and the fee is $10 per person.
⚠ All other hikers, including flip-floppers and southbound thru-hikers, who wish to overnight in the Park should make reservations in advance. Common options, listed in order of their proximity to KSC are **Abol Campground**, **Daicey Pond Campground** (cabins $55D/up) and **Foster Field Group Area**, just north of Katahdin. Note that Abol Campground in the Park, Abol Pines at Abol Bridge and the privately run Abol Bridge Campground are three distinct entities.

P If you are driving to Baxter: gates open 6am. Maine residents enter for free; $14 per vehicle for non-residents. KSC parking is limited to 25 cars and you will not be allowed to enter if the lots are full. Day-use parking reservations are highly recommended and can obtained for KSC, Abol or Roaring Brook Campgrounds by phone up to three weeks in advance, for a $5 fee. There is no long-term parking in Baxter. Check with local taxi and shuttle services for info on long term parking outside the Park.

Cell phone reception is unlikely anywhere in the park other than on Katahdin, so do not count on calling for a ride from KSC. Even where there is reception, do not place calls from the summit or within earshot of other hikers. Please use a cell phone only If there is an emergency.

Pets are not allowed in the park.

⌁ Connie McManus 207-723-6795 Privately run kennel service; pickup/drop off at Abol Bridge.

SoBo	NoBo		Elev
39.9	2145.4	Prentiss Brook	698
38.6	2146.7	Side trail east to sand beach on shore of Nahmakanta Lake	684
38.2	2147.1	**Wadleigh Stream Lean-to**, stream can be dry during summer. 29.6◄21.5◄10▶◄8.1▶19.6▶33.0	717
37.2	2148.1	Spring	809
36.3	2149.0	Nesuntabunt Mountain, short side trail east to view of Katahdin, 16 mile line-of-sight distance to Katahdin summit from here.	1520
35.8	2149.5	View	1180
35.1	2150.2	Wadleigh Pond Rd (gravel)	1028
34.4	2150.9	Crescent Pond west end	1008
33.6	2151.7	Pollywog Gorge, side trail overlooking gorge	900
32.6	2152.7	Pollywog Stream N45 46.774 W69 10.320 P. Cross stream on logging road bridge.	681
30.6	2154.7	Outlet stream from Murphy Pond	971
30.1	2155.2	**Rainbow Stream Lean-to**, baseball bat floor. 29.6◄18.2◄8.1▶11.5▶24.9▶0.0 Tenting on hill behind lean-to. Excellent swimming hole upstream.	1023
28.2	2157.1	West to Rainbow Lake dam	1109
28.0	2157.3	Stream.	1071
26.3	2159.0	Rainbow Lake Campsite, spring west 30 yards.	1100
25.1	2160.2	Stream.	1080
24.8	2160.5	Unmarked trail leads 0.2W to Rainbow Lake Camps (private)	1124
24.5	2160.8	Trail 0.7E to Rainbow Mountain	1146
22.9	2162.4	Side trail 0.1E to Little Beaver Pond, 0.7E to Big Beaver Pond	1086
21.1	2164.2	Rainbow Ledges, view of Katahdin	1517

SoBo	NoBo			Elev
18.6	**2166.7**	**Hurd Brook Lean-to,** baseball bat floor 29.7◄19.6◄11.5◄►13.4►0.0►0.0	☽ 💧 ∠ (6)	720
18.1	**2167.2**	Small spring.	💧	791
15.9	**2169.4**	Bog bridge		624
15.4	**2169.9**	Golden Rd (paved), Nobo east on road, **Millinocket, ME** (19E)	(pg.220)	609
15.1	**2170.2**	Abol Bridge crosses west branch N45 50.111 W68 58.158 of Penobscot River. Parking on east side of road between bridge and trailhead.	P 📷 (pg.220)	578
14.7	**2170.6**	End of Golden Rd, Nobo veer left on dirt road		620
14.6	**2170.7**	Abol Stream Trail to east, footbridge, Baxter State Park Boundary	💧	606
14.3	**2171.0**	Information board, Abol Pond Trail east, registration for The Birches Campsites		595
14.0	**2171.3**	Footbridge, Katahdin Stream, Foss and Knowlton Trail to east	💧	591
13.2	**2172.1**	Foss and Knowlton Brook, footbridge	💧	598
10.5	**2174.8**	Lower fork of Nesowadnehunk Stream Both forks of this stream may require fording. There is a highwater bypass.	💧	626
9.5	**2175.8**	Upper fork of Nesowadnehunk Stream	💧	808
8.7	**2176.6**	Short side trail to view of Big Niagara Falls	📷	951
8.4	**2176.9**	Side trail west to Toll Dam and Little Niagara Falls	💧	1054
7.7	**2177.6**	Daicey Pond Nature Trail to west, parking area and privy north of trailhead	P ☽	1096
6.9	**2178.4**	Tracy and Elbow Pond Trails to west, Daicey Pond Nature Trail to east	💧	1119
6.2	**2179.1**	Grassy Pond Trail to west (two intersections).		1082
5.8	**2179.5**	Footbridge, stream	💧	1059
5.3	**2180.0**	Perimeter Rd		1090
5.2	**2180.1**	Katahdin Stream Campground **The Birches Lean-tos & Campsite** (0.2E) thru-hikers only, $10PP pay at KSC ranger station or info board (9.1S). 33.0◄24.9◄13.4◄►0.0►0.0►0.0	💧 ⛺ ∠ (16)	1106
4.0	**2181.3**	Owl Trail to west, footbridge, stream	💧	1563
3.9	**2181.4**	Katahdin Stream Falls	☽ 💧	1647
3.0	**2182.3**	Spring	💧	2399
2.6	**2182.7**	Pass "The cave" small slab cave		2850
1.6	**2183.7**	The Gateway, The Tableland		4518
1.0	**2184.3**	Thoreau Spring, Abol Trail to east	💧	4620
0.0	**2185.3**	**Katahdin**, Baxter Peak, Northern Terminus of the AT	(pg.220-221)	5268

SoBo NoBo 1000 2000 3000 4000 5000 6000 Elev

MILLINOCKET, ME

↑N Pop. 5,203 (2000)
N45.39.433, W68 42.533
Mag. Dec. 17° 18'W

1.4 mi

(23.9 mi. to Katahdin Stream)

Ice Fish Inn

Keybank

Central Laundry

Circle-K with Dunkin Donuts

Subway

Hannaford with Pharmacy

Baxter Park Inn

157   11

Appalachian Trail Cafe and Trail Connection 🛜 🍴

Smoke & Beverage Shop

Rite Aid
Katahdin Inn

House of Pizza
Family Dollar
Serenity Salon
IGA
McDonald's
Baxter Park HQ

Pamola Motor Lodge
Hang Wong (AYCE 11-2)

Hotel Terrace & Ruthies

Library 207-723-7020 M & Th 9-6,
Tu & W 10-6 (closed F, Sa, Su)

True Value

Katahdin Valley Health Center

PO (04462): 207-723-5921
M-F 7-11 & 2:15-4:15
Sa 8-12

LanMan's Lounge

220
ME

Russ's Barbershop

Angelos Pizza 🍴

Pins & Cues

Scootic In 🍴

Blue Ox Saloon

Millinocket Regional Hospital 207-723-5161

Pelletier Loggers Family Restaurant

Lankhorst Chiropractic

Rideout's Market

A.T. Lodge & Ole Man's Gear Shop

Katahdin Cabins

2169.9, 2170.2   Golden Rd, Abol Bridge

🔥🍴🚐📷✉ **Abol Bridge Campground & Store**

207-447-5803 ⟨www.abolcampground.com⟩ Open 7am-8pm all months except December and April. Campsites (includes shower) $16.05S, $25.68D includes tax. Shower w/o stay $5. Visa/MC accepted. Breakfast sandwiches and subs, sodas, ice cream, long-term resupply, white gas/oz and Heet. Phone can be used for $1/minute. **The Northern Restaurant** serves lunch and dinner 11-8 Wed-Sun. ⚠ $10 maildrop fee, send well in advance: P.O. Box 536 Millinocket, ME 04462

🔥 **Abol Pines** $8+tax ($4+tax ME residents) self-register tent sites and shelters across the street from Abol Bridge Store, south of Golden Road. Provided by Maine Dept. of Conservation.

Millinocket: Paul (OleMan) & Jaime (NaviGator) Renaud provide many hiker services from two locations. Call 207-723-4321 for all services in this block ⟨www.appalachiantraillodge.com⟩ credit cards accepted.

🛏📷🚿🔥⛺🚌🅿🛜🖥✉ **The Appalachian Trail Lodge** Bunkroom $25, private room $35S, $55D, family suite call for rates. Showers for nonguests $3. Coin laundry. Free daily shuttle from Baxter park, from Sept 1, till Oct 15, between 3pm – 4:30pm. Licensed and insured shuttle service for hire to and from bus in Medway, into 100-Mile Wilderness or Monson, food drops. Slackpack in 100-Mile Wilderness, other shuttles by arrangement, free parking. No pets. SoBo special: pickup in Medway, bed in bunkroom, breakfast at AT Cafe', and shuttle to KSC. $70pp, by reservation. Maildrops for guests: 33 Penobscot Avenue, Millinocket, ME 04462.

🥾 **Ole Man's Gear Shop** Full line of gear at the lodge; packs, bags, fuel, stoves, poles, Southbound A.T. Guide and more.

🍴 **The Appalachian Trail Cafe** Serves B/L/D

📷🛜🖥 **Trail Connection** Above Cafe; computer, wireless, specialty coffee.

2185.3   Katahdin, Baxter Peak, *Millinocket, ME 04462* (24E)

Trail's End Festival September 12-14 with vendors, food, and entertainment. Hardcore trail work on Friday.

🛏🍴📶 **Hotel Terrace & Ruthie's Restaurant** 207-723-4545 $59.95S, $65.95D, $6EAP. Ruthie's serves B/L/D.

🛏⛺📶🖥 **Katahdin Inn** 207-723-4555 $70S, $80D +tax, $10EAP, indoor heated pool and hot tub.

🛏🍴📶✉ **Pamola Motor Lodge** 800-575-9746 $69S $79D, cont. breakfast. **Hang Wong** Chinese restaurant on site with AYCE lunch buffet. Pets $10. Maildrops: 973 Central Street, Millinocket, ME 04462.

🛏📶✉ **Katahdin Cabins** 207-723-6305 ⟨www.katahdincabins.com⟩ Skip & Nicole Mohoff run eco-friendly cabins with continental breakfast, TV, DVD, frig & mwave. 2013 prices: $65 up to 3 persons, $85 up to 5. No smoking. Gas grill, bikes free for use, community room, accepts CC/cash/checks. Maildrops: 181 Medway Rd, Millinocket, ME 04462.

🛏📶⛺ **Baxter Park Inn** 207-723-9777 $89.99D, $10EAP, pets $10, hot tub, pool.

🛏📶✉ **Ice Fish Inn** 207-723-9999 $120-135 double occupancy room includes full hot breakfast. Maildrops: PO Box 136, Millinocket, ME 04462.

🔌🚿⛺📶🅿 **Wilderness Edge Campground** 207-447-8485, Tent sites $10PP, shower without stay $3, tax included. WiFi in office, coin laundry, free parking for section hiking guests. At edge of town on road to Baxter SP.

🍴⛺ **Pelletier Loggers Family Restaurant** 207-723-6100 Open Wed-Sun 11am-9pm. Laundry adjacent open 7 days 8am-8pm.

■◉ **LanMan's Lounge** Relaxing place with TV, restroom; pack storage $5.

🚌 **Maine Quest Adventures** 207-447-5011, 207-746-9615 ⟨www.mainequestadventures.com⟩ pick up at Medway bus station and drop off at Katahdin Stream or Abol Bridge. Shuttles to Monson and parts of the 100-Mile Wilderness. Food Drops can be arranged.

🚌 **Bull Moose Taxi** 207-447-8079 Medway to Millinocket $16, Millinocket to KSC $55. Fares are per ride, $1 EAP up to 4 persons. Covers all of Maine.

✈ **Katahdin Air** 866-359-6246 ⟨www.KatahdinAir.com⟩ One-way flights to a number of trailheads from White House Landing to Monson. $65-135 per person, includes shuttle from Abol Bridge to seaplane base.

Getting to Katahdin

⚠ Flip-floppers and southbound hikers need a reservation to stay in Baxter State Park. See park rules on pg. 217.

Most routes to Katahdin are through Bangor, Maine, which has an airport and bus terminal. Bangor is 91 miles from Baxter SP. Shuttle services will pick you up in Bangor, but it is more economical to take **Cyr Bus Lines** to Medway, 31 miles from Baxter State Park. Hikers often layover in Millinocket, 24 miles from Katahdin Stream Campground, the closest parking area to Katahdin.

Bangor, ME - Medway, ME

🚌 **Cyr Bus Lines** 800-244-2335 ⟨www.cyrbustours.com⟩ One-way routes 7 days $12. Cash, credit cards accepted. Routes below are to Concord Hub near airport; bus also stops at Greyhound station 20 min later (arrival) or 20 min sooner on departure.
Medway 9:30am (station at Irving store) to Bangor 10:50
Bangor 6:30pm to Medway 7:40pm
🚌 **Concord Trailways** 207-945-4000 ⟨www.concordtrailways.com⟩ Hub near Bangor airport, service to South Station in Boston.
🚌 **The Appalachian Trail Lodge, Maine Quest Adventures, and Bull Moose Taxi,** all listed in Millinocket, provide transportation from Medway to Millinocket and Katahdin.

There is an edition of this book made specifically for southbound hikers. The southbound edition, and other A.T. books and DVDs are sold on the website:

www.theATguide.com

221

ME

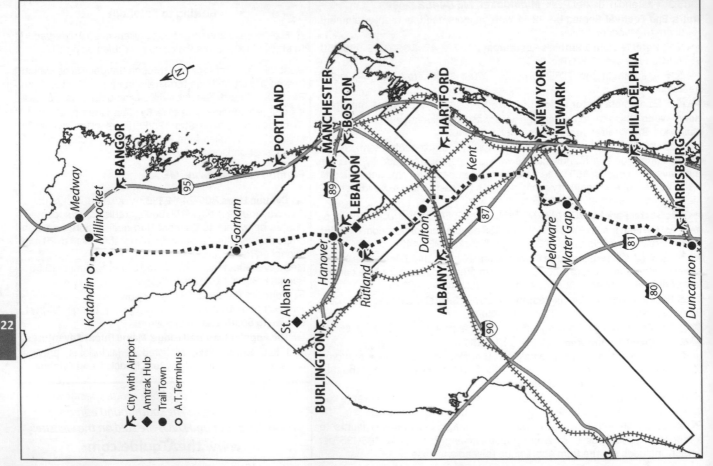

N

Medway
BANGOR
Millinocket
Katahdin
95
Gorham
Hanover
PORTLAND
MANCHESTER
BOSTON
LEBANON
St. Albans
BURLINGTON
Rutland
Dalton
ALBANY
90
87
Kent
HARTFORD
Delaware
Water Gap
80
81
NEW YORK
NEWARK
PHILADELPHIA
HARRISBURG
Duncannon
89

City with Airport
Amtrak Hub
Trail Town
A.T. Terminus

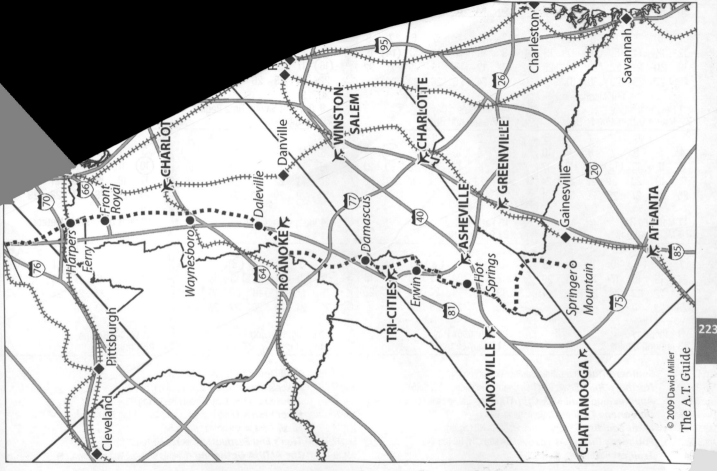

95

WINSTON-SALEM ✈

CHARLOTTE ✈

26

Charleston ◆

Savannah ◆

◆ Danville

CHARLOT ✈

66

Front Royal

70

Daleville

77

40

GREENVILLE ✈

20

Gainesville ◆

ATLANTA ✈

85

Harpers Ferry

Waynesboro

64

ROANOKE ✈

Damascus

ASHEVILLE ✈

Hot Springs ○

Springer Mountain ○

76

TRI-CITIES ✈

Erwin ●

81

75

Pittsburgh

KNOXVILLE ✈

CHATTANOOGA ✈

Cleveland

The A.T. Guide

JANUARY

Su	M	Tu	W	Th	F	Sa
			1	2	3	4
5	6	7	8	9	10	11
12	13	14	15	(16)	17	18
19	**20**	21	22	23	24	25
26	27	28	29	30	31	

Full Moon

1 New Year's Day
20 Martin Luther King Jr. Day

FEBRUARY

Su						
2	3	4	5	6	7	8
9	10	11	12	13	14	15
16	**17**	18	19	20	21	
23	24	25	26	27	28	

14 Valentine's Day
17 Presidents' Day

MAY

				Th		
			1	2	3	
4	5	6	(7)	8	9	10
11	12	13	(14)	15	16	17
18	19	20	21	22	23	24
25	**26**	27	28	29	30	31

11 Mother's Day
26 Memorial Day

JUNE

1	2	3	4	5	6	7
8	9	10	11	12	(13)	14
15	16	17	18	19	**20**	**21**
22	23	24	25	26	27	28
29	30					

15 Father's Day
21 Summer Begins

JULY

6	7					
13	14					
20	21					
27	28	29				

4 Independence Day

SEPTEMBER

	1	2	3	4	5	6
7	8	(9)	10	11	12	13
14	15	16	17	18	19	20
21	22	**23**	24	25	26	27
28	29	30				

1 Labor Day
23 Autumn Begins

OCTOBER

			1	2	3	4
5	6	7	(8)	9	10	11
12	**13**	14	15	16	17	18
19	20	21	22	23	24	25
26	27	28	29	30	**31**	

13 Columbus Day
31 Halloween

NOVEMBER

2	3	4	5	(6)		
9	10	**11**	12	13	14	
16	17	18	19	20	21	
23	24	25	26	**27**	28	
30						

2 Daylight Saving Time Ends
11 Veterans Day   **27** Thanksgiving

DECEMBER

					5	(6)
					12	13
			17	18	19	20
		23	24	**25**	26	27
	29	30	31			

21 Winter Begins
25 Christmas

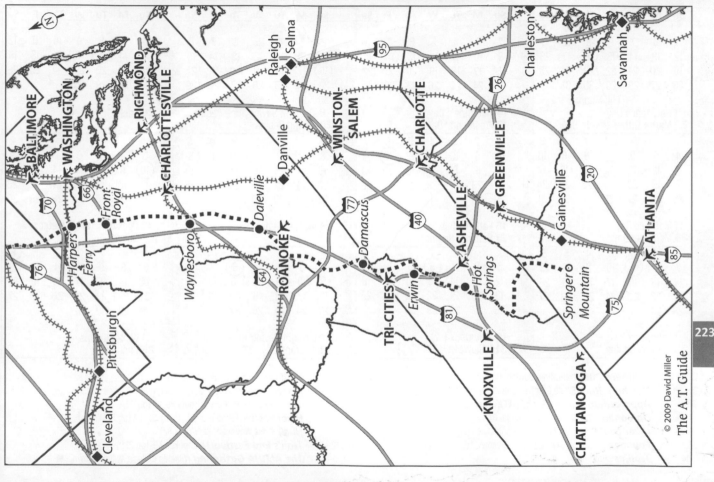

BALTIMORE

WASHINGTON

RICHMOND

CHARLOTTESVILLE

Raleigh

Selma

WINSTON-SALEM

CHARLOTTE

Charleston

Savannah

Danville

Front Royal

Daleville

Harpers Ferry

Waynesboro

ROANOKE

Damascus

ASHEVILLE

GREENVILLE

Gainesville

ATLANTA

Pittsburgh

TRI-CITIES

Erwin

Hot Springs

Springer Mountain

Cleveland

KNOXVILLE

CHATTANOOGA

95

26

20

77

40

66

70

76

64

81

85

75

223

© 2009 David Miller

The A.T. Guide

JANUARY

Su	M	Tu	W	Th	F	Sa
			1	2	3	4
5	6	7	8	9	10	11
12	13	14	15	(16)	17	18
19	**20**	21	22	23	24	25
26	27	28	29	30	31	

Full Moon

1 New Year's Day
20 Martin Luther King Jr. Day

FEBRUARY

Su	M	Tu	W	Th	F	Sa
						1
2	3	4	5	6	7	8
9	10	11	12	13	(14)	15
16	**17**	18	19	20	21	22
23	24	25	26	27	28	

14 Valentine's Day
17 Presidents' Day

MARCH

Su	M	Tu	W	Th	F	Sa
						1
2	3	4	5	6	7	8
9	10	11	12	13	14	15
(16)	17	18	19	**20**	21	22
23	24	25	26	27	28	29
30	31					

9 Daylight Saving Time Begins
20 Spring Begins

APRIL

Su	M	Tu	W	Th	F	Sa
		1	2	3	4	5
6	7	8	9	10	11	12
13	14	(15)	16	17	18	19
20	21	22	23	24	25	26
27	28	29	30			

20 Easter

MAY

Su	M	Tu	W	Th	F	Sa
				1	2	3
4	5	6	7	8	9	10
11	12	13	(14)	15	16	17
18	19	20	21	22	23	24
25	**26**	27	28	29	30	31

11 Mother's Day
26 Memorial Day

JUNE

Su	M	Tu	W	Th	F	Sa
1	2	3	4	5	6	7
8	9	10	11	12	(13)	14
15	16	17	18	19	20	**21**
22	23	24	25	26	27	28
29	30					

15 Father's Day
21 Summer Begins

JULY

Su	M	Tu	W	Th	F	Sa
		1	2	3	**4**	5
6	7	8	9	10	11	(12)
13	14	15	16	17	18	19
20	21	22	23	24	25	26
27	28	29	30	31		

4 Independence Day

AUGUST

Su	M	Tu	W	Th	F	Sa
					1	2
3	4	5	6	7	8	9
(10)	11	**12**	13	14	15	16
17	18	19	20	21	22	23
24	25	26	27	28	29	30
31						

12 Peak of Perseids Meteor Shower

SEPTEMBER

Su	M	Tu	W	Th	F	Sa
	1	2	3	4	5	6
7	8	(9)	10	11	12	13
14	15	16	17	18	19	20
21	22	**23**	24	25	26	27
28	29	30				

1 Labor Day
23 Autumn Begins

OCTOBER

Su	M	Tu	W	Th	F	Sa
			1	2	3	4
5	6	7	(8)	9	10	11
12	**13**	14	15	16	17	18
19	20	21	22	23	24	25
26	27	28	29	30	**31**	

13 Columbus Day
31 Halloween

NOVEMBER

Su	M	Tu	W	Th	F	Sa
						1
2	3	4	5	(6)	7	8
9	10	**11**	12	13	14	15
16	17	18	19	20	21	22
23	24	25	26	**27**	28	29
30						

2 Daylight Saving Time Ends
11 Veterans Day   **27** Thanksgiving

DECEMBER

Su	M	Tu	W	Th	F	Sa
	1	2	3	4	5	(6)
7	8	9	10	11	12	13
14	15	16	17	18	19	20
21	22	23	24	**25**	26	27
28	29	30	31			

21 Winter Begins
25 Christmas

Jan 17-20	**Southern Ruck**	Nantahala Outdoor Center (pg.24)
Jan 31-Feb 2	**Northern Ruck**	Bears Den Trail Center, Bluemont, VA (pg.95)
Mar 7-9	**Appalachian Trail Kick-Off (ATKO)**	Amicalola Falls (pg. 6)
Mar 14-16	**Dahlonega Trail Fest,**	Dahlonega, GA
Mar 28-29	**Hiker Fool Bash**	Sapphire Inn, Franklin, NC (pg.18)
Apr 3-5	**Founder's Bridge AT Festival**	Bryson City, NC (pg.24)
Apr 11-14	**Trailfest**	Hot Springs, NC (pg.32)
May 16-18	**Trail Days**	Damascus, VA (pg.51)
May 16-18	**Hiker's Celebration**	Marion, VA (pg.56)
Jun 6-7	**Troutville Trail Days**	Troutville, VA (pg.68)
Jun-7	**Hiker Festival**	Pine Grove Furnace SP, PA (pg.106)
Jun-14	**Hiker Fest**	Waynesboro, VA (pg.82)
Sep 12-14	**Trail's End Festival**	Millinocket, ME (pg.220)
Oct 10-12	**The ALDHA Gathering**	Williams College, Williamstown, MA